MW00526083

Catholicism & Evolution

A History from Darwin to Pope Francis

Catholicism & Evolution

A History
from Darwin *to* Pope Francis

⊕

by
Michael Chaberek, O.P.

First published in the USA
by Angelico Press

First published in Polish as *Kościół a ewolucja*
(Warszawa: Wydawnictwo Fronda, 2012)

For information, address:
Angelico Press
4709 Briar Knoll Dr.
Kettering, OH 45429
angelicopress.com

ISBN 978-1-62138-137-2 (pbk)
ISBN 978-1-62138-138-9 (cloth)
ISBN 978-1-62138-139-6 (ebook)

I, Mark Padrez, O.P., Prior Provincial of the Western Dominican Province, hereby grant the *Nihil Obstat* and *Imprimatur* to *Catholicism and Evolution* by Michal Chaberek, O.P.

The *Nihil Obstat* and *Imprimatur* are official declarations that this book is free of doctrinal or moral error. No implication is contained herein that I, who have granted the *Nihil Obstat* and *Imprimatur*, agree with the contents, opinions, or statements expressed.

3/12/14

Cover Image:
Cathedral of Monreale, Palermo, Sicily:
Mosaic of the Creation of Adam, 1180s
Cover Design:
Michael Schrauzer

CONTENTS

Acknowledgments

Work on the American edition of "Catholicism and Evolution" was a long process involving many individuals to whom I would like to express my very great appreciation. No human work is perfect, but there are some individuals whose valuable and constructive editorial input made this work significantly better. For all the remaining shortcomings of this book the author, and he alone, remains responsible. Specifically, I would like to express my deep gratitude to Professor Jay W. Richards, whose time and effort at early stages helped to significantly improve the translation of this work. I am also greatly indebted to Professors Jonathan Wells and Michael Behe, who helped me—a non-biologist—accurately discuss the scientific matters treated in this work. Special thanks should also be given to all those who provided me with technical and moral support during the most intensive work on the manuscript, especially the staff of the Discovery Institute and my Dominican community in Seattle. Above all, however, I would like to extend words of particular gratitude to Bruce Chapman, without whose initiative, patient guidance, enthusiastic encouragement, and useful critiques the publication of this book would not have been possible.

Introduction

Beginning with the 1859 publication of Charles Darwin's *Origin of Species*, the discussion about evolution has been a constant ingredient in modern life, predictably flaring up with each decennial anniversary of its publication. Why did this one book arouse more interest, polemic, passion, and argument than all other works on natural science of the 19th and 20th centuries combined? That is the question this book intends to address.

Darwin was the first naturalist to propose a systematic and scientific theory explaining the entire biological complexity of the world without reference to supernatural or intelligent causes.[1] The English scholar was mainly interested in finding a purely natural answer to the question of the origin of biodiversity on Earth—that is, the origin of species. The new concept provoked both support and opposition in the scientific community as well as in the clerical circles of various Christian denominations.

It is difficult for a contemporary believer to understand the reactions of religious leaders of the time. Indeed, many Christians have come to terms with the possibility that God may have used evolution in creating the world. Drawing on older accounts, Christian scholars have developed various concepts of causality which, they claim, can reconcile the "randomness" of evolutionary processes with purposive divine action. Modern exegetes explain difficult passages from the Book of Genesis, using historical and critical methods that often do more to "explain away" than to explain. But even if we define the literary genre of the first chapters of Genesis as a poetic hymn telling of God's glory, this does not solve the issue of evolution. It does, however, serve to allow the idea of evolution to be considered within a theological framework. Finally, as more and more discretion in biblical interpretations is accepted, the inspired text suddenly comes to appear as so ambiguous that neither truth nor dogma can be validated by God's word.

1. In fact, a theory identical to Darwin's was simultaneously developed by another scholar, Alfred Russel Wallace (1823–1913). However an informal agreement at the Linnaean Society of London gave priority to Darwin as a person enjoying greater respect. Later, Wallace—contrary to Darwin—began to pursue a concept of evolution directed by a higher intelligence. More on the life and work of Wallace can be found in M.A. Flannery, *Alfred Russel Wallace: A Rediscovered Life* (Seattle: Discovery Institute Press, 2011).

This was not always the case. For almost two thousand years, the universal belief of Christians (and Jews) was that God used His power to create the various species separately, that He created man directly from the dust of the earth, and that He took Eve from Adam's side. The Holy Bible was interpreted as a true historical account, and the constancy of species was seen as a manifestation of God's Wisdom, which ordered this world according to "measure and number and weight" (Wisdom 11:20). This understanding of creation permeated the Western culture of Darwin's time.

When Darwin proposed a new explanation of "beginnings," the generic idea of evolution as the transformation of living beings into different living beings was not unknown. Ancient Greek philosophers were already familiar with the search for a material cause of all reality. Naturalistic and emanational cosmogonies dominated ancient pagan cultures—ideas that the Church Fathers combated with great zeal in the early Christian era. Darwin's key contribution was not species transformism or materialism, but a proposed *mechanism* that suggested that a purely natural, scientific answer to the question of origins had been found. Thus, the idea proposed by Darwin challenged not only science but also longstanding religious beliefs. In that context, it is no wonder that this new theory provoked opposition and discussion, and indeed continues to do so to this day.

Many Catholic theologians now claim that the Church never had a problem with Darwin's theory. It is often said that Darwin's work is not a challenge to faith, as it is a scientific rather than a religious concept. Some even claim that evolution presents a better picture of God than the theory of direct creation, since a God who works through "secondary causes" is more perfect than one who would have to create everything separately, and, in a way, intervene in His own work.[2]

But is it really possible to reconcile evolution with the Book of Genesis, and, if so, what would the resultant concept of creation look like? What are the limits of science in addressing questions about the origins (of the world, species, man), and what should be accepted from revelation and theology? These questions are significant, since they touch upon the Christian understanding of creation as well as the essential questions faced by every human being: Where did I come from? How did the world come to be? Where is it headed? The answers to these questions shape our views of man, of the world, and of God himself.

2. For example, this perspective is assumed in three major publications treating the topic of Catholicism and evolution: *Darwin and Catholicism*, ed. Louis Caruana (London: T&T Clark, 2009); *Roman Catholicism and Modern Science*, ed. Don O'Leary (New York: Continuum, 2007); and Mariano Artigas, Thomas F. Glick, Rafael A. Martinez, *Negotiating Darwin: The Vatican Confronts Evolution* 1877–1902 (Baltimore: John Hopkins University Press, 2006).

In this book I argue that the Catholic Church has not taken an unambiguous stand on evolution. Catholicism currently lacks a straightforward answer to the question of whether evolution, understood as the origin of species, is compatible with the Church's teaching.

Furthermore, until at least the middle of the 20th century, the Church maintained a coherent and clearly expressed position (on the level of the ordinary teaching) on the issue of the direct creation of man, with reference to the soul and the body. Therefore, the opinion that the Catholic Church never had any difficulty with Darwin's theory contradicts what is found in Church documents. It is my intention to demonstrate that the present teaching of the Church allows a plurality of views on this matter; in fact, the Church currently authorizes mutually exclusive ideas, such as theistic evolution and progressive creationism. This necessitates further analysis of the problem, and discussion on the matter is by all means justified.

Three Levels of the Debate

The subject of evolution may be considered on three fundamental levels: scientific, philosophical, and theological. Each level relates to slightly different problems.

On the level of natural science, the essential question is whether biological macroevolution (a process of the generation of totally new higher taxonomic groups, like genera and families) is or can be empirically confirmed to be occurring in the natural world. The problem is that significant macroevolutionary change is believed to occur only over long periods of time—on the order of millions of years. Therefore, it is not possible to observe them in the span of a few decades or even the few centuries available to scientific observation. As a result, one must employ indirect methods of verification. This, strictly speaking, is the subject of evolutionary biology. Scientists still have not reached a consensus on whether life could have originated on its own, and whether one or a few spontaneously generated organisms could have given rise to the entire diversity of species, including man. Recent studies conducted by researchers associated with the intelligent design movement have produced new challenges for some evolutionary theses commonly recognized by science.

As far as philosophy is concerned, the controversy is about the possibility of the transformation of species, that is, whether a given kind of organism can, under the influence of genetic mutations or external environmental factors, transform into an organism of a completely different kind. Classical metaphysics claimed that no being by nature tends to lose its nature; on the contrary, each being seeks to preserve what it is. St. Thomas Aquinas, like Aristotle, believed that an accidental change *cannot* result in a change of nature. Therefore, it is impossible to transform from one nature to another by way of small accidental changes. In Darwin's theory, however, each being by nature strives to become something else. Thus, over time, a bacterium is supposed to turn into a plant, a reptile into a bird, a monkey into a man.

Moreover, evolution assumes that a lower cause may produce higher effects, thus making all nature subject to the law of spontaneous emergence of increased organization. Meanwhile, according to classical metaphysics, no being can cause more perfection (actuality) than it already has. The lesser can come from the greater, but not the greater from the lesser. Problems such as the transformation of species by means of accidental changes, or the emergence of completely new natures through the natural process of animal generation, are rarely raised in today's discussions on evolution. The probable reason is the general crisis in philosophical thinking and the abandonment of classical metaphysics in mainstream philosophy. The current philosophical discussion is primarily concerned with accommodating evolution in terms of modes of divine causality. For example, there is an attempt to resolve the problem of "insufficient causality" in evolution by adopting two-way (bottom-up and top-down) causation working in nature and leading to the generation of entirely new living forms. The literature addresses such ideas as the possibility of reconciling the randomness of evolutionary processes with purposeful divine action, or the participation of higher Intelligence in the emergence of the natural world by means of natural evolution.

From the point of view of this work, the most important area of research is found on the third, theological level. Since the announcement of Darwin's theory, essentially two periods of discussion in Catholic theology followed. The first period coincided roughly with what has been called "the Modernist crisis" and lasted from the 1890s to the 1920s. At that time, scholars attempted to combine evolution with the classical Church doctrine on creation, which produced the concept of theistic evolution. Later on, particularly in the 1950s and 1960s, the discussion shifted its focus to polygenism—the concept that human individuals now living did not all descend from a single, original human ancestral pair. The topic of evolution returned in the late 20th and early 21st centuries. This present debate (and its often white-hot intensity) may eventually lead to the necessity of doctrinal settlement in the Church, a move that would hopefully define with greater precision the scope and bounds of Catholic orthodoxy.

Rapid developments in biochemistry are raising many obstacles to the common evolutionary scenario, and theologians now face the need to reinvestigate the original doctrine of the Church and explore whether theistic evolution is in fact compatible with the Christian view of creation. Another challenge is the harmonization and integration of intelligent design theory into Catholic theology—a task that until now has not been seriously considered. This present work is primarily historical in nature, and as such it does not seek to fill these gaps. Nevertheless, the analysis of the dispute around evolution presented in the first chapter points to intelligent design theory as the adequate scientific background for further development of the doctrine of creation within Catholic theology.

Since the late nineteenth century, evolution has been the topic of numerous scientific and popular-scientific studies. In 1998, the opening of the Vatican archives of the Congregation for the Doctrine of the Faith gave access to information never before available to historians. The archives contained the documents of the Sacred Congregation of the Index. These documents revealed firm opposition of the Church to the new concept of creation emerging among theologians at the end of the 19th century. As yet, this material has been the subject of only a few papers and a single book, entitled *Negotiating Darwin: The Vatican Confronts Evolution.*[3] While the articles are fragmentary in nature, the book contains a comprehensive study of the documents, along with a background of debates and numerous quotations from the sources. It is sufficient to constitute the basis for the greater part of the fourth chapter of our work.

In the first two chapters, we introduce definitions of basic terms and outline the dispute between evolutionism and creationism in natural science. Some space is devoted to presenting intelligent design theory as a modern alternative to neo-Darwinism. The rest of the book is concerned with the issue of evolution in the Catholic Church. The dispute in Catholicism can be divided into two stages, according to the changing attitude to evolution in theological circles and documents of the Magisterium. So chapters three through five describe the "inefficient rejection of evolutionism in 1860–1909," whereas chapters six through nine discuss the "moderate acceptance of theistic evolution in 1950–2015." Thus the book presents all substantial opinions and positions that have appeared in Catholicism on the subject of evolution over the course of the past 150 years.

3. M. Artigas, T.F. Glick, R.A. Martínez, *Negotiating Darwin: The Vatican Confronts Evolution*, (Baltimore: The Johns Hopkins University Press, 2006). One of the papers worth noting is Brian W. Harrison, "Early Vatican Responses to Evolutionist Theology," *Living Tradition* 93 (May 2001). http://www.rtforum.org/lt/lt93.html (01.24.15).

1

The Controversy About Evolution
Its Origin, Characteristics, and Current Status

The History of Modern Evolutionism: Basic Terms ("Evolution" and "Species")

IN HIS PRESENTATION of the philosophical concept of evolution, Étienne Gilson pointed out that the word evolution refers to *un-folding* (Latin: *e-volvere*), as opposed to folding or *in-volution* (*un-rolling* of the *in-rolled*/*de-velopment* of the *en-veloped*). Therefore, in his opinion, the only philosophical concept that justifies the use of this term is the idea of *logoi spermatikoi* (seed-like reasons) mentioned by Stoics and such writers as St. Justin, St. Augustine, and St. Bonaventure. "Unfolding" assumes an earlier existence in some kind of hidden, "folded" form. For this reason, Gilson correctly acknowledged that the notion of "creative evolution" is "contradictory and impossible."[1] Charles Darwin knew that evolution in the traditional sense did not mean the emergence of anything new. However, his own theory described the origin of completely new species. The word did not match what he had in mind. For this reason he introduced the term "evolution" only in his later works, after the cultural change of the term's meaning.

In science, we can find several related but distinct definitions of the term "evolution."[2] In the most general sense, evolution refers simply to change

1. E. Gilson, *From Aristotle to Darwin and Back Again*, transl. by J. Lyon (Notre Dame: Notre Dame University Press, 1984), 50. Gilson also writes: "If the word evolution does not signify the contrary, or the inverse movement, from that of an in-volution, it does not signify anything intelligible. It is not certain that the present chaotic state of scientific evolutionism is not but the deferred effect of this original fault. Darwin at first avoided it. In a sense he was never personally responsible for it" (52). Gilson indicates that the person responsible for popularizing the faulty interpretation of evolution was H. Spencer (87).

2. S.C. Meyer, S. Minnich, J. Moneymaker, P.A. Nelson, and R. Seelke speak of these three meanings of biological evolution in *Explore Evolution: The Arguments for and Against Neo-Darwinism* (Melbourne & London: Hill House Publisher, 2007), 8.

through time. So, for example, astronomers refer to the "evolution" of stars, by which they mean not natural selection or biological descent but simply the way different stars change over time. In biology, evolution can refer to (1) changes within given species, or what is called microevolution; (2) Darwin's specific mechanism of change—random variation and natural selection; (3) the descent of some group of organisms from a common ancestor; and, closely related to this, (4) the idea that, through natural changes and descent alone, one kind of organism can become an entirely new life form, that is, a new natural species (macroevolution). In its broadest sense, evolution becomes a total theory of reality, encompassing not only such concepts as cosmic evolution (emergence of stars and planets), chemical and biochemical evolution (rise of life from inorganic matter), and biological evolution, but also the evolution of language, law, ethics, and every manner of human activity. In the broadest sense, then, evolution becomes a general scientific and philosophical paradigm that can be extended to almost any aspect of nature or culture. This work shall interpret "evolutionary theory" or "evolution" as biological macroevolution, while at times including chemical evolution in the interpretation. Obviously, there are many detailed concepts of biological and chemical evolution, but they differ in mechanisms rather than in effects. Thus, for the purposes of this work, it is not as important to determine which evolutionary mechanisms are more probable—e.g., Lamarckian, Darwinian, or neo-Darwinian ones. The important components to our definition are: (1) evolution means a purely natural process; (2) evolution means macroevolution. The present study is primarily concerned with philosophical and theological implications of evolution in this sense.

The second notion that requires precision is that of "species." In the contemporary debate, there are four basic meanings of this term. From a philosophical point of view, two notions of "species" are possible: (1) *an ontological concept*, i.e., a logical subcategory of the higher rank "genus" (scholars who claim that "there are no real species," or that the idea of species is untenable, actually use the word "species" in this sense); (2) *a metaphysical concept*, a logical subcategory of a higher rank of "genus," but which in addition is composed of units that share an abstractly defined common nature or substantial form. In a scientific sense, we can also speak of (3) *biological species*. According to the now commonly recognized definition of Ernst Mayr, a biological species signifies all populations in which specimens are prospectively able to interbreed in a natural environment and produce fertile offspring.[3]

There is also the idea of (4) *natural species*, that is, those used as a basis for the classification of living organisms until roughly the second half of the 19th century-

3. E. Mayr, *Systematics and the Origin of Species from the Viewpoint of a Zoologist* (New York: Columbia University Press, 1942).

tury. From a biological point of view the limits of a natural species are determined by taxonomic genus or, in some cases, family. From a metaphysical point of view natural species are composite living beings (i.e., composed of matter and form) sharing the same nature or substantial form. From a theological perspective natural species could be considered biblical "kinds" (Gr. *genos*, Heb. *l'mînô*). Thus, natural species as described both by Linnaeus (who spoke of their unchangeability), and by Lamarck, Buffon, or Darwin (who challenged their existence) is in a certain way an intermediate concept between biological and metaphysical species. The concept of "natural species," even if considered obsolete today, is best able to communicate the idea of some kind of fixed biological reality. It is also well adapted to interdisciplinary studies, where disparate areas of knowledge need to refer to the same reality. For this reason I shall adopt this definition of species, unless expressly indicated otherwise by the context.

The Birth of the Evolutionary Paradigm in Modern Thought

In the middle of the 18th century, naturalists professed a coherent and biblically consistent opinion on the origin of species. The most famous naturalist of the period was the Swedish scientist Carl Linnaeus (1707–1778). According to Linnaeus, species are constant and have all been created by God in the same form as they currently exist.[4] This idea, however, was not unique to Linnaeus. It had been commonly held since antiquity by natural philosophers as well as theologians. As conformity with the Scriptures was the basic principle of all studies of the Christian era, the claim of the constancy of species was adopted from Genesis on an *a priori* basis. For Linnaeus, the constancy of species was also an empirical fact based upon research rather than exclusively a religious belief.[5] Nevertheless, the theory of the Swedish scholar was challenged in the works of Georges-Louis Leclerc de Buffon, who first agreed with Linnaeus, but then (in 1761) decided that under the direct influence of the environment, species might have undergone complex structural modifications.[6] Similar ideas were expressed by the German biologist Gottfried Reinhold Treviranus as well as Erasmus Darwin (1731–1802), the grandfather of Charles Darwin.

4. "There are as many species as there are different forms that were created at the beginning." [Species tot numeranus quot diversae formae in principio sunt creatae.] C. Linnaeus, *Philosophia botanica* (Stockholm, 1751), 99.

5. "Contemplating the works of God, it is plain to everyone that organisms produce offspring perfectly similar to the parents," C. Linnaeus, *Systems* (Leipzig, 1748), 21, in H. Muckermann, "Evolution," *Catholic Encyclopedia*, vol. 5 (New York: The Encyclopedia Press, 1909), 655.

6. Cf. H. Muckermann, "Evolution," 655–56. While speaking about the first "theories of change," one should take note of an interesting claim about the origin of life forms made already by Descartes (1596–1650). Even though he was an ardent supporter of the separate creation of species and direct creation of the human body, in *The Principles of Philosophy* he speculates about the possibility of

In *Zoonomia* (1794), his major work on biology, Erasmus Darwin includes a chapter entitled "On Reproduction." He writes there as follows:

> Would it be too bold to imagine, that in the great length of time, since the earth began to exist, perhaps millions of ages before the commencement of the history of mankind, would it be too bold to imagine, that all warm-blooded animals have arisen from one living filament, which THE GREAT FIRST CAUSE endued with animality, with the power of acquiring new parts, [...] and thus possessing the faculty of continuing to improve by its own inherent activity, and of delivering down those improvements by generation to its posterity, world without end![7]

The elder Darwin also authored a poem entitled "The Temple of Nature," in which he presents a literary vision of the procession of Nature from microorganisms, through a mythological past, to advanced society. His intention was not to present a scientific truth, but rather—as he himself said—"to amuse, by bringing distinctly to the imagination, the beautiful and sublime images of the operations of Nature."[8] The poem, like other works of his, mentions the concept of life being born in oceanic waves or in waterside mud in the form of small organisms that over many generations gradually develop new and improved organs, grow into families of species, and eventually form organisms capable of movement, thought, and feeling. The works of this medic and poet of the Enlightenment contain a complete concept of biological evolution.

Another scholar who challenged Linnaeus's belief in the constancy of species was the French military man, physician, and botanist Jean-Baptiste Lamarck (1744–1829). In his primary work, *Philosophie Zoologique*, published the year Charles Darwin was born (1809), Lamarck presents his own comprehensive idea of the origin of biological diversity. In his opinion, nature can produce life spontaneously (abiogenesis). Then these "simplest organic bodies," through

---

explaining the origin of species with natural processes. "[I]f we want to understand the natures of plants or of men, it is much better to consider how they might gradually grow from seeds than to consider how they were created by God as going concerns at the start of the world. In this spirit perhaps we can think up some very simple and easily grasped principles that can function as the seeds (so to speak) from which the stars, the earth, and indeed everything we observe in this visible world demonstrably could have grown. We know for sure that they didn't arise in this way, but we'll be able to explain their nature much better in this way than if we merely described them as they now are or as we believe them to have been created." R. Descartes, *The Principles of Philosophy*, III, 45. Translated by J. Bennett. http://www.earlymoderntexts.com/pdfs/descartes1644part3.pdf (2 March 2015).

7. E. Darwin, *Zoonomia or the Laws of Organic Life*, 2nd edition, vol. 1 (London, 1794), 505.

8. *The Temple of Nature or, the Origin of Society: A Poem, with Philosophical Notes* (Baltimore, 1804). In the preface, the author writes: "The Poem, which is here offered to the Public, does not pretend to instruct by deep researches of reasoning; its aim is simply to amuse, by bringing distinctly to the imagination, the beautiful and sublime images of the operations of Nature, in the order, as the author believes, in which the progressive course of time presented them."

"organic movement" and under the influence of a "sufficient lapse of time" and "circumstances which were necessarily favourable," give rise to even the most complex beings. For plants, the influence of the environment is the main driver for changes, whereas for animals it is new needs and activities. Organs emerging in response to these new needs then develop through use or disappear through atrophy. Consequently, Lamarck rejected the idea of constant species: "What we call species have been created in this way imperceptibly and successively among them; they have a constancy which is only relative to their condition and cannot be as old as nature."[9] Therefore, the concept of species is only relative and actually impossible to define. Despite accepting spontaneous generation and the emergence of all life forms from a few primitive models, Lamarck still upheld the idea of the Creator as a general causative principle of the process. According to him, nature does not have the power to create the entire complex and ordered world of life.[10]

Some scholars immediately opposed the emerging theories of evolution. For example, William Paley (1743–1805), addressing the concept of spontaneous

9. Lamarck summarized his view in the following six points: "(1) All organic bodies of our earth are true products of nature, which she has brought forth successively over a long period of time. (2) In her progress, nature began, and begins again every day, by creating the simplest organic bodies, and she does not directly create anything except by this process, that is to say, by these first beginnings of organic structure which are designated by the expression "spontaneous generation." (3) The first beginnings of animals and plants were formed in appropriate places and circumstances. Once the faculties of a commencing life and of organic movement were established, these animals and plants of necessity gradually developed organs, and, in time, they diversified these organs, as well as their parts. (4) The faculty of growth in each portion of an organic body is inherent in the first effects of life; it gave rise to different ways of multiplication and reproduction of individuals. In this process, the progress acquired in the composition of the organic structure and in the shape and diversity of parts was maintained. (5) With the help of a sufficient lapse of time, of circumstances which were necessarily favourable, of changes which every point on the surface of the earth has successively undergone, in a word, with the assistance of the power which new situations and habits have for modifying the organs of a body endowed with life, all those which exist now have been imperceptibly shaped just as we see them. (6) Finally, after a sequence of events like the above, living bodies have each experienced greater or lesser changes in the condition of their organic structure and their parts. What we call species have been created in this way imperceptibly and successively among them; they have a constancy which is only relative to their condition and cannot be as old as nature." J.B. Lamarck, *Zoological Philosophy*, trans. by I. Johnston (Nanaimo, BC: Malaspina University-College, 1999), 68.

10. "Dare one carry the systematic spirit so far as to say that it is nature alone which has created this astonishing diversity of means, tricks, dexterity, precaution, and patience, so often illustrated to us by the industry of animals? Is not what we observe in this respect in the class of insects alone a thousand times more than sufficient to make us feel that limiting the power of nature would not permit her to produce on her own so many marvels and to impress on us the most persistent belief that here the will of the supreme Author of everything was necessary and alone sufficed to bring into existence so many admirable things?" Ibid., 69–70.

generation of different life forms as formulated by Buffon and others, argued that

> No changes, like those which the theory requires, have ever been observed. All the changes in Ovid's *Metamorphoses* might have been effected by these appetencies, if the theory were true: yet not an example, nor the pretense of an example, is offered of a single change being known to have taken place. Nor is the order of generation obedient to the principle upon which this theory is built.[11]

These first evolutionary theories were purely speculative and independent of prospective empirical corroboration. Individual scholars supplemented the missing facts with poetic or imaginative visions, but were unable to pinpoint credible causes or clear mechanisms of how species could actually progress from one to another.

When in 1830 Étienne Geoffroy Saint-Hilaire (1772–1844) presented his doctrine concerning the unity of organic plan and structure in all living beings (later known as homology) to the French Academy of Sciences, he was challenged by another French botanist, Georges Cuvier (1769–1832). According to Saint-Hilaire, the main cause of changes was *monde ambient*—the surrounding world or environment. He also claimed that nature can generate abrupt changes in embryonic structure. Cuvier, on the other hand, was the author of a modern taxonomy, and a supporter of the constancy of species. His main work, *Théorie de la terre* (1821), included the analysis of fossil records. He realized that we usually discover single bones instead of whole organisms, and that fossils provide information about skeletons, and not about soft body parts. Nevertheless, he highly valued fossil records in studies of the history of Earth. He claimed that species, genera, and classes are so different from each other that even a small bone fragment enables the classification of a given organism in the appropriate species.[12] Over the course of his studies he considered why modern species could not have emerged from those found in the fossil record: "Yet to these persons [promoting species transformism] an answer may be given from their own system. If the species have changed by degrees, we ought to find

11. W. Paley, *Natural Theology* (Boston, 1854), 242.

12. "The smallest articulating surface of bone, or the smallest apophysis [a curve at the edge of a bone], has a determinate character, relative to the class, the order, the genus, and the species to which it belonged; insomuch, that when one possesses merely a well preserved extremity of a bone, he can, by careful examination, and the aid of a tolerable analogical knowledge, and of accurate comparison, determine all these things with as much certainty as if he had the entire animal before him. I have often made trial of this method upon portions of known animals, before reposing full confidence upon it, in regard to fossil remains; and it has always proved so completely satisfactory, that I have no longer any doubts regarding the certainty of the results which it has afforded me." G. Cuvier, *Essay on the Theory of the Earth*, 5th ed. (Edinburgh-London, 1827), 92.

traces of these gradual modifications. Thus, between the palaeotheria [*palaeotheriidae*—an extinct genus of mammals] and our present species, we should be able to discover some intermediate forms; and yet no such discovery has ever been made."[13]

Nonetheless, Cuvier was interested in the degree to which species may change. In further studies he argued that they could undergo minor and negligible changes, and that domestication caused an increase in these changes. He also addressed the argument that species might have evolved over a very long period of time, asserting that the necessary length of time is in fact inaccessible to our investigation:

> I am aware that some naturalists lay great stress upon the thousands of ages which they call into action by a dash of the pen; but, in such matters, we can only judge of what a long period of time might produce, by multiplying in idea [i.e., in imagination] what less time produces. With this view, I have endeavoured to collect the most ancient documents relating to the forms of animals; and there are none which equal, either in antiquity or abundance, those that Egypt furnishes.... I have examined with the greatest attention the figures of quadrupeds and birds sculptured upon the numerous obelisks brought from Egypt to ancient Rome. All these figures possess, in their general character ... a perfect resemblance to the species represented, such as we see them at the present day.[14]

Having analyzed numerous examples, Cuvier concluded: "There is nothing, therefore, to be derived from all the facts hitherto known, that could, in the slightest degree, give support to the opinion that the new genera which I have discovered or established among the fossil remains of animals ... might have been the sources of the present race of animals, which have only differed from them through the influence of time or climate."[15] As a scientist, Cuvier did not thus draw a conclusion about creation, but only stated that the existing body of scientific evidence can justify neither transformation of one species into another nor common descent. In contrast to his adversary, Cuvier based his studies on positive facts, proving that neither the fossils nor the mummies brought by Napoleon from Egypt confirm the modification of species. In France, the works of Cuvier temporarily put an end to speculations about evolutionary origins of life and brought academic attention again to the exclusive study of positive facts.[16]

13. G. Cuvier, *Essay on the Theory of the Earth*, 103.

14. Ibid., 110. Cuvier defined species as "the individuals which descend from each other, or from common parents, and those which resemble them as much as they resemble each other" (ibid., 104).

15. Ibid., 112.

16. Cf. H. Muckermann, "Evolution." More on the subject in T.A. Appel, *The Cuvier–Geoffroy Debate: French Biology in the Decades before Darwin* (Oxford: Oxford University Press, 1987).

At the turn of the 19th century, British scientific circles were generally unfavorable towards evolutionary ideas. The traditional worldview left the answer to the question about the origins to the Scriptures and religion. Old British universities were staffed with Anglican clergymen and open only to students belonging to the Church of England.[17] According to the calculations of the Anglican bishop James Ussher (1581–1656), the Earth was created on October 22, 4004 BC, on Saturday, at 6:00 PM. These kinds of results were accepted by most natural philosophers and theologians until the end of the 18th century.[18] For Protestant scholars, scientific data had to agree with the Scriptures—after all, the Bible was recognized as the sole standard of truth (*sola Scriptura*). What troubled the researchers was Noah's ark. Its dimensions were known, and its capacity was calculated on the basis of descriptions from the Book of Genesis. It was widely believed that the fossil record proved that the majority of animals died in the Flood that covered the whole Earth. The academic mood—as well as the social sphere as a whole—was characterized by the absolutism of the rising Victorian age. Outwardly, nobody favored new ideas on the origin of life, though the old theory served mainly as a dummy, crafting the pretense of a coherent worldview. Writers and thinkers suggesting alternative solutions were disdained and their ideas silenced.[19] Nevertheless, evolutionary works were circulated in academic communities through private channels, and were discussed and modified according to the emerging views of subsequent authors. It might be said that this situation revealed an expansive dichotomy between official and new opinions.

The year 1844 saw the publication of *Vestiges of Creation*,[20] a work whose author was carefully concealed. In 1884, upon publication of the book's twelfth edition, it was announced that the author was Robert Chambers, a bookseller and amateur geologist from Edinburgh, who had died in 1871. The book made a significant impact: only at the end of the 19th century was the total number of

17. W. Stephen, *The Evolution of Evolution: Darwin, Enlightenment and Scotland* (Edinburgh: Luath Press, 2009), 15.

18. Cf. Iacobo Usserio Armachano, *Annales Veteris Testamenti a prima mundi origine deducti* in *The Whole Works of the Most Rev. James Ussher, D.D.*, vol. 8 (Londini: 1650), 7. Similar conclusions were reached by such scholars as Pico della Mirandola, Johannes Kepler, and Isaac Newton. See G. B. Dalrymple, *The Age of Earth* (Stanford: Stanford University Press, 1991), 13ff.

19. See the history of publication of three evolutionary works in the same year (1813), written by physicians W.C. Wells, J.C. Prichard, and W. Lawrence. Cf. S. Skowron, *Narodziny wielkiej teorii*, 96–98. In addition to these authors, A.R. Wallace and P. Matthew proposed the idea of the emergence of species from natural causes in *On Naval Timber and Arboriculture, with critical notes on authors who have recently treated the subject of planting* (Edinburgh & London, 1831); R. Chambers, *Vestiges of the Natural History of Creation* (London, 1844).

20. R. Chambers, *Vestiges of the Natural History of Creation*, 2nd ed. (New York: Wiley and Putnam, 1845). All quotations come from this edition.

copies sold of *Vestiges* surpassed by those sold of Darwin's *The Origin of Species.*[21] It was a book that actually reached the common people. Because Prince Albert read the book aloud to the young Queen Victoria, some speculated that the prince himself might be its author. Its light, popular-scientific style, free of excessive argumentation and complex biological detail, gave the work the status of a family novel, often read for entertainment in elite circles.[22] Nevertheless, the content of its four hundred pages was revolutionary and not easy for many readers to accept. The title, suggesting the "vestiges of creation," was a diplomatic one, as the true intention was to show that God did not create various forms of life but only constituted fundamental natural laws according to which subsequent organisms appeared gradually due to natural causes.

The book begins modestly. In its first chapters the author presents basic information about geology (such as the formation of continents) and gives examples of various organisms found in the fossil record. Chambers also notes that from a biological point of view these organisms could be arranged in a chain—from the simplest to the most advanced. Up to this point every traditionally-minded reader would agree with the author.

In chapter twelve, however, Chambers moves from biology to theology, and proposes a change to the commonly held belief in the separate creation of species:

> A candid consideration of all these circumstances [the existence of many levels of biological forms over a long period of time] can scarcely fail to introduce into our minds a somewhat different idea of organic creation from what has hitherto been generally entertained. That God created animated beings, as well as the terraqueous theatre of their being, is a fact so powerfully evidenced, and so universally received that I at once take it for granted. But in the particulars of this so highly supported idea, we surely here see cause for some re-consideration. It may now be inquired: in what way was the creation of animated beings effected? The ordinary notion may, I think, be described as this,—that the Almighty Author produced the progenitors of all existing species by some sort of personal or immediate exertion. But how does this notion comport with what we have seen of the gradual advance of species, from the humblest to the highest? . . . Some other idea must then be arrived at in regard to *the mode* in which the Divine Author proceeded in the organic creation. Let us seek in the history of the earth's formation for a new suggestion on this point. We have seen powerful evidence, that the construction of this globe and its associates . . . , was the result, not of any immediate or personal

21. W. Stephen, *The Evolution of Evolution*, 27.

22. Ibid., 23. Cf. also J.A. Secord, *Victorian Sensation: The Extraordinary Publication, Reception, and Secret Authorship of Vestiges of the Natural History of Creation* (Chicago: University of Chicago Press, 2000), 168–69.

> exertion on the part of Deity, but of natural laws which are expressions of His will. What is to hinder our supposing that the organic creation is also the result of natural laws, which are in like manner an expression of his will?[23]

Thus, the author of *Vestiges* posited the existence of *laws* built into nature, laws that govern the formation of Earth's surface, such as erosion and uplifts. Next he extrapolated these laws, by pure deduction, to the origins of animate beings. In a later part of the work he presented data that suggested the automatic emergence of life from inorganic matter, as well as its development as far as man, human language, and civilization. Moreover, he argued that ethnic groups represented different levels of development. The Negroid race he deemed the least developed and the Caucasian race the most developed.[24]

Chambers also argued in favor of spontaneous generation. For instance, he noted that crystals have complex internal structures that are symmetrical, or—as in the case of *arbor dianae*—resemble a bush. Another argument for him was the electric discharges observed in the darkness that resemble the structure of trees or single leaves: "These phenomena seem to say that the electric energies have had something to do in determining the forms of plants."[25] Admittedly, even at that time, these arguments must have entertained little credibility.

Even as the book became popular, it also provoked heated criticism. The anonymous author was described with epithets such as credulous, superficial, skeptical, imaginative, childlike, crazed, hypothetical, fantastical. Words of reprehension came both from the Church of England (Bishop Wilberforce) and from important scientists (Buckland, Sedgwick, Murchison, Lyell).[26] Given these reactions, it is clear why Chambers did not want to reveal his name. He chose to enjoy a calm life until the end of his days in the scientific circles of the Royal Society of Edinburgh and the Geological Society of London.

Chambers' work became a wedge driven into the traditional view of the origin of species. One might say that it prepared the cultural background for Darwin's theory. It kindled a discussion, expanded the mental horizons of a wide group of readers, and declared loudly and clearly what others might only have imagined. After *Vestiges*, no theory of nature was shocking.

Another, quite different publication helped Darwin's ideas to spread quickly: Charles Lyell's (1797–1875) *Principles of Geology* (1830–1833). Successive volumes of this classic in its field accompanied the young Darwin on his trip around the

23. R. Chambers, *Vestiges*, 115–16.

24. The remarks concerning the hierarchy of races used in the book are immediately striking. Nowadays such observations are commonly rejected as ethically unacceptable. Nevertheless, the use of such expressions as early as the first works on the evolution of species shows that this idea was dangerous and liable to abuse from the very beginning.

25. Ibid., 125.

26. Cf. W. Stephen, *The Evolution of Evolution*, 28.

world. Which elements of Lyell's doctrine might have influenced the mind of the British naturalist?

First of all, it was Lyell who came up with a natural explanation of the shaping of forms on the Earth's surface. He based his studies on the idea that many phenomena can be explained by the ordinary action of nature:

> Many appearances, which for a long time were regarded as indicating mysterious and extraordinary agency, are finally recognized as the necessary result of the laws now governing the material world; and the discovery of this unlooked for conformity has induced some geologists to infer that there has never been any interruption to the same uniform order of physical events.[27]

Thus Lyell rejected both Cuvier's catastrophism and the idea that sudden leaps occur in natural history. As Lyell was accustomed to say, *natura non facit saltum*—nature does not take leaps. This was the basic statement of Lyell's doctrine known as "uniformitarianism."

However, Lyell argued that the laws governing the material world had a limited scope of action: they concerned only the formation of inanimate parts of creation. In volume three of his work Lyell directly addressed the question of species being shaped by the influence of laws imposed on matter by God. It is a "widespread opinion," he observes, stemming from "naturalists' desire to dispense, as far as possible, with the repeated intervention of a First Cause."[28] Having presented the Lamarckian theory of transformism, Lyell wrote that researchers who propagate the theory without being aware of its limitations "give full rein to speculation." They apply transformism to nearly all phenomena, claiming that the "outward form, internal structure, instinctive faculties, nay, that reason itself may have been gradually developed from some of the simplest states of existence—that all animals, that man himself, and the irrational beings, may have had one common origin; that all may be parts of one continuous and progressive scheme of development."[29] After showing how far the transformists extrapolate their conclusions, Lyell then proceeded to pinpoint what he takes to be "defective in evidence" and "fallacious in reasoning."

First, he responded to the transformists' argument that species do not exist because classification of many plants and animals is difficult. He observed that such difficulties arise primarily from our insufficient knowledge about the organisms in question. Thus, they cannot be used as the key argument in challenging the very existence of species. According to Lyell, Lamarck was wrong in his presentation of the generally accepted idea of species. It is not true, in Lyell's

27. C. Lyell, *Principles of Geology: An Attempt to Explain the Former Changes of the Earth's Surface, by Reference to Causes Now in Operation*, vol. 1 (London: 1832), 85.

28. C. Lyell, *Principles of Geology*, vol. 3, 6th edition (London: 1840), 23.

29. Ibid., 26–27.

opinion, that naturalists commonly believe that the organization of an animal or plant remains entirely constant and unchangeable in any part.[30] Of course, naturalists assumed that various external factors may to some degree affect the formation of organisms.

Therefore, the next stage in Lyell's refutation of transformistic views was an attempt to determine how far these changes might reach. He referred to the example of domesticated animals, which undergo the greatest modification as a result of conscious and purposeful human action in the course of breeding. He then proved, however, that despite many years of breeding, neither dogs nor horses nor camels depart very far from their original forms—to which they quickly revert after being reintroduced into the wild.[31] Though no records concerning animals can be found in the works of ancient philosophers—to the chagrin of modern researchers—the Egyptian cemeteries have, in fact, become such a record. Lyell mentioned hundreds of mummified animals taken by French researchers during Napoleon's occupation of Egypt, which were then brought to Paris and thoroughly described by Cuvier and others. In every case, however, the analysis revealed that the identity of the ancient species corresponded exactly with that of the modern ones, both domestic and wild.[32] Thus, Lyell concluded that the theory of species transformation contradicted the facts.

Since the doctrine of the distinguished geologist went essentially against Darwin's expectations, one might ask what Darwin might have learned from Lyell. Why did Darwin repeatedly quote him, even though he was usually reluctant to recognize his predecessors? Perhaps it was just a pretense of compliance on Darwin's part with the undisputed scientific authority of the early 19th century.

Undoubtedly, Darwin was drawn to certain methodological novelties that he found in *Principles of Geology*. For instance, he willingly embraced the search for natural rather than supernatural explanations of phenomena. Moreover, Lyell excluded catastrophes or rapid processes as explanations. Instead, he introduced the key assumption that changes occur gradually and complementarily by virtue of certain laws.[33] This idea helped Darwin establish gradual processes in biology. Another significant element in Lyell's work that shaped Darwin's thinking is evident in the extended title of Lyell's book: *Principles of Geology: An Attempt to Explain the Former Changes of the Earth's Surface by Reference to Causes now in Operation*. This suggested the new, powerful idea that

30. Ibid., 33.

31. "The greatest departure from a common type—and it constitutes the maximum of variation as yet known in the animal kingdom—is exemplified in those races of dogs which have a supernumerary toe on the hind foot with the corresponding tarsal bones; a variety analogous to one presented by six-fingered families of the human race" (ibid., 35).

32. Ibid., 37.

33. C. Lyell, *Principles of Geology*, vol. 1, 90ff.

we can draw conclusions concerning any part of the distant past from current observations. Lyell believed this method to be highly reliable. Thus, during the decade prior to the publication of *The Origin of Species* (1859), Darwin had at his disposal a complete system of ideas regarding evolution.

From his childhood, Charles Darwin (1809–1882) was fascinated by nature. He eagerly observed and collected various plants and animals. His poor ability to work systematically prevented him from graduating from medical school in Edinburgh, where his father had sent him at the age of sixteen. Therefore, with further encouragement from his father, he went to Cambridge to study theology and thus prepare himself for the function of a pastor of the Church of England. Over the course of three years of studies, he read many books (among them William Paley's *Natural Theology*), and made observations in the fields of geology and entomology. This time he did graduate, receiving a basic degree in theology, thus completing his formal academic training. In 1831, soon after graduating, he set out on a five-year research expedition around the world. The mission of the ship, *The Beagle*, was to add greater precision to the maps of the western coast of South America. The young naturalist Darwin was to act as assistant to the captain and as an expert on the natural world. During the journey he read the consecutive volumes of Lyell's *Principles of Natural Geology* and collected specimens of previously unknown plants, insects, and fossils, which he sent to Europe for further analysis. He also kept a detailed journal, which when published became his first major work.[34] Upon his return to England, he settled in Down, south of London, where he lived for the rest of his life, preparing subsequent publications far from the bustle of the city. In 1859 he published his breakthrough work, *The Origin of Species*, in which he laid out the foundations of his own theory of species transformism. Though he was not the first to write about the possibility of the generation of species through transformism, Darwin was the first to claim that he had discovered the mechanism governing this process.[35] It was a significant novelty in relation to all the previous theories. But what were the elements of Darwin's new idea?

Darwin and *The Origin of Species*

The first part of the theory is the relativization of the concept "species." Species, to Darwin, is just a "strongly-marked and well-defined" variety,[36] and an origi-

34. Why, however, was the journal only published three years after Darwin's return? According to Walter Stephen, that time was full of opportunities to correct the text in order to adjust it to the conclusions. *The Evolution of Evolution*, 16.

35. Cf. note 1 in the Introduction.

36. C. Darwin, *The Origin of Species, by Means of Natural Selection, or the Preservation of Favoured Races in the Struggle for Life* (London: John Murray, 1859), 55.

nating variety is nearly the same as a distinctive species. According to Darwin, there is no criterion for differentiating species, since both physical features and fertility are relative and difficult to define.

The second part of the theory is based on an observation taken from Thomas Malthus's *Essay on Population*, which states that every species of plant or animal produces many more offspring than are able to survive. If a given species happened to avoid obstacles, such as a limited supply of food, it would procreate at an exponential rate and quickly cover the earth.

This gives rise to the third part of the theory: the constant struggle for life among all specimens (either within a single species or between different species). The objects of struggle consist of basic resources: food, space, light, and so forth. For Darwin, nature does not represent the previously perceived harmony and order of the Creator's work, but is beset by perpetual strife and adversity. The effect of this struggle is the death of most offspring and "the survival of the fittest."

The fourth part of Darwin's proposal is natural selection—a process of gradual elimination of less-fit individuals in each population, and the survival of those that enjoy any kind of existential advantage over others.

Darwin's conclusion is that, over a sufficiently long period of time and succession of countless generations, one species may transform, through random variation and natural selection, into another, thus representing a higher level of organization. This aspect of the theory, more than any other, has been subject to constant dispute, dating from the publication of *The Origin of Species* to the present.

Until the time of Darwin, the diversity and apparent design of life on Earth spontaneously referred people to God as its source. For Christians, the biblical description of creation was a certain answer to the question: "Where do all things come from?" Darwin knew that he was not only presenting a new scientific theory, but also challenging predominant religious beliefs. Some of his statements suggest that replacing the previous supernatural explanation of the origin and diversity of life with a natural one was an essential goal of his work. For Darwin, referring to "separate acts of creation" was a tautology, an absence of explanation,[37] no better than saying "just because" or preferring an unreal cause to the *vera causa*.[38] At one point he clearly sets creation and natural selection in opposition to one another:

37. "I believe this grand fact can receive no sort of explanation on the ordinary view of independent creation." C. Darwin, *The Origin of Species*, 398. "The relations just discussed [...] are, I think, utterly inexplicable on the ordinary view of the independent creation of each species, but are explicable on the view of colonisation from the nearest and readiest source, together with the subsequent modification and better adaptation of the colonists to their new homes" (ibid., 406).

38. "Undoubtedly there are very many cases of extreme difficulty, in understanding how the same

> He who believes in separate and innumerable acts of creation will say, that in these cases it has pleased the Creator to cause a being of one type to take the place of one of another type; but this seems to me only restating the fact in dignified language. He who believes in the struggle for existence and in the principle of natural selection, will acknowledge that every organic being is constantly endeavouring to increase in numbers; and that if any one being vary ever so little, . . . and thus gain an advantage over some other inhabitant . . . , it will seize on the place of that inhabitant.[39]

This passage demonstrates two theses (which are also evident in other assertions by Darwin). First, he believed that invoking the creative act of God is not a sufficient answer to the question of the origin of species. It only repeats, if in a more sophisticated way, the statement that species do exist, without providing any positive knowledge. Second, he understood his idea of natural selection and random variation as competing with the idea of creation. Interestingly, both views are presented here as matters of *belief* rather than *knowledge*. Therefore, they are closely positioned on the epistemological level and compete with each other as mutually exclusive options. This further suggests that the distinction, sometimes emphasized by theologians, between "the theory of evolution" and "evolutionism" is not well founded. Some theologians claim that evolutionism is an error, but the theory of evolution, if kept within scientific boundaries, is acceptable. We see that Darwin himself did not make this distinction; his theory was simultaneously natural and theological, and these two aspects could not be separated.

One might argue that the only consequence of the new theory was to eliminate discrete creative acts from the origin of species. In fact, the theory reorganized the earlier, thoroughly theistic, approach to nature. Up to that point, nature was considered a harmonious whole—each detail of nature reflected the divine mind in the plan of creation. For instance, in his *Natural Theology* (1802), Paley saw a certain scheme and purpose designed by the perfect Intelligence in every detail of human, animal, and plant structure. Nature in its entirety was for him the expression of God's benevolence and creativity.[40] Darwin's work, by intention, was a sustained polemic against precisely these conclusions.

species could possibly have migrated from some one point to the several distant and isolated points, where now found. Nevertheless the simplicity of the view that each species was first produced within a single region captivates the mind. He who rejects it, rejects the *vera causa* of ordinary generation with subsequent migration, and calls in the agency of a miracle" (ibid., 352). "To admit this view [of the special creation of species] is, as it seems to me, to reject a real for an unreal, or at least for an unknown, cause" (ibid., 167). "Such facts as the presence of peculiar species of bats, and the absence of all other mammals, on oceanic islands, are utterly inexplicable on the theory of independent acts of creation" (ibid., 477–78).

39. Ibid., 185–86.

40. Cf. W. Paley, *Natural Theology*, e.g., 253–54.

Until the 18th century, there was a particular philosophical paradigm in use, in which the beauty and rationality of the world refers to God as its creator, and everything visible has an omnipotent and intelligent cause. Natural philosophers in particular believed that the very possibility of species classification, their complementariness and systematization into logical sequences, is more than coincidental. Classification itself demonstrated a plan and was a clear sign of the divine mind at work. For Darwin, this "wonderful fact"[41] had quite a different explanation:

> Naturalists try to arrange the species, genera, and families in each class, on what is called the Natural System. But what is meant by this system? . . . The ingenuity and utility of this system are indisputable. But many naturalists think that something more is meant by the Natural System; they believe that it reveals the plan of the Creator; but unless it be specified whether order in time or space, or what else is meant by the plan of the Creator, it seems to me that nothing is thus added to our knowledge. Such expressions as that . . . the characters do not make the genus, but that the genus gives the characters, seem to imply that something more is included in our classification than mere resemblance. I believe that something more is included; and that propinquity of descent,—the only known cause of the similarity of organic beings, is the bond, hidden as it is by various degrees of modification, which is partially revealed to us by our classifications.[42]

The understanding of nature as a reflection of beauty was the biggest challenge for Darwin's worldview. If there is beauty, it must have an author. Pre-Darwinian thinking about nature can be illustrated with a following syllogism:

> Harmony and rationality require a rational cause (major premise);
> The world is rationally organized (minor premise);

41. "It is a truly wonderful fact . . . , that all animals and all plants throughout all time and space should be related to each other in group subordinate to group, in the manner which we everywhere behold. . . . On the view that each species has been independently created, I can see no explanation of this great fact in the classification of all organic beings; but, to the best of my judgment, it is explained through inheritance and the complex action of natural selection" (*The Origin of Species*, 128–29).

42. Ibid., 413. "On this same view of descent with modification, all the great facts in morphology become intelligible, to whatever purpose applied" (456–57). "This tendency in the large groups to go on increasing in size and diverging in character, together with the almost inevitable contingency of much extinction, explains the arrangement of all the forms of life, in groups subordinate to groups, all within a few great classes, which we now see everywhere around us, and which has prevailed throughout all time. This grand fact . . . seems to me utterly inexplicable on the theory of creation" (471). "It is so easy to hide our ignorance under such expressions as the plan of creation, unity of design, etc., and to think that we give an explanation when we only restate a fact" (481–82). "We shall never, probably, disentangle the inextricable web of affinities between the members of any one class; but when we have a distinct object in view, and do not look to some unknown plan of creation, we may hope to make sure but slow progress" (434).

Therefore, the world is explained through referring to the rational cause or the greatest reason (conclusion).

Darwin did not argue with the conclusion but simply removed the major premise by stating that order in nature does not require a higher reason to be explained:

> *Natura non facit saltum.* We meet with this admission in the writings of almost every experienced naturalist.... Why, on the theory of Creation, should this be so? Why should all the parts and organs of many independent beings, each supposed to have been separately created for its proper place in nature, be so invariably linked together by graduated steps? Why should not Nature have taken a leap from structure to structure? On the theory of natural selection, we can clearly understand why she should not.[43]

According to Darwin, either the world is in a state of constant struggle or it constitutes a field for the operation of nature's laws; but in neither case need it reflect any supernatural order. In his argument, the apparent presence of "imperfection" within nature figures prominently. Among some examples is the case of the bee, which, by stinging in order to save its life, inevitably loses it. This, along with several other instances, was sufficient proof for Darwin that nature is imperfect. And because natural selection could not be expected to achieve perfection, natural selection was the better explanation for natural phenomena.[44] The notion that all nature is "egoistic" is the basis of his theory: "If it could be proved that any part of the structure of any one species had been formed for the exclusive good of another species, it would annihilate my theory, for such could not have been produced through natural selection."[45] Any trace of altruism in nature, according to Darwin, would have proved "absolutely fatal to the theory."[46]

But this reasoning was somewhat inconsistent. For instance, Darwin's own example of the bee that kills a prospective enemy of other insects and dies doing so meets the criterion of unselfishness that is so destructive to his theory. Another example would be a bird that produces loud warnings against immi-

43. Ibid., 194.

44. Cf. *The Origin of Species*, 188–89. "Natural selection will not produce absolute perfection, nor do we always meet, as far as we can judge, with this high standard under nature. [...] If our reason leads us to admire with enthusiasm a multitude of inimitable contrivances in nature, this same reason tells us, [...], that some other contrivances are less perfect. Can we consider the sting of the wasp or of the bee as perfect [...]?" Ibid., 202.

45. Ibid., 201.

46. "The foregoing remarks lead me to say a few words on the protest lately made by some naturalists, against the utilitarian doctrine that every detail of structure has been produced for the good of its possessor. They believe that very many structures have been created for beauty in the eyes of man, or for mere variety. This doctrine, if true, would be absolutely fatal to my theory" (ibid., 199).

nent danger. The warnings benefit other creatures, but reduce the bird's own chance of survival.

Contradictory evidence such as this did not make Darwin abandon his theory, since it is more philosophical and axiological than biological in its nature and intention. Darwin and later Darwinists presented his work as a neutral scientific explanation for the diversity and complexity of organisms. But his continual use of the argument from imperfection and against special creation demonstrates that his work is as much theological—or atheological—as scientific. This is perhaps unsurprising, given that theology was the only subject in which he received academic qualification. In any case, a complete assessment of Darwinism must account not only for its scientific theses, but for its philosophical and theological content as well.

From Darwinism to Neo-Darwinism

One of the key problems in Darwin's theory is the source of advantageous novelties in subsequent generations of living beings. By itself, the claim that natural selection preserves the fittest organisms and destroys the unfit ones is a tautology. To the question of which organisms would survive, Darwin replies: the fittest. But to the question of which organisms are the fittest, the answer was: the ones that survive. The idea of "species" is similarly problematic. At the beginning of his work, Darwin claims that species are variable, and that borders between species and varieties are fluid to the point of being indefinable. The adoption of such postulates opens the way to the theory of species transformism. The entire theory is based on the assumption of a common and presumably limitless "tendency of departing from the original type," i.e., the claim that succeeding generations exhibit new traits. Those new traits at first distinguish offspring within the species, but the accumulation of new features over many generations leads to the emergence of new varieties—new species, genera, families, orders, etc. However, the same diversification must also lead to the consolidation of features in order to make a new species distinct from the others. Paradoxically, then, for Darwin variability within a species is responsible both for departure from a species and for the consolidation of features constituting a species.

For decades, honest interpreters of Darwin have recognized that his explanations were based on circular reasoning, tautologies like that of the *survival-of-the-fittest*, and contradictions, in which opposite effects were attributed to the same action. The problem faced by Darwinism concerned the way in which "blind" nature was supposed to shape one-directional and apparently purposeful changes sufficient to guide the postulated evolution of new species, organs, and body plans. In terms of classical metaphysics, Darwin's explanations were generally reductive, since he excluded *a priori* final and formal causes from his studies. In fact, he conflated the efficient cause (*causa efficiens*) with the material cause (*causa materialis*). Therefore, the main question he needed to answer was: What material cause produces novel advantageous traits in organisms?

When trying to answer the question of biological novelties, Darwin had only a few examples, most of which did not explain the origin of advantageous changes but assumed their previous existence.[47] Eventually, he admitted:

> Our ignorance of the laws of variation is profound. Not in one case out of a hundred can we pretend to assign any reason why this or that part differs, more or less, from the same part in the parents.[48]

In 1866, an Austrian religious, the Augustinian friar Gregor Mendel (1822–1884), published a work entitled *Experiments on Plant Hybridization* wherein he presented the results of many years' observations of interbreeding varieties of pea plants (*pisum sativum*). In this work, Mendel formulated the fundamental laws of heredity (Mendel's laws), which to this day constitute the basis of genet-

47. Darwin claimed that variability was determined, for example, by conditions of living that might particularly influence the reproductive system. If the parents' system changes to a minor extent, the offspring may change significantly. Similarly, a minor variation during the embryonic period may result in a major variation in an adult specimen. At another point Darwin suggested that natural selection takes part in variation: "When a variation is of the slightest use to a being, we cannot tell how much of it to attribute to the accumulative action of natural selection, and how much to the conditions of life" (*The Origin of Species*, 133). However, Darwin's referral to selection in an attempt to explain the causes of selection is just circular reasoning. On the other hand, by invoking the "conditions of life" as a generator of variability he returned to Lamarck's concept, according to which an animal was able to develop new features by effort of its will in reaction to the environment. This concept is tantamount to claiming that, for example, a squirrel, by jumping from tree to tree for many millions of generations, would gradually transform into a bird. Darwin assumed what later proved to be largely wrong—that acquired traits are hereditary. Darwin also looked for the origin of new traits in the mechanism of "acclimatization," or changes resulting from species' adjustment to new climatic conditions. Acclimatization, however, does not explain where the new characteristics come from, but only restates the fact that natural selection may possibly preserve animals best adapted to the new environment, therefore those who already possess these characteristics. Another source of variability, Darwin thought, was the "reappearance of lost traits" or the so-called "tendency to reversion." In this case, though, he assumes the previous existence of such traits without explaining their actual origin. A similar problem pertains to what he referred to as "correlation of growth," i.e., the process by which an animal's organs were adjusted to other, previously transformed (e.g., enlarged) organs. But the question is not whether organs change together (or correlate) but: What makes them change? Where are the sources of variation? Darwin also noticed that "uncommonly developed parts tend to be more variable." Again, this finding says nothing about the sources of variation. Darwin was aware that his explanations were insufficient, so he tried to fill the gaps with the statement that changes occur very slowly: "New varieties are very slowly formed, for variation is a very slow process, and natural selection can do nothing until favourable variations chance to occur, and until a place in the natural polity of the country can be better filled by some modification of some one or more of its inhabitants" (177). Eventually, there was nothing left but to assume that the advantageous novelties appeared by chance.

48. Ch. Darwin, 167.

ics.[49] Mendel's discoveries at first did not attract much notice from biologists, who regarded his ideas as useful only for plant growers. In 1900, however, his work was brought to light by three scientists: Hugo de Vries (1848–1935), Carl Correns (1864–1933), and Erich Tschemark (1871–1962). The studies of these pioneering geneticists show that much of heredity is governed by strict laws. For the first time, genetics had confirmed the extraordinary stability of species, and also proved that traits acquired by chance in individual development cannot be inherited by offspring.

This was a serious threat to the theory of biological macroevolution—the theory lost the only source of possible variability, without which natural selection could achieve nothing. In subsequent years Darwin's idea encountered obstacles in various subfields of biology.[50] First of all, intermediate links between individual species were found to be missing from the fossil record. Large groups of organisms appeared suddenly, as though out of nowhere, and continued for millions of years in unchanged forms (*stasis*). The fossil record, then, contradicted the theory of gradual development of species from a single common ancestor.[51] Later studies proved that the law of recapitulation (postulated by Ernst Haeckel) was unfounded.[52] As a result, Darwinists faced stiff resistance on the scientific front even as their power in popular mass culture was on the ascent.

49. Mendel, an avid scientist, obviously knew Darwin's theses but opposed them, leaning towards the theory of independent creation. For more on this subject see B.E. Bishop, "Mendel's Opposition to Evolution and to Darwin," *Journal of Heredity* 87 (1996): 205–13. L.A. Callender, "Gregor Mendel: An Opponent of Descent with Modification," *History of Science* 26 (1988), 41–75.

50. This problem is signaled by Michael Behe in his book *Darwin's Black Box: The Biochemical Challenge to Evolution* (New York: Free Press, 2006). Recent years have seen many publications concerning the scientific problems of Darwinism in the 20th century. Pioneering works on the subject include the now-classic book by Michael Denton, *Evolution: A Theory in Crisis: New Developments in Science are Challenging Orthodox Darwinism* (London: Burnett Books, 1985). Cf. note 79.

51. The discussion among paleontologists of the existence of intermediate links between various fossils and contemporary organisms continues to this day. Currently, even many evolutionary biologists admit that the fossil record does not fit the scenario of gradual, minor modifications, but rather the sudden emergence of large groups of entirely new organisms. See: http://www.veritas-ucsb.org/library/origins/quotes/Discontinuties.html (January 20, 2015). The problem of missing links and the so-called "Cambrian explosion" (the sudden appearance in fossil records of the major animal types within a geologically short period) is discussed in the film *Darwin's Dilemma*, http://www.darwinsdilemma.org/ (January 25, 2015) and a book by Stephen Meyer, *Darwin's Doubt* (New York: HarperOne, 2013).

52. The law of recapitulation states that individual development repeats the evolution of the species (ontogeny recapitulates phylogeny). This law was postulated by Darwin but popularized by Haeckel who, in order to prove it, used falsified drawings of various animal embryos. The "mythological" nature of Haeckel's embryos has been analyzed by Jonathan Wells in his *Icons of Evolution* (Washington, DC: Regnery Publishing, 2002), 81–110. The law of recapitulation has no scientific justification but is still preserved in many textbooks. The last place a reader would expect to find this

Harvard professor of anatomy Thomas Dwight provided an interesting account of the situation in academic circles at the time. In a book first published just before his death (1911), he writes about the forced introduction of Darwin's theory into science:

> The tyranny of the Zeitgeist in the matter of evolution is overwhelming to a degree of which outsiders have no idea; not only does it influence (as I must admit that it does in my own case) our manners of thinking, but there is the oppression as in the days of the terror. How very few of the leaders of science dare to tell the truth concerning their own state of mind. How many of them feel forced in public to do a lip service to a cult they do not believe in![53]

In 1941, a group of intellectuals determined to reconcile Darwin's theory with the findings in genetics assembled at a meeting held by the Geological Society of America. Among the representatives of science were the geneticists George Ledyard Stebbins and Theodosius Dobzhansky; zoologists Ernst Mayr and Julian Huxley (the grandson of T.H. Huxley); palaeontologists George Gaylord Simpson and Glenn L. Jepsen; as well as population geneticists Ronald A. Fisher and Sewall Wright. These scholars devised a new version of Darwinism, officially referred to as "the synthetic theory of evolution," or popularly "neo-Darwinism." This synthesis led to the adoption of evolution through natural selection as the unifying principle of all biology.[54] In the years following, various specialists began to incorporate the neo-Darwinist synthesis into their respective fields.

As all the previous candidates for explaining the origin of variability conflicted with the evidence from biology, genetic mutations were invoked as the generators of change. Darwin referred to so-called "monstrosities" as one of the possible sources of variability (this idea had already been mentioned by Robert Chambers in his *Vestiges*).[55] However, the early Darwinists knew that strong mutations (macromutations) lead to the generation of debilitated individuals, which are eliminated rather than preserved by natural selection. Therefore, they attributed little importance to them. Paradoxically, neo-Darwinists subse-

fraud is a Catholic encyclopedia. However, even in the latest edition (2003) of the *New Catholic Encyclopedia*, Haeckel's drawings are featured under the entry *Evolution* without any correction. See *New Catholic Encyclopedia*, 2nd Edition, vol. 5, ed. B.L. Marthaler et al. (Washington, DC: Catholic University of America Press, 2003), 492.

53. T. Dwight, *Thoughts of a Catholic Anatomist* (New York, London: Longmans Green & Co., 1911), 20.

54. Cf. B. Leith, *The Descent of Darwin: A Handbook of Doubts about Darwinism* (London: Collins, 1982), 14.

55. The term "monstrosities" was applied to bigger changes that are now known to be the result of specific genetic errors. In humans, a known "monstrosity" was the occurrence of six fingers or toes. Incidentally, this was the ailment of Robert Chambers himself. He knew, however, that this kind

quently adopted mutations as the main source of innovation in their revamped theory, since only mistakes in the genetic code—random mutations—could be passed on to offspring. These two factors—random mutation and natural selection—are the core of the neo-Darwinian explanation for the origin of the astounding diversity and complexity of creatures.[56]

Of course, errors in the reproduction of genetic material do occur, and this is where micromutations take place. These consist in a faulty duplication of a fragment of a gene sequence. As a consequence, the organism may lose a trait, which may be a minor and insignificant loss, or a loss great enough to lead to a serious genetic disease resulting in the painful death of an individual. In the second half of the 20th century, laboratories in the USA, Europe, and the USSR conducted thousands of experiments aimed at demonstrating that new species could form by the accumulation of beneficial mutations through natural selection. But whether the mutations were created by artificial laboratory conditions or by happenstance in nature, it was found that they did not give rise to any advantageous biological novelties.[57] Each erroneous reproduction of the genetic material results in the usually irreversible loss of information necessary for the proper functioning of an organism. If a population of a given species is too small to overcome the loss of genetic information by interbreeding many different specimens from different environments, then the population degenerates. More and more offspring are born weak and ill, fertility of the population decreases, and biologists begin to devote efforts (often futile) to prevent the species from becoming extinct. Over millions of years, species lose information that they seem to have had in the most complete form in the beginning. Observation of nature does not reveal the improvement of species as much as it does their degeneration and extinction. The process might be likened to a constant rewriting of the same piece of text. If a copyist misspells a word or a letter, the

of mutation was not to his advantage (the extra fingers were not functional). Moreover, he witnessed this feature disappear in his family in subsequent generations. The conclusion that should have come to mind was that mutations could not be responsible for the emergence of functional anatomical novelties. Another relationship known to Darwin was the deafness of white, blue-eyed cats. We know today that this coincidence is due to a damaged gene that simultaneously determines hearing, eye color, and fur color. But for Darwin and the early evolutionists, occurrences of this type were a great mystery and a possible beginning for new breeds and species.

56. Cf. C. H. Waddington, "Theories of Evolution" in *A Century of Darwin*, ed. S. A. Barnett et al. (London: Mercury Books, 1962), 10–18.

57. It is often claimed that resistance to antibiotics in bacteria is an example of advantageous novelties caused by mutations. In fact, those mutations do not produce any novelty in the organisms but only alter one of the key proteins in such a way that the antibiotic can no longer recognize it and destroy its function. The alteration of the protein is advantageous only relatively, when the antibiotic is present. But the resistant strains of bacteria are not able to compete with the non-resistant (non-mutated) ones shortly after the antibiotic is removed. Cf. *Explore Evolution*, 100–105.

next one rewrites it with these errors. Of course, an intelligent scribe could correct the words in order to restore the original information. However, nature is blind: it copies what it receives, and thus cannot make up for any loss on its own.

Most evolutionists were aware of this problem, so as early as the 1950s the answer to the theory's shortcomings was the claim that random events in nature may produce any kind of effect, including the generation of inconceivably complex biological structures. Therefore, the core of the contemporary debate on evolution is the question of what chance is and what it can lead to.[58] This is the context in which statements of evolutionists should be interpreted, such as George Gaylord Simpson's "Man is the result of a purposeless and natural process that did not have him in mind."[59]

Sometimes artificially induced mutations are cited as evidence of the power of mutations to generate biological novelties. A famous example is the four-winged fruit fly. In the late 1970s, geneticist Ed Lewis succeeded in breeding a fruit fly (Drosophila melanogaster) with two pairs of wings instead of one. The fly was an effect of controlled genetic mutations. In the USA, it quickly became a textbook example of how mutations may lead to the macroevolution of organisms. However, the example of the fruit fly was encumbered with many difficulties. First, the new pair of wings appeared in the place of another pair of organs—the halteres, which in a normal specimen are responsible for its balance in flight. Second, the new pair of wings was not attached to any muscles and was therefore useless. It was also no novelty, but only a copy of a structure already existing in the organism. Finally, the breeding process required a series of three controlled mutations and artificial reproduction of specimens that would not have survived in normal conditions. Therefore, the example was based on purposeful action of scientists and was no proof that such a situation could occur in the natural environment. The mutant fly was not able to fly well, so it could not procure food in the wild. It would have been the first to be eliminated through selection. Even before Lewis engineered his four-winged fruit fly, evolutionary biologist Ernst Mayr wrote about flies with other major mutations: "[T]hey are such evident freaks that these monsters can be designated only as 'hopeless.' They are so utterly unbalanced that they would not have the slightest chance of escaping elimination." See E. Mayr, *Animal Species and Evolution* (Cambridge: Cambridge University Press, 1970), 251–53. Quoted in J. Wells, 177ff.

58. Darwin expressed an ambiguous view of the role of chance: "New varieties are very slowly formed, for variation is a very slow process, and natural selection can do nothing until favourable variations chance to occur" (*The Origin of Species*, 177). "I have hitherto sometimes spoken as if the variations [...] had been due to chance. This, of course, is a wholly incorrect expression, but it serves to acknowledge plainly our ignorance of the cause of each particular variation" (ibid., 131). Neo-Darwinists have not shared Darwin's hesitation. One of the most famous evolutionists of the era wrote: "Since they [mutations] constitute the only possible source of modifications in the genetic text, itself the sole repository of the organism's hereditary structures, it necessarily follows that chance alone is at the source of every innovation, of all creation in the biosphere. Pure chance, absolutely free but blind, at the very root of the stupendous edifice of evolution: this central concept of modern biology is no longer one among other possible or even conceivable hypotheses. It is today the sole conceivable hypothesis, the only one that squares with observed and tested fact. And nothing warrants the supposition—or the hope—that on this score our position is likely ever to be revised." J. Monod, *Chance and Necessity: Essay on the Natural Philosophy of Modern Biology*, trans. A. Wainhouse (New York: Vintage, 1971), 112.

59. G.G. Simpson, *The Meaning of Evolution*, rev. ed. (New Haven: Yale University Press, 1967), 345.

One of the most famous criticisms of "what chance can do" comes from a distinguished but also controversial astronomer and mathematician, Fred Hoyle (1915–2001). Hoyle[60] calculated that the probability of the random occurrence of enzymes necessary for the production of even a single amoeba is $1{:}10^{40000}$. (By comparison, the probability of randomly drawing a specified atom in the entire universe is $1{:}10^{80}$.) Hoyle's calculations were later confirmed by more advanced research.[61]

Since Hoyle's first results, scientists have often returned to the "probability of the spontaneous origination of life." It should be noted here that, in itself, such a concept is elusive. When trying to calculate the probability of something that did not exist before, we have no defined universe. Starting out from the notion of accidental emergence, one might theoretically assume that life could have originated in many different ways, although no one knows what anything other than protein-based life would look like. By undertaking calculations of this sort, scientists define the domain based on their knowledge of what already exists. However, it takes a virtually infinite number of factors to generate even a single cell. For this reason no calculations can really account for the probability of the emergence of life. This is why all of these calculations refer to the probability of generating only one specific fragment of an organic compound and not a living being. It is a necessary, albeit insufficient, condition for the generation of life as such. This means, however, that the road from even the most accurate calculations to the actual probability of the origination of life is incredibly long.

Returning to Hoyle's calculations, one should now realize their import. Let us assume, for the sake of simplification, that the probability of winning the national lottery[62] is $1{:}10^7$. Consequently, the odds of origination of the enzymes in the simplest cell are roughly equal to those of winning the lottery 6000 times in a row. Supposing that there are a hundred drawings per year (twice a week excluding holidays), the probability of the birth of a cell is approximately the same as that of winning the desired combination of six digits twice a week, with no exception, for 60 years.[63] However, as Hoyle only calculated the odds of origination of basic compounds for a simple organism, one would have to

60. Hoyle calculated that the probability of random emergence of roughly 2000 enzymes which are necessary for even the simplest organism is one in 10^{40000}. Cf. F. Hoyle, Ch. Wickramasinghe, *Evolution from Space: A Theory of Cosmic Creationism* (New York: Simon & Schuster, 1984), 24 and 130.

61. Cf. S.C. Mayer, *Signature in the Cell: DNA and the Evidence for Intelligent Design* (New York: HarperOne, 2009), 213.

62. The exact odds of winning the Polish national lottery (Lotto) are 1:13,983,816.

63. Another comparison: Let us imagine that John cast a single specified atom into the universe (not the solar system or our galaxy, but one of the billions of galaxies) and asked Mary to find it with her eyes covered. Mary found the atom without making a mistake. John was surprised but he decided

assume that such events recurred millions of times in history. The history of the world is much too short to contain it all. For this reason, some critics of Darwinism call it "the atheists' faith."[64] Hoyle himself, having obtained his result, wrote that it alone "is enough to bury Darwin and the whole theory of evolution."[65] Hoyle was not a religious person. He reached his conclusions on the need for intelligence in the origin of life purely through physics and mathematical speculation.

to test Mary's luck and asked her to do it again. This time, he cast the atom somewhere else and Mary found it again. Such a scenario is impossible by chance, and the problem would be further aggravated if Mary locates the atom 500 times in a row. The transformation and calculation of the probability of organism generation has become a kind of a game for some scientists. For instance, 20th-century cosmologist Carl Sagan estimated that the probability of the origination of a man would be $1{:}10^{2000000000}$. But Borel's law of probability states that events less probable than $1{:}10^{50}$ never occur in the real world; see C. Sagan, F. H.C. Crick, L.M. Muchin, *Communication with Extraterrestrial Intelligence* (*CETI*), ed. C. Sagan (Cambridge: MIT Press, 1973), 45–46. On the background of Borel's estimate, see W. Dembski, *The Design Revolution* (Nottingham: InterVarsity Press, 2004), 84–85.

64. An example of such faith can be found in one of R. Dawkins's books: "The origin of life is a flourishing, if speculative, subject for research. The expertise required for it is chemistry and it is not mine. I watch from the sidelines with engaged curiosity, and I shall not be surprised if, within the next few years, chemists report that they have successfully midwifed a new origin of life in the laboratory. Nevertheless it hasn't happened yet, and it is still possible to maintain that the probability of its happening is, and always was, exceedingly low—although it did happen once!" See R. Dawkins, *The God Delusion* (New York: Mariner Books, 2008), 164–65.

65. Hoyle was to say, "The likelihood of the formation of life from inanimate matter is one to a number with 40,000 naughts after it [...]. It is big enough to bury Darwin and the whole theory of evolution. There was no primeval soup, neither on this planet nor any other, and if the beginnings of life were not random, they must therefore have been the product of purposeful intelligence." Cf. Lee Elliot Major, "Big Enough to Bury Darwin," *The Guardian* (23 August 2001), http://www.guardian.co.uk/education/2001/aug/23/highereducation.peopleinscience (January 25, 2015). At another point Hoyle likened the idea of the generation of higher forms of life through evolution to a "tornado sweeping through a junk-yard assembling a Boeing 747 from the materials therein." See F. Hoyle, "Hoyle on Evolution," *Nature* 294 (November 12, 1981), 104–105.

2

From Biblical Creationism to Intelligent Design

From Biblical Creationism to Scientific Creationism

THE TURN OF the 20th century was a difficult time for Christian denominations all around the world. Christianity came to be opposed by an intellectual trend in culture, referred to—first by Protestants, and then by Catholics—as "modernism." For Protestants, modernism was primarily a synonym for the strong criticism of the Bible, initiated primarily in Germany by David Friedrich Strauss (1808–1874). This intellectual struggle affected all churches and ecclesial communities in the world and presented a serious challenge to religious leaders. The modernists attempted to undermine the principles of Christian faith from various directions (e.g., philosophy, dogmatics, biblical studies). Conservative Protestants in America answered this by attempting to define Christianity anew by identifying its central and incontrovertible truths. In 1910, the General Assembly of the Presbyterian Church decided on the fundamental principles of faith, known as *Five Fundamentals*. The same year saw the publication of a larger version of *The Fundamentals* in a collection of ninety essays on basic dogmatic issues (1910–1915).[1]

Three essays were directly concerned with Darwin and evolution. In one of them, George F. Wright writes of the impossibility "to get any such proof of evolution as shall seriously modify our conception of Christianity. The mechanism of the universe is so complicated that no man can say that it is closed to divine interference."[2] In another essay, Henry H. Beach asks: "As a purely aca-

1. https://archive.org/details/fundamentalstest17chic (January 20, 2015). An abridged version of *The Fundamentals* to which I shall also refer the reader was published in 1990.

2. G. F. Wright, "The Passing of Evolution" in *The Fundamentals* (Grand Rapids: Kregel Publications, 1990), 625. One should also note that Wright directly admits the interpretation of a "creation day" as a period of time, not necessarily 24 hours long. Thus, he was not a determined supporter of

demic question, who cares whether a protoplastic cell, or an amoeba, or an ascidian larva, was his primordial progenitor? It does not grip us. It is doubtful whether any purely academic question ever grips anybody. But the issue between Darwinism and mankind is not a purely academic question."[3] The authors of *The Fundamentals* primarily attacked the philosophical implications of Darwinism, which were strong within this doctrine from the very start. They also looked somewhat condescendingly upon the claims of scientific evolutionists, openly defying them with the biblical account of creation.

These so-called fundamentalists adopted the principle of integral interpretation of the Scriptures. Beach further argued, "We cannot depend on the Bible to show us *how to go to heaven* if it misleads us as to *how the heavens go* regarding the origin, nature, descent and destiny of brutes and men."[4] Thus, according to the early fundamentalists, the Bible not only states that "God had created the world" but also tells "how He did it." Nevertheless, it should be added that Protestant fundamentalism has always been focused on doctrine and intellect, attempting to determine the inviolable truths of faith. Political implications, though noticeable, have never stepped out of the framework of American democratic order. This is what has always distinguished Protestant fundamentalism from other fundamentalisms, such as the Islamic one, which is a unified political and theological vision.

young earth creationism (ibid., 613). In his essay, Wright also stresses the thought that evolution is an ancient view, going back as early as pagan antiquity, and that as such it re-emerges at different points of history. "Evolution is not a new thing in philosophy, and such is the frailty of human nature that it is not likely to disappear suddenly from among men. The craze of the last half century is little more than the recrudescence of a philosophy which has divided the opinion of men from the earliest ages. In both the Egyptian and the East Indian mythology, the world and all things in it were evolved from an egg; and so in the Polynesian myths. But the Polynesian had to have a bird to lay the egg, and the Egyptians and the Brahmans had to have some sort of deity to create theirs. The Greek philosophers struggled with the problem without coming to any more satisfactory conclusion. Anaximander, like Professor Huxley, traced everything back to an infinity which gradually worked itself into a sort of pristine mud [...], of which everything else evolved; while Thales of Miletus tried to think of water as the mother of everything, and Anaximenes practically deified the air. Diogenes imagined a mind stuff (something like Weissmann's biophores, Darwin's gemmules possessed with affinity for each other, and Spencer's vitalized molecules) which acted as if it had intelligence; while Heraclitus thought that fire was the only element pure enough to produce the soul of men. These speculations culminated in the great poem of Lucretius entitled, *De Rerum Natura*, written shortly before the beginning of the Christian era [...]. Modern evolutionary speculations have not made much real progress over those of the ancients. They are, in their bolder forms atheistic; while in their milder forms they are deistic—admitting, indeed, the agency of God at the beginning, but nowhere else" (ibid., 624–25).

3. H.H. Beach, "Decadence of Darwinism" in *The Fundamentals*, 4, ch. 5 (this essay is absent from the paper issue from 1990); http://www.ntslibrary.com/PDF%20Books%20II/Torrey%20-%20The%20Fundamentals%204.pdf (January 25, 2015).

4. *The Fundamentals*, 4, ch. 5.

In 1925, in keeping with the trend of American religious revival, the state of Tennessee passed a bill proposed by John Washington Butler. The bill declared it "unlawful for any teacher in any of the . . . public schools of the State which are supported . . . by the public funds of the State, to teach any theory that denies the story of the Divine Creation of man as taught in the Bible, and to teach instead that man has descended from a lower order of animals."[5] In practice, the bill stifled the evolutionists' endeavors to present their theory as a scientifically proven fact and essentially rejected the notion of man's descent from lower animals for being incompatible with the Book of Genesis. The passing of that law soon led to the court case now known as the "Scopes Monkey Trial," which became an icon of the struggle—as popularly depicted—between an old-fashioned town full of religious fanatics and a wider world of educated scientists.[6] The defendant John Scopes, a teacher who presumably taught Darwin's theory against the law, was elevated to the rank of a martyr fighting for academic freedom. However, an analysis of the case based on the sources reveals that popular-science literature contains a number of myths and simplifications concerning the whole issue.[7]

Since the Scopes trial, there have been a few dozen trials concerning the teaching of evolution. In recent cases (such as Kitzmiller vs. Dover, 2005) the

5. H.W. House, "Darwinism and the Law" in *Intelligent Design 101: Leading Experts Explain the Key Issues*, ed. H.W. House (Grand Rapids: Kregel Publications, 2008), 180.

6. This kind of simplified picture of the case has been furthered by the 1955 film and play by J. Lawrence and R.E. Lee, entitled *Inherit the Wind*. The play ran on Broadway until 1957. It was revived in 1996 and ran until 2009. H.W. House lists fourteen discrepancies between the film and the facts. *Intelligent Design* 101, 189–190.

7. The new law passed in Tennessee attracted the attention of the American Civil Liberties Union, an organization established a few years earlier and concerned with the protection of constitutional liberties. After the bill was passed, the ACLU decided to test its significance and began to search for a candidate, a teacher who would be willing to conduct a lesson on Darwin against the provisions of the law. The organization promised to cover the costs of the trial and provide financial help to the defendant. Some business people from the small town of Dayton decided to take advantage of the situation. They wanted to stimulate the local economy and looked for a way to attract crowds to the town. The ACLU's offer seemed interesting, so they found a sports teacher (and occasional substitute in other subjects), John Scopes, whom they convinced to act as the defendant. Scopes himself asked three students to testify against him, though—as he later confessed in a secret interview with a journalist—he never actually conducted a lesson on Darwin. The trial began on May 25, attracting crowds of journalists and spectators from all over the country. A monkey dressed in a suit was walked around the town, performing tricks for money, and popcorn and hot dogs were on sale. The courthouse was full and the town became famous in the international press. The prosecutor was William J. Bryan, a famous orator and three-time Democratic presidential candidate. The lawyer representing Scopes on behalf of ACLU was Clarence Darrow. The case was in fact a dispute between the views represented by the two men. Bryan voluntarily subjected himself to a hearing by the advocate, so that, as he said, "the Christian world may know that any atheist, agnostocist or unbeliever can always ask me about my faith in God, and I will answer." Bryan was promised a chance to question Darrow

idea under scrutiny was not the replacement of evolution with the biblical record but promotion of so-called "balanced education." Opponents of the theory demanded that the teaching of scientific arguments be supplemented with information about scientific controversy and opposing arguments.

The promotion of the neo-Darwinian synthesis had its peak at the 100th anniversary of the publication of Darwin's *The Origin of Species*. An international celebration was held at the University of Chicago on November 24–28, 1959. Among many prominent figures (mostly Americans) were two British guests: Julian Huxley and Charles Darwin (the grandson of the naturalist). The ceremony included a few lectures and discussion panels. Each day was devoted to a different subject—cosmic evolution, evolution of life, evolutionary origin of man, evolution of societies, of religion and ethics. The event included the premiere of the musical *Time Will Tell*, about the life and work of Darwin. There were screenings of films on evolution, and the symposium enjoyed wide publicity in the media.

On Thanksgiving Day (November 26), the conference participants assembled in the university chapel, where Huxley, standing at the pulpit, announced the end of the idea of creation: "[A]ll aspects of reality are subject to evolution," he declared, "from atoms and stars to fish and flowers, from fish and flowers to human societies and values—indeed, that all reality is a single process of evolution. . . . The earth was not created; it evolved. So did all the animals and plants that inhabit it, including our human selves, mind and soul as well as brain and body."[8] Huxley's speech was controversial, but it was prophetic in

as well, but this never happened. In the course of the hearing, Darrow tried to have Bryan state a thesis about literal interpretation of Genesis, but the latter was not of such view and leaned rather towards progressive creationism. Scopes's defenders mentioned—as proofs of evolution—the examples of the Piltdown man and Heidelberg man, later exposed as frauds. Dr. K. F. Mather listed Neanderthals and Cro-Magnon people as the missing intermediate links and quoted the law of recapitulation: "ontogenesis repeats phylogenesis." Before it was time for Darrow to be heard, he interrupted the trial and confessed that the charges were justified. The situation became quite curious as the advocate now demanded that his client be sentenced. This way, Darrow avoided the hearing and also prevented Bryan from making a final statement in which the prosecutor would surely have used many strong arguments, and his testimony of faith would have gained publicity. But the defense had intended to lose the case primarily in order to take appeal. If Scopes had been acquitted, it would not have been possible to take an appeal and make a precedent, leading to the abolishment of the law in Tennessee. Thus the teacher was sentenced to a $100 fine. Appeal was taken to the Supreme Court of Tennessee, which overruled the sentence due to a formal error in the decision of the lower court. As it turned out, the Dayton judge had no right authority to determine the amount of the fine, as it had been the within the competence of the jury to do so. This way, the Tennessee bill was abolished, but the civic efforts to limit the teaching of evolution have never ceased in some regions of the USA. Account based on H. W. House, *Darwinism and the Law*, in *Intelligent Design* 101, 177–214.

8. J. Huxley, "The Evolutionary Vision: The Convocation Address" in *Evolution after Darwin* (Chicago: University of Chicago Press, 1960), 249–61, at 249; cf. 252–53.

demonstrating the power of Darwin's theory at the time, which extended far beyond the biological realm. A century after its inception, the theory of evolution was enjoying an undisputed victory in mass-culture and pervading the minds of regular people. Yet, already in the 1950s, the new Darwinian synthesis was opposed not only by biblical fundamentalists but also by scholars speaking in the name of science. One might wonder, then, why their voices were not heard at an event in which scientific issues were discussed.[9]

Less than a year later, two authors, John C. Whitcomb, a Protestant biblical scholar, and Henry Morris, a geologist and engineer, published a book entitled *The Genesis Flood*. The publication opened a new phase in the controversy. At the beginning of the volume, the authors made the following declaration: "In harmony with our conviction that the Bible is the infallible Word of God, verbally inspired in the original autographs, we begin our investigation."[10] The book attempts to convince the reader that the flood described in Genesis occurred globally and that the essential chronology of the flood explains empirical data such as the layers of the geological strata. Whitcomb first presents a few biblical arguments, from the Old as well as the New Testament, supporting this interpretation. Then he gives the floor to Morris, who attempts to correlate biblical data with scientific studies, particularly in the field of geology. According to both authors, the doctrine of uniformitarianism was not sustainable in the face of the scientific data available at the time.

The book offers somewhat sophistical arguments in favor of the necessity of a global flood to explain the arrangement of geological layers. The flood could not have been a local occurrence, argue Morris and Whitcomb, as water always strives to reach an equal level everywhere. Moreover, it would not have been able to cover the mountaintops (Genesis 7:19) had the flood only occurred in a certain region. The authors also consider the capacity of the ark and the possibility of its holding all the animals. They opt for the view that God had created the world during six twenty-four hour days, and the Earth's entire history (calculated using biblical genealogies) is less than 10,000 years old. Thus they support the view now referred to as young earth creationism (YEC), a school known to this day as "scientific creationism."

Scientific Creationism

The supporters of scientific creationism generally embraced natural science

9. Among scientists who challenged some or all of the neo-Darwinian claims were biologists Richard Goldschmidt, Pierre-Paul Grassé, Otto Schindewolf, Søren Løvtrup, and Ernst B. Chain (Nobel Prize laureate); mathematicians Marcel-Paul Schützenberger and Wolfgang Smith; and historians Jacques Barzun and Richard Weaver.

10. J. C. Whitcomb and H. Morris, *The Genesis Flood: The Biblical Record and its Scientific Implications* (Philadelphia: Presbyterian & Reformed, 1960), 1.

and called upon scientific research in attempting to prove their interpretation of the scriptures. Until that time, wherever there was a conflict between science and Holy Scripture, biblical creationism gave absolute priority to the Bible. According to scientific creationism, "the book of nature" and the book of divine revelation cannot be incompatible. Nevertheless, in the event of any difficulties reconciling scientific data with the letter of Genesis, priority was given to the latter. Conflict between the two showed that science still knows too little about the world, and that only when science converges with biblical teaching does the former achieve true understanding. It was an undeniable novelty for Bible scholars to probe into scientific research and willingly use the work of natural scientists. Before that, the fight was between scientific evolutionists and creationists, who simply asserted the biblical view without taking any interest in what science had to say. The standpoint of the "fundamentalists" of the 1920s is summarized in the statement: "It is so, because the infallible Bible says it is so." In contrast, the opinion of scientific creationists might be expressed as follows: God has revealed Himself to man in His Word, which we accept as it is; and science will eventually confirm this.

Scientific creationism developed in great detail among conservative Protestants in the second half of the 20th century. Soon, creationist organizations began to arise, focusing on scientific and biblical studies.[11] In 1963, a group of ten American scholars established the Creation Research Society. The number of its members quickly rose to 650, and each of them had to hold at least a Master's degree in a scientific discipline. In 1972, Morris set up the Institute for Creation Research, which has been a resilient organization for science and publicizing to this day. Not all of the few dozen institutions established in the USA and elsewhere in the world have shared the Young Earth Creationist views of Whitcomb and Morris. Differences between various kinds of creationism were often the subjects of heated debates and the objects of pity and ridicule from evolutionists. Without a doubt, the popularity of creationist organizations was stimulated by the ideological offensive of Darwinian materialism in the media and science, which encouraged scholars sharing a belief in creation to seek out others with similar views and form research groups. Today's public sees the creation versus evolution debate through the prism of disputes fought in the 1960s, 1970s, and 1980s. It was in those years that every kind of creationism came to be associated with fundamentalism and anti-science.

By the late 1980s there were dozens of books in the stream of scientific creationism. There were also a few Catholic authors supporting creation science, such as J.W.G. Johnson, who published the book *The Crumbling Theory of Evo-*

11. Currently in the USA there are at least 73 creationist organizations, followed by another 35 elsewhere in the world. See: http://www.creationism.org (January 25, 2015).

lution in 1982, followed by *Evolution?* in 1987. Johnson devotes much space to criticism of uniformitarianism and a defense of the literal geology and chronology of the flood. He recalls doubts concerning the C-14 carbon dating method, questions continental drift theory, and seeks to confirm the Earth's young age with the use of polonium radio-halos. He also extrapolates his findings to issues of culture and civilization, concluding that progressive evolution is also not possible in these fields.

In addition to his critique of modern science, Johnson goes on to criticize the philosophical concept of the "Omega Point" found in the works of Pierre Teilhard de Chardin, S.J. In this context, he writes of the "contamination of Christianity with evolutionism" and of theistic evolution. He emphasizes the inconsistencies between the ideas of the French Jesuit and the official view of the Catholic Church, pointing out the elements of pantheism and relativism in the works of Teilhard. Among his many arguments against evolution, Johnson includes the second law of thermodynamics, which implies that it is impossible for simpler systems to give rise to more complex ones using only the powers contained in the system. With reference to the "evolution of man," Johnson debunked the many fraudulent "intermediate links" between apes and *Homo sapiens* such as the Piltdown Man popularized by Teilhard. In sum, the work of Johnson had several advantages, particularly in the way it criticized the overreach of evolutionism; it was, however, less successful in providing a positive answer to scientific questions about origins. Like Whitcomb's *Genesis Flood*, it became entangled in aporias and overinterpretations of scientific facts, and placed too much emphasis on a literal and global interpretation of the Genesis flood.[12]

In 1985, biochemist Michael Denton published *Evolution: A Theory in Crisis*,[13] which occupied an intermediate standpoint between scientific creationism and intelligent design theory. Denton abandoned the attempts at reconciling the Bible with natural science and instead focused on the biochemical issues of evolution. Based on the latest findings in genetics, he proved the impossibility of combining organisms into a single phylogenetic tree. He was the first to frame

12. We say here "literal and global" to express the idea of the deluge covering literally all peaks on the Earth's surface (as scientific creationists maintained). But the deluge could also have been global in a slightly different sense—the same as when we speak about "global economy" or "global warming." It doesn't mean that all peaks were literally covered with water, but that this event affected all Earth and all humans.

13. See M. Denton, *Evolution: A Theory in Crisis. New Developments in Science are Challenging Orthodox Darwinism* (Great Britain: Burnett Books, 1985). In his book, Denton systematically discusses the major issues of evolution. He indicates scientific problems with the neo-Darwinian theory in paleontology and genetics; he disproves an argument from homology, mentions the difficulties of classification within Darwinism, and emphasizes the role of the philosophical paradigm in the theory of evolution.

the debate over evolution in empirical terms, and stressed that the problem lies primarily in the scientific weakness of the evolutionary theory itself, regardless of religious concerns.

From Scientific Creationism to Intelligent Design

In 1991 Phillip E. Johnson, a law professor at the University of California at Berkeley, published his book *Darwin on Trial.* Fifteen years later, the author wrote about his work: "Much to my pleasant surprise, this book turned out to be the match that lit the tinder beneath a stockpile of dry logs. This is not to my credit; the logs had been piled high, and the tinder gathered. Darwinian naturalists had accumulated a large stock of public discontent."[14] It turned out that Johnson's book gave rise to something of a social movement among scientists and philosophers, which came to be known as the intelligent design movement. Jay W. Richards expressed Johnson's message in the following way: "One reason why this book is so important is that Phil understood how to frame the issue properly, in a way that can actually win the debate. Rather than getting mired in disputes about the proper interpretation of Genesis 1 or the nature of science, he argued that we should simply consider the evidence for Darwinism empirically."[15] Thus the publication marked a new stage in the debate about the theory of biological evolution, and purely materialistic or mechanistic accounts of origins more generally.

Among the opponents of Darwinian evolutionism there had emerged a group of people, including many scientists, who were not interested in the creationist disputes over the shift of tectonic plates after the flood, or which peak of the Ararat Mountains houses Noah's ark. At the same time, Darwinists began gathering together more and more scientific doubts about the theory they propagated. Dissensions started growing in their own circle, and some of them began to criticize the neo-Darwinian synthesis openly and call for an alternative.[16] Aside from the problems that had remained unsolved since Darwin's time, the development of new subfields of biology presented fresh difficulties to what critics saw as an increasingly "obsolete theory." Information about these problems did not reach the general public, since the Darwinists enjoyed media support and Darwinian evolution prevailed in textbooks and academia. Until

14. P. Johnson, "Bringing Balance to a Fiery Debate" in *Intelligent Design* 101, 21–40, 23.

15. J. W. Richards, "Why Are We Here? Accident or Purpose?" in *Intelligent Design* 101, 131–152, 133.

16. An example of an unsolved debate among evolutionists was the criticism of the evolutionary interpretation of the fossil record conducted by Stephen J. Gould, N. Eldredge, and S. Stanley. These scientists proposed their own explanation in the form of the punctuated equilibrium theory. However, "orthodox" Darwinists rejected this doctrine, and Gould was severely criticized. Fundamental doubts in various fields were also reported by Fred Hoyle, R. Goldschmidt, and others.

at least the mid-1980s it was believed that, imperfect as it is, Darwin's theory was still the only sensible answer to the question of the origin of life's complexity. Scientists do not abandon a theory—even a very defective one—if there is no viable alternative that arranges and explains facts more efficiently. However, before 1990, the only obvious alternative to Darwinism was found in biblical or scientific creationism—which no Darwinist would consider, not least because creationism provided a "religious" answer to a "scientific" question.

In March 1992, just a few months after the publication of Johnson's *Darwin on Trial*, a conference was held at Southern Methodist University, which was the first to gather the leading figures of the emerging intellectual movement among American scientists. It was an occasion when the following professors met: lawyer Phillip Johnson, biochemist Michael Behe, philosopher of science Stephen C. Meyer, and analytic philosopher and mathematician William Dembski.

It was already two years since the establishment of Seattle's Discovery Institute—one of the American think tanks promoting the ideals of representative democracy and free market economics. In 1995, the Discovery Institute held a conference entitled "The Death of Materialism and the Renewal of Culture," which again assembled individuals interested in anti-evolutionary ideas. This is how the Center for Science and Culture, a program of Discovery Institute, was born. The Center sponsors research exploring the limits to Darwinian explanations and the development of intelligent design as an alternative to Darwinism and materialism.

In 1998 the Center prepared a five-year plan called the *Wedge Document*—an internal brochure sent out privately to scientists, philosophers, and business people who might prospectively be interested in supporting the initiatives of the Institute. Phillip Johnson repeatedly declared that the movement intended to drive a wedge (thus the term *wedge strategy*) into the materialistic monolith of contemporary science—the biological sciences in particular. Johnson believed that the scientific disciplines had been unreservedly captured by the proponents of a single, and rather poorly founded, theory. However, as this theory had the monopoly, Johnson argued that a "wedge" needed to be driven into it, which could then open up space to develop an alternative theory. As he wrote:

> My goal has been to unite the divided theists and open-minded skeptics of religion and divide the united evolutionist community. The neatest way to divide Darwinists is to point out the line that separates philosophical naturalists from those who are actually open to looking at the evidence carefully.[17]

17. P. Johnson, "Bringing Balance to a Fiery Debate," 32.

During more than a decade of its activity, the "wedge strategy" produced amazing fruits of cooperation among adherents of very different religious and political views around the common idea of intelligent design. At the same time, though, it terrified the leading personages of evolutionary ideology, who often resorted to personal attacks on their critics. This problem was so acute that even leading Darwinian philosopher Michael Ruse referred to Daniel Dennett and Richard Dawkins as "absolute disasters in the fight against intelligent design," for using a "plain silly and grotesquely immoral" way to blame Christianity as the root of evil, when in fact "we are in a fight, and we need to make allies in the fight, not simply alienate everyone of good will."[18] This statement by Ruse demonstrates the power of the challenge Darwinists faced from other scholars.

Despite the controversy, intelligent design (ID) has gained popularity as an alternative approach to the interpretation of natural facts. Evolutionists were forced to seek the support of hesitant people—but the eccentric remarks of Dawkins and Dennett concerning God and Christianity were making that harder to accomplish. At the same time, ID proponents were busy encouraging real cooperation among experts in various fields of science and philosophy, regardless of their varying religious views. In this way the wedge strategy has proved successful. Intelligent design has divided scientists, not according to the classic pattern of conservative Christians versus liberals and atheists, but according to the pattern of ideological, Darwinian materialism versus open-minded critical thinking about the so-called "scientific consensus." Currently, the prominent figures within the movement include agnostics (D. Berlinski), Protestants (Dembski, Johnson, and Meyer), Catholics (Behe and Richards), Jews, Buddhists, and even a follower of Rev. Moon (Jonathan Wells).

The late Anthony Flew (d. 2010) was an atheist philosopher who presented his extraordinary erudition in numerous debates on the existence of God over several decades. One might say that through his publications and appearances he was a scientific icon of atheism in the English-speaking culture of the second half of the 20th century. Near the end of his life, however, he changed his position, converting to deism and opening up to the possibility of supernatural revelation. He expressed his change of views several times, particularly in the introduction to the fourth edition of his work *God and Philosophy*. In a 2004 interview, Flew said:

> I think that the most impressive arguments for God's existence are those that are supported by recent scientific discoveries.... I think the argument to

18. It is a piece of correspondence published by W. Dembski (with the author's consent) on his blog post of February 21, 2006. See W. Dembski, *Remarkable Exchange between Michael Ruse and Daniel Dennett*. http://www.uncommondescent.com (January 25, 2015).

> intelligent design is enormously stronger than it was when I first met it. . . . It now seems to me that the findings of more than fifty years of DNA research have provided materials for a new and enormously powerful argument to design.[19]

Anthony Flew did not speak about a religious conversion, but about changing his philosophical views under the influence of ID arguments. The new theory provided him with rational, scientific, and convincing arguments in favor of theism.

Elements of Intelligent Design Theory

Specified Complexity

A frequent mistake made in discussions about intelligent design is to claim that the theory is just a new, "disguised" version of creationism, and that it offers nothing more than criticism of Darwinian evolutionism. In fact, ID—much like Darwinism—is more than just one of many scientific theories. It is a new paradigm of science and philosophy alternative to neo-Darwinism. Researchers associated with the ID movement do not limit their work to criticizing Darwinism. First of all, these scientists differ in their approach to various elements of Darwin's theory. Some of them—Michael Behe, for instance—do not reject the idea of common descent, or the significant role of natural selection in the development of genomes. All ID scientists recognize that natural selection explains *some* features of organisms. However, they all believe that natural selection and random mutations cannot explain the entire complexity of the organic world. What is more, these scientists are aware of the limitations of methodological naturalism in the approach to the mystery of life. On this basis, they defend an open philosophy of science, which postulates that a scientist should go wherever empirical facts take him, even if these facts lead to an intelligent cause.

It is crucial to grasp the difference between creationism and intelligent design theory. The nature of scientific creationism is well expressed by the subtitle of Whitcomb's book, *Genesis Flood: The Biblical Record and its Scientific Implications.* The biblical record offered specific scientific implications for which creationism attempted to find scientific evidence. Things are different with intelligent design. The dispute is fought on a scientific and philosophical level. The question is whether the world is a product of blind processes, as postulated by Darwinism, or an effect of intelligent agency. Does experimental research help us find in the world the effects of random or purposeless pro-

19. See: A. Flew, G. R. Habermas, "My Pilgrimage from Atheism to Theism," *Philosophia Christi* (Winter 2004), 197–212; http://www.epsociety.org/library/articles.asp?pid=33 (January 26, 2015).

cesses, or of planned actions, "designs" that could only have been devised by some kind of intelligence?

What ID theorists do not do, however, is specify the identity of this intelligence. As scientists, they pursue the idea that the effects of intelligent agency can be tested empirically, and that the action of an intelligent factor is a better explanation (or indeed the only explanation) of a number of natural phenomena, especially on the molecular level of biology. Such an approach may have theological implications—like many other natural theories—but it does not of itself lead to any religious doctrine, nor does it presuppose the existence of God.

For example, according to Stephen C. Meyer, ID allows for concepts which claim that life on Earth came from some kind of extraterrestrial intelligence. Any religious or philosophical view may be compatible with ID, provided it rejects chance and necessity as the primary causes of the emergence of organized structures. This is ID theory in its minimalist sense. This "minimum" does not even determine whether the world was created or exists eternally. Neither does it speculate about the origin and essence of this intelligence. It focuses specifically on a common attribute of all intelligent agents, whether human, non-human, or divine.

It seems that after more than a century of controversy, scientists have finally managed to establish an appropriate level of debate that does not juxtapose religious and scientific visions, but rather considers two separate scientific paradigms. As William Dembski, one of ID's pioneers, has written:

> What has kept design outside the scientific mainstream these last 130 years is the absence of precise methods for distinguishing intelligently caused objects from unintelligently caused ones. For design to be a fruitful scientific theory, scientists have to be sure they can reliably determine whether something is designed. Johannes Kepler, for instance, thought the craters on the moon were intelligently designed by moon dwellers. We now know that the craters were formed naturally. This fear of falsely attributing something to design only to have it overturned later has prevented design from entering science proper.... Scientists are now able to avoid Kepler's mistake.[20]

According to Dembski, scientific progress makes it possible to develop new theories, which in turn have the strength to change the paradigms. After long predominance, Darwinism is facing the same process of science development which a century ago significantly restricted design inference in natural science.

One might ask if ID is an entirely new concept. The answer will depend on

20. W.A. Dembski, "Introduction: Mere Creation," in *Mere Creation: Science Faith and Intelligent Design*, ed. William Dembski (Nottingham: InterVarsity Press, 1998), 16. Cf. *The Design Revolution*, 33–34.

which aspect of the theory one takes into consideration. Signs of intelligent activity in the natural world have been recognized since pagan antiquity, in the Bible and Christianity, and in the works of certain founders of modern science, such as Copernicus and Newton. The latter, having presented his opinion about the structure of the planetary system, wrote:

> Though these bodies may, indeed, continue in their orbits by the mere laws of gravity, yet they could by no means have at first derived the regular position of the orbits themselves from those laws. . . . [Thus] this most beautiful system of the sun, planets, and comets, could only proceed from the counsel and dominion of an intelligent and powerful Being.[21]

Clearly Newton attributed the operation of the planetary system to laws of nature, but to explain its origin one needed to appeal to intelligent causality.

The entire history of European philosophical and scientific thought confirms that man is able to recognize traces of higher intelligence in the universe. The period of Darwinism's prevalence was possibly the first moment in history when natural scientists tended to disregard what had seemed obvious to their predecessors. Nevertheless, Dembski's reservation remains valid. No ancient, medieval, or modern approach to design could be confirmed as strongly as that of today. Moreover, none was as thoroughly separated in its scientific content from philosophical and theological assumptions and implications. Many of the previous searches for design came close to pretenses (for instance, some of Paley's examples in biology) because those who proposed them lacked an adequate scientific background. In effect, design has sometimes seemed to have been imposed on the evidence more than inferred from the evidence. Therefore, the contemporary platform of intelligent design offers a new quality, one able to compete with the naturalistic concepts that have dominated science since the 19th century.

Currently, there is general agreement among scientists that life on the molecular level depends not only on physics and chemistry but also on information. Even Richard Dawkins admitted that a single cell nucleus contains more information than the thirty volumes of *Encyclopedia Britannica*.[22] Intelligent design

21. Sir Isaac Newton, *Newton's Principia Mathematica, Motte's Translation Revised*, trans. Andrew Motte, rev. Florian Cajori, 1934, 1686, 543–544. In his *De revolutionibus orbium coelestium* (*On the Revolutions of the Heavenly Spheres*), Copernicus wrote: "For when a man is occupied with things [astronomy] which he sees established in the finest order and directed by divine management, will not the unremitting contemplation of them and a certain familiarity with them stimulate him to the best and to admiration for the Maker of everything, in whom are all happiness and every good?" Nicholas Copernicus' *Revolutions*, Book 1, Introduction. English text available at: http://www.geo.utexas.edu/courses/302d/Fall_2011/Full%20text%20-%20Nicholas%20Copernicus,%20_De%20Revolutionibus%20%28On%20the%20Revolutions%29,_%201.pdf (January 26, 2015).

22. R. Dawkins, *The Blind Watchmaker* (New York: W.W. Norton, 1986), 116.

theory states that information cannot be generated by laws of nature or chance events, but must have its source in an intellect capable of choosing between alternatives, and that information can be distinguished from what-it-is-not by rigorous and objective scientific testing.

The origins of this concept can be found in William Paley's *Natural Theology*. The most famous example in his argument concerns a watch found by accident. If we walk through the moors and notice a watch on the ground, we will not be satisfied with the answer to the question of how it came to be there that it has gotten there by chance, or that it has just been lying there forever. Such a precise and purposeful mechanism could not have come into being by chance. On the other hand, positing that it has always existed merely evades the question as to where it came from. Today, in order to explain the biochemical argument, one might use another example. If we walk on the beach and find scratched into the sand the words "John loves Mary," we spontaneously presume that this is not a product of a blind or random movement of waves, wind, or animals. Assuming that there are 26 letters in an alphabet, plus the space sign—and not factoring in capital letters—the probability of arrangement of this simple sentence is 1 in 27^{15}. It is an incredibly small number, yet this inscription has meaning—it conveys information! Low probability and meaningful pattern, taken together, lead us to infer design. Now, if we realize that a single cell nucleus contains information equivalent to at least hundreds of thousands of such sentences, we can safely conclude that such information cannot have been generated only by chance or necessity, or a combination of both.

Piotr Lenartowicz, considering such "probabilistic miracles," wonders why evolutionary scientists accept the possibility of the occurrence of such events. Lenartowicz argues that such an event, though its mathematical probability is higher than zero, is actually impossible in the real world. According to Lenartowicz, scientists who accept the possibility of "probabilistic miracles" make the mistake of uncritically projecting mathematical considerations upon the physical world, and therefore ignore the obvious difference between random and selective choice. If such a "probabilistic miracle" really occurred, one might use statistical analysis to prove that it was a selective event rather than a random one.

The chance of throwing "six" with one die in one throw, for example, is 1 in 6. The probability of getting a thousand "sixes" when throwing one die a thousand times is very small, 1 in 6^{1000}. The probability of getting a thousand "ones" or "twos" or "threes" (etc.) in a row is exactly the same. In fact, the probability of any sequence of any natural number between 1 and 6 is equal and is always 1 in 6^{1000}. This means that the mathematical probability of getting a thousand "fours" in a row is extremely small, but is not smaller than obtaining any other such string with any other sequence of numbers. Yet, anyone who threw a die a thousand times and got a "four" a thousand times would be quite surprised and even suspicious about the quality of the die. In fact, no one would believe that this was a random event. However, nobody would be suspicious if "four" came up occasionally, maybe two or three times in a row. If the sequence of numbers was even more probable than a thousand "fours" in a row (for example, if "fours" appeared three times more often than other digits), a more mathematically inclined person would ask that a statistical test on randomness be applied to verify whether the die is fair or not. And the test would immediately show that the die must have been altered (weighted on the "three" face), for otherwise the total number of each digit's appearance should be roughly the same—about 1/6 of a thousand (~166). Thus, probability calculus—a theoretical tool—is in this case inadequate and misleading, because it leaves us with an impression that any outcome of throwing a die is equally probable in the real world. In fact, the larger the probabilistic resources (more throws of a die) the less probable it will be to get the same digits in a row, or any other pattern. With each extra throw, the total number of appearances of each digit will tend to approximate more closely 1/6 of the total number of throws. This fact diminishes (not increases) the possibility of getting any spectacular, that is, meaningful, outcome.

A more familiar example, called the "dactylographic miracle," describes monkeys tapping a computer keyboard. Lenartowicz points out that monkeys cannot type even a simple sonnet at random, for when the keys are being pressed randomly, the probability of hitting any symbol is exactly the same. Whereas each text in any given language is subject to various limitations (e.g., there must be a space after a punctuation sign, numbers occur much less frequently than letters, etc.). Therefore, text can only be composed through selective treatment of the keyboard, of which monkeys are incapable.[23] Again, the rule is: the more taps, the lesser chance to get a meaningful pattern. But since every language must have some patterns, the probability decreases as the number of random taps grows. This also explains why random events can produce some very short meaningful phrases or words (like "you," "be," "on") but never complete phrases, let alone books.

The crucial question for intelligent design theory concerns the possibility of detecting design. People can indeed spontaneously detect designs in everyday life. But is there any objective and precise method to distinguish between the

23. See: P. Lenartowicz, "O 'cudach' probabilistycznych, czyli fakt selekcji i odmowa poznania tego faktu" ["On Probabilistic 'Miracles,' that is, the Fact of Selection and Refusal of Recognition of This Fact"] in *Vivere et Intelligere. Wybrane prace Piotra Leartowicza SI z okazji 75-lecia jego urodzin* [Selected Works of Piotr Lenartowicz SJ on the Anniversary of His 75th Birthday], ed. J. Koszteyn (Kraków: Wyd. WAM, 2009), 569–608.

products of intelligence and other events that do not require intelligent causation?

In recent years, a method of identifying designs in nature has been proposed by William Dembski. He distinguishes between two different types of reasoning regarding intelligent causation: design argument and design inference:

> The design argument is at its heart a philosophical and theological argument. It attempts to establish the existence and attributes of an intelligent cause behind the world based on certain features of the world. By contrast, the design inference is a generic argument for identifying the effects of intelligence regardless of the intelligence's particular characteristics and regardless of where, when, how or why the intelligence acts.[24]

Design inference is thus different from the more theological arguments of thinkers like Saint Thomas Aquinas or William Paley.

The Explanatory Filter, proposed by Dembski, is a three-step intellectual tool which enables one to determine whether a given event, object, or element of nature—like biological structure—should be explained by design or rather by chance and necessity (law of nature). Dembski describes it as follows:

> (1) At the first stage, the filter determines whether a law can explain the thing in question. Law thrives on replicability, yielding the same result whenever the same antecedent conditions are fulfilled. Clearly, if something can be explained by a law, it had better not be attributed to design. Things explainable by a law are therefore eliminated at the first stage of the Explanatory Filter.
>
> (2) Suppose, however, that something we think might be designed cannot be explained by any law. We then proceed to the second stage of the filter. At this stage the filter determines whether the thing in question *might not reasonably be expected to occur by chance*. What we do is posit a probability distribution, and then find that our observations can reasonably be expected on the basis of that probability distribution. Accordingly, we are warranted attributing the thing in question to chance. And clearly, if something can be explained by reference to chance, it had better not be attributed to design. Things explainable by chance are therefore eliminated at the second stage of the Explanatory Filter.
>
> Suppose finally that no law is able to account for the thing in question, and that any plausible probability distribution that might account for it does not render it very likely. Indeed, suppose that any plausible probability distribution that might account for it renders it exceedingly unlikely. In this case we bypass the first two stages of the Explanatory Filter and arrive at the third and final stage.

24. W. Dembski, *The Design Revolution*, 77.

> (3) The third stage of the Explanatory Filter therefore presents us with a binary choice: attribute the thing we are trying to explain to design if it is specified; otherwise, attribute it to chance. In the first case, the thing we are trying to explain not only has small probability, but is also specified. In the other, it has small probability, but is unspecified. It is this category of *specified things having small probability that reliably signals design.* Unspecified things having small probability, on the other hand, are properly attributed to chance.[25]

Now, how does the Explanatory Filter work in the case of some simple, everyday events? For instance, seeing a statue of a national hero in a city, nobody doubts that it was intelligently designed. What makes one arrive at this conclusion instantly? Normally we do this directly and intuitively rather than inferentially, but if we follow the formal path of the Explanatory Filter, we ascertain the following: (1) the arrangement of the material (such as bronze) in the statue does not display any simple, repetitive pattern that could be determined by a law of nature. Neither is there any determination in the material itself to take this particular shape. (2) The particular arrangement of elements in the statue is complex and highly improbable. (3) The complexity is specified, as there is an independent model (a historic figure in this case) corresponding to the statue. Thus, the statue has been designed.

If we apply the Explanatory Filter to the biological realm we will arrive at the same conclusion: (1) The arrangement or sequence of nucleotide bases inside a DNA double helix is not determined by chemical properties. Thus, there is no law of nature that would determine the particular sequence of nucleotide bases. (2) The sequence of nucleotide bases forms the DNA code, which is often compared to letters building sentences in human language. As was said, long strings of letters are extremely complex and highly improbable. (3) Finally, DNA code is a source of information for the cell to build proteins with specific functions that then build or regulate the work of cellular organella. Therefore, DNA is not just complex but also specified. The conclusion is that it must have been designed.

DNA and RNA chains contain information that can now be deciphered and described with letters corresponding to particular nucleobases (T, G, C, A). Scientists can also synthesize, process, and further specify genetic information with respect to intended aim. Genetic engineering, as it is called, is a rapidly developing branch of biochemistry. The condition for the work of these bio-

25. W. Dembski, "The Explanatory Filter: A Three-Part Filter for Understanding How to Separate and Identify Cause from Intelligent Design," an excerpt from a paper presented at the 1996 Mere Creation conference "Redesigning Science"; http://www.arn.org/docs/dembski/wd_explfilter.htm (26 January 2015).

chemical engineers is a design existing in biological structures. If scientists did not acknowledge the existence of a design in the form of intelligible, purposeful genetic information, they would not be able to modify it according to their own plan, which would make void the entire branch of science.

The fundamental question in determining whether intelligent design is a science or not is whether it can be verified (falsified or confirmed) that a given natural structure or event is a product of intelligence. Detecting design is crucial for many human activities. It is performed, for instance, when archeologists establish whether a given piece of stone is an ancient tool or just a pebble shaped by wind and water, copyright and patent offices identify theft of intellectual property, insurance companies recognize fraud, detectives employ circumstantial evidence to incriminate a guilty party, scientists identify cases of data falsification, or statisticians and computer scientists distinguish random from non-random strings of digits. The claim of intelligent design theorists is that, just as scientists can detect human designs, so can they also detect designs embedded in nature. Opponents of this claim either reject the rational structure of reality or claim that design is only apparent (things look as if they were designed, but are not). But if the first were true, then no complex specificity could be discovered in nature, and genetic engineering would be no more than a game of roulette. And if the second were true, the question would follow, why do things that were not designed in fact look as if they were designed? And if they look and act as if they were designed, why wouldn't we then acknowledge that they were designed?

Currently, most inventions are first created with the use of computers, i.e., through mathematical description. Airplanes are entirely computer-designed, and only after the design is completed is a model tested under real-world conditions. Just as man is able to make a design and then transfer it to physical reality, it is possible also to identify a design in nature and transfer it to a computer. This is what happens when genetic codes are deciphered. The specified complexity of information contained in genes implies that it originated from an intelligent source. This is where the competence of science ends, as do also the postulates of intelligent design theory.

Irreducible Complexity

In 1996, Michael Behe published *Darwin's Black Box*, which is now commonly recognized as a stepping-stone in the critique of neo-Darwinism and the case for intelligent design.[26] Behe's term "black box" refers to any natural phenome-

26. It should be noted that ten years before the publication of Michael Denton's *Evolution: A Theory in Crisis* and twenty-one before that of Behe's *Darwin's Black Box*, the Polish Jesuit Piotr Lenartowicz (1934–2012) pointed out the problem of complexity discovered on biochemical level. In

non in which we know only input and output data (effects), but are ignorant of what happens inside the system. For 19th-century science, the cell was such a black box. It was not possible to see the mesmerizing complexity inside cells. Input data—that cells absorb nourishment, are sometimes sensitive to light, and so forth—was known. Output data—that cells divide, move, and eventually die—was also known. This was the information available to observers at the time; but the inside of these micro-globules remained a complete mystery. For Darwin, Ernst Haeckel, and other early evolutionists, a cell was a simple, homogeneous blob of protoplasm. Based on their lack of knowledge, they believed these "protoplasm bubbles" could emerge spontaneously, and that their function is determined by the emergence of a higher level of material organization. But as time passed the progress of the sciences, especially genetics and biochemistry, led to the discovery of the exquisitely orchestrated complexity of cell structure and processes. Scientists realized that what they were dealing with is a microcosm, an entire galaxy of sequences, organelles, functions, transformations, and relationships. Evolutionary biology attempted to explain the origin of hooves, beaks, fins, and wings; but, as Behe writes, "The real work of life does not happen at the level of the whole animal or organ; the most important parts of living things are too small to be seen. Life is lived in the details, and it is molecules that handle life's details."[27]

Behe recalled the dispute between Francis Hitching and Richard Dawkins on the evolution of the defense system of the bombardier beetle. Hitching demonstrated how the beetle skillfully releases from its abdomen two chemical substances that, when combined, produce an explosive mix that strikes an enemy, and asked how such a clever system could have evolved. Dawkins' reply is that both of the compounds as well as their catalyst occur in organisms. "The bombardier beetle's ancestors," he argues, "simply pressed into different service

---

his doctoral paper presented at the Pontifical Gregorian University in 1975, he discusses a "postulate of the complexity of the genetic material." See his *Phenotype-Genotype Dichotomy: An Essay in Theoretical Biology* (Roma: Pontificia Universitas Gregoriana, 1975), 143–46. He also considers the "multidimensional complexity" (ibid., 111). He argues that "modern molecular biology is quite aware of the fact that the dynamic events underlying the structural developmental changes observed during the life cycle are not only based upon the non-random dynamism, but even exclude the random dynamism in principle.... The only adequate explanation in sight seems to imply a dynamic, active agent, integrating heterogeneous events into the spatially and temporally multidimensional reality of the life cycle. The agency seems to be necessarily stable, i.e., independent of phenotypic influences.... The nature of this agent remains obscure" (ibid., 230). In 1986, Lenartowicz, in the book *Elementy filozofii zjawiska biologicznego* (Kraków: WAM, 1986), presented the concept of "functional integrity"—the idea that all parts in cellular devices must be present at once to perform a function. In the second edition of his book, Behe remarks that he had not been aware that in 1986 the biologist M.J. Katz used the expression "irreducible complexity" before him, with reference to biochemical systems (M. Behe, *Darwin's Black Box*, 221).

27. M. Behe, *Darwin's Black Box*, 4.

chemicals that already happened to be around. That's how evolution works."[28] Commenting on this unusual debate, Behe points out that none of the authors grasped the gist of the matter. The question is: how could complex biochemical systems have emerged by a blind and gradual process? Rather than focus on the entire organism, with its broad scope of complexity—perhaps beyond our ken at the moment—Behe argues that we can answer the question on the molecular level, where our understanding is more complete.

The key to understanding Behe's argument is the concept of an irreducibly complex system. He defines this as "a single system composed of several well-matched, interacting parts that contribute to the basic function, wherein the removal of any one of the parts causes the system to effectively cease functioning."[29] Certain cells contain organs such as cilia and flagella, complex systems of parts and processes coordinated to work together for specific functions. If any of their basic elements is missing, then the system as a whole will fail to function. In other words, their components are mutually dependent on each other. In order to determine whether a given system is irreducibly complex, one needs to: (1) recognize the function and all the key elements of the system (open all the "black boxes"); (2) check whether all elements of the system are necessary for its function.

Behe's primary example of an irreducibly complex system is a mousetrap. A mousetrap is a simple mechanism, composed of just five elements, but it is only able to perform its function when all five elements are simultaneously in their places. The trap has a base (piece of wood), a spring, a frame that hits the mouse, a restraining pin, and a pin fastener that is released by the mouse. Just as the trap does not work if all elements are not immediately in their places, a cilium or a flagellum does not do its job if all the protein structures are not properly coordinated and performing their respective functions—that is, are exactly where they should be. Of course, many of these structures (such as microtubules) can be found in other places of the cell—as can many similar proteins. However, according to Behe, evolutionary biochemistry has no idea how these elements could be simultaneously modified, complemented with the unique proteins, and combined into a functional whole. The problem with major evolutionary innovation is that, if the Darwinian mechanism is to achieve it, each "small change" must provide some survival advantage to the organism that possesses it. Otherwise, natural selection would not favor it. In particular, the gradual Darwinian process of random mutation and natural selection is incapable of producing irreducibly complex systems, since natural selection could only "select" them once the system is functioning as an integrated whole.

28. R. Dawkins, *The Blind Watchmaker*, 87.
29. M. Behe, *Darwin's Black Box*, 39.

It is theoretically possible that some features of organisms could be explained in terms of gradual modification. These are the types of systems that exhibit what Behe has called "cumulative complexity" (such as AMP biosynthesis), but the process of their gradual emergence would be extremely vulnerable to failure and thus nearly impossible. Aside from theoretical speculations, there is no positive evidence that even these reducible systems were produced in this way. Still, the irreducible complexity would need to come by a different route. The most likely candidate is an intelligent agent that can foresee the intended function and produce a system that fulfills it. No blind or Darwinian process has recourse to such foresight. The discovery of irreducible complex systems in organisms, therefore, is not only a strike against Darwinian explanation, but a piece of positive evidence for intelligent design.

In *The Origin of Species* Darwin himself showed how to disprove his theory, writing that "if it could be demonstrated that any complex organ existed, which could not possibly have been formed by numerous, successive, slight modifications, my theory would absolutely break down."[30] In spite of the fact that contemporary biochemistry has found many examples of such "organs," any of which, according to Darwin, ought to demolish the theory, allegiance to Darwinian explanations nonetheless seems to remain unshaken, at least at the textbook and popular levels. This is because the universal claim of the "scientific community" is that biochemistry explains how irreducibly complex structures could have emerged.

This claim, however, turns out to be unfounded. In the second edition of his book, Behe questions the significance of scientific literature concerning biochemical evolution. Based on computerized publication databases, he demonstrates that in the tens of thousands of papers published on these issues, no explanation has ever been offered of how irreducibly complex systems could have arisen. An overwhelming majority of these papers are concerned with the analysis and comparison of protein sequences. They appear very professional and are full of scientific methods and terms, yet other than describing "what has been discovered," they offer no answer to the question: "How did it originate?" In most papers, biochemists simply compare protein sequences and, on this basis, conclude that a given gene must have evolved from another. But this is nothing more than the old argument from homology (as old as Darwin), only applied at a molecular level. It rests on the shaky and often disproven assumption that similarity attests to common origin. In fact, this argument is a vicious circle: structures (genes, organs, limbs) are similar to each other because they have originated from a common ancestor. But how do we know they have a common ancestor? Because they are similar. This reasoning

30. C. Darwin, *The Origin of Species*, 189.

assumes the truth of the thing it seeks to prove. Similarity might be the result of common descent, but by itself it cannot provide evidence of such descent, just as the coincidence of two similar-looking people does not necessarily prove they are siblings.

Behe points out that there are also some publications that do not stop at comparing DNA sequences, but also try to answer the important question concerning how molecular machines originate. As there are very few of them, he discusses each one separately and demonstrates that when scientists get to the details of biochemical evolution they become "dreamers." They start using vague metaphors, and replace references to real chemical compounds with schematic terminology such as "part A" and "part B." The articles are full of speculation and presupposition—"maybe," "probably," "possibly," etc.—and are reminiscent of the speculations and conjectures of Darwin and his first followers.[31]

The origin of irreducibly complex systems has, then, never been properly explained, and the literature taking up this important question is surprisingly limited in proportion to the vast number of publications on molecular biology. The origins and evolution of life are as great a mystery for today's science as they were two hundred years ago. Science has made huge progress in explaining *how* life works, as far as we can observe it, but has not answered the question of *where* this life—in its basic forms—originates. In contemporary theology, the findings of biochemists such as M. Behe, and Stephen C. Meyer and P. Lenartowicz's work on cells, also present a serious challenge to theistic evolutionists who integrate Darwinian conclusions into their theology.

The Limits of Evolution

In 2007 Michael Behe published a second book, entitled *The Edge of Evolution*. This time, the author's goal was to determine what Darwinian mechanisms actually do in the world of biology. "In the past hundred years," Behe writes, "science has advanced enormously; . . . now that we know the sequences of many genomes, now that we know how mutations occur, and how often, we can explore the possibilities and limits of random mutation with some degree of precision—for the first time since Darwin proposed his theory."[32] Behe analyzes well-known cases of the adaptation of organisms to natural conditions by means of mutations that occur accidentally through genome replication in procreation. But Behe mentions many other examples, also well-documented, in

31. Cf. M. Behe, *Darwin's Black Box*, 173–183.

32. M. Behe, *The Edge of Evolution: The Search for the Limits of Darwinism* (New York: Free Press, 2007), 3.

which mutations occurring over a comparably long time, with massive populations and much higher rates of reproduction, were not able to overcome certain biological barriers.[33] Somewhere among these examples, Behe argues, can be found the limits of evolution.

Behe showed that the "improvements" experienced by such organisms, such as malarial parasites, are just as random as the mutations causing them. Just as sediments accumulating on a riverbed may sometimes cause the riverbed to dam up and form a natural reservoir, one accidental duplication of genes may enhance the function of certain proteins, and another mutation may knock out a protein which, in a certain selective environment, may make a bacterium resistant to a certain antibiotic. These changes tend to negatively affect the functions of the same proteins. Moreover, none of the four possible types of mutation (substitution, insertion, deletion, or duplication) leads directly to the development of some kind of functional novelty, but introduces a change potentially (and only relatively) advantageous, and may be accompanied also by some biological disadvantages.

Behe further demonstrates that the difference between relatively effective mutations observed in nature and the (actually unattainable) results postulated by Darwin's theory can be measured by determining the number of changes necessary for a single mutation to develop a new functional feature. Developing resistance to a new drug requires only one change in the DNA of a malarial parasite. In many organisms such changes occur easily. In such a case, the Darwinian process of natural selection preserves the changes. Even if unmutated specimens (of malarial microorganisms, for example) die from a new drug, the mutated ones are able to survive, reproduce, and eventually dominate the population. This is the process through which viruses (such as HIV) and bacteria

33. The examples discussed by Behe include malaria microorganisms and arctic fish. The former can only reproduce in tropical temperatures, and thus do not occur in the North. On the other hand, arctic fish should presumably freeze in saltwater. This is because even if the water does not freeze because of the salt content, its temperature falls below zero, which should kill the fish. However, during the estimated 10 million years of evolution, they have acquired resistance to low temperatures. Now, Behe's question is this: How did the fish—with a much slower rate of reproduction and fewer offspring than the bacteria—manage to develop the desired characteristic, while malaria failed to adapt to low temperature? These two cases illustrate the boundaries of evolution. The answer to the question has been provided by recent research. The mechanism that prevents the fish from freezing is quite simple, and its development was a result of single gene duplication. Such mutations occur relatively often. Subsequent duplication of the same gene further increased the fish's resistance to low temperatures. Over many years, their DNA developed a sequence of nine identical genes. Each of these minor changes was advantageous, and so it spread out to the whole population. On the other hand, malaria would require the development of new genes and more complex mutations that would have to occur simultaneously to produce adaptation to the lower temperatures. And so, malaria, in contrast to the fish, have made no progress in this advantageous direction over millions of years. Ibid., 15–16 and 79–83.

become drug-resistant, insects become resistant to some poisons, and arctic fish "reinforce" the mechanism that prevents their blood from freezing. However, the problem concerns the emergence of new intracellular structures and highly complex mechanisms, which require not just a single point mutation or duplication of a given gene, but the simultaneous development of many coordinated genetic changes.

At a few points in the book, Behe reiterates that only the studies of recent years show how inconceivably complex, and at the same time precisely tailored, are the mechanisms at the foundations of life. When the cell was understood to be no more than a simple blob of protoplasm (Haeckel, Darwin), it was possible to postulate that it had originated spontaneously. The more details science reveals about cell structure, the less sufficient Darwinian mechanisms prove in explaining its genesis. Hence Behe concludes that, while random mutations can explain some minor changes within organisms, they cannot explain the development of more complex cellular mechanisms or new organic structures. At the same time, non-random mutations, intelligently designed and directed, might surely have farther-reaching consequences, though this does not mean they could lead to the emergence of life in all its diversity.

In recent years, scientists inclined toward intelligent design have initiated a number of studies aimed at finding the precise limits of random mutations and natural selection in the development of new structures. The latest achievements include the research done by Douglas Axe and Ann Gauger of the Biologic Institute in Redmond, Washington. In one of their experiments, Axe and Gauger attempted to generate new functional proteins through random mutations of other functional proteins. For this purpose, they adopted two simple proteins as the basis of their research, and tried to determine the number of changes to the genetic code (mutations) needed for the gene of one protein (Kbl_2) to encode the function of another protein ($BioF_2$). The proteins were chosen in such a way as to demonstrate the highest level of similarity in structure and the same kind of function. Thus, the transition from the function of one protein to the function of another should be quite easy as it reflects one of the shortest possible evolutionary steps. Nevertheless, it turns out that a successful functional conversion would require seven or more nucleotide substitutions in one step (one generation). In nature, single substitutions are quite frequent; double substitutions are very rare; and triple substitutions are virtually non-existent. These studies conclude that it is impossible to change even one functional protein into another functional protein through random mutation, given the known size and age of the universe.[34] And proteins are the basic

34. An article on this subject, D. Axe, A. Gauger, "The Evolutionary Accessibility of New Enzyme Functions: A Case Study from the Biotin Pathway," was published in *Bio-Complexity* 1 (2011), 1–17.

building material of the cellular machinery. If Darwinism cannot explain adaptations and innovations at this level, then higher levels are vastly out of reach of the meager tools of natural selection and random mutation.

Based on the most current research in biology, scientists have come up with four groups of arguments undermining the mechanisms of Darwinian evolution: (1) the informative nature of DNA; (2) the existence of irreducibly complex systems; 3) the impossibility of protein evolution; and 4) the impossibility of common descent.

Directions in Intelligent Design Theory Development

The key components of the intelligent design debate can be summarized in the following seven points:

1. *Doubt about the power of random mutations and natural selection.* The new movement started out because of the dissatisfaction of a group of scientists and scholars (in the USA and elsewhere) with the scientifically dominant idea that all the biodiversity in nature can be explained by the rather primitive neo-Darwinian mechanism of random mutations and natural selection.

2. *Criticism of the alleged evidence for evolution.* Doubts about Darwinian evolution have been intensified by the critical revision of the popular evidence presented in its support. In the course of re-examination (often conducted only in the last ten or fifteen years) it was discovered that many of these "classic" evidences for evolution were in fact: (a) based on erroneous assumptions (e.g., Miller-Urey experiment, the fruit fly mutation), and/or (b) intentionally misleading (Haeckel's embryos, pithecanthropus, and other "humanoid" forms), and/or (c) the postulated conclusions were unfounded extrapolations of experimental results (peppered moth experiments, Darwin's finches, etc.). I consciously ignore the extensive literature on this subject, as it goes beyond the framework of ID and concerns the broader issue of critical thinking in science (one book disclosing the unsatisfactory character of classical "textbook" evidence for Darwinian evolution is *Icons of Evolution* by Jonathan Wells). No doubt, researchers cooperating with the Discovery Institute have helped expose many myths; nevertheless, this field of activity is only a negative background for more important research.

3. *Rejection of methodological naturalism as a basic scientific principle.* Since the 19th century, virtually everyone in scientific circles agrees that effective scientific research can only proceed through a purely naturalistic approach to the natural world. However, as some ID experts remind us, many significant discoveries in the history of science were made in a broadly theistic and

"[W]e estimate that some 10^{30} or more generations would elapse before a *bioF*-like innovation that is paralogous to *kbl* could become established. This places the innovation well beyond what can be expected within the time that life has existed on earth, under favorable assumptions."

Christian perspective, which provided a stimulus for studying nature. This is confirmed by the unquestionable success of science in Christian Europe. The most distinguished minds in the history of science were open to the existence of non-material reality and this belief did not hinder their scientific investigations. In contrast, naturalism, which constitutes the basis for Darwinian explanations, is a limited methodology when it comes to stimulation of new research. Some important discoveries of recent times are even contrary to Darwinian predictions (e.g., the function of "junk DNA"). One could suggest that they would never have been made if scientists remained exclusively within the framework of Darwinism. This is why researchers associated with ID propose to abandon naturalism, which, according to them, is not essential to scientific endeavor, and may even be harmful to science in the long run.[35]

4. *Examining the limits of the evolutionary mechanisms.* Currently, no one is questioning the occurrence of "some kind" of evolution. Changes to organisms are observed in biology and this fact is indisputable. But Darwinism postulates much more than what can actually be observed in nature or in the laboratory. Thus the question engaging ID experts is not whether evolution occurs at all, but rather what its mechanisms are and how far it is able to transform existing organisms. Research shows that Darwinian mechanisms can transform existing genomes. However, the neo-Darwinian theorem goes far beyond that—it claims that all organisms, both living and extinct, as well as life itself, and eventually the whole world and human psyche, were established through the same simple mechanisms. Experiments show, however, that the capacity of mutation and selection is, in fact, limited, and that beneficial changes may also entail some losses. The key question concerns the origin of information in the cell nucleus (even if it only meant the first piece of information in the cell nucleus of a common ancestor). The precise definition of the possible capacity of Darwinian evolution is still an open issue, although the results obtained so far do not bode well for the future of the neo-Darwinian theory.

5. *Examination of structures that could not have developed through a gradual process.* A positive aspect of ID studies includes the discovery of irreducibly complex systems and other mechanisms (e.g., AMP biosynthesis), whose structure in itself excludes gradual development through minor transformations. Identification of these structures casts an entirely new light on the organization of life. At least some of its fundamental elements had to arise by way of large and sudden leaps (entire, ready-made, fully functional systems).

35. To be precise: abandoning naturalism in this context does not mean allowing supernatural and immediate divine causality in the universe, but rather considering intelligent causality as one of three possible causes (the other two being chance and necessity) responsible for the emergence of life on Earth in its current forms.

6. *A proposition for the improvement of an outdated theory.* The proponents of intelligent design are not trying to reject Darwin's theory completely, but, instead, are seeking to modify it. Doubtless, there is a limited extent to which the theory is true, but it dates back to the 19th century and, just like the theories from other scientific domains, it has suffered some degree of expiration. Its explanatory power is too weak to account for phenomena observed under the electron microscopes of the 21st century. Darwin's theory may be compared to Newton's mechanics, which eventually were replaced by Einstein's general theory of relativity. Newton's theory remained valid, but only with reference to a narrow range of phenomena (at low speeds and in small spaces). In order to explain broader phenomena, we needed a new and more general theory. In biology this broader theory is intelligent design.

7. *A new scientific paradigm.* Discovering that at least some elements of nature are the product of intelligence leads to new, unexpected inspirations in research. It turns out that the world is intelligible and rationally ordered and thus worth exploring. If necessity and chance were the only foundation of everything, one should not expect to discover anything surprising, beautiful, or different. Intelligent design proves to be a new, more adequate, and more inclusive paradigm in science, which currently involves not only biology but also astronomy and physics, and is extending to other disciplines.[36]

The Arena of the Current Debate

Main Standpoints in the Creation/Evolution Dispute

Looking at the history of the debate on the origin of species, one may notice that the past 150 years have produced a few quite different opinions on the subject. Today's researchers choose between four principal solutions.[37] A brief presentation of each of them might help the reader orientate himself on the "argument map."

Atheistic evolution

Proponents of atheistic evolution do not ask about the very beginning of the

36. An example of astronomic research within the framework of ID is shown in the book *The Privileged Planet* (Washington: Eagle Publishing Company, 2010) by J. Richards and G. Gonzalez. The authors attempt to overthrow the Copernican principle stating that everything in the cosmos is equal and there are no "privileged" places. Relatively recent research has shown that the earth's place in the galaxy, and in the solar system, is structured in a very specific way that makes the earth the only known place in the known universe that meets all the conditions for the existence of advanced forms of life.

37. The three theistic standpoints presented here are thoroughly discussed in J. P. Moreland, J. M. Reynolds, *Three Views on Creation and Evolution* (Grand Rapids, MI: Zondervan Publishing House, 1999). In addition to these three positions, I have described a fourth—atheistic evolution.

universe, but instead assume its eternal existence in one form or another. Atheistic evolution claims that all life forms—indeed, life itself—have developed in the course of spontaneous material processes. According to this approach, life developed through chemical and biochemical evolution, which means that random collisions of molecules, governed by certain law-like regularities, led to the emergence of the first microorganisms. Next, the mechanisms of genetic mutations and natural selection (and perhaps other unguided processes) caused the diversification of these primitive forms of life (proto-organisms) into all species known today, both living and extinct.

Most of the pioneers of the theory of evolution did not own up to atheism directly. For their purpose, T.H. Huxley coined the term "agnostic." However, as these scientists often signaled their skepticism or hostility towards institutionalized religion, their opinions were usually deemed atheistic.[38] This dual attitude is especially noticeable in the case of T.H. Huxley and E. Haeckel. In the course of his life, Darwin himself went through a transformation from religious beliefs to agnosticism in the Huxleyan sense. An explicitly atheistic standpoint was only formed in the period of neo-Darwinian synthesis of the 1940s and 1950s. At that time atheistic evolution in the strict sense was endorsed by such scholars as Ernst Mayr, Julian Huxley, Jacques Monod and George Gaylord Simpson.[39] Nowadays, its most recognizable supporters are Richard Dawkins and Jerry Coyne.

Theistic evolution

The second view is referred to as "theistic evolution," "continuous creationism," "evolving creation," "evolutionary creationism," "one-time creation," "directed

38. See T.H. Huxley, "Agnosticism and Christianity," in *Lectures and Essays* (London: Macmillan and Co., 1903). E. Haeckel was a particularly ardent opponent of institutionalized religion. See for example his three lectures given in Berlin: *Kampf um den Entwicklungs-Gedanken: drei Vortrage gehalten am* 14, 16, *und* 19. *April* 1905 *im Saale der Sing-Akademie zu Berlin*. English edition: E. Haeckel, *Last Words on Evolution*, trans. J. McCabe (London: A. Owen, 1906).

39. Cf. E. Mayr, "How I Became a Darwinian," in *The Evolutionary Synthesis*, ed. E. Mayr, W.B. Provine (Cambridge: Harvard University Press, 1998), 413–22. At the 100th anniversary of the publication of *The Origin of Species*, Julian Huxley (the grandson of T.H. Huxley) said the following: "Evolutionary man can no longer take refuge from his loneliness in the arms of a divinized father-figure whom he has himself created [...]. The evolutionary vision is enabling us to discern, however incompletely, the lineaments of the new religion that we can be sure will arise to serve the needs of the coming era." J. Huxley, "The Evolutionary Vision: The Convocation Address," in *Evolution after Darwin: The University of Chicago Centennial*, ed. Sol Tax et al., vol. 3, *Issues in Evolution: The University of Chicago Centennial Discussions* (Chicago: University of Chicago Press, 1960), 249–261, at 253 and 260. Particularly significant are Simpson's repeated confessions about his complete loss of faith through accepting evolution, the reduction of man to a purely material level, and the claim that science and religion are in constant, insurmountable conflict. See his *This View of Life* (New York: Harcourt, Brace & World, 1964).

evolution," or—as Howard van Till puts it—"creation's functional integrity."[40] This approach affirms the divine origin of the world—that in the first moment of creation, the world was brought forth out of nothingness. However, this approach further assumes that the world had been programmed in such a way that it progressed to its current form by virtue of its own laws and capacities (secondary causes). Evolution—cosmic, chemical, and biological—has developed the world we live in today, along with all living organisms, which share a single common ancestor (LUCA, *Last Universal Common Ancestor*). Man shares a common origin with lower species, but is unique in having a spiritual dimension and a desire to know God. Theistic evolution is different from deism, insofar as it assumes that the entire process of world development is subject to Divine Providence and is part of the biblical *fiat* as the manifestation of God's creative power and blessing. Moreover, it credits God with the power to interfere directly with His creation; it does state, though, that God does not use this power, instead leaving the history of the cosmos and life entirely to secondary causes, namely, evolution.

Theistic evolution has its origins in the concepts of Erasmus Darwin, William Paley, Robert Chambers, and Charles Darwin. The first Catholic theologians to adopt the term "theistic evolution" were the Jesuit Erich Wassmann and Fr. John A. Zahm.[41] Other Catholic pioneers of this view include St. George Mivart, Dalmace Leroy, and Raffaello Caverni.

One should immediately take note of three peculiarities of this approach, which make it inherently unstable.

First, hypothetically, one might assume that guided evolution is the work of both God and natural processes, which complement each other so perfectly that the supernatural influence is unnoticeable from the biological point of view. This way, evolution would be a series of minor divine interventions, altogether giving the impression of a natural process. However, such a view represents not theistic evolution but rather a specific version of progressive creationism (where God acts supernaturally on nature).

Second, in contrast to the first position, one could assume that God "front-

40. H. J. Van Till, "Basil, Augustine, and the Doctrine of Creation's Functional Integrity," in *Science and Christian Belief* 8 no. 1 (April 1996), 21–38, 21. A quite thorough definition of theistic evolution (TE) based on six criteria is provided by Francis Collins in *The Language of God* (New York: Free Press, 2006), 200ff. The author himself, however, suggests a different name: BioLogos (ibid., 203).

41. Erich Wassmann (1859–1931) attempted to demonstrate the essential differences between theistic and atheistic evolution. Therefore, one may assume that he was the one to coin the term "theistic evolution," at least in Catholic circles. See his *The Berlin Discussion of the Problem of Evolution* (London: Kegan Paul, Trench Trubner & Co., 1912), 23ff. J. A. Zahm (1851–1921) presented a complete treatise on theistic evolution in *Evolution and Dogma* (Chicago: D.H. McBride & Co., 1896), 279, 304, 312ff.

loaded" the information for the first organism, or just programmed the initial cosmic conditions, and thus "pre-planned" evolution, which from then on acted on purely natural grounds. But this stance boils down to deism.

Third, one might conclude that the same effect comes simultaneously and identically (i.e., in the same respect) from the supernatural work of God and the natural agency of secondary causes. In this form, theistic evolution leads to ontological monism, as an identity between the two causal actions equals an identity between the agents.[42] Monism itself may be either materialistic (when supernaturality is identified with the natural order), panentheistic (when the natural order becomes part of God), or pantheistic (when nature is identified with God).[43] None of these solutions can be considered Christian. In the contemporary debate it is becoming more and more difficult to define a clear difference between theistic evolution and monism of any kind.

Progressive creationism[44]

This concept assumes that both the universe and different species, including man, were created by means of special operations performed directly by God rather than in the course of natural processes or as a result of secondary causes. This view adopts the scientific concept of *deep time* (old age of the universe), currently estimated at about 13.7 billion years. The negative framework for progressive creationism is marked by the two following points: (1) there was more than one act of creation, which means that God created the universe and vari-

42. This is why Thomas Aquinas claimed that "It is impossible for two complete causes to be the causes immediately of one and the same thing" (*S.Th.*, I,52,3,c).

43. Materialistic monism was the view held, for instance, by Ernst Haeckel. See his *Monism as Connecting Religion and Science*, transl. J. Gilchrist (London: Adam and Charles Black, 1894). In recent times panentheistic ideas have been developed by A. Peacock and J. Zycinski, who tend toward a pantheistic interpretation of creation.

44. Nowadays, one of the most famous supporters of this standpoint is the American astrophysicist and pastor Hugh Ross. See, among others, his *Creation and Time: A Biblical and Scientific Perspective on the Creation-Date Controversy* (Colorado Springs: NavPress, 1994). This concept is also discussed in an article by E. Scott, "The Creation/Evolution Continuum," http://ncse.com/creationism/general/creationevolution-continuum (January 28, 2015). According to Hugh Owen, "[p]rogressive creationism is the belief that God created matter and energy and intervened periodically and supernaturally over long ages of time to produce the variety of life forms in the universe." Owen claims that this view does not reveal specific divine action, and just as in the case of theistic evolutionism, leads to confusion of the order of creation with the order of Providence. For this reason, Owen seeks some kind of intermediate standpoint between the progressive and "radical" (as he calls it) creationism embraced by some Protestants. Eventually, he endorses the short history of the Earth, which—according to our classification—makes him an advocate of YEC. Cf. H. Owen, "Beyond Creationism: Towards a Restoration of Catholic Creation Theology," in *Logos Review* (Summer 2009), 2, 7. The problem with Owen's standpoint is that he fails to explain how direct creative acts of God present in progressive creationism are different from the creative acts present in his own concept; http://www.logosinstitute.org/LR4_Beyond_Creationism_Logos_Review.pdf (28 January 2015).

ous forms of life through separate acts of creation out of nothing or through formation from previously created matter; and (2) these acts did not all occur simultaneously, that is, they might have taken place over the period of many years.

Different forms of progressive creationism define in greater detail the number of creative acts and the degree to which originally created species were able to diversify further. The essence of this view is the belief that not only did the universe have an absolute beginning, but each distinct nature was formed directly by God. Within the general idea of progressive creationism there are some questions open to further investigation. These are, for example, the extent to which created natures are able to diversify according to the laws of nature; whether God directly created many specimens of each species, or just a pair of each; and whether He shaped them from the matter He previously created, or added new matter.

In the past, progressive creationism was usually considered the same as concordism—the attempt to reconcile scientific and biblical data at all costs. As these attempts often led to various misunderstandings, concordism was commonly rejected. The difference between progressive creationism and concordism is that the primary goal of the former is not to reconcile science and the Bible at all costs. Progressive creationists interpret Genesis in such a way that, while preserving the literal and historical sense, they leave room for justified criticism of the text, and acknowledge true scientific discoveries (e.g., old age of the universe, heliocentrism, multitude of galaxies). Among representatives of this approach are 19th-century geologists such as Georges Cuvier, William Buckland, and Louis Agassiz, as well as contemporary Protestant scholars such as Bernard Ramm, Gleason Archer, and Hugh Ross. Progressive creationism was present also in Catholic thought of the 19th century. Its supporters (though they did not use the exact term) included theologians from the Roman School, such as dogmatist Rev. Franz Hettinger (1819–1890); scientist and theologian Giambattista Pianciani, S.J. (1784–1862); biblical scholar Rev. Johann B. Holzammer (1828–1903); and more recent scholars such as Rev. Patrick O'Connell.

As with theistic evolution, one may try to reconcile progressive creationism and evolutionary theory. Some imagine that God intervened in a supernatural way, so as to make a reptile give rise to the first bird through a kind of natural process. This means, for instance, that the first bird hatched from a reptilian egg, or that one specific reptilian species was a descendant of an amphibian, or that new species emerged thanks to the supernatural mutation of a genome at the moment of fertilization. In this way, God would create new species, but creation would be completely concealed within natural generation, and thus there would be no vestiges of creation in natural history. Nevertheless, this view is hard to maintain because it either suggests that God operates in a completely chaotic way or assumes that things can happen in the natural order in ways that are entirely impossible by solely natural causes. The arrival of the exemplary reptile is not just a matter of a different embryo in the egg but of the egg as a whole and of countless other factors. The same applies to all complete natures, as they are unique wholes and not just different arrangements of similar organic parts. Therefore, either God would have had to constantly suspend all laws of nature—which would exclude "natural evolution"—or the leaps would have had to be so large that we should rather assume the creation of complete species as wholes, which brings us back to the classic concept of creationism.

Young Earth Creationism (YEC)

YEC claims that the creation account in Genesis is a literal description of how the universe came into existence. It not only assumes that God directly formed the human body and created species (as in progressive creationism), but also that the world is no more than 10 thousand years old. Young earth creationism interprets the six days of creation as six 24-hour periods, six natural days. This idea has its roots in 17th-century Protestantism. Before that, there were many theologians who postulated a young age of the world; however, their views were not put forward in opposition to scientific data, but rather stemmed from the poor scientific knowledge of the time.[45] After Darwin came forward with his theory, the young earth standpoint was explicitly defined in turn-of-the-century American Protestantism. Nevertheless, the concept of young earth creationism has become increasingly rare among scientists and scholars. Its contemporary supporters include Protestant theologians John Whitcomb and Ken Ham, scientists from the Creation Research Society, Eastern Orthodox philosopher John M. Reynolds, Eastern Catholic theologian Hugh Owen, and Roman Catholics such as J.W.G. Johnson and Rev. Victor P. Warkulwiz.

The four standpoints above are not an exhaustive description of views on origins, which range from complete naturalism to Biblicism. Still, the four views presented here are sufficient for the purpose of this study. Atheistic evolution searches for answers to all questions exclusively within the limits of the physical world, while young earth creationism is largely a fideistic concept, though it sometimes seeks connections with science in so-called scientific creationism. The two middle-ground views, i.e., theistic evolution and progressive creationism, try to integrate both scientific knowledge and the biblical message.

45. It is widely believed that the Church Fathers were young earth creationists. In fact their opinions on the length of the days in Genesis differed. Saint Augustine, for instance, did indeed opt for a young age of the universe, but he also rejected the interpretation of the biblical day of creation as a 24-hour day.

The Emergence of Theistic Evolution in Western Culture

Having presented the four principal views in the debate on the origin of species, it is now time to ask about the genesis of theistic evolution, which is a relatively new concept, dating back to the late 19th century, although nowadays it is the most popular one among Christian theologians.

One of Charles Darwin's goals was to prove that phenomena previously attributed to God's creative power have only natural causes. Thus it might be surprising that it was Darwin himself who suggested—in *The Origin of Species*—the possibility of theistic evolution:

> Authors of the highest eminence seem to be fully satisfied with the view that each species has been independently created. To my mind it accords better with what we know of the laws impressed on matter by the Creator that the production and extinction of the past and present inhabitants of the world should have been due to secondary causes. . . . When I view all beings not as special creations, but as the lineal descendants of some few beings . . . , they seem to me to become ennobled.[46]

It turns out, however, that Darwin did not arrive at this conclusion by himself. The complete idea can be found in the works of his grandfather Erasmus, who, in his *Zoonomia*, suggested that evolutionary thinking goes back as far as Plato (who believed that all humans and animals had originally been hermaphroditic, and that sex-differentiation took place later). Nevertheless, Erasmus Darwin named David Hume as the direct author of the evolutionary approach:

> The late Mr. David Hume, in his posthumous works, places the powers of generation much above those of our boasted reason; and adds, that reason can only make a machine, as a clock or a ship, but the power of generation makes the maker of the machine.[47]

If Erasmus Darwin understood Hume's works correctly, it would mean that it was Hume who propagated the philosophical principle that a lower cause—that undefined "power of generation"—can lead to higher outcomes in the form of ever more advanced organic structures. At the same time, it is not reason (an intelligent agent) that is responsible for the origination of these structures, but a merely material or organic process of generation.

The way Erasmus Darwin interpreted Hume is important, as it casts light on the genesis of Charles Darwin's idea. For the elder Darwin, Hume

> concludes that the world itself might have been generated, rather than created; that is, it might have been gradually produced from very small begin-

46. C. Darwin, *The Origin of Species*, 488–89.
47. E. Darwin, *Zoonomia*, xxxix, iv, 8, 509.

> nings, increasing by the activity of its inherent principles, rather than by a sudden evolution of the whole by the Almighty fire.—What a magnificent idea of the infinite power of the Great Architect! The Cause of Causes! Parent of Parents! *Ens Entium*! For if we may compare infinities, it would seem to require a greater infinity of power to cause the causes of effects, than to cause the effects themselves. This idea is analogous to the improving excellence observable in every part of the creation.[48]

To Erasmus Darwin, the idea of an evolutionary origin of the world meant a certain improvement of the concept of God as the First and Supreme Being. According to him, more power is in the one who generates causes of effects than the one who directly generates the effects themselves. However, this opinion does not take into consideration an essential sense of the Christian notion of creation. In classical Christian thought, although God's wisdom is expressed by His use of secondary causes, the highest rank is given to immediate acts of completely free creation *ex nihilo*. The view held by Erasmus and his followers was actually of deistic provenance, and it practically boiled down to the statement that because the generation of causes is better, God does not generate results but only causes. In 1817, Erasmus's work was put on the papal *Index of Prohibited Books* in the more severe category of condemned books.[49] It was the first official measure taken by the Church with reference to the idea of biological macroevolution. Erasmus Darwin did not promote atheistic evolution, but his view was discarded nonetheless.

The question to be asked now is: apart from Erasmus Darwin and David Hume, can we identify other sources of the idea of evolution as a process begun by God? The answer is yes. The concept of theistic evolution (in a quite developed form) can be found in the first entirely "evolutionist" publication, Robert Chambers' *Vestiges* (1844). Having described the vast variety of life forms that can be arranged by taxonomy, Chambers proposed a new explanation of these facts as an alternative to the then-commonly accepted view. Up to that point, the official idea was that of the independent creation of species, but the amateur naturalist from Edinburgh was not satisfied with such theology:

> How can we suppose an immediate exertion of this creative power at one time to produce *zoophytes*,[50] another to bring in one or two crustaceans, again to produce crustaceous fishes, again perfect fishes, and so on to the end? This would surely be to take a very mean view of the Creative Power—

48. Ibid.

49. The papal *Index of Prohibited Books* is divided into two categories: (1) books suspended from publication until corrected; and (2) books prohibited or condemned. More on the subject in H. Wolf, *Index: Der Vatikan und die Verbotenen Bücher* (München: Beck, 2006), 260.

50. In the 19th century, this was the term used with reference to various underwater animals resembling plants, e.g., sea anemones (a type of coral).

> to, in short, anthropomorphize it, or reduce it to some such character as that borne by the ordinary proceedings of mankind.[51]

In view of all "proofs provided by nature" and problems with the "anthropomorphization of Creative Power," Chambers proposed an alternative solution—the generation of species by virtue of natural laws. If the earthly order, as seen for example in the arrangement of geological layers, is an effect of the laws of nature, then there is nothing contrary to the idea that the organic order could also have been formed by similar laws. As Chambers asked,

> How can we suppose that the august Being who brought all these countless worlds into form by the simple establishment of a natural principle flowing from his mind, was to interfere personally and specially on every occasion when a new shell-fish or reptile was to be ushered into existence on one of these worlds? Surely this idea is too ridiculous to be for a moment entertained.[52]

Aware that he would be criticized by believers, he hastened to add:

> It may be objected that the ordinary conceptions of Christian nations on this subject are directly derived from Scripture, or, at least, are in conformity with it; to which I would respectfully answer, that the Mosaic record appears, when perused with an awakened mind, much more in conformity with the present view than with that which has been so long entertained. All the procedure is there represented primarily and pre-eminently as flowing from commands and expressions of will, not from direct acts. . . . Thus, the scriptural objection quickly vanishes, and the prevalent ideas about the organic creation appear only as a mistaken inference from the text, formed at a time when man's ignorance prevented him from drawing therefrom a just conclusion."[53]

In but a single page, Chambers provided an interpretation of the Book of Genesis that overturned 1800 years of interpretative tradition.

Chambers did not admit the possibility of the separate creation of species, as he deemed it unthinkable for a Supreme Being to have descended so low as to create a slug or some sea plant. According to Chambers, the Supreme Being could not have been so petty. This provokes a question: what vision of God stands behind Chambers's ideas? Was it the God of Abraham, Isaac, and Jacob, the God involved in history and caring for each being, even the smallest? Or, rather, does he think of God as the "supreme idea," an abstract and unrealistic *Ens Entium*, serving as nothing more than the intellectual principle necessary for explaining the origins of natural laws? This question about the vision of God in theistic evolution is also relevant to today's debate.

51. R. Chambers, *Vestiges of Natural History of Creation*, 157.
52. Ibid., 158–59.
53. Ibid., 159–60.

The ideas of Erasmus Darwin were challenged by William Paley, an Anglican theologian living at the end of the 18th century.[54] In his main work, *Natural Theology* (1802), Paley presented a number of arguments against the possibility of random emergence of all natures. In nearly all biological phenomena Paley recognized the products of the operation of some kind of intelligence. Paley's book was thus a polemic against Hume and Erasmus Darwin, who had stated that it is the "law of generation," not intelligence, that creates life. In Paley's words, "It is a perversion of language to assign any law as the efficient, operative cause of anything. A law presupposes an agent; for it is only the mode according to which an agent proceeds."[55]

The most famous example in Paley's argument concerns a watch found by accident. If a man walks through the moors and notices a watch on the ground, he will not be satisfied with the answer that it got there by chance, or that it has just been sitting there forever. Such a precise and purposeful mechanism could not have come into being by chance. However, positing that it has always existed seems merely to evade the question of whence it came. Explaining his "metaphor of the watch," Paley concluded that an intelligent being may be so clever that it not only creates one watch, but also designs it in such a way as to make it generate other watches. Such a great contrivance would make the intelligent cause even more perfect.[56] But Paley did not stop at this metaphor. In his philosophy, he went a step further, stating that God, in order to demonstrate his wisdom even more distinctly, subjected himself to his own self-established laws which he had imposed on his creation:

> Whatever is done, God could have done without the intervention of instruments or means: but it is in the construction of instruments, in the choice and adaptation of means, that the creative intelligence is seen.... God, therefore, has been pleased to prescribe limits to his own power, and to work his ends within those limits. The general laws of matter have perhaps the nature of these limits; its inertia, its reaction; the laws which govern the communication of motion ... the laws of magnetism, of electricity; and probably others, yet undiscovered. These are general laws; and when a particular purpose is to be effected, it is not by making a new law, nor by the suspension of the old ones ... but it is, by the interposition of an apparatus, corresponding with these laws, and suited to the exigency which results from them, that the purpose is at length attained. As we have said, therefore, God prescribes limits to his power, that he may let in the exercise, and thereby exhibit demon-

54. For more on W. Paley's opposition to E. Darwin's ideas, see John T. Baldwin, "God and the World. William's Paley Argument from Perfection Tradition: A Continuing Influence," *The Harvard Theological Review* 85, no. 1 (Jan. 1992): 109–20.

55. W. Paley, *Natural Theology*, 8.

56. Ibid., 12–13.

stration of his wisdom. For then, i.e., such laws and limitations being laid down, it is as though one Being should have fixed certain rules; and, if we may so speak, provided certain materials; and, afterwards, have committed to another Being out of these materials, and in subordination to these rules, the task of drawing forth a creation: a supposition which evidently leaves room, and induces indeed a necessity for contrivance. Nay, there may be many such agents, and many ranks of these. We do not advance this as a doctrine either of philosophy or of religion; but we say that the subject may safely be represented under this view, because the Deity, acting himself by general laws, will have the same consequences upon our reasoning, as if he had prescribed these laws to another."[57]

Based on this statement, it might seem that Paley allowed for the idea of bottom-up evolution as defined by E. Darwin or Hume, i.e., development occurring through material causes. However, such an interpretation would be inaccurate. First of all, Paley's aim was to demonstrate the idea that the arrangement of the world, and particularly of living beings, arises from supreme principles (intelligence) rather than from low-rank, material, or vitalistic causes such as the power of generation. Second, he ruled out the possibility of chance as a cause in the emergence of important elements of the functioning reality.[58] Third, Paley consistently argued that generation is not a law but a process, which means that it requires purposeful action and, in itself, explains nothing, but rather demands an explanation.[59] Therefore, Paley philosophically disqualified what later became the foundation of neo-Darwinism—the possibility of new life forms being generated by means of random mutation and natural selection. What, then, was Paley's contribution to the development of theistic evolution? In at least three aspects, the Anglican theologian opened the gate to this doctrine.

First, according to Paley, natural structures could have been designed as "self-organizing" and transferring their intrinsic design to subsequent levels of being. This way, when some initial laws are bestowed upon the world, nature's further existence and development is, to a great degree, autonomous. Without a doubt, this idea echoes the predominance of Newton's mechanics in Europe at the time, as well as further development of naturalism in the Enlightenment.

57. Ibid., 26–27.

58. "This is always to be computed, when the question is, whether a useful or imitative conformation be the produce of chance, or not: I desire no greater certainty in reasoning, than that by which chance is excluded from the present disposition of the natural world. Universal experience is against it. What does chance ever do for us? In the human body, for instance, chance, i.e., the operation of causes without design, may produce a wen, a wart, a mole, a pimple, but never an eye. Amongst inanimate substances, a clod, a pebble, a liquid drop might be; but never was a watch, a telescope, an organized body of any kind." Ibid., 38–39.

59. Ibid., 236.

As made evident in the above-quoted passage, the reason Paley sought the idea of "fixed laws" was his intention to demonstrate the Divine contrivance.

Second, Paley caught himself in a kind of philosophical trap: for in order to exalt God's contrivance, Paley demanded that God limit his power. In a way, God needed to restrict his power by withdrawing from creative action in order to manifest his contrivance through the operation of secondary causes. This erroneous thinking probably had its roots in the Protestant trend of juxtaposing God's attributes—nature and providence, grace and will, etc. In any case, in a more classical approach—e.g., according to Thomistic synthesis—such juxtaposition would make no sense, as God's attributes converge in a single divine substance. Nevertheless, the echo of this error reverberates still in the concept of theistic evolution.

Third, in the end, struggling to salvage the idea of design in nature as a kind of "metaphysical minimum," Paley abandoned a number of theological implications. For instance, he decides that the power of creation can be passed on by the Supreme Being to lower beings, a view that bears a striking resemblance to the early heresies and pagan emanationist ideas condemned by the Church Fathers. The theologian did make it clear that it was not his intention to present a religious or philosophical doctrine of any kind, but only a concept that would conform to the idea of design. On this account he can be called a pioneer of today's theistic evolution in its attempt at combining bottom-up and top-down, primary and secondary, causation in the work of creation. In contrast, one might say that by excluding chance as the main drive in the development of the universe, Paley also became the author of the early version of intelligent design theory.

After Darwin, the idea of "evolution started by God" was promoted by some of the main supporters of Darwinism. Huxley, for instance, wrote that

> As a natural process, of the same character as the development of a tree from its seed, or of a fowl from its egg, evolution excludes creation and all other kinds of supernatural intervention. As the expression of a fixed order, the conception of evolution no less excludes that of chance. It is very desirable to remember that evolution is not an explanation of the cosmic process, but merely a generalized statement of the method and results of that process. And, further, that, if there is proof that the cosmic process was set going by any agent, then that agent will be the creator of it and of all its products, although supernatural intervention may remain strictly excluded from its further course.[60]

60. T.H. Huxley, "Prolegomena to Evolution and Ethics," in *Evolution and Ethics and Other Essays* (New York: Macmillan, 1894), 6.

Huxley's view is equivalent to the claim that God used evolution, that is, that God transferred the role of developing the world, particularly various kinds of organisms, to so-called secondary causes. Nevertheless, God still remains the Creator, as he had created the process of evolution itself; moreover, evolution does not require any further supernatural "interventions." Today this concept (although authors rarely refer directly to Huxley's writings) is the most popular among Christian theologians.

Different versions of theistic evolution were postulated during the nineteenth century by such scholars as Richard Owen and Charles Kingsley, an Anglican clergyman, as well as by Frederick Temple, the Archbishop of Canterbury. Owen did not adopt natural selection as the main drive for change (which gave rise to an argument with Darwin), but he defended theistic evolution from the philosophical point of view, assuming the existence of some kind of archetypical scheme in God's mind that determined the law of continuous emergence of new life forms.[61] Soon, Darwin's ideas began to penetrate the Church of England. Kingsley, for one, wrote to Darwin, commenting on *The Origin of Species*: "I have gradually learnt to see that it is just as noble a conception of Deity, to believe that He created primal forms capable of self-development into all forms needful *pro tempore* and *pro loco*, as to believe that He required a fresh act of intervention to supply the *lacunas* which He Himself had made."[62] Another Anglican clergyman, Frederick Temple, supported Darwin from the very beginning. In 1869, upon acceding to the Archbishopric of Canterbury, Temple became the first Christian hierarch to recognize the compatibility of evolution with the Christian notion of creation, even though the theory had been condemned by the Church of England. In 1884, he stated that "this doctrine of Evolution is in no sense whatever antagonistic to the teachings of Religion."[63]

Based on these statements, one might conclude that from the very beginning the first evolutionary authors tried to address the problem of reconciling evolution with the idea of creation that was so deeply rooted in the culture they lived in. In fact, the origin of theistic evolution lies in pagan mythologies and

61. Cf. J. H. Brooke, "The Wilberforce–Huxley Debate," in *Science and Christian Belief*, vol. 13, no. 2 (2001): 127–141.

62. *The Life and Letters of Charles Darwin, Including an Autobiographical Chapter*, vol. 2, ed. F. Darwin (London: John Murray, 1887), 288.

63. See fourth lecture given in Oxford in 1884. See Frederick, Lord Bishop of Exeter, *The Relations between Religion and Science: Eight Lectures Preached Before University of Oxford in Year* 1884 (New York: Macmillan and Co., 1884). Temple also wrote: "[T]he doctrine of Evolution leaves the argument for an intelligent Creator and Governor of the world stronger than it was before. There is still as much as ever the proof of an intelligent purpose pervading all creation. The difference is that the execution of that purpose belongs more to the original act of creation, less to acts of government since. There is more divine foresight, there is less divine interposition; and whatever has been taken from the latter has been added to the former." Ibid., 122–23.

Enlightenment-age deism, which was explicitly suggested by the pioneers of the concept—David Hume and Erasmus Darwin. The idea later evolved into a "demythologized" (and more scientific) form in the writings of agnostic naturalists such as Robert Chambers, Charles Darwin, and Thomas Huxley. The next chapters will demonstrate how the idea has gradually pervaded and dominated mainstream Catholic theology.

3

Early Statements of the Magisterium on Evolution

Genesis, Content, and Reception of the Synod of Cologne (1860)

In 1859 the Archbishop of Cologne, Cardinal Johannes von Geissel, appealed to the Holy See for permission to convene a synod in his own ecclesiastical province. He obtained consent from Pope Pius IX, and for the next few months the diocese made preparations for the conference. The archbishop convened the synod on February 25, 1860, and the meeting was held from April 29 to May 17 of the same year. The synod covered four dioceses and was attended by four diocesan bishops (including Geissel), their four auxiliary bishops, and twelve canons, as well as representatives of universities, religious superiors, and rectors of seminaries. They met in five general sessions, during which the texts of decrees were prepared and then passed by unanimous votes. In July 1860 the cardinal sent the documents to the Holy See requesting an official examination (*recognitio*). In December 1861 Cardinal Prospero Caterini, Prefect of the Congregation of the Council, responded by praising the work of the synod and adding some remarks. Pope Pius IX also answered in person in April 1862, with words of commendation for the results achieved. After this official acceptance from the Holy See, Cardinal von Geissel promulgated the acts of the synod in July 1862. The acts consisted of 250 pages of text in Latin, divided into two large parts and containing an appendix with excerpts of ecclesiastical documents to which the main body of text referred. The first part of the records (80 pages) treated of Catholic doctrine (*De doctrina catholica*), and the second (70 pages) discussed Church regulations (*De disciplina ecclesiastica*). The structure of the records implies that the synod was of a doctrinal and disciplinary nature.

Our interest is in the first part of the acts. The titles in the first part concern the following topics: religion and faith in general, the one God and the Trinity of Persons, creation, man, Christ as the Restorer of the human race, the Church of Christ, grace, sacraments, and the future life. The fourth title, *On Man* (*De Homine*), was composed of four chapters (XIV–XVII), the first of which was entitled: *On the Origin of the Human Race and Human Nature* (*De humani generis origine hominisque natura*). The chapter begins as follows:

> Our first parents were created immediately by God. Therefore we declare that the opinion of those who do not fear to assert that this human being, man as regards his body, emerged finally from the spontaneous continuous change of imperfect nature to the more perfect, is clearly opposed to Sacred Scripture and to the Faith.[1]

The doctrinal definition presented by the synod contained all elements necessary for the rejection of the theory of the evolutionary origin of the human body. Charles Darwin's main work, *The Origin of Species*, had been published in England six months before the synod, and its German translation was already available the year in which the synod took place. Darwin's other book, *The Descent of Man*, was not published until 1871. In *The Origin of Species* he did not speak directly about man, but extended the mechanisms of natural selection to the whole animated world, claiming that his theory "will throw light on the origin of man and his history."[2] The synod fathers were familiar with Darwin's concepts, the topic of evolution then being the hottest issue in scientific circles of Europe. Ideas can spread faster than the books that contain them, and in the case of Darwin's work the publicity was almost instantaneous. Evolutionary ideas were not unknown to any educated person.

Under these circumstances, the synodal statement should be viewed as a direct reaction of the local Church to the discussion going on in the world of science. The synod rejected the suggestion that the bodies of the first human parents might have originated by way of a change from "imperfect nature to the more perfect"—which was exactly what evolutionary theories assumed—regardless of the specific mechanisms governing the process. The synodal decree obtained the unreserved acceptance of Rome, as it contained nothing more than what was part of the ordinary Catholic teaching. Two questions, then, shall be raised in the context of the document: (1) What is the formal significance of the resolutions of the Synod of Cologne? (2) How was it interpreted by Catholic theologians who sought to accommodate Darwinism?

In order to evaluate the doctrinal rank of the Cologne pronouncement, one

1. "Primi parentes a Deo immediate conditi sunt. Itaque Scripturae sacrae fideique plane adversantem illorum declaramus sententiam, qui asserere non verentur, spontanea naturae imperfectioris in perfectiorem continuo ultimoque humanam hanc immutatione hominem, si corpus quidem spectes, prodiisse." *Acta et decreta Concilii Provinciae Coloniensis* (Coloniae, 1862), 30.

2. Ch. Darwin, *The Origin of Species*, 488.

needs first to discuss the relationship between universal and local teaching. One should bear in mind that this issue can be analyzed either from today's point of view or from that of the time the given document was published. To avoid anachronism, I shall refer to a classical textbook in canon law, *Ius decretalium*, by Franz Xavier Wernz, first published in 1899 and reissued many times thereafter. According to Wernz, the procedures governing synodal decisions at the time did not require any confirmation or approval from the pope. The records, as in the case of the Synod of Cologne, were to be sent to Rome, where they were normally passed to the Congregation of the Council for examination (*recognitio*). The approval of the Congregation did not mean, Wernz explains,

> that each and every question mentioned in the records is thus approved or considered as legally binding, as it is assumed that they might also contain false or invalid judgments. Nevertheless, one should not underestimate *recognitio*, as if it gave no authority to the records and decrees of provincial synods. It is thus an authentic testimony of a higher authority that a synod had been convened and conducted legally and that nothing worthy of reproof (*censura*) was found in the examination of its decrees. Such decrees still remain the decisions of a synod, but it is easier to enforce them or defend them from those who put them into question.[3]

The problem with the Cologne statement is that it has the form of a definition of faith, the type used in the case of conciliar documents or papal statements *ex cathedra*, but it is not supported with the same rank of authority. Admittedly, a synod has no right to establish a definition of faith, but as the Church had always affirmed the instant and direct (rather than evolutionary) creation of man, none of the hierarchs examining the records had any objections to the definition in question. In the years that followed, many theologians writing about evolution mentioned the Cologne statement, which had in a sense become a bone of contention. The theologians claiming that the Church has never made a statement against evolution have not opposed the synodal definition directly. They usually first considered the question of its importance, with an eye to downgrading it, and the issue of its interpretation, tending to blur its concepts and their meanings. Theologians representing the opposite view usually overestimated the rank of the Cologne statement.

The animated discussion concerning the 1860 definition is understandable. Until the publication of Pius XII's encyclical *Humani Generis* (1950), the Cologne statement remained the only public act[4] of the teaching Church

3. F.X. Wernz, *Ius decretalium ad usum praelectionum in scholis textus canonici sive iuris decreatlium*, vol. 2, *Ius constitutionis Ecclesiae Catolicae* (Rome: S.C. de Propaganda Fidei, 1899), 1091.

4. The ecclesiastical acts fall into two groups: public (addressed to the universal or particular Church) and private (addressed to a single person.)

directly addressing the matter of the evolutionary origin of the human body. Therefore, the statement initially assumed greater significance than it should have, and after *Humani Generis*, its status changed to the opposite: it has now been completely forgotten.

As early as the 1890s, evolutionary theologians solved the "problem" of the Cologne statement by claiming that the word *spontanea* ("spontaneously," "by itself") only excludes those evolutionary concepts that disregard Divine cooperation in the process of evolution. Consequently, there would be no difficulty in accepting evolution as long as the necessity of God's action for the emergence of the process was recognized also. This is the way the "problem" of the statement was handled by Dalmace Leroy, a Dominican priest.[5] Rev. John A. Zahm, for his part, entirely ignored the Cologne decree. The only Church document cited in his work is the Constitution of the First Vatican Council, *De Fide Catholica*, which he saw as completely consistent with the theory of evolution.[6] The Cologne definition was completely dismissed by Rev. H. Dorlodot—the first Catholic evolutionist whose works were not questioned by the Church.[7] Rev. John A. O'Brien followed this path also and fails to mention the Cologne decree in his study *Evolution and Religion* (1930).[8] Thus, the first theologians supporting evolutionism usually ignored the Cologne decree despite the fact that it was the only public act of the Church referring directly to the subject of human evolution at the time.

In 1932, seventy years after the Cologne synod, Rev. Ernest Messenger argued that

> If we read this decree carefully, we shall see that the Fathers of the Council of Cologne do not condemn the origin of Adam's body by organic evolution if this evolution is not regarded as purely spontaneous up to its term inclusively. In other words, this Council does not condemn the hypothesis, provided an immediate intervention on the part of God is postulated in order that the embryonic Adam should attain to the last disposition calling for information by rational soul. Furthermore, since dogmatic decrees are always to be interpreted strictly, it is clear that the hypothesis of a Divine intervention affecting the manner of appearance, for instance, by accelerating the process of evolution while at the same time respecting the complete causality of secondary causes, would not come under the condemnation. We might even suggest that the Fathers of the Council, who cannot have been

5. Cf. M. Artigas, T.F. Glick, R.A. Martínez, *Negotiating Darwin*, 23. Cf. D. O'Leary, *Roman Catholicism and Modern Science: a History* (New York: Green Press, 2006), 47.

6. J.A. Zahm, *Evolution and Dogma* (Chicago: D.H. McBride & Co., 1896), 312–13 and 221–23.

7. Cf. H. Dorlodot, *Darwinism and Catholic Thought*, trans. E. Messenger (London: Burns, Oates and Washbourne, 1922).

8. J.A. O'Brien, *Evolution and Religion*, 2nd ed. (New York: The Century Co., 1932).

> unacquainted with the ideas of St. Augustine, wished to avoid condemning such a hypothesis, for they take care to add to the adjective *spontanea* the two verbs *continuo ultimoque*.[9]

Obviously, no Church hierarch having anything to do with the Cologne statement had interpreted it the way Messenger presented it. Nevertheless, it is Messenger's opinion that has proved durable, while the synodal decree has been essentially abandoned. The very fact that Messenger made an attempt at such a far-fetched reinterpretation of the statement proves that it had been an obstacle to the idea that "God used evolution" in creating the first human body. Did Messenger's reinterpretation really reconcile the Cologne decree with the concept of the evolution of Adam?

Like other authors, Messenger believed that the decree only excluded evolution as a purely natural process without the need for any divine action. It should be noted, however, that such a claim concerning any process would be essentially un-Christian, as Christians believe that everything that goes on in the world is subject to God's providence. Thus the important question is not whether evolution as described in the decree is a purely natural process, or one guided or inspired by God in some way, but whether evolution can be an acceptable alternative to direct creation. As I have shown in the first chapter, Darwin saw evolution as an alternative to many separate acts of creation producing various species. Similarly, the hypothesis of the evolution of Adam stands in opposition to the statement that "our first parents were created immediately by God." The synod excluded the idea of evolution as opposed to direct creation.

In Fr. Messenger's evolutionary concept of the origin of the human body, the substantial unity of form and matter becomes problematic. According to traditional Christian anthropology, the human soul is not just the mind or will of a man, but constitutes his individual form, that is, it is responsible for the whole individual being. St. Thomas defended the thesis that there can only be one form in one man.[10] This means that the same soul is responsible for all the properties of the body—intellectual, sensual and vegetative ones, the living process itself, and even essential physical features of the body. This metaphysical truth is the basis for the Christian recognition of the true unity of spirit and body of each human being.

However, the truth of the substantial unity of man is a challenge to the concept of the evolutionary generation of the human body from lower animals. This is because, if *this body* can only be integrated with *this soul*, it becomes obvious that the integration with another body would entail a change of the

9. E.C. Messenger, *Evolution and Theology: The Problem of Man's Origin* (New York: Macmillan Company, 1932), 226–27.

10. Cf. Thomas Aquinas, *S.Th.*, q. 76, a. 3–4.

bodily substance. The emergence of Adam from any animal ("hominization"), regardless of whether it is an embryo or an adult specimen (a so-called "hominid"), would imply an actual transformation. Therefore, from this metaphysical point of view, it is simply impossible to obtain the body of Adam suitable to receive human form in the process of material evolution, because without *this soul*, there cannot be *this particular body.* In consequence, each evolutionary hypothesis postulating the "emergence of the body from a lower living matter," which subsequently is given a soul directly by God, is inconsistent with traditional Christian anthropology. If the soul is given directly by God, the emergence of Adam would require direct action by God—both with respect to the body and the soul, as it is an act of creation of a new being composed of form and matter. Therefore, not only an ontological (*viz.* regarding substance) but also a physical (*viz.* regarding body) "leap" is indispensable.

Being aware of this problem, Messenger used it to his advantage by claiming that the evolutionary hypothesis also involves "direct" Divine action in the formation of the body at the moment of infusion of the soul into a living being (so-called special transformism). This way, he could argue that Adam's body evolved, though at the same time it was "immediately created." Messenger's idea formally bypassed the problem of the word *immediate* (immediately) used in the synodal definition. But would the synodal fathers actually allow this kind of interpretation?

Messenger's interpretation of the Cologne definition did not eliminate all discrepancies. In fact it provoked new ones. The scholar departs from the realistic evolutionary hypotheses proposed by biologists, according to which the human body originated in the course of "purely natural" processes. Messenger was aware that through purposeless biological processes evolution would have never led to the generation of a body apt for integration with a rational soul. This is why he writes about the "acceleration of the process of evolution" by God himself. However, if God intervened to advance the process, it would no longer be "natural evolution" as postulated by Darwin, but rather some form of creationism. If God acted simultaneously as the primary and secondary cause, we would arrive at monism, because if the actions are identical, the agents too must be identical. If a secondary cause in the form of evolution led to the generation of the body required by the rational soul (as Messenger suggested), matter would generate the form, and spirit would be just a function of matter. Such a view would represent a return to Haeckel's materialistic monism. Messenger's interpretation, then, encounters so many obstacles that it cannot constitute the golden mean between naturalistic and classical Christian doctrine. His solution is also anachronistic, as the synodal fathers never even considered the sophisticated concepts he developed, but simply addressed the opposition between evolution and creation of the first human body.

In order to reconcile the synodal definition with the theory of evolution, theologians could possibly modify the meaning of terms such as *condo* ("create"), *spontanea* ("spontaneously"), *immediate* ("immediately," "directly"), or *continuo ultimoque* ("continually until eventually"). However, if such a method of interpretation was permitted for other Church decrees, it is doubtful whether any dogma would preserve its essential content. Terms should be interpreted according to their most natural meaning, so long as it is not proved beyond doubt that they are to be understood otherwise. Moreover, a synodal definition should be interpreted as an integral whole, with each term being clarified in the context of the other terms.

Admittedly, the Cologne decree was devised with "German precision" and contains all the elements necessary for stating that Adam's body had been created in a direct act: The fathers first asserted that "our first parents were created immediately by God." It is the definition of the positive doctrine that contradicts any account that denies immediate creation. Next, lest any ambiguity remain, they explained which approach is contradictory to this doctrine; namely, the notion of Adam becoming himself by way of a change.

There are four possible charges against the synodal definition. First is the claim that in the evolutionary scenario man did not emerge by way of any change, because the word "man" refers to the compound of body and soul. And if man came into being only at the moment of receiving a soul, the evolution of the body is permitted—as up to that point there is no man, but only an evolving "preexisting living matter". This is why the fathers added the expression "as regards the body" (*si corpus spectes*), i.e., they referred all elements of the anti-evolutionary definition, not to Adam as a compound of body and soul, but to his body. Second, one might propose that there are various mechanisms of evolution and that the synodal definition concerns only some of them. Third, one could also say that the definition focuses only on materialistic or atheistic theories. These interpretations, however, also fail, because the synodal fathers defined evolution in abstract philosophical terms, not in specific biological terms. The statement does not mention natural selection, heredity, common descent, or survival of the fittest. What it does mention is the transformation from "imperfect nature to the more perfect." This expression includes the essence of all macroevolutionary concepts. All the theories in existence in 1860 (just like the slightly later Darwinism) assumed that the human body originated through small and slow changes of the body of some kind of animal, until it eventually became entirely human. The fathers clearly intended to deny precisely that idea.

Still, one might argue that even the Bible itself speaks of two divine acts: first, God forms the body; second, God breathes into the man the breath of life (Gen 2:7). Thus arises the fourth possibility: that the Holy Scriptures also allow some sort of transformation from "imperfect nature to the more perfect." In order to disqualify this interpretation, the fathers added the words "continuously, until eventually" (*continuo ultimoque*), which refers to a process rather than two distinct acts. The Cologne decree was very precise by itself, although, through a certain manipulation of the meanings of terms, the statement could be deprived of important content, as was done for example by Fr. Messenger.

The First Vatican Council (1870) and the Encyclical *Arcanum* (1880) of Leo XIII

In 1868, Pius IX issued the bull *Aeterni Patris*, convoking the First Vatican Council. Based on a number of previously operating theological assemblies, the pope established five deputations (commissions of synodal fathers) whose work was to prepare drafts of decrees. Each deputation (of faith, church discipline, religious orders, Eastern Rite and mission, and political and church affairs) was composed of twenty-two experts headed by one cardinal. The deputations prepared fifty-one documents that were to be subjected to discussion and voting by the fathers. The Council was interrupted after the fourth official session (July 18, 1870) due to the Italian invasion of the Papal States. In the end, the Council managed only to adopt two dogmatic constitutions: *Dei Filius*, on the Catholic faith; and *Pastor Aeternus*, on the Church of Christ, which established the dogma of papal infallibility.

As far as the topic of evolution is concerned, the constitution *Dei Filius* is of some importance, as the document briefly discusses the subject of creation. The Council states as follows:

> This sole true God . . . with most free volition, immediately from the beginning of time fashioned each creature out of nothing, spiritual and corporeal, namely angelic and mundane; and then the human creation, common as it were, composed of both spirit and body.[11]

The canons with anathemas added at the end of the constitution were even more explicit. According to Canon 5,

> If anyone does not confess that (a) the world and all things which are contained in it, . . . were produced, according to their whole substance (*secundum totam suam substantiam*), out of nothing by God; or (b) holds that God did not create by his will free from all necessity, but as necessarily as he necessarily loves himself; or (c) denies that the world was created for the glory of God: let him be anathema.[12]

11. *Dei Filius*, ch. I, 18.
12. Ibid., can. 5.

The conciliar teaching constitutes at least a threefold challenge to evolution understood as the method of God's creation of the world. First, it states that creatures in all their substance are created immediately by God. This formula teaches that no being, except for God himself, has the power to create, and that the creation of each new substance (i.e., new kind of being) is wholly and directly performed by God. Therefore, not only were the first matter and the laws of nature created, but also the diversity of things. This of course does not refer to every individual being, for many beings were not formed directly by God but by virtue of secondary causes, such as generation. Generation, however, does not produce new natures; rather, it only transmits the natures God had initially created out of nothing. The Vatican Council repeats here traditional Church doctrine already established in medieval times. In response to this, theistic evolutionists claimed (and claim) that everything was made by God, but not necessarily by him directly. Therefore, they argue, the participation of evolution in creation is not in disagreement with the conciliar text.

The second challenge for theistic evolutionists comes from the statement that God is completely free in creating. He does not create out of any necessity. Contrasted with this, in evolutionary theory it is the laws of nature (i.e., some sort of necessity) that determine the origin of species. Theistic evolutionists countered that view by saying that, as God is the maker of natural laws, one can conclude that the creation of beings in accord with these laws is still an expression of His free will.

The third point of disharmony between evolution and the conciliar canons concerns the beauty of the natural world. The world exists for God's glory. According to the Christian interpretation, the world is thus an expression of His wisdom and goodness. But the world made according to Darwinian principles is a manifestation of a constant struggle between all beings—of large-scale death and destruction giving rise ever so slowly to new beings. Life is the product of determinism and chance (cf. Chapter One, under "Darwin and *The Origin of Species*") rather than of God's wisdom and goodness.[13] To this claim, the evolutionists answered that since the world is subject to the effects of sin, the "struggle for life" might be its consequence.

13. The Darwinian scenario of the origins of the world is in even greater disagreement with the statement of the Council of Florence (Session 11 (8.1), February 4, 1442): "Most firmly it [the Holy Church] believes, professes and preaches that the one true God, . . . is the creator of all things that are, visible and invisible, who, when he willed it, made from his own goodness all creatures, both spiritual and corporeal, good indeed because they are made by the supreme good, but mutable because they are made from nothing, and it asserts that there is no nature of evil because every nature, insofar as it is a nature, is good." Latin text in *Dokumenty Soborów Powszechnych*, ed. A. Baron, H. Pietras, vol. 3, 582–584; English text: http://www.dailycatholic.org/history/17ecum11.htm (January 28, 2015).

And so, each of the challenges could be matched with an evolutionary response. It should be noted that the council's pronouncement excludes evolution in principle (understood as the emergence of totally new organisms from previously existing ones). Nevertheless, it is too general to serve as the final argument in contemporary debates. It provides a broader framework for possible future definitions of faith.[14]

It is a little-known fact, but one crucial for our subject, that apart from the two final documents, there was also one draft of a dogmatic constitution that was not subjected to vote during the Council because of its interruption. The schema of *De doctrina catholica* includes the following passage:

> This, our Holy Mother the Church believes and teaches: When God was about to make man according to His image and likeness in order that he might rule over the whole earth, He breathed into the body formed from the slime of the earth the breath of life, that is, a soul produced from nothing. . . . And blessing the first man and Eve his wife who was formed by divine power from his side, God said: Increase and multiply, and fill the earth (Gen 1:28).[15]

This passage would raise to the rank of official doctrine (i.e., infallible and solemn teaching) the following three truths: direct creation of man from the dust of the earth; creation of the human soul directly by God; and the creation of the first woman in no other way than by God's power from Adam's side.

A draft that is not enacted by the council has no binding force. Still, we should not ignore the fact that such a fragment was included in the draft of a dogmatic constitution. Had the text been enacted, it would have been a logical complement of the interpretation of faith given in *Dei Filius*. When assessing its value we should bear in mind, however, that the preparatory commissions were composed of the most trustworthy experts, proficient in theology, including many bishops.[16] This statement is thus an important testimony of traditional Catholic teaching. The records of the First Vatican Council do not mention any

14. Sometimes the decisions of Vatican I are claimed by theologians to oppose the theory of evolution. It is so in the case of Father Johannes Grun, who sees anti-evolutionary expressions in the decrees of Lateran IV (1215), Florence (1439–1442), and Vatican I (1870). J. Grun, "Metaphysics to the Rescue: Rediscovering the Authentic Meaning of Conciliar Teaching on Creation," in *International Catholic Symposium on Creation, October* 24–25, 2002 (Rome: Kolbe Center, 2002), 79–141.

15. "Haec credit et praedicat Sancta Mater Ecclesia: Facturus Deus hominem ad imaginem et similitudinem suam, ut praeesset universae terrae, corpori de limo terrae formato inspiravit spiraculum vitae, animam scilicet de nihilo productam. [. . .] Primo autem homini et Haevae uxori, e costa eius divinitus formatae, benedicens ait: Multiplicamini et replete terram (Gen. 1:28)." "Schema reformatus constitutionis de doctrina catholica," c. 2, in *Acta et Decreta Sacrorum Conciliorum Recentiorum*: Collectio Lacensis, vol. 7 (Freiburg: Herder, 1890), 554–55.

16. In this context, B.W. Harrison openly concludes: "After all, those preparing doctrinal statements for an Ecumenical Council, are, obviously, drawn from among those regarded by the Holy See as the most learned bishops and the most erudite and trustworthy theologians available. If they are

of the fathers having reservations regarding the above-quoted formula. On the contrary, the first version of the text did not include the phrase about Eve being "formed by divine power from his [Adam's] side" (*e costa eius divinitus formatae*). The clause was added in a second draft, which suggests that the theologians, having thoroughly analyzed the issue, decided to make the doctrinal formulation even more explicit, so that it clearly opposed the evolutionary origin of Eve. (The matter of Adam's origin had already been sufficiently explained in the first wording of the draft.) It is also worth noting that the council discussions concurred with the early publications on the evolution of the human body from lower animals, such as Huxley's *Evidence as to Man's Place in Nature* (1863) and Haeckel's *Natürliche Schöpfungsgeschichte* (1868). Darwin's *The Descent of Man* was not published until 1871, so it could not have influenced the debate.

We can now summarize the discussion as follows. To begin, lay agnostic scientists came up with the idea of man having originated from lower animals. These concepts were immediately rejected by the Synod of Cologne. Next, the experts preparing the general council resolved to confirm the Catholic doctrine of the creation of man. As the debate in lay circles gathered steam, Church experts, having conducted their analysis, improved the text of the constitution to help protect the truth of the origin of both the first man and the first woman. The Council was unfortunately interrupted, but the testimony of Church faith was recorded in the prepared documents. We can safely conclude, therefore, that it was the intention of Vatican I to reject the theory of human evolution from lower animals and contrast it with the religious truth of immediate creation.

This interpretation is confirmed by the 1880 encyclical of Leo XIII, *Arcanum divinae sapientiae*, on marriage. The pope asserts that:

> The true origin of marriage, venerable brothers, is well known to all. Though revilers of the Christian faith refuse to acknowledge the never-interrupted doctrine of the Church on this subject, and have long striven to destroy the testimony of all nations and of all times, they have nevertheless failed not only to quench the powerful light of truth, but even to lessen it. We record what is to all known, and cannot be doubted by any, that God, on the sixth day of creation, having made man from the slime of the earth, and having breathed into his face the breath of life, gave him a companion, whom He miraculously took from the side of Adam when he was locked in sleep. God

---

not in position to know what the ordinary Magisterium of the Church has been up till their own time, who ever would be?" B.W. Harrison, "Did Woman Evolve from Beasts? A Defense of Traditional Catholic Doctrine," in *International Catholic Symposium on Creation*, 161. In his paper, Harrison presents the thesis that, in view of both the old and the modern documents of the Church, the truth about the creation of Eve directly from Adam's rib is part of infallible Catholic doctrine.

thus, in His most far-reaching foresight, decreed that this husband and wife should be the natural beginning of the human race, from whom it might be propagated and preserved by an unfailing fruitfulness throughout all futurity of time.[17]

The text is a clear expression of Catholic doctrine. The pope regarded the truths concerning the origin of the first human couple as "well known to all" and "never-interrupted." Nevertheless, he decided to remind the faithful of them, because of the "revilers of faith" disputing the "doctrine which cannot be doubted by any." Who were these "revilers of faith" attempting to "quench the light of the truth"? We know that the encyclical was a response to the then-questioned legislation guaranteeing the indissolubility of marriage; it was also a voice in the argument about mixed marriages during the Prussian *Kulturkampf.* There were thus many political enemies of the Church against whom the papal encyclical was directed. However, in the above-quoted passage, the pope is not speaking of political issues but of the "true origin of marriage," built upon the foundation of the truth about woman's creation from Adam's rib. Thus the enemies undermining this truth were naturalists using alleged scientific proofs to impose the idea of an evolutionary origin of man. The expression of Leo XIII, stating that Eve had been created in a "miraculous" way (*mirabiliter*), means that she had not been created by the power of nature, which therefore precludes her evolution. Also, Leo XIII mentions the origination of mankind from a single human couple constituting "the natural beginning of the entire human family." In this way, then, the pope's statements are directly aimed against both evolution and polygenism.

Rev. Brian W. Harrison remarks that, up until the late 20th century, the *Arcanum* encyclical had not appeared in the church debates. This, he argues, is "perhaps the most weighty of all magisterial interventions for the direct, supernatural formation of the first woman. Like Pope Pelagius' sixth-century profession of faith, it seems to have fallen into oblivion, and is never cited, even by those theologians who would certainly have been most happy to enlist it in their cause if they knew about it."[18] Harrison suggests the reason might be due to the simple fact that the statement on the creation of man is included in an encyclical on marriage. Theologians studying the topic of evolution and cre-

17. "Nota omnibus et nemini dubia commemoramus; posteaquam sexto creationis die formavit Deus hominem de limo terrae, et inspiravit in faciem eius spiraculum vitae, sociam illi voluit adiungere, quam de latere viri ipsius dormientis mirabiliter eduxit. Qua in re hoc voluit providentissimus Deus, ut illud par coniugum esset cunctorum hominum naturale principium, ex quo scilicet propagari humanum genus, et, numquam intermissis probationibus, conservari in omne tempus oporteret." Leo XIII, *Arcanum divinae sapientiae* in *AAS*, 12 (1879; reprt. 1968), 386.

18. B.W. Harrison, "Did Woman Evolve from Beasts?," 162. On the teachings of Pope Pelagius I, see Appendix.

ation probably omitted the pastoral encyclical by definition, even without knowing its content. In this way, one of the most important statements on the subject has been almost completely forgotten. The statement by Leo XIII is of a doctrinal rank and has never been revoked in subsequent decrees. Thus it is also binding in the current debate.

4

The Rise of Catholic Evolutionism

George Mivart's "Christian Evolutionism"

Papal Affirmation of the Book On the Genesis of Species

In 1871, twelve years after the publication of Darwin's *The Origin of Species* and parallel to the publication of his other work, *The Descent of Man*, the English biologist St. George Mivart published his book *On the Genesis of Species.*

Mivart was born to an Anglican family but converted to Catholicism in 1844. This decision expelled him from Oxford academic circles, forcing him to resort to private education and studies in Catholic facilities. His teachers included George Waterhouse and Richard Owen. Mivart even cooperated with Thomas H. Huxley, who helped him gain the position of a lecturer at the St. Mary's Hospital Medical School, where he worked until his retirement in 1884. He was a member of the Zoological Society and the Linnean Society, and in 1867 was elected a member of the Royal Society. As a biologist studying the origin of species, Mivart was among the closest friends of Charles Darwin. He corresponded with him and scrutinized his works, while conducting research of his own.

However, around the year 1868, studies on the taxonomy of primates led him to a conclusion that morphologically similar classes and orders must have originated independently of each other. At the same time, he rejected the idea of natural selection for religious reasons. He expressed his feeling about the rejection in a letter to Darwin:

> After many painful days and much meditation and discussion, my mind was made up, and I felt it my duty first of all to go straight to Professor Huxley and tell him all my thoughts, feelings, and intentions in the matter without the slightest reserve, including what it seemed to me I must do as regarded the theological aspect of the question.... As soon as I made my meaning clear, his countenance became transformed as I had never seen it.... He was

> kind and gentle as he said regretfully, but most firmly, that nothing so united or severed men as questions such as those I had spoken of.[1]

This "transformation of Huxley's countenance" was, in a way, an expression of the changed attitude of the entire scientific community gathered around Darwin.

Mivart presented the development of his views in *On the Genesis of Species* in the following manner:

> The author of this book can say that, though by no means disposed originally to dissent from the theory of Natural Selection, if only its difficulties could be solved, he has found each successive year that deeper consideration and more careful examination have more and more brought home to him the inadequacy of Mr. Darwin's theory to account for the preservation and intensification of incipient, specific, and generic characters. That minute, fortuitous, and indefinite variations could have brought about such special forms and modifications . . . , seems to contradict not imagination, but reason.[2]

The British scientist must have had solid grounds based on research to publicly reject the theory supported by his best friends and co-workers. When he did so, he was "excommunicated."

Five years after the publication of his work, Mivart received the degree of doctor of philosophy from Pope Pius IX himself. In 1884, he was also granted an honorary doctorate in medicine by the Catholic University of Louvain in Belgium. These distinctions enforced the social and academic status of the researcher in Catholic circles. Some scholars believe that the first distinction was given because of the papal endorsement of Mivart's attempt to combine Christianity with some general idea of evolutionary origin of species.[3] In fact, the true reason for Mivart's distinctions remains uncertain. In order to investigate this issue objectively, we need to determine precisely what the British biologist wrote in his book.

On the Genesis of Species is comprised of twelve chapters. Eleven of them contain a rather critical portrayal of various elements of the theory of biological evolution, particularly directed against Darwin's ideas. In a summary of his charges,[4] Mivart states that natural selection can by no means be responsible

1. Cf. R.J. Richards, *Darwin and the Emergence of Evolutionary Theories of Mind and Behavior* (Chicago: University of Chicago Press, 1987), 355.

2. St. G. Mivart, *On the Genesis of Species* (New York: D. Appleton and Company, 1871), 74.

3. The authors of *Negotiating Darwin*, despite introducing a few distinctions, are headed in the same interpretative direction; cf. ibid., 236. This interpretation is endorsed also by A. Siemieniewski in the article "Postawa Kościoła wobec teorii ewolucji: *Semper Idem*" [The Church's View on the Theory of Evolution: *Semper Idem*], in *Wrocławski Przegląd Teologiczny* 17, no. 1 (2009), 39–58; http://www.dbc.wroc.pl/Content/14112/wpt2009-1.pdf (January 29, 2015).

4. St. G. Mivart, 34.

for the formation of new species and generic features. He expresses his support for the traditional idea of specified limits to species changeability, which he argued were confirmed by the fact that the supposed intermediate forms are missing from the fossil record. In his opinion, the geographical distribution of some species only introduces further difficulties. He rejects Darwin's newly announced theory of pangenesis, which constituted—in Mivart's words—"nearly an explanation *obscurum per obscurius*." However, such a critical attitude toward evolution is not evident in the content of individual chapters, which discuss more thoroughly the issues broached in the introduction. The text of the book, therefore, is quite ambiguous, and different readers might be prompted to defend contradictory views on the basis of Mivart's statements. It seems that the general idea behind the work is that macroevolution is neither proved nor disproved by the facts. If, however, macroevolution actually occurs, it does not happen by virtue of the mechanisms proposed by Darwin. On the one hand, then, Mivart stands in clear opposition to Darwin's theory; on the other, he allows, at least hypothetically, for the possibility of transformism and common descent of species.

Finally, Mivart also presents his view on the origins of man:

> In this way we find a perfect harmony in the double nature of man, . . . his soul arising from direct and immediate creation, and his body being formed at first (as now in each separate individual) by derivative or secondary creation, through natural laws. By such secondary creation, i.e., by natural laws, for the most part as yet unknown but controlled by Natural Selection, all the various kinds of animals and plants have been manifested on this planet.[5]

Thus, Mivart was a supporter of the evolution of the human body from lower animals, and also inclined towards the natural emergence of species.

Only on two points (in the first and last chapter) in his three-hundred-page book does he mention matters of theology. He concludes that those aspects of the theory of evolution, though at the time scientifically unproven, are reconcilable with Christianity. In chapter twelve, referring to theological issues, he first devotes much space to the criticism of Herbert Spencer's philosophical concept of evolution, and then tackles Darwin's charges against creation. Eventually he gets to his own idea of theistic evolution, which takes up just three pages. Two more pages argue that there are no objections from the teachings of St. Augustine and St. Thomas that would prohibit recognizing the evolutionary origin of species. The most controversial topic, namely, the evolution of man, consists of two sentences, which might have been overlooked even by careful

5. Ibid., 305.

readers. It should thus be noted that nearly the entirety of the work for which Mivart was awarded a doctorate by Pius IX was a robust criticism of Darwin's theory, which was surely appealing both to the pope and to the censors designated by Rome.

More detailed studies are needed to determine if the main (and, actually, the only) argument in favor of the alleged pro-evolutionary attitude of Pius IX has not been exaggerated by some researchers. It is quite possible that the pope commended Mivart's book not because of these few pages promoting theistic evolution, but in spite of them.

As Mivart's concept was the first Catholic attempt to reconcile theology and evolution, it requires a synthetic presentation. First, the scholar distinguished three senses of "creation":

> In the strictest and highest sense, Creation is the absolute origination of anything by God without preexisting means or material, and is a supernatural act. In the secondary and lower sense, creation is the formation of anything by God *derivatively*; that is, that the preceding matter has been created with the potentiality to evolve from it, under suitable conditions, all the various forms it subsequently assumes. . . . This is the natural action of God in the physical world, as distinguished from His direct, or, as it may be here called, supernatural action. In yet a third sense, the word *Creation* may be more or less improperly applied to the construction of any complex formation or state by a voluntary self-conscious being who makes use of the powers and laws which God has imposed, as when a man is spoken of as the creator of a museum, or of his own fortune, etc. Such action of a created conscious intelligence is purely natural, but more than physical, and may be conveniently spoken of as hyperphysical.[6]

Thus, according to Mivart, creation may be defined as: "(1) direct or supernatural action; (2) physical action; and (3) hyperphysical action—the two latter both belonging to the order of nature."[7]

Next, Mivart states that, since evolution belongs to the natural order, it has nothing to do with creation in the first sense. Furthermore,

> With secondary or derivative creation, physical science is also incapable of conflict; for the objections drawn by some writers seemingly from physical science are, as has been already argued, rather metaphysical than physical. Derivative creation is not a supernatural act, but is simply the Divine action by and through natural laws. To recognize such action in such laws is a religious mode of regarding phenomena, which a consistent theist must necessarily accept, and which an atheistic believer must similarly reject. . . . The

6. Ibid., 269.
7. Ibid.

> conflict has arisen through a misunderstanding. Some have supposed that by creation was necessarily meant either primary, that is, absolute creation, or, at least, some supernatural action; they have therefore opposed the dogma of creation in the imagined interest of physical science. Others have supposed that by "evolution" was necessarily meant a denial of Divine action, a negation of the providence of God. They have therefore combated the theory of evolution in the imagined interest of religion. It appears plain, then, that Christian thinkers are perfectly free to accept the general evolution theory.[8]

In this way, Mivart tries to harmonize two ideas that were irreconcilable according to the majority of theologians at the time.

The significance of Mivart's thought—the first attempt to incorporate evolutionary thinking in Catholicism—merits a commentary indicating its three fundamental difficulties:

1. Mivart identifies three meanings of "creation." However, such a distinction is not found in the writings of the Church Fathers, in St. Thomas, or in dogmatic decisions of medieval councils. The distinction is thus quite foreign to the Catholic tradition, which only knows creation in the first sense mentioned by Mivart, i.e., creation from nothing (*creatio ex nihilo*), which is not a change of any kind (*creatio non est mutatio*). The traditional understanding of "second creation" refers to a supernatural, direct act of God, who produced new natures by working on previously formed matter. Therefore, the solution of the author is based on the relativization of the traditional concept of creation.

2. Mivart's reasoning is circular. He first defines creation in the second sense as a natural process, but then claims that a natural process (evolution) is not in opposition to creation understood in the same, second sense.

3. Creation in the third sense—as the co-operation of free subjects—disagrees with the teachings of the Church Fathers. According to Aquinas and the Fathers, no one but God can be called a Creator. For instance, for St. Augustine, "it is blasphemy to believe or to say (even before it can be understood) that any other than God is creator of any nature."[9]

The acceptance of Mivart's book in some church circles might have been shaped by two favorable reviews published in 1871 and 1872 in the *Dublin*

8. Ibid., 278–79.

9. St. Augustine, *City of God*, Book XII, ch. 24. In Chapter 25, Augustine adds: "We do not call gardeners the creators of their fruits, [...]. Nay, not even the earth itself do we call a creator, though she seems to be the prolific mother of all things [...]. We ought not even to call a woman the creatress of her own offspring." It is obvious that Augustine does not exclude here figurative or metaphorical usage of the terms "creator/creation" referring to creation. However, Mivart does not postulate figurative usage, but analogical. This was the sense of introducing three meanings of "creator/creation" in his book. And this is why his concept contradicts traditional Christian teaching.

Review, a major Catholic periodical. The anonymous author of these articles emphasized, however, that recognition of the evolutionary origin of the first man is unfounded, whereas the concept of man's creation is based on the Bible, the agreement of theologians, and Sacred Tradition. Nevertheless, the author did not seem to view direct creation as a defined truth of the faith.[10]

Mivart's Departure from Catholic Orthodoxy

A certain tension first appeared between George Mivart and the Catholic hierarchy in England between 1885 and 1887. Mivart published articles in *The Nineteenth Century* and the *Dublin Review*, suggesting that Catholics should be free to study the scientific issues present in the Bible. According to him, Galileo's case demonstrated that God had entrusted scientific matters exclusively to scientists, rather than to theologians and congregations of the Holy See.

John Cuthbert Hedley, Bishop of Newport, and Fr. Jeremiah Murphy disagreed with him. Bishop Hedley noted that Mivart was partly right, but extrapolated the case of Galileo beyond its significance and drew erroneous, far-reaching conclusions. Fr. Murphy, however, wrote that, contrary to what Mivart said, Catholicism and evolution are in conflict, so there is no need to abandon the literal interpretation of the Bible concerning the creation of man as long as evolutionists do not produce sufficient proofs of their theory.

In a further stage of the discussion, Mivart attacked Murphy's position, calling it "intolerably pernicious." Mivart argues that, according to Murphy, a theologian persistently maintains that a literal biblical interpretation is true, but at the same time leaves open the possibility of abandoning literal interpretation immediately when some "inconvenient" evolutionist provides a contrary claim with a "sufficient proof." "This to me is a revolting position," writes Mivart, "at once skeptical and shocking from the indifference to truth it makes manifest."[11]

Murphy answered with another long article, which is important because it was representative of the arguments and opinions of most theologians of the time. According to Murphy, revealed truths about the creation of Adam are clear and precise, and if they are to be read literally, they leave no room for evolution. Church Tradition and theologians are entirely in agreement about this

10. St. G. Mivart, "Notices of Books: *On the Genesis of Species*," in *Dublin Review* (January–April 1871): 482–86. The second paper is a favorable review of four pro-evolutionary books, including Darwin's *The Descent of Man* and Mivart's *On the Genesis of Species*. The main thesis of the article is that nothing in the theory of evolution is in conflict with faith: "Evolution and Faith," in *Dublin Review* (July–October 1871), 1–40.

11. Cf. St. G. Mivart, "Letter from Dr. Mivart on the Bishop of Newport's Article in Our Last Number," *Dublin Review* (January–April 1888): 182. (Cf. M. Artigas, T. F. Glick, R. A. Martínez, *Negotiating Darwin*, 245).

matter. "And what is the ground for contradicting it here? The evolution theory—a theory, however, confessedly not proved, not even provable, but pointed out as scientifically probable by analogy—a misleading guide."[12] Fr. Murphy not only refers to the complete agreement within tradition, but also claims that the immediate creation of Adam is part of the ordinary doctrine of the Church. For this reason, the editor of the *Dublin Review* decided to add a short note at the end of the article, stating that immediate creation of the human body is commonly taught by theologians, but that it had not yet been clarified whether it is only their opinion or is a truth revealed by God and binding on the conscience of believers: "The question is not whether they [theologians of the past] considered their interpretation of Genesis as true, but whether they taught that it was an article of faith. This, we venture to think, has not yet been placed beyond doubt."[13]

Despite the public disagreements between Mivart and the clergy, his evolutionary views provoked no official demand for recantation, nor did they provoke condemnation by the Church. Mivart's true problems began when he published texts on strictly theological matters. In 1892–1893, again in *Nineteenth Century*, he published three articles, the first entitled "Happiness in Hell."[14] His basic idea is that it is possible that damned souls experience some kind of happiness in hell. Mivart claims, among other things, that the condemned can enjoy the low desires they succumbed to during their lives; that they can have friends and will gradually return to some form of unity with God. In this series, and in later publications, Mivart adds still other theses in conflict with Church doctrine. By the end of his life, he decides that most people are not capable of committing a mortal sin. He also questions the virginal conception of Jesus and the perpetual virginity of Mary, the reality and transmission of original sin, redemption as the actual price for the sins of man, the biblical account of the resurrection of Jesus, eternity of punishment in hell, the inspiration and integrity of the Bible, the authority of the Church in the interpretation of the Scriptures, and more.

Mivart's articles from 1892–1893 were added to the Index, and the scholar himself surrendered to the decision of the Congregation on August 10, 1893. However, as early as 1899, probably under the influence of an incurable disease that might have limited his ability for conscious action, he initiated a campaign against the Church. He demanded an explanation from the Congregation of

12. Cf. J. Murphy, "Dr. Mivart on Faith and Science," *Dublin Review* (January–April 1888): 407. (Cf. *Negotiating Darwin*, 246).

13. Ibid., 411. (Cf. *Negotiating Darwin*, 247).

14. St. G. Mivart, "Happiness in Hell," in *Nineteenth Century* 32 (1892): 899–919; "The Happiness in Hell: A Rejoinder," in *Nineteenth Century* 33 (1893), 320–38; "Last Words on the Happiness in Hell: A Rejoinder," in *Nineteenth Century* 33 (1893), 637–51.

the Index concerning the decision from six years before, and in various publications proposed further claims contrary to settled teaching. In correspondence with his ordinary, the Archbishop of Westminster—Cardinal Herbert Vaughan—he confesses that he had come to the conclusion that Catholic doctrine and natural science are fatally antagonistic, so that no one in their right mind could agree with the Catholic Church. Having refused to sign a confession of faith received from Cardinal Vaughan, Mivart put himself outside the Church; however, he was never formally excommunicated. On January 18, 1900, the cardinal issued a letter to the diocese, denying the scholar the right to sacraments. Mivart died of diabetes on April 1 of the same year.

Regarding evolution, one may identify two stages of Mivart's thought. In the first, he accepted Darwinism and travelled in circles propagating the new theory. In the second period, he criticized Darwin's ideas, but not the evolutionary origin of species itself. After in-depth studies, Mivart decided Darwinism was indefensible, but he still believed evolution as such was possible. His conversion to Catholicism inspired him to try to reconcile evolution with revelation. In his major work, he proposed, on the one hand, fundamental criticism of the ideas of Darwin and Spencer, and on the other a synthesis of evolution and faith, which he believed was viable for Christians. We know that Pius IX appreciated his attitude, but we do not know if this was because of the theistic evolution found in Mivart's writings or rather his criticism of other evolutionary thinkers, which constitutes the core of his work.

It should be noted that Mivart received the title of doctor of philosophy from the pope, and the title of doctor of medicine from the University of Louvain. Neither of the distinctions was of a strictly theological nature, but the concept of theistic evolution certainly was theological. Thus, if Pius IX had really approved Mivart's theological opinions (and not just his scientific criticism of evolution), he should have distinguished him with some kind of theological degree. In view of ecclesiastical debates at the time, as well as the mode in which Pius IX is known to have acted in such cases, we should rather assume that the criticism of Darwinism alone was the sufficient reason for the pope's appreciation of Mivart's work. One testimony of Pius IX's stance on Darwin's theory can be found in a private letter to the French naturalist Constantine James, who published a critical book on Darwinism. The pope commented on James's work in these words:

> [Dr. James] refuted so well the aberrations of Darwinism. . . . A system that is repugnant at once to history, to the tradition of all peoples, to exact sciences, to observed facts, and even to reason itself, would seem to need no refutation. But the corruption of this age, the machinations of the perverse, the danger of the simple, demand that such fancies, altogether absurd though

> they are, should—since they borrow the mask of science—be refuted by true science.[15]

This fragment reveals the attitude of Pius IX to the theory of evolution and confirms his tactic of supporting scientists who criticized evolution. During the pontificate of Pius IX, institutional endorsement of the Church was also given to a few other local anti-evolutionist initiatives, such as the establishment of the journal *Academia* in England by Cardinal Wiseman.[16] Therefore it is highly likely that his strong criticism of Darwinism was the sole reason for Pius IX to distinguish the English scholar.

The Unknown Prohibition of Raffaello Caverni

The Principal Theses of De' nuovi studi della filosofia

As a young man, Raffaello Caverni (1837–1900) studied in Florence. There, he discovered his vocation, entered a seminary, and was ordained a priest in 1860. He spent ten years at the Firenzuola seminary as a professor of physics and mathematics. In 1871, he was transferred to the parish of Quarate, a small village near Florence, where, thanks to the proximity of the city, he continuously conducted research and released publications concerning the history and philosophy of science. The most famous work of Caverni was his pioneering, six-volume *Storia del metodo sperimentale in Italia* (*History of the Experimental Method in Italy*). That work, about four thousand pages in length, gave its author a certain notoriety, especially after he received the top prize in a competition held by the Royal Institute of Science in Venice. Caverni criticized Galileo, which put a distance between some scientists and the monumental work of the Italian priest; as time passed, however, he has been almost completely forgotten.

At the end of the 1860s, when Darwin's new ideas were provoking heated debates in the academic community, Caverni also focused his interest on evolution. In 1875 and 1876, he published a few articles that were then collected in a book entitled *De' nuovi studi della filosofia* (*New Studies of Philosophy*, 1877).[17] Its main contention is that it is possible to reconcile evolution with Christian doctrine. Caverni emphasizes the need for divine creative action and the active intervention of God, who through His providence controls natural processes in order to reach foreseen ends. In order to harmonize this theory with the bibli-

15. Pius IX, A letter to Constantine James of May 17, 1877. Quotation after: T. F. Glick, *What about Darwin?* (The John Hopkins University Press, 2010), 347.

16. See P. M. Thompson, *Between Science and Religion: The Engagement of Catholic Intellectuals with Science and Technology in the Twentieth Century* (Lanham: Lexington Books, 2009), 4.

17. R. Caverni, *De' nuovi studi della filosofia: Discorsi a un giovane studente* (Firenze: Carnesecchi, 1877).

cal account, he makes a distinction between two aspects of the Bible—the divine and the human. The divine aspect, in his opinion, includes truths of faith and is infallible, whereas the human aspect could contain claims that through the study of nature could be found to be wrong. According to this approach, the Bible can be fallible in what it says about nature. Caverni also cites Galileo's opinion that it was not the purpose of the Bible to teach people about matters of science, but rather to show them the way to heaven.[18] Caverni concludes that science has complete freedom in the search for the origin of species, although he also states that if the limits of natural science are marked by nature, the natural sciences exceed their competence by speaking about the spiritual world.[19] This distinction helps him exclude man from the evolutionary process (as man has a spiritual soul) and thus avoid the most controversial ideas. Therefore, he promotes a version of theistic evolution that excludes the evolutionary origin of man, entails finality, and affirms God's activity in the universe.

Already in the same year, Caverni's book encountered full-scale criticism by the Jesuit Francesco Salis Seewis, who published a lengthy two-part article in *La Civiltá Cattolica*.[20] Meanwhile, the editors of the periodical began to publish articles by Pietro Caterini, S.J. (a total of 37), which constitute a synthesis of Catholic criticism of evolutionism.[21] Essentially, Caverni's critics rejected his approach to the Bible and defended the truth of the full infallibility of the sacred text. They also detailed the scientific errors and philosophical difficulties of Darwin's theory. Francesco Salis Seewis depicted quite accurately the position of the majority of theologians:

> Darwinism is a seed of unbelief, the result of considering nature without God and of the tendency to exclude God from science. All the laws that Darwin dreamed up have the result of making divine action superfluous. Darwin scarcely concealed the equivalence of his theory and the atheistic, materialist principles that have been professed afterward by his followers and successors without any qualification.[22]

18. Ibid., 24–28.

19. Ibid., 172.

20. F. Salis Seewis, "Review of *De' nuovi studi della Filosofia: Discorsi di Raffaello Caverni a un giovane studente*," *La Civiltá Cattolica* 10, no. 4 (1877), 570–80; 10; no. 5 (1878), 65–76. [References to original late-19th-century articles and documents of the Congregation of the Index included in this work are taken from *Negotiating Darwin*. English translation is based on the text of that study. Notes contain references to original articles and documents, helping the reader to find it in the relevant archives].

21. A few years later, the articles were published as a separate compilation: P. Caterini, *Dell'origine dell'uomo secondo il transformismo: Esame scientifico filosofico teologico* (Prato: Giachetti 1884).

22. F. Salis Seewis, "Review of *De' nuovi studi della Filosofia*," *La Civiltá Cattolica*, 10, no. 5 (1878), 66. (Cf. M. Artigas, T.F. Glick, R.A. Martínez, *Negotiating Darwin*, 36.)

In turn, Caterini does not stop at criticism of Caverni's openness to evolutionary ideas. At one point he states: "It is revealed doctrine that the first parents of humankind were produced by the immediate operation of God, not only insofar as the soul is concerned, but the body also."[23] In support of his thesis, Caterini refers to the Bible, the Church Fathers, and the "common agreement of theologians," including Hettinger, Perrone, Palmieri, Mazzella, Hurter, Dupasquier, and Bertie. Finally, Caterini concludes that the doctrine of transformism is rife with theological errors and in complete disagreement with Catholicism. From the point of view of science and reason, he argues, transformism is a collection of philosophical absurdities, confused ideas, unfounded theses, exaggerated data, and false conclusions. The last sentence of the long series of articles reads: "In sum, transformism considered theologically is a gross and manifest error contrary to faith. Examined philosophically it is a fantastic dream, a strange *a priori* system, opposed to observations and facts of nature."[24]

Indirect Condemnation of Darwinism

Late in 1877, the Archbishop of Florence, Eugenio Cecconi, having investigated the case on the diocesan level, submitted a reservation against Caverni's book to the Vatican Congregation of the Index. The Congregation appointed an expert, Tommaso Maria Zigliara, a prominent Dominican Thomist whom Leo XIII would make a cardinal at the beginning of his pontificate (1879). In May 1878, Zigliara presented his three-part examination of Caverni's work.[25]

In the summary of his review, Zigliara states that Caverni, in attempting to emphasize the difference between man and animal, gets lost in imprecise concepts. The more he tries to extricate himself from the confusion, the closer he moves to materialism—not because it had been his intention, but because it was the true nature of his theory. Caverni's three major errors are theistic evolution, a rejection of the infallibility of divine revelation with respect to the natural world, and the claim that the human soul might be the effect of divine influence on an animal brain. All three errors justify the book's placement on the Index. Zigliara also recommends that the Florentine priest be stopped from publishing his announced second book about the origins of man.[26] Caverni's case was soon on the agenda of the Congregation of the Index. The decision to renounce the book was unanimous. The experts present on the occasion included Tommaso Maria Zigliara and Rev. Luigi Tripepi, the future Cardinal

23. "Come entrino la fede e la teologia nella questione trasformistica, XLI," *La Civiltá Cattolica* 4 (1880), 171. Cf. *Negotiating Darwin*, 38.

24. Ibid.

25. ACDF, Index, *Protocolli*, 1878–1881, vol. 71.

26. *Negotiating Darwin*, 43–44.

and expert of the Congregation in the case of D. Leroy. Next, the decision of the preparatory body was passed on to the general meeting of the Congregation of the Index, which took place on July 1, 1878. Their conclusion is set forth in the clearest terms:

> [Caverni's work] merits serious and special attention. In it, Darwinism is expounded and partly approved, [stating] that it has many points of contact with religious doctrine, especially with Genesis and other books of the Bible. Until now the Holy See has rendered no decision on the system mentioned. Therefore, if Caverni's work is condemned, as it should be, Darwinism would be indirectly condemned. Surely there would be cries against this decision: the example of Galileo would be held up; it will be said that this Holy Congregation is not competent to emit judgments on physiological and ontological doctrines or theories of change. But we should not focus on this probable clamor. With his system, Darwin destroys the bases of revelation and openly teaches pantheism and abject materialism. Thus, an indirect condemnation of Darwin is not only useful, but even necessary, together with that of Caverni, his defender and propagator among Italian youth.[27]

The decision to ban Caverni's book was made unanimously by nine cardinals present at the general meeting. Afterwards it was presented to the pope, who personally approved the decree on July 10, 1878. When Caverni heard his book was about to be renounced, he wrote a letter to the rector of his family town: "You should know that in the current controversies between science and faith I have sought to intrude a bit as a peacemaker, and with regard to Darwin I have said that once it is demonstrated that man cannot come from the monkey, it matters little for religion to accept the Darwinian system of transformation of species for the other animal species. This is the substance of all my heresies."[28] Once notified about the book's listing on the Index, the author surrendered to the decision. The Index worked in such a way that when a given author surrendered to the resolution of the Church, his work—as it had already been published—was added to the list. However, the entry included a note that the author had surrendered to the decision.

Three years later Caverni released his book on the origin of man,[29] arguing in it that the scientific data concerning this matter is uncertain and thus no hypotheses should be drawn about the age of mankind. Furthermore, he assures believers that they could follow the scientific debate on this issue without fear, as the empirical sciences have no grounds to contradict what God has

27. ACDF, Index, *Protocolli*, 1878–1881, vol. 73. After M. Artigas, T.F. Glick, R.A. Martínez, *Negotiating Darwin*, 47.

28. Letter from S. Pagnini, *Profilo di Raffaello Caverni* 1837–1900 (Firenze: Pagnini e Martinelli, 2001), 40–41. (Cf. *Negotiating Darwin*, 49.)

29. R. Caverni, *Dell'antichitá dell'uomo secondo la scienza moderna* (Firenze: Cellini, 1881).

generously revealed. Such an approach to the topic did not face any negative reaction from Church authorities.

Until recently, Caverni's case was almost completely unknown to historians. The authors of *Negotiating Darwin* (M. Artigas, T.F. Glick, R.A. Martínez) argue that the renunciation of Caverni's book was completely ineffective.[30] Why was that? The reason is rather trivial. The title of the book does not mention evolution or Darwinism, and its content is quite varied. The Index entry, however, does not specify the reason for renunciation, only the title and information about the author. As the reports prepared for the Congregation remained confidential, there was no sufficient ground for claiming that theistic evolution had been the main reason for the renunciation. Usually it was the Italian periodical *La Civiltá Cattolica* that gave publicity to affairs related to teaching evolution. However, in this case even the editors of that periodical did not know the motives of the Congregation and so refrained from commenting for fear of making a mistake. As the second work of Caverni aroused no controversy, and he himself remained obedient to the Church, there was no scandal such as usually accompanied Church decisions of this kind. In this way the rejection of Caverni's evolutionism has not been preserved historically. Moreover, the case was probably outshone by other, more glaring events from the last decade of the 19th century. Only the 1998 opening of the archives of the Congregation of the Doctrine of Faith—which contains documents of the previously abolished Congregation of the Index—led researchers to realize that the first indirect condemnation of Darwinism by the Church had been quickly forgotten and remained obscure until that point.

Dalmace Leroy's Idea of "Restricted Evolution"

Dalmace Leroy was born in 1828, in Marseille. In 1852, he made his solemn profession as a Dominican friar. He performed various functions in the order until his death in 1905. He served as deputy superior of the novitiate, a prior in Flavigny, provincial's assistant, and chaplain. Throughout his life he was interested in philosophy and natural history. In 1887, he published the book *L'évolution des espèces organiques* (*The Evolution of Organic Species*). Its favorable reception encouraged him to extend the publication with supplemental material on various controversial issues. Consequently, four years later he released *L'évolution restreinte aux espèces organiques* (*Evolution Limited to Organic Species*). The title was meant to indicate that the author was not going to address the origin of man.

30. Cf. *Negotiating Darwin*, 50.

At the beginning, Leroy writes: "I think the idea of evolution will run the same course as that of Galileo; it will initially alarm the orthodox, but once emotions have calmed, truth will be distinguished from the exaggerations of both sides. . . . Let us know how to give to Caesar what is Caesar's, and to invite Caesar that he, in turn, give to God what is God's."[31] After this introduction, the author includes two letters supporting his views and praising his publication: one written by geologist Albert Cochon de Lapparent, the other by a famous Dominican preacher, Jacques-Marie Monsabré.

In the first chapter, Leroy distances himself from a godless type of evolution according to which matter is eternal; and on its own, over a long period, evolved into the world and living species without any divine intervention. The second chapter begins with a declaration of orthodoxy and a listing of points upon which the author agrees with the traditional view of creation:

> I must declare at the outset that I agree with the ideas and principles of the partisans of the fixity of species on the most important points. Like them, I accept primordial creation out of nothing from cosmic matter through all-powerful, divine action, as well as the creation of physical forces, together with the admirable laws that govern them. Like them, I attribute the introduction of life on Earth to the special intervention of a prime cause. Like them, I recognize and salute the incessant action of divine Providence in the universe, unfolding in accord with a grand plan that reveals an infallible intelligence. . . . Like them, in sum, I admit the existence of specific types susceptible of perpetuating themselves by generation: but instead of attributing the origin of each one of the five or six hundred thousand known organic types to a special act of creation and of declaring them immutable, I only recognize a relative fixity in them, and I consider them the result of evolution from previous types, with the exception of the first ones.[32]

According to Leroy, evolution started from a few created organisms (polyphyletic evolution), proceeded to the vast variety of all plants and animals, but then ended before the emergence of man.[33] This "limitation," however, actually differed very little from the concept of Darwin himself. In *The Origin of Species*, Darwin does not speak of the origination of life from inorganic matter. Neither does he speak of the evolution of man. Both authors most likely applied a certain strategy in presenting their views, hoping their opponents would take an

31. D. Leroy, *L'évolution restreinte aux espèces organiques* (Paris: Delhomme et Briguet, 1891), 2 (English quotations after *Negotiating Darwin*, 55).

32. Ibid., 31.

33. According to the idea of polyphyletic evolution, God created a few primitive organisms or first representatives of the largest taxonomical groups (like phyla). Although it is a quite limited version of the macroevolutionary story, still it entailed the idea of transformation of species, which was unacceptable for traditional Catholic philosophy and theology.

apparent compromise for granted, and that the passage of time would help them maintain and popularize their views.

In the same second chapter Leroy reminds the reader that there cannot be any inconsistency between science and revealed truth, and proposes to study whether limited evolution contradicts faith. In subsequent chapters he tries to prove that limited evolution is not in disagreement with religious orthodoxy. In dealing with the Bible, the Tradition, Church doctrine, and theology, he always concludes that no authority opposed his view. In the tenth chapter, summarizing his analysis, he explains that "It is appropriate to emphasize in passing that the matter has been judged, and there is no need to return to this subject. Thus, the question is reduced to a problem of philosophy and natural history."[34]

It is true that Leroy declares he does not intend to bring up the issue of the origin of man, but in fact his digressions head in that direction. The origin of man aroused the greatest interest in the fields of both science and religion. For example, Leroy first establishes the ground of his discussion by granting man an immaterial and immortal soul. If man has a soul of this kind, then the origin of his body—according to Leroy—is of no great importance. So, could the body have originated through evolution? Leroy answers:

> My reply leaves no doubt: no, this is not admissible . . . in religious teaching, which here takes precedence over all the facts of science. There is an order of things that so proclaim. No, man's body does not derive from animals but is the result of a direct intervention by the Creator. We have said that religious teaching is based on four sources: the Holy Scripture, the Church Fathers, the decisions of the Church, and theology; if I interrogate each one of them separately, I might not find the question completely decided; but taken together, they assume a luminosity that banishes all doubt.[35]

But immediately after this statement Leroy again refers to the Bible, finding that it lacks anything opposing the evolution of man from lower animals. The Bible claims that God formed Adam's body from the dust of the earth, but says nothing about the manner in which He did so. It might have happened by virtue of secondary causes, i.e., evolution. In Leroy's opinion the Church Fathers do not address this question, and the Synod of Cologne only condemns atheistic evolution. The formation of the first human body would not occur spontaneously (*spontanea*), but rather "under Divine influence."

Finally, however, the French Dominican identifies the key argument against the possibility of an evolutionary origin of the human body. He finds this in the "problem of the substantial unity" of man (signaled in Messenger's case), this

34. Ibid., 275.
35. Ibid., 257 (Cf. *Negotiating Darwin*, 58).

time based on Thomas Aquinas. The author interprets St. Thomas's thought as follows:

> According to the Angelic Doctor, every corporeal substance is composed of two agents, one essentially active and other purely passive, form and matter. In this association, it is form that supplies all the nature or quiddity of the substance. Saint Thomas says: *Cum forma sit tota natura rei* [As is the form, so is the whole nature of the thing]; matter, as absolutely neutral, is capable of taking any form. It is scarcely necessary to say that in the living compound called the human body, the soul is the form. In these conditions, it is evident that the human body could not arise from the transformation of an animal. For it to have effectively derived from animality, it would be necessary that the human soul, that is, the form which constitutes the whole nature, also originate in the transformation. But this is impossible because, in contrast to what happens in animals, the [human] soul can only come directly from God. Thus, Catholic theology . . . formally rejects the opinion that would have the human body come from animals. . . . It is only after the infusion of the soul, and because of the infusion itself, that man is constituted a living being. Before infusing the spirit, there was nothing human, not even the body, inasmuch as human flesh cannot exist without the soul, which is its substantial form. . . . Thus, the Bible—interpreted by theology—tells us that man's body cannot be derived from lower nature.[36]

On the next pages, Leroy again invokes the authority of the Church Fathers, who view the origination of the human body as a special intervention of the first cause—i.e., God. Having supported his own view with Church tradition, Leroy then discusses the scientific difficulties that arise in negating the animal origin of man. In his opinion the anatomical differences are too substantial for such a scenario to be acceptable.

A reader who has reached this point in Leroy's book could plausibly stand convinced that evolution must have stopped at the animal stage, but just seven pages from the end, Leroy takes an unexpected turn:

> Now it may seem that everything has been said on this subject. Nevertheless, there is one more point to consider. The human body is composed of matter and form, and the soul, in substantial form, comes directly from God, of course. But where does the matter come from? It is also certain it comes from the mud of the earth—Scripture and tradition clearly say so. But does this mud receive the infusion of the human soul instantly, that is, without any preparation? Such is the question that we can still ask.[37]

In further discourse, the theologian states that he does not wish to be a pioneer

36. Ibid., 259–61.
37. Ibid., 266–67.

in this view, but has only tried to analyze it in order to determine the aspects under which it could be accepted or rejected. Even though at the end he reiterates that the human body had been made through a direct act of God's power, his previous analyses in fact provided support for the opposite thesis. On the last pages he writes

> Have I succeeded in making the theory of evolution less suspect? I hope so, but I have few illusions. Although it may be shown that certain objections are insubstantial, there will always be some who persist in repeating them. I expect, therefore, that I will still hear it repeated that evolution, even the limited form, is in opposition to the Bible and the teachings of the Church, that it is not supported by any scientific fact; and that to seek to explain, insofar as possible, the formation of the world without miracles, is to propose Creation without God. For this there is only one remedy: time. It is too much to expect that the problem could be discussed freely at this time. Thirty years ago one could not have done it without risk. Each generation needs to become accustomed to new ideas before being able to do them justice. This is the case of the system of limited evolution [...]. I expect, nevertheless, that it will survive the test.[38]

Even before the book was submitted for examination by the Congregation of the Index, Leroy was drawn into a polemic with the Jesuits Joseph de Benniot, Joseph Brucker, and François Dierckx. Benniot and Brucker published critical articles after the release of the first edition of *L'évolution* in 1887. What deserves special attention is the argument with Brucker and Dierckx (Benniot died in 1889, without responding to Leroy) about the origin of Eve.

In an article published in *Études*, Brucker (making reference to Leroy) writes that there were theologians at that time who dared claim that the Church Fathers had not dogmatized the truth about the direct formation of the body of Adam.[39] In the second edition of his book, Leroy responds that the quotations from the Fathers mentioned by Brucker are not convincing. In a nine-page review of the book released in late 1891,[40] Brucker responded by presenting two problems which—despite some corrections—remained in the book: the origin of the first woman and the origin of Adam's soul. Brucker asks how the French theologian understood the creation of the first woman, since the Bible so clearly speaks of her direct formation from the body of Adam. In response,

38. Ibid., 283 (*Negotiating Darwin*, 60).

39. J. Brucker, "L'origine de l'homme d'après la Bible et le transformism," *Études* 26 (May 1889): 28–50, 46. Brucker's reasoning is based on the theological principle that if a given truth had been unanimously taught by the Fathers, it became a truth of the faith. This principle is confirmed several times by the Magisterium. The Church Fathers were entirely in harmony about the origin of man. Thus Bruckner concludes that they had given this idea the rank of a truth of the faith.

40. J. Brucker, "Bulletin Scripturaire," *Études* 28 (September–December 1891): 488–97.

Leroy decided that God followed different patterns in the case of Adam and Eve. With reference to Adam He used evolution, while Eve was created directly. He also admitted that he could not say why had it been so.[41]

The second polemic against Leroy—from the Jesuit F. Dierckx—criticized the French Dominican for the inconsistency of his explications. According to Dierckx, Leroy's answer is skillful but only shuffles appearances, without solving the essence of the difficulty. Dierckx writes:

> What is distasteful in Leroy's theory is that, wishing to please all schools, he takes with one hand what he discards with the other, all arbitrarily, running the risk of not pleasing anyone. What spoils it is that, in order not to break violently with Catholic doctrines, he limits himself to applying evolution to Adam's body, while admitting for Eve the so feared miracle of immediate creation by God. It is disappointing that he interprets the biblical text about Eve literally, while he strives to seek a metaphorical meaning for the formation of Adam. . . . What should be demonstrated is that the Creator wanted to form Eve with his own hands and to leave to the care of secondary causes the formation of the body of Adam. That is what Leroy should have proved, and he does not prove it.[42]

The Intervention of the Congregation of the Index

The polemics of Benniot, Brucker, and Dierckx with the French Dominican had nothing to do, however, with the book being reported to the Congregation of the Index. That denunciation came from Mr. Ch. Chalmel, a man foreign to Vatican circles. In June 1894, Chalmel wrote a letter to the Vatican in which, having listed the main theses of the book, he asked if the new interpretation of Genesis had been approved by the Congregation, and if the literal interpretation that the Church always endorsed should be now abandoned. The prefect of the Congregation, Cardinal Serafino Vannuttelli, entrusted the review of the book to a new consultant, Teofilo Domenichelli, from the order of Franciscan Observants. At the end of August, Domenichelli's 27-page report was ready.

After summarizing the argument of the book, the reviewer proceeds to evaluate the denunciation, stating that most of the objections arose from misunderstanding or over-interpretation of certain words. For instance, Leroy does not write that Genesis was an old patriarchal poem needing to be read metaphorically. This opinion of Leroy, according to Domenichelli, refers only to the style of the initial pages of the book, and to the "manner" in which God created material objects. Such moderate claims of Leroy regarding exegesis would only

41. Cf. *Negotiating Darwin*, 64.
42. After *Negotiating Darwin*, 64.

have been reproachable if the Church had always attributed literal meaning to the entirety of the biblical text. However, according to Domenichelli, the six days of creation may be interpreted in an allegorical sense. In support of this thesis Domenichelli refers to the then-recent encyclical *Providentissimus Deus* (November 18, 1893) on the interpretation of the Holy Scriptures. Next, he shores up Leroy's opinion with the authority of Aquinas who (according to Domenichelli) only appreciated the "fact of creation" as important for the faith, while regarding the "manner" of creation as accidental.[43] Quoting a few Church Fathers, he agrees that they recognized the possibility of various interpretations of the account of creation. So the discussion as to whether it should be read literally or allegorically, remains open to theologians and should not be banned. In view of today's knowledge, such a literal interpretation would have been simply absurd. Therefore, Chalmel's allegation concerning the interpretation of the Bible should be rejected.

Next, Domenichelli proceeds to examine the issue of evolution. He states that despite its brilliant arguments, Leroy's book failed to convince him to adopt evolutionist views, which he regards as hypothetical and lacking solid foundations, at least in part. However, it is not the function of the Congregation of the Index to judge the book on scientific grounds, but by reference to Church doctrine. Moreover, many contemporary Catholic scholars allow evolution as agreeing with the Catholic faith, provided certain limits are imposed, especially concerning the independent creation of each human soul. Taking into account the nuances mentioned by Leroy, the theory of evolution is completely harmless as regards the truth of God the Creator and Administrator of the world. On a final note, Domenichelli writes:

> My report should be used only if you decide either not to prohibit the book or to postpone the judgment. If a decision to prohibit it were to prevail, then another report should be made, fuller and more profound than mine, which is very short and should not be used to condemn the work.[44]

Still referring to evolution, Domenichelli suggested that according to evolutionary theory, a lower cause would have had a higher effect, which would stand in conflict with the basic laws of reason and reality. He stated also that it is a philosophical rather than theological reservation, and so he would not consider it at all. Moreover, he notes that the Church Fathers and Scholastics affirm the spontaneous generation of some species of animals from inorganic matter. It is true that Louis Pasteur (1822–1895) invalidated this thesis, but if such a total

43. Domenichelli provided a reference to St. Thomas's commentary to Peter Lombard's *Sentences* (*Super Sent.* lib. 2, d. 12, q. 1, a. 2, co).

44. ACDF, Index, *Protocolli*, 1894–1896, 86:16; after *Negotiating Darwin*, 70.

"heterogenesis" was not forbidden by the Fathers, then surely Leroy's "much more limited evolutionist heterogenesis" deserved less criticism.

At the end of his report, Domenichelli broached the most controversial question, namely the evolution of man. He acknowledges that the Bible says that man was made from the dust of the earth, but does not specify how this happened—whether through an immediate act of God, or through the operation of natural causes, allowed by God. The Synod of Cologne, recognized by Rome, only rejected spontaneous transformation without God's participation.[45] And because the human body is created through the infusion of the soul, it does not originate from an animal but is always an effect of immediate action of God. According to Domenichelli, Leroy's arguments in favor of the spiritual nature of man are not weakened by his acceptance of the evolution of the human body. Thus, Rome's expert employed the metaphysical problem of the substantial unity of form and matter—just as Leroy did—to introduce the evolution of the body, while attempting to maintain the direct creation of man. Moreover, Domenichelli made no distinction between the order of the creation of natures and their subsequent transmission through generation.

Despite his many positive remarks, Domenichelli also found it difficult to agree with Leroy that evolution might have prepared the matter that subsequently became a human body through the infusion of the immortal soul. Genesis might be interpreted this way, but the unanimity of the Church Fathers, Doctors, and theologians is so great that it is more reasonable and safe to hold to their view. In this matter the French theologian "reaches a limit beyond which speculation is transformed into condemnable temerity."[46] At the end, he notes the various mitigating circumstances: since its first edition seven years earlier, Leroy's book had not encountered any problems; other publications had appeared containing even stronger statements written by Catholic writers; and a renunciation of the book would have caused great harm to the author, his order, and those who quoted the book. If *L'évolution* contains condemnable errors, they should be specified in a separate act, while the book itself should be "dismissed [from the ban] (Latin *dimittatur*)."[47]

In conclusion, Domenichelli does not see any problem in Leroy's approach to the interpretation of the Holy Scriptures and Tradition with respect to the possibility of species transformism. What raises doubts is Leroy's treatment of the formation of the first human body, which approaches the limits of ortho-

45. At this point it is worth noting that Domenichelli did not fully present the Cologne decision, which not only stated that the generation of the body had not been spontaneous, but also that the first parents had been created directly by God.

46. ACDF, Index, *Protocolli*, 1894–1896, 86:23 (cf. *Negotiating Darwin*, 71).

47. Ibid., 27.

doxy. Taking into account all external circumstances, however, the reviewer recommends against an official renunciation of the book.

This was the report received by the consultants and secretary (a Dominican, Marcolino Cicognani) gathered at the preparatory meeting of the Congregation of the Index on September 13 1894. *L'évolution* was one of four works discussed that day, and eventually the seven persons attending the meeting made a unanimous decision to suspend the judgment and appoint someone else to write a report that would reconsider the issue. A few days later—following an exchange of opinions and a serious debate—a general meeting of the Congregation upheld the decision, committing the investigation of the case to two new consultants: Ernesto Fontana and Luigi Tripepi. This time the experts were asked to answer three questions: (1) What criteria of exegesis are recognized by Leroy with reference to Genesis? (2) What is his interpretation of the evolution of organic species? (3) What is his view on the origin of man?

At the end of October, Fontana's report was submitted to Cicognani. The fact that it contained fewer than five pages may be ascribed to the author having just been made Bishop of Crema (a small town near Milan), where his new duties absorbed most of his time. Initially, Fontana stated that he did not detect anything against faith and morals in the book, but he did find it inappropriate that Leroy would be so eager to defend a hypothesis which—even if not in conflict with the faith—is uncertain and contested even by many naturalists.

In answer to the first question, he writes that "The author says explicitly and absolutely that, when the biblical text is susceptible to diverse interpretations and neither dogmatic definitions nor the consensus of the Church Fathers determine one of them, scientists are free to apply to it the meaning that science gives it."[48] According to Fontana, the criterion "cannot be reproached or condemned; but I think it dangerous and somewhat impertinent."[49] To the second question, Fontana replies that the evolutionary system limited to plants and lower animals is "neither absurd nor condemnable."[50] Arguing from classical philosophy, he maintained that since animal and plant forms are not spontaneously generated, they can be subject to changes dependent on the environment in which they live:

> It is admissible that forms that are not subsistent, inherent in matter, and, even more, immersed in matter and unable to exist and act if not "in" and "with" matter, might suffer those affections that matter suffers owing to climate, nutrition, and the circumstances in which the individual organism lives. Supposing, as the author supposes, that the creative act may have

48. ACDF, Index, *Protocolli*, 1894–1896, 123:2 (*Negotiating Darwin*, 78).
49. Ibid.
50. Ibid., 3.

> placed in the individuals of the primitive types aptitudes and potentials as embryonic, to be developed, evolution is not impossible.[51]

Eventually, Fontana decided that he could not fully answer the question of whether evolution could lead to the emergence of new species (as postulated by Leroy), or just to accidental changes within existing species. According to him the second option was supported by most naturalists; nevertheless, the problems with determining the essence of species, breed, kind, and variety make it impossible to find the right answer.

In response to the last question, Fontana did not see any obvious error in Leroy's approach. Nevertheless, he pointed out three difficulties: (1) The author of the book does not state explicitly that when God infused in the "living matter" a spiritual soul in order to make man, the purely sensitive soul, which animated that matter before, completely disappeared. This might lead to the "fatal error of Rosmini," who claimed that the human soul can naturally develop (in ontogenesis) from sensitive to rational when the idea of being is presented to it.[52] (2) His treatment of the substantial unity of the human being is not clear. (3) Lastly, Fontana raises a concern rarely mentioned in the debates of the time, but of fundamental importance to the understanding of man. In Leroy's view, Fontana argues,

> the human body would have its origin in the body of a beast, raised . . . to the highest grade of perfection, but still a beast. The author does not ever use, here, the word beast or animal; he always uses the term organized matter; but matter most perfectly organized . . . , is it not a beast? Now, this hypothesis is repugnant and clashes with Christian and human feeling; in what refers to

51. Ibid. Two remarks should be added to Fontana's statement. First, it is true that an individual form (of an animal or plant) cannot exist without matter except in thought. However, it is not individual form (*forma individuata*) that determines species-specific features—it is substantial form (*forma substantialis*) that does so. On the other hand, for the substantial form, the influences mentioned by Fontana are only of an accidental nature, which cannot determine the essence of a being. Therefore, if Fontana's argument was to support transformation of species it would be based on the confusion of the individual form and the substantial form. But apparently Fontana considered evolution very narrowly, probably much more so than Leroy. He wrote about the development of potentialities that God had introduced to the original types at the beginning of creation. Such a concept of evolution would have little in common with Darwinism, and would not help to defend Leroy's transformism.

52. Among the 40 of Rosmini's theses condemned by the Holy Office in 1888 were the following: "(20) It is not inconsistent that the human soul, in order that it may be multiplied by human generation, may thus be conceived as proceeding from the imperfect, namely from the sensitive grade, to the perfect, namely to the intellectual grade. (21) When being is capable of being intuited by the sensitive principle, by this influence alone, by this union with itself, only sensing this first, but now, at the same time understanding, it is brought to a more noble state, it changes its nature, and becomes understanding, subsisting, and immortal" (DS 1910–1911).

> myself, I cannot tolerate it. Darwin and his followers tolerate it, because in some way it is similar to theirs.[53]

Thus the expert of the Congregation, in addition to all the scientific, religious, and philosophical considerations, also put forward a sort of moral argument against the proposed hypothesis. The animal origin of man, regardless of how it might be described, would stand in conflict with human dignity as recognized in Christianity and true humanism. Fontana ended his report as follows:

> I dare not propose that the book of the learned Leroy be placed on the Index of Prohibited Books, but I declare my wish that the author be seriously warned for the intemperance and impertinence of his ideas, which will please those evolutionists who are also atheists and materialists, but cannot be acceptable to true Catholics.[54]

At the end of 1894 (December 8), the secretariat of the Congregation received the second report, a 54-page text by Tripepi. This document requires more attention, as it synthesized the entire anti-evolutionary argumentation of the Catholic Church in the late 19th century.

Tripepi begins by answering the most important question, i.e., about the origin of man. He first approaches evolution from the scientific point of view, demonstrating that the arguments of its supporters are frequently contradictory—that they also never go beyond hypotheses, proving neither the reality nor the logical necessity of evolution. Moreover, he observes, the contemporary arguments are actually old arguments that are based on arbitrary premises and disagree with experience. According to Tripepi, "evolutionism is nowadays abandoned and refuted as false and absurd by the same rationalists and unbelievers who previously supported it."[55] Referring to a textbook by Cardinal Mazzella (*De Deo creante*), Tripepi concludes that the action through which God formed the body of the first man is different from the first creation of matter:

> On the basis of the authority of Sacred Scripture, understood according to the unanimous interpretation of the holy Fathers, [Catholic theologians] respond with one voice that man's body was formed by the direct and immediate action of God, distinct not only from the first creation of matter, but also from the concurrence which God, as first Cause, gives to the operation of secondary causes.[56]

Thus, theologians identified three actions of God in the creation of man: (1) creation of matter, (2) formation of the body, and (3) infusion of the soul. This

53. ACDF, Index, *Protocolli*, 1894–1896, 123:4 (*Negotiating Darwin*, 79).
54. Ibid., 5.
55. ACDF, Index, *Protocolli*, 1894–1896, 125:9 (*Negotiating Darwin*, 80).
56. Ibid., 11. Quotation after B.W. Harrison, "Early Vatican Responses to Evolutionist Theology."

is how they distinguish the formation of man from the formation of other beings.

Tripepi also replies to evolutionary theologians who claim to appropriate St. Augustine's concept of *rationes seminales*. With respect to the creation of man, the Bishop of Hippo only meant a passive potentiality in the original matter, which required direct Divine action to actualize this potentiality. Tripepi cites St. Thomas's opinion from the *Summa Theologiae*: "The first formation of the human body could not be by the instrumentality of any created power, but was immediately from God."[57] Thus the first human body was the subject of the direct work of God, who acted as a special efficient cause—not in the same way as in creation out of nothing, but in a manner attributable exclusively to God. Tripepi mentions that until recently this had been the view of all Catholic theologians. It is a fact that some of them, such as Fabre d'Envieu, Gmeiner, Zahm, and Mivart, hold different opinions; but, as he writes: "These cannot at all diminish the complete, solemn, uninterrupted, and universal agreement of theologians on this issue."[58]

Furthermore, he notes that the opinions of individuals of doubtful theological reputation can never outweigh the accord of the Roman school based on serious studies of the Church Fathers and Christian philosophers. Having listed the arguments "from authority," Tripepi recalled the decisions of the First Vatican Council that truths recognized as part of the Catholic faith do not need to be explicitly confirmed by separate document. It is enough if they are present in ordinary and universal teaching as revealed by God.[59] Similar importance is ascribed to long-lasting and common agreement of theologians. But even if the direct creation of the human body had not ranked as a truth of the faith, it still would not mean, Tripepi claimed, that it might be challenged. There are views that are blatantly heretical, and there are those that are close to heresy, erroneous, or imprudent. Meanwhile, [some people who claim to be Catholic scholars] "themselves can be carried away by their studies, and first establish their

57. *S. Th.*, I, q. 91, a. 2.

58. ACDF, Index, *Protocolli*, 1894–1896, 125:14 (*Negotiating Darwin*, 81).

59. "Wherefore, by divine and Catholic faith all those things are to be believed which are contained in the word of God as found in Scripture and tradition, and which are proposed by the Church as matters to be believed as divinely revealed, whether by her solemn judgment or in her ordinary and universal magisterium" (*Dei Filius*, III, 34). Tripepi's view agreed with what Pius IX wrote in his letter *Tuas libenter* (1863). The pope went even further than the council formulation: "it is not sufficient for learned Catholics to accept and revere the aforesaid dogmas of the Church, but that it is also necessary to subject themselves to the decisions pertaining to doctrines that are issued by the Pontifical Congregations, and also to those forms of doctrine held by the common and constant consent of Catholics as theological truths and conclusions, so certain that opinions opposed to these same forms of doctrine, although they cannot be called heretical, nevertheless deserve some theological censure" (DS 2880).

theories without consulting the teachings of revelation, and later strive to accommodate revelation to their theories."[60]

After presenting the arguments based on Tradition, Tripepi returns to the interpretation of the Bible, emphasizing that the literal sense of the text is what should primarily be respected. As a case in point, Genesis 1:26–27[61] does not mention any mediation between God and the first man and woman: "indeed, such mediation is excluded; for He [God] alone created the man whom He created in His own image and likeness."[62] Gen 2:7 clearly specifies two divine actions:

> [God] disposed the already-created clay of the earth in a form which was apt, or required, to be informed by the soul; then He breathed in his face the breath of life. Moreover, it is said that only after the infusion of the soul did the body moulded from clay possess life: and man became a living soul. Thus, prior to that it had no life at all. Therefore, it could not have come about through evolution from any animal.[63]

Tripepi also calls upon other passages from the Old Testament speaking of the creation of man, but none of them bears any trace of mediation.[64] Next, he embarks on the issue of the creation of Eve, which was such a mystery to Leroy himself that he had to accept her direct creation in the polemic with the Jesuits. According to Tripepi, the fact of immediate creation of Eve "casts new light on the generation of Adam."[65]

Next, Tripepi refers to Leroy's claim that the evolution controversy would reprise the case of the controversy over Galileo. The Roman consultant notices, however, that there is a substantial dissimilarity between these two cases. In

60. ACDF, Index, *Protocolli*, 1894–1896, 125:17.

61. "Then God said: 'Let us make man in our image, after our likeness. Let them have dominion over the fish of the sea, the birds of the air, and the cattle, and over all the wild animals and all the creatures that crawl on the ground.' God created man in his image; in the divine image he created him; male and female he created them."

62. ACDF, Index, *Protocolli*, 1894–1896, 125:17.

63. Ibid., 17–18.

64. Job 10:8–9: "Your hands have made me, and fashioned me wholly round about, and do you thus cast me down headlong on a sudden? Remember, I beseech you, that you have made me as the clay, and you will bring me into dust." 33:4: "The Spirit of God has made me, And the breath of the Almighty gives me life." 33:6: "Behold, I belong to God like you; I too have been formed out of the clay." Sir 17:1: "God created man of the earth, and made him after his own image." Wis 7:1: "I myself am a mortal man, like all others, and of the race of him, that was first made of the earth." Ps 119:73: "Your hands have made me and formed me." 2 Macc 7:28: "I beseech you, my son, look upon heaven and earth, and all that is in them, and consider that God made them out of nothing, and mankind also." Particularly in the last passage, the Bible emphasizes that when God creates, He does not use secondary causes. Neither does the genealogy of Jesus (Lk 3:38) introduce any intermediate creation between Adam and God.

65. ACDF, Index, *Protocolli*, 1894–1896, 125:20.

Galileo's case, the mistake was made in the way his discovery was presented, rather than his theory as such. Galileo, he says, "found support not only in scientific arguments of fact and reason, but also in many well-interpreted scriptural texts, in ancient Fathers and Doctors, Pontiffs and theologians, even some before him."[66]

After reiterating that Caverni's book had already been renounced 16 years earlier, and mentioning numerous contemporary authorities who rejected the evolution of the human body, Tripepi concludes:

> It seems to me, with all that has been said, that the doctrine generally professed by the Church is clear. . . . Even though these matters have not yet been defined dogmatically, transformism, if it is limited only to the origin of the human body, prepared and destined to receive the soul, does not seem reconcilable with Catholic doctrine.[67]

Concerning the evolution of species, Tripepi addresses two arguments—one of a scientific and the other of a theological nature. According to him, evolution is a system abandoned even by the oldest and most prominent followers of Darwin. Moreover, evolutionism, he says, is regarded as barely a hypothesis, still lacking a solid foundation:

> If one considers it only as an aspect of human natural science, leaving aside the teachings of revealed doctrine, this system can be considered and shown to be false. Furthermore there are many contradictions among its followers; its arguments can be considered gratuitous hypotheses and prove nothing either in regard to facts or to logical reasoning. The system is contrary to great and firm philosophical principles and to facts which show that specific types (species) are absolutely irreducible, and varieties of a species should not be confused with transformation of species.[68]

In support of his claim the consultant invokes such scientific authorities as Mazzella, Brucker, Rossignoli, Ballerini, Vigouroux, Bonniot, De Mandato, Agassiz, and Lavaud de Lastrade. The latter individual, indeed,

> demonstrates at length that the doctrine which teaches that animal and plant species can change from one to another through a slow transformation, viewed scientifically and independently of its consequences, is a false doctrine that must be rejected, because it contradicts: 1. experience and observed facts; 2. history; 3. paleontology; 4. common sense; 5. the most important naturalists.[69]

66. Ibid., 26 (*Negotiating Darwin*, 83).
67. Ibid., 31.
68. Ibid. (*Negotiating Darwin*, 84).
69. Ibid., 35.

It should be noted that Tripepi was familiar with the scientific research of the time and that the doctrine of evolution was still not commonly accepted. Moreover, many arguments used by the scholars he mentions had never been replied to by the evolutionists. We may thus assume that for Tripepi evolution is in disagreement with science. This conviction undoubtedly facilitated his theological judgment.

Then, Tripepi returns to the interpretation of the Holy Scriptures. In his opinion, the theory of evolution conflicts with the natural understanding of the biblical text. In the Genesis account, creation is attributed directly to God, even if it is not specified for each species separately. Furthermore, it contains a statement that God created plants and animals "according to their kinds" (Gen 1:11; 12:24), which is in conflict with the hypothesis of the evolution of species. St. Augustine, St. Thomas, and Suarez understood creation as the formation of separate species from the beginning.

Tripepi also mentions two other difficulties, this time of a philosophical nature: (1) No being, by virtue of its own nature, seeks to lose its nature. But this is exactly what is meant by the change of species, if the change of being entails the destruction of the previous being. (2) The transformation of species would suggest that living beings have capacities or powers surpassing their own natures.

He then notes a difference between the emergence of man and the formation of other organic species in Scripture. With respect to the animals and plants, the Bible uses expressions such as "let the earth bring forth" (Gen 1:12) and "let the water bring forth" (Gen 1:21), leaving open the possibility that secondary causes had something to do with their creation. However, "the primordial determination of species by means of the act of God the Creator seems to indicate, rather, a law whereby each species is from that moment fixed and immutable."[70]

In answer to the third question, Tripepi attempts to determine the compliance of Leroy's exegetic criteria with Church doctrine. At one level he decides he does not see any errors in the French Dominican's claim that Genesis is not a science textbook, and that the six days of creation may be interpreted allegorically. After all, this was the standpoint already presented by some Church Fathers. Leroy goes beyond those interpretations, however, by adding that Genesis is poetic in style and as such should not be interpreted literally. For Tripepi, Genesis is an historical account, which states not only *that* God created the world, but also *how* he did so. In particular, the Bible speaks clearly about the manner of creation of plant and animal species. Genesis should not, then, be stripped of its truth by recognizing only its metaphorical language, as proposed by Leroy. Each language, even that of science, needs to make use of metaphors,

70. ACDF, Index, *Protocolli*, 1894–1896, 125:43–44 (*Negotiating Darwin*, 85).

but "it is completely different to say that there are metaphors in the first pages of Genesis, and to say that these pages *are* metaphors (*ces métaphores*), so that the literal meaning would be irrational. Not this: these are two immensely different things."[71]

In defense of his claim, Tripepi quotes the encyclical by Leo XIII, *Providentissimus Deus*, which appealed to readers "not to depart from the literal and obvious sense, except where reason makes it untenable or necessity requires."[72] "Neither of these two cases," Tripepi writes,

> applies here; thus it cannot be said that it is irrational to take the first pages of Genesis literally. If Creation is accepted, it cannot be said it is irrational to admit the particular mode given by the literal sense.... God could create. Could he not have created and acted in the way indicated by the literal sense? Who might dare to say so?[73]

Thus, according to the Roman consultant, there have not been sufficient reasons to abandon the literal sense as the proper understanding of the Biblical account of creation. Allegory might have been used with respect to the "day" of creation, but not to the creation of plant and animal species:

> On this point, up to now the Church Fathers and theologians are morally agreed to exclude evolutionary theory and take the words of Scripture in a literal sense, for that is precisely the most natural, obvious and proper sense.[74]

At the end of the report Tripepi mentions a certain weakness with contemporary Catholics, theologians in particular:

> There are Catholics who value and fear so-called modern science too much, and to whom it seems that because of it they can almost put aside our beliefs. They concede too much to the word of man, and try too hard to associate it with the word of God, robbing it, at times, of practically all its meaning.[75]

Taking into account all the arguments, Tripepi recommends that steps be taken against the publication of Leroy's book. He leaves it to the cardinals to decide whether it should be banned or the author only be warned by his superiors, and asked to withdraw the book from sale and revoke the censured theories. The latter solution seems better to Tripepi, because it recognizes the good intentions, as well as the intellectual and moral values, displayed by the scholar.

71. Ibid., 47 (*Negotiating Darwin*, 86).

72. "A litterali et veluti obvio sensu minime discedendum, nisi qua eum vel ratio tenere prohibeat vel necessitas cogat dimittere." *Providentissimus Deus* in *AAS* 26 (1893–1894), 282.

73. ACDF, Index, *Protocolli*, 1894–1896, 125:47.

74. Ibid., 48–49.

75. Ibid., 52.

It would not be good if Leroy were openly condemned while similar books remained in free circulation.

The two reports on Leroy's case (by Fontana and Tripepi) were presented at the second preparatory meeting, held in January 1895. This time there were fifteen participants, including Domenichelli—the author of the first and most favorable report. The new reports represented two differing perspectives, but neither was particularly favorable to Leroy's theses. As Cicognani wrote in his memorandum, there was a heated debate on the French Dominican's book, during which arguments for and against it were considered with great prudence. The decision of the preparatory assembly was that "the doctrine, as it is found in the book, should be proscribed."[76] Thus the gathered experts chose the stronger of the two measures suggested by Tripepi. The discussion must have been stormy, for one of the participants—Dominican Enrico Buonpensiere—decided to write down his own arguments and add them to the three existing reports.

The principal thesis of the 8-page text by Buonpensiere was that evolutionism is beyond any doubt an entirely fallacious theory, from the point of view of both science and philosophy. Among other things:

> Evolutionism, as all Catholic philosophers teach, is resolutely condemned by ontological and empirical science. In ontology, the essence of any object is an immutable type, that is, incapable of any change (*evoluzione*), whether toward the greater or toward the lesser. In empirical science there is an inexorable law of hybridization, which maintains living species distinct, in such a way that from the pairing of two organisms belonging to different species no fruit will be obtained, or else such fruit is totally infertile.[77]

Was Buonpensiere right? Darwin maintained that species were just well-distinguished varieties, and that varieties were the origin of new species. According to Darwin's theory, species should deviate further and further from the original types over time. Nevertheless, the examples he gave in support of his claim were never anything more than cross-breeds within a single natural species (or taxonomical genus). Therefore, the law of hybridization could be broken only within a very limited scope. Darwin believed that a longer period of time would demonstrate that species (i.e., natural species) are able to cross. However, as he did not "have" such a long period of time on his hands, his claim was no more than an extrapolation based on limited observations. What he demonstrated was hybridization, not the emergence of new natural species.[78]

Buonpensiere's report was attached to the other three and submitted, along

76. *Negotiating Darwin*, 90 and 92.
77. ACDF, Index, *Protocolli*, 1894–1896, fol. 118: in *Negotiating Darwin*, 92.
78. Cf. *The Origin of Species*, ch. 2.

with the decision of the preparatory meeting, to the Prefect of the Congregation of the Index, so that the cardinals received four reports on Leroy—two negative and two moderately positive. On January 25, 1895, the second general meeting was held. Discussion of the book by the French Dominican was the fourth item on the agenda. The decision of the Congregation was as follows: the book should be deemed banned, but the decree on it kept unpublished. Through the Master of the Order, the author should be asked to publicly revoke his theses and withdraw the remaining books from bookstores. Of the ten cardinals present, one submitted a dissenting opinion. He thought the book should not be condemned and that the author should only be reprimanded by the Master of the Order.

Under these circumstances, Leroy was summoned to Rome for questioning. At the end of February he sent a letter to the editors of *Le Monde* containing a relevant correction. In early March the French journal printed his "act of submission," in which the Dominican states:

> Now I learned that my thesis, examined here in Rome by the competent authority, has been judged untenable, above all for that which refers to the human body, which is incompatible both with scriptural texts and with the principles of sound philosophy.[79]

Until the opening of the archives of the Congregation in 1998, this letter was the only public testimony offering evidence of the decision of the Church authorities. It did not specify, however, who made the decision, nor did it state any specific reasons. The fact that the decision renouncing the publication remained essentially secret, and the title of the book was never listed in the Index, certainly played down the importance of the whole event. The Church's negative stance on evolution could not be known more objectively by theologians.

Submission to the decision of the Congregation was only a superficial act of the French Dominican, who never retracted his claims. While still in Rome he asked the pope for permission to read Tripepi's report. After getting acquainted with the arguments used in the discussion, he wrote a long letter to the Prefect of the Congregation, Cardinal Vennutelli, in which he reintroduced his thesis on the changeability of species. Based on the arguments of a few researchers he claimed that natural science proves the evolution of species against the principles of classical philosophy. He also restated that evolution can be reconciled with the Holy Scriptures. But he entirely put aside the matter of the origin of man. There was no official response to the letter.

79. A copy of the letter is kept in the Congregation's archives (ACDF, Index, *Protocolli*, 1894–1896, fol. 134: After *Negotiating Darwin*, 101).

Two years later, Leroy again attempted to rehabilitate his ideas. He wrote a letter to the Prefect of the Congregation, stating that he had reedited his book, taking into account Tripepi's remarks. The prefect agreed to investigate the new version of the work and appointed an Augustinian, Angelo Ferrata, as the consultant. In mid-1897, Ferrata submitted his report to the Congregation. He listed the errors repeated by the author and concluded that he saw nothing that could change the previous judgment about the book. However, the prefect found Ferrata's report incomplete and ordered the preparation of another one, this time by Buonpensiere. The sixth and final report was over fifty pages long and, like Tripepi's text, is a collection of classic Catholic arguments. If in his first text Buonpensiere had focused mainly on philosophy, in the second report he invoked theological arguments. Having presented numerous reasons, he decided that despite the introduction of a few new ideas, the number of errors in the book had not been reduced, indeed had even increased. Leroy again surrendered to the decision to ban his book from printing. Nonetheless, he continued to publicly maintain his original views.[80]

In 1898, the theologian published an article in which he reiterated his argument in favor of the evolution of the first human body. Each material substance, he argued, is composed of form and matter. The form expresses the nature of the substance. Two substantial forms cannot co-exist in the same being. A rational soul is a form of the human body in an exclusive and direct way—this is beyond doubt, because this doctrine had been independently confirmed by the Council of Vienna.[81] Therefore, the agent who infuses the form (in this case, a human soul) into the material substrate is the one who directly and immediately forms the body of a man, regardless of the origin of the substrate. Thus was it possible to believe that the body of the first man was formed directly by God, and that the divine action referred to the substrate was prepared by evolution.

In the next year, Leroy published a review of Jean Guibert's *L'origine des espèces* (*The Origin of Species*).[82] In the second part of the review he states that

80. Cf. *Negotiating Darwin*, 100–12.

81. The Council of Vienna (1311–1312) stated the following against the errors of Pietro Olivi: "We reject as erroneous and contrary to the truth of the catholic faith every doctrine or proposition rashly asserting that the substance of the rational or intellectual soul is not of itself and essentially the form of the human body [...]. We define that anyone who presumes henceforth to assert, defend, or hold stubbornly that the rational or intellectual soul is not the form of the human body of itself and essentially, is to be considered a heretic." See http://www.ewtn.com/library/COUNCILS/VIENNE.HTM#09 (January 31, 2015).

82. J. Guibert, *Les Origines, questions d'apologétique. Cosmogonie. Origine de la vie, origine des espèces, origine de l'homme. Unité de l'espèce humaine. Antiquité de l'espèce humaine. État de l'homme primitive* (Paris: Letouzey et Ané, 1896). Leroy's review was published in *Revue Thomiste* 7 (1899): 735–41.

there are two views on this matter in Catholicism. One is Brucker's opinion, followed by Guiberti; the other is the idea of the human body as a substrate prepared by evolution before the infusion of the soul. As long as there is no final decree of the Church on this matter, both views are maintainable. By spreading such theses, Leroy acted against the decisions he knew had already been made. However, the fact that his book had not been officially condemned allowed other Catholic scholars to cite it as reference, and this in turn has consolidated the opinion that the Church has no objection to the evolutionist perspective.

The French Dominican made one more attempt at publishing a modified version of his book. In 1901 he petitioned the secretary of the Congregation to reconsider his case. Again, he was rebuffed. Therefore, in early 1902 he sent a declaration of his obedience, which also contained a request: "I want to know whether it is the theory of evolution itself that is rejected, or only the manner in which I have treated it. I have reason to believe that it is mainly that manner that caused the rejection."[83] With this letter, the correspondence ended.

Dalmace Leroy's work was not added to the Index, even though it was condemned. The ideas he proposed faced continuous if qualified opposition by the Congregation of the Index. Although the author did not forfeit his formal unity with the Church, his position was hardly one of obedience to the decisions issued.

John A. Zahm's Advanced Concept of Theistic Evolution

Another priest whose evolutionist views faced unfavorable reception in the Church was an American member of the Congregation of the Holy Cross, John Augustine Zahm. Zahm's case deserves broader discussion for at least two reasons. For one, he was the first to explicitly present the full concept of theistic evolution, which in its essential form is currently the dominant view among theologians. Secondly, the investigation by the Congregation of the Index most accurately illustrates the atmosphere, mode of action, and attitude of the Church towards evolutionism at the time.

John A. Zahm was born in New Lexington, Ohio (USA) in 1851. In 1867 he began studies at the University of Notre Dame in Indiana, where he eventually joined the Congregation of the Holy Cross, receiving ordination in 1875. From the very start he was interested in scientific issues, and soon became a lecturer, and later dean, of the Department of Sciences, rising eventually to the post of vice-chancellor of the University. Beginning in the early 1890s he published

83. ACDF, Index, *Protocolli*, 1900–1902, 199. See *Negotiating Darwin*, 116.

books on the relationship between theology and natural science. In 1896, he became the Procurator General of the Congregation, and afterwards (1898–1906) held the office of provincial. Outside his intellectual work and service for the Congregation, he traveled frequently, was interested in archeology, and collected maps and relics of nature. He died in 1921, in Munich, where he had stopped on his journey to the Holy Land.[84]

The Release and Content of *Evolution and Dogma*

February 1896 saw the publication of the English edition of Zahm's book *Evolution and Dogma*, which soon became the reason for his personal problems and complicated political intrigues at the Vatican. Concurrently with the book's release, the author arrived in Rome to take the office of Procurator General of his order. Six months later, the French and Italian versions of the book were published. The Italian translation obviously enhanced the work's influence in Roman circles. Zahm also became involved in a movement of the American clergy who referred to themselves as "Americanists."[85]

84. Zahm was among the planners of an expedition to South America, attended by former US President Theodore Roosevelt and his son Kermit. The trip, involving Zahm and 18 other people, aimed at exploring a longer section of Rio da Dúvida (River of Doubt). It was a total disaster. Three people died. The President himself contracted malaria, which weakened him so much that he was not able to leave the boat upon reaching human settlements. Late in his life, Zahm planned to make a trip to the Middle East in order to explore the Holy Land and write a book on the archeology of the region.

85. Americanism was a combination of theological and sociological views that entered Catholicism in the second half of the 19th century. The essence of this theological view was to prioritize the active virtues (activity, missionary involvement) over the passive ones (moderation, humility), and the natural over the supernatural. Americanism also postulated full religious freedom (not only tolerance) and, especially in Europe, the limitation of papal influence in individual countries. Pope Leo XIII accused it of neglecting monastic rules of life and attempting to adapt the Church to the requirements of contemporary culture. The term "Americanism" derived from a group of Catholics from the USA and France, who characterized themselves by this name. The pope criticized some excesses of that standpoint in his letter *Testem benevolentiae* (1899), where he wrote: "[W]e are not able to give approval to those views which, in their collective sense, are called by some Americanism. But if by this name are to be understood certain endowments of mind which belong to the American people, just as other characteristics belong to various other nations, and if, moreover, by it is designated your political condition and the laws and customs by which you are governed, there is no reason to take exception to the name. But if this is to be so understood that the doctrines which have been adverted to above are not only indicated, but exalted, there can be no manner of doubt that our venerable brethren, the bishops of America, would be the first to repudiate and condemn it as being most injurious to themselves and to their country. For it would give rise to the suspicion that there are among you some who conceive and would have the Church in America to be different from what it is in the rest of the world." Leo XIII, *Testem benevolentiae*, http://www.papalencyclicals.net/Leo13/l13teste.htm (February 1, 2015).

The issue of Zahm's "Americanism" was probably entangled from the very beginning with questions of the orthodoxy of his evolutionist views. The essence of that movement was to modernize the Church through the observation of lay societies treated as exemplary models of spirituality and liberty. According to some scholars, Americanism, later condemned by Pope Leo XIII (1899), was more popular in Europe (particularly in France) than in America itself.[86] As early as January 1897, the publication of *Evolution and Dogma* triggered action on the part of the Holy Office—a higher-ranking body than the Congregation of the Index. Nevertheless, the Holy Office entrusted the case to the Congregation of the Index, a relevant authority, and this ended the connection between Zahm's case and the Holy Office. In addition, the publication was opposed by Archbishop Otto Zardetti, former Bishop of Saint Cloud, Minnesota (USA), who had lived in Rome since 1895.

Zahm's book consists of two parts. Part one is entitled "Evolution: Past and Present," and describes the history of the evolutionist idea from antiquity. Next, the author presents evidence in support of evolution and scientific objections against it. The second part, "Evolution and Dogma," refers to the relationships between evolution and other views: monism, agnosticism, and Catholic doctrine. At the core of the book is the idea that evolution is in no way discordant with Christianity, as the former leaves room for Divine action, does not exclude creation, and even sublimates our concept of God. "Many . . . look on the theory of Evolution with suspicion," Zahm argues,

> because they fail to understand its true significance. . . . It deals not with creation, with the origin of things, but with the *modus creandi*, or, rather, with the *modus formandi*, after the universe was called into existence by Divine Omnipotence. . . . Evolution must postulate a Creator not only for the material which is evolved, but it must also postulate a Creator, *Causa causarum*, for the power or agency which makes any development possible. God, then, not only created matter in the beginning, but He gave it the power of evolving into all forms it has since assumed or ever shall assume. . . . We must also believe that creative action and influence still persist, that they always have persisted from the dawn of creation, that they, and they alone, have been efficient in all the countless stages of evolutionary progress from atoms to monads, from monads to man. . . . Evolution is the grand and stately march of creative energy, the sublime manifestation of . . . the first, creative, legislative and directing Cause.[87]

Clearly, the American theologian and scientist viewed evolution as the general principle of all physical reality. According to him, evolution guarantees a "bet-

86. Cf. *Negotiating Darwin*, 159ff.
87. J.A. Zahm, *Evolution and Dogma* (Chicago: D.H. McBride & Co., 1896), 431–33.

ter image" of God, as it assumes the constant cooperation between the Creator and creation, and it implies the necessity of creation on account of the existence of an evolving universe.[88]

At one point in *Evolution and Dogma*, Zahm asks, "Can we, then, consistently with the certain deductions of science and philosophy, and in accordance with the positive dogmas of faith—can we as Christians, as Catholics, who accept without reserve all the teachings of the Church, give our assent to theistic evolution? This is a question of paramount importance."[89] Answering his own question, the American clergyman explains that the foundations of theistic evolution were adopted and defended by the most prominent doctors of the Greek and Latin Church. As examples he points to St. Gregory of Nyssa and St. Augustine. "According to the Doctor of Hippo," he writes, "God did not create the world as it now appears, but only the primordial matter of which it is composed. Not only the diverse forms of inorganic matter, rocks, minerals, crystals, were created by the operation of secondary causes, but plants and animals also were the products of such causes."[90] In this context, Zahm asks a series of rhetorical questions:

> Has any modern philosopher stated more clearly the salient facts of organic Evolution? Has anyone insisted more strongly on the reign of law in nature, or discriminated more keenly between the operations of the Creator and those of the creature? Has anyone realized more fully the functions of a First Cause, as compared with those of causes which are but secondary or physical? . . . Modern scientists have, indeed, a far more detailed knowledge of the divers forms of terrestrial life . . . but they have not, with all their knowledge . . . been able to formulate the general theory of Evolution a whit more clearly, than we find it expressed in the writings of the Doctor of Grace, who wrote nearly fifteen centuries ago.[91]

Zahm associates Augustine with the modern theory of evolution, even though the majority of his contemporary Catholic theologians were convinced of the opposite—that is, that the Bishop of Hippo not only would not have supported the theory, but would have rejected it in his claims about the creation of different natures as having been distinguished right from the beginning.[92]

The American priest expresses no less admiration for Thomas Aquinas's

88. Ibid., 435–38.

89. Ibid., 279.

90. Ibid., 280–81.

91. Ibid., 283–84.

92. Because of his concept of *logoi spermatikoi* ("seedlike reasons," or "primeval reasons"), St. Augustine has been regarded as the precursor of theistic evolution from the very inception of Darwinism. In 1926, a Catholic philosopher, Michael McKeough, wrote: "The gradual appearance of living beings upon the earth through the operation of natural laws and secondary causes, constitutes a

theological concepts. "Indeed," he writes, "so exhaustive and so complete is [Thomas's] treatment of the origin and Evolution of the material universe and all it contains; so clear and so conclusive is his argumentation, that his successors have found but little to add to his brilliant propositions respecting the genesis of the world and its inhabitants."[93] What was so captivating about St. Thomas's views? According to Zahm, it was his acceptance of the concept of "primordial reasons" (*rationes seminales*), which provide, he assumed, the foundations for the modern theory of evolution. He also found a link between the ancient concept of primordial (or rational) reasons and modern physical findings:

> The physical forces—heat, light, electricity and magnetism—would, doubtless, in modern scientific terminology, correspond to the *seminales rationes* of the Angelic Doctor, as they are efficient in producing changes in matter and in disposing it for that gradual Evolution which has obtained in the material universe. In the beginning, then, God created primordial matter, which was actuated by various substantial forms. With the elements thus created were associated certain *seminal influences*—certain physical forces, we now should say—and the various compounds which subsequently resulted from the action of these forces, on the diverse elements created, were the product of generation and not of creation. There was development, Evolution, under the action of second causes, from the simple elements to the highest inorganic and organic compounds; from the lowest kinds of brute matter to the highest bodily representatives of animated nature; but there was nothing requiring anew creative action or extraordinary interventions, except, of course, the human soul.[94]

Having outlined this putatively Thomistic vision of the emergence of the world, the author argues that Aquinas interpreted the Biblical account of creation in evolutionary terms. Eventually, Zahm states that there is nothing uncertain, ambiguous, or misleading in the teachings of either St. Augustine or St. Thomas in reference to the creation and evolution of all beings:

satisfactory philosophical basis for evolution and merits for him [Augustine] the title of the Father of Evolution." See *The Meaning of rationes seminales in St. Augustine* (Washington, DC: Catholic University of America, 1926), 109–10. However, Augustine and Darwin spoke of evolution in two different senses. First of all, Augustine recognized the creation of all beings "according to their kinds" at the beginning of the world, even if some of them were to develop gradually afterwards. In Darwinian evolution, new species appear gradually over millions of years by virtue of natural laws. The debate on Augustine and the theory of evolution flared up anew in the 1990s, when J. Wells and J.M. Reynolds got involved in a polemic with the ideas of H. van Till.

93. J.A. Zahm, *Evolution and Dogma*, 284–85.

94. Ibid., 289–90.

> Theistic Evolution, in the sense in which it is advocated by St. Augustine and St. Thomas, excludes also Divine interference, or constant unnecessary interventions on the part of the Deity, as effectually as it does a low and narrow Anthropomorphism. . . . Only the crudest conception of derivative creation would demand that the theist should necessarily, if consistently, have recourse to continued creative fiats to explain the multifold phenomena connected with inorganic or organic Evolution.[95]

The author recognizes the difference between the concepts of the two doctors and the theory of evolution in the modern sense, but he believes they only failed to include it in their writings for lack of modern knowledge.[96]

According to Zahm, it is clear that "far from being opposed to faith, theistic Evolution is on the contrary supported both by the declarations of Genesis and by the most venerable philosophical and theological authorities of the Church."[97] On the other hand, the doctrine of "special creation" is only a supposition, unsupported by any serious Church authority.[98] "Which of the two theories is the more probable," he asks,

> evolution or special creation? Both of them, it must be admitted, rest upon a certain number of postulates; . . . For our present purpose it will here suffice to repeat the answer of the Abbé Guillemet, who tells us that Evolution, as against special creation, has this in its favor, that it explains and coordinates the facts and phenomena of nature in a most beautiful and simple manner; whereas the theory of special creation not only explains nothing and is incapable of explaining anything, but, by its very nature, tends to impede research, to bar progress, or, as he phrases it, it forces science into a blind alley.[99]

According to Zahm, then, there is no intermediate solution between evolution and special creation, no possibility of reconciliation or compromise: "We must be either creationists or evolutionists."[100]

95. Ibid., 304–5.

96. "Of course no one would think of maintaining that any of the Fathers or Doctors of the Church taught Evolution in the sense in which it is now understood. They did not do this for the simple reason that the subject had not even been broached in its present form, and because its formulation as a theory, under its present aspect, was impossible before men of science had in their possession the accumulated results of the observation and research of these latter times. But they did all that was necessary fully to justify my present contention; they laid down principles which are perfectly compatible with theistic Evolution. They asserted, in the most positive and explicit manner, the doctrine of derivative creation as against the theory of a perpetual direct creation of organisms." Ibid., 312–13.

97. Ibid., 312.

98. Ibid., 135.

99. Ibid., 419.

100. Ibid., 75.

Of course the American priest regards creationism as the view that there were multiple creative acts throughout the history of the world, whereas evolutionism as he understands it is the theistic version thereof, assuming initial creation. The important thing is that, according to Zahm, the same thing cannot both be created and be the product of evolution at the same time and in the same respect. Such a standpoint would have to lead to monism, which he contests just as zealously as he does "special creation."

Proceeding to the scientific aspects of evolution, Zahm offers the main arguments used by Darwin: those based on classification, morphology, embryology, geographical distribution, and geological succession of forms.[101] Nevertheless, Zahm names three major problems with the new hypothesis. First, no one had ever observed an example of change of one species into another. The answer to this objection, Zahm claims, had already been given by Lamarck, who argued that the constancy of species is observed in their living environments, which have not changed for a long time. Second, the fossil record does not show any intermediate links between species. In response, Zahm repeats Darwin's claim about the imperfection of the record and the fact that intermediate forms die soonest, making them hard to identify in fossil layers. The third objection concerns impossibility of cross-breeding between species and the fact that even if we manage to cross-breed specimens within a single family, the offspring are infertile. Zahm admits that this is a serious objection, but states (following Darwin) that the concept of species is generally uncertain and hard to define.[102]

From the point of view of religion, the more important questions are concerned with the origin of life and man. With reference to the former issue, Zahm recognizes the fact that Pasteur's experiments excluded spontaneous generation.[103] He adds, however, that some scientists (Haeckel, Fiske) still maintained it was possible, and so perhaps one day it would be possible to prove that such a process had taken place or even still occurs from time to time in the present world.[104] For Zahm, neither the possibility of spontaneous generation nor the attempts at its creation in a laboratory are in conflict with Christian doctrine.[105] In support of this claim the scholar appeals to the Church Fathers and Scholastics. This latter thesis of Zahm's encountered firm criticism from the Jesuit Francesco Salis Seewis, who immediately published

101. Ibid., 134.

102. Ibid., 143–93.

103. Zahm considers synonymous terms such as spontaneous generation, abiogenesis, generatio aequivoca, heterogenesis, and autogenesis (cf. 41).

104. Ibid., 329.

105. Ibid., 338.

four articles in *La Civiltá Cattolica*, explaining what Aristotle, Thomas Aquinas, and the Scholastics have to say about spontaneous generation.[106]

At the beginning of the sixth chapter, "The Simian Origin of Man," Zahm argues—invoking the authority of Rudolf Virchow[107]—that so far not even the slightest proof had been found of the simian origin of man. Nevertheless, the idea of human evolution from a simian ancestor was plausible to him.[108] He even anticipates the fear some may feel that evolution would diminish man's dignity:

> Evolution, far from depriving [man] of his high estate, confirms him in it, and that, too, by the strongest and noblest of titles. It recognizes that although descended from humble lineage, he is the beauty of the world, and the paragon of animals; . . . the highest term of a long and majestic development, and replaces him in his old position of headship in the universe.[109]

Analyzing the origin of the human soul, Zahm claims, in accordance with tradition, that the soul is created directly by God with respect to each human being. But what about the body of the first man? "In other words," Zahm writes, "is man, as to his body, the direct and special work of the Creator's hands, or is he the descendant of some animal, some anthropoid ape or some missing link of which naturalists as yet have discovered no trace?"[110]

He answers that we need to follow the law of analogy. If there is nothing contrary to the Catholic faith in either the evolution of species or in the emergence of life from inanimate matter, there cannot be any similar conflict with reference to the human body. Even though there is not a single trace of a scientific proof of the evolution of man, Zahm is convinced that "[a]nalogy and scientific consistency, we are told, require us to admit that man's bodily frame has been subject to the same law of Evolution, if an Evolution there has been, as has obtained for the inferior animals."[111] The American priest's argument, then, is purely deductive, based on "analogy" and "cohesion" rather than on demonstrable evidence from natural science. In support of his thesis he refers to the

106. F. Salis Seewis, "La generazione spontanea e la filosofia antica," in *La Civiltá Cattolica*, 16th ser., 11 (1897), 142–52; "Sant'Agostino e la generazione spontanea primitiva," ibid., 421–38; "S. Tommaso e la generazione spontanea primitiva," ibid., 676–91; "Le origini della vita sulla terra secondo il Suarez," in *La Civiltá Cattolica* 16th ser., 12 (1897), 168–76.

107. Rudolf Virchow (1821–1902) was one of the most distinguished German biologists of the 19th century; he is famous for developing cell theory. For most of his academic career, he challenged Darwin's theory, promoted in Germany, primarily by arguing with E. Haeckel.

108. J. A. Zahm, *Evolution and Dogma*, 342.

109. Ibid., 435.

110. Cf. ibid., 350.

111. Ibid., 352.

work of St. George Mivart, who had been made a doctor of philosophy by Pope Pius IX himself.[112]

Zahm's characteristic approach is revealed when he discusses the creation of the human body as presented by St. Thomas. Following the tradition of the Fathers, Aquinas believes that the human body was created directly by God, though he also speculated about some possible assistance of angels. If St. Thomas allows any participation of angels, then, Zahm argued, he could also permit the aid of other factors.[113] Therefore, Zahm concludes, the evolution of the body is not necessarily in conflict with the teachings of St. Thomas. The American theologian facilely proceeded from the "possibility of some kind of assistance of angels in direct creation" to "absence of objection to derivative creation" in Aquinas's thought.

Zahm is aware of a "metaphysical difficulty" related to the substantial unity of the man whose body would have been developed through evolution, and whose soul would have been given directly by God.[114] He does not deem it an unconquerable obstacle, but at the same time he fails to provide any positive solution. For Zahm, the evolution of the body does not require any "Divine additions." He expresses it clearly by invoking the view of the Spanish Cardinal Zeferino Gonzáles (1831–1894), who had claimed that many theological objections to the theory of the evolution of man would have disappeared, if one had assumed that God had completed the work of evolution in the final phase of development of the body by making a direct intervention of some sort. Zahm believes otherwise: "If we are to admit the action of Evolution at all, in the production of Adam's body, it appears more consistent to admit that it was competent to complete the work which it began."[115]

At the end of his book, the author also discusses the issue of purpose and design in nature. Evolution undermined the classical argument of design, but it introduced a much richer and more interesting concept of finality. Darwin was the first to explain the relationships between organisms and their hierarchy and functions in connection to what we might expect from the First Cause:

> The result has been that we have now a higher, a subtler, a more comprehensive teleology than the world has ever before known. We have a teleology which is indissolubly linked with the teachings of revealed truth; a teleology which, while receiving light from Evolution, illumines, in turn, this grand

112. Ibid., 353.

113. Ibid., 355. Thomas actually does allow the assistance of angels, but only to the extent to which they had gathered dust of the earth in the adequate place, which God used to form the first man directly by His own power. In the same way, Aquinas argues, the angels will bring together ashes of the saints on the day of the resurrection of bodies. Cf. *S.Th.* I, 91, a.1, ad 1.

114. J.A. Zahm, *Evolution and Dogma*, 358.

115. Ibid., 360.

> generalization, and shows us that Evolution, when properly understood, is a noble witness to a God who, unlike the God of the older Deism, that simply sets the machine of the universe in motion, and leaves it to work by itself is, on the contrary, One who, in the language of Holy Scripture, is not only above all, but through all, and in all.[116]

The American priest, therefore, sees no problem with finality within evolutionism. On the contrary, he believes the theory to be a blessing for Christian theology. For Zahm, evolution as a general principle of all reality helps sublimate our understanding of Divine Providence.

The Debate about the Book

The first review of *Evolution and Dogma* was published in the Belgian journal *Revue des Questions Scientifiques* in July 1896.[117] The author, Jean-François-Albert du Pouget, known as the Marquis de Nadaillac, begins by praising Zahm for his approach to evolution. He emphasizes that the American clergyman distinguishes evolution itself from its atheistic, agnostic, materialistic, and pantheistic interpretations, suggesting a theistic evolution that does not go against the doctrine of the Church. Nevertheless, Nadaillac notices a few problems with Zahm's ideas.

First of all, he disagrees with Zahm's claim that evolutionism had been anticipated by the Church Fathers and St. Thomas: "The conclusion of this learned theologian evidently exceeds his premises. It strikes me as difficult to tease evolution, as we currently understand it, out of the words of the philosophers of antiquity or doctors of the Church, and we would not know how to find in their theses any support for the doctrines of Lamarck or Darwin. . . ."[118] Next, the French reviewer completely rejects abiogenesis, about the possibility of which Zahm had speculated. On the genesis of the human body, he states that the question is unanswerable from the scientific point of view. Calling upon the concept of Cardinal González, he agrees with Zahm that accepting some partial divine intervention in the formation of the body is incoherent and has little to do with the scientific notion of evolution. However, the punchline of the article is the statement that, despite the hypothetical compliance of evolution and Catholic doctrine, there are insufficient scientific proofs in support of the hypothesis. We do not know what process might have directed it, he says, and we do not know its causes. The impossibility of one species transforming into

116. Ibid., 377.

117. M. de Nadaillac, "Review: *L'évolution et le Dogme*," *Revue des Questions Scientifiques* (July 1896), 229–46 (*Negotiating Darwin*, 134).

118. Ibid., 231.

another in the process of generation, the infertility of hybrids, uncertainty of arguments based on natural selection, the unknown role of the natural environment, and the impossibility of inheritance of acquired features—all these things make evolution difficult even for evolutionists themselves. "Doctor Zahm's book has great merit," he concludes, "but, if I may be permitted to say so, it takes too much as truths already acquired what are hypotheses that ought to be proven. . . . If I am not very disposed to accept the conclusions of the evolutionist school, neither can I reject them in any absolute way."[119] One should note, therefore, that according to the French scholar, the scientific foundations of evolution are too slight to provide the basis for far-fetched theological conclusions.

The second favorable review was released in October of the same year in the *Dublin Review*—a reputable Catholic journal of the English-speaking world.[120] The piece was signed with the pseudonym "F. David," which referred to the Franciscan David Fleming, who was employed at the Vatican Curia and a personal acquaintance of Zahm and his friends. Fleming commends the author for his clarity and skill in formulating theses. He believes that we should not perceive as contrary to faith a view according to which in the beginning the Creator inspired matter with the potentiality necessary for the emergence of organic life, and then left it to evolve and diversify over time, according to laws imposed by the same Creator. Fleming furthermore applauds Zahm's frequently used terms "derivative creation" or "mediated creation," referring to the formation of particular organisms from other organisms. "The point of this argument," he writes, "is, that if the Scholastics had all the facts before them which we have, they would not have the slightest hesitation in admitting that all the organic species at present existing are the outcome not of direct and immediate, but of derivative and mediate creation."[121] The Franciscan likes the idea of theistic evolution, as—like Zahm—he believed that it is more perfect to create beings that are able to generate further beings than to create species directly. Evolution provides an exceptionally beautiful and harmonious vision of the Divine effective causality. Like Zahm, Fleming distinguishes the general idea of evolution from specific theories explaining it. These theories need not be correct, and their mechanisms may raise many doubts, but this cannot lead to the rejection of evolution itself as purportedly against faith or reason. Thus both scholars can be viewed as increasingly inclined to make a distinction between the "fact" of evolution, which is undeniable, and the "mechanism," which so far

119. Ibid., 245.

120. F. David [David Fleming], "Review of *Evolution and Dogma*," *Dublin Review* 119 (July–October 1896), 245–55.

121. Ibid., 248 (*Negotiating Darwin*, 136).

is not well-founded. Indeed, as Fleming writes, "It seems to us that, as matters stand at present, the theory of Evolution has passed from the state of being merely possible to the state of probability.... It is quite evident to us that there is no incompatibility between Evolution and Theism...."[122]

At the end of his review Fleming approaches the most important problem, that is, the matter of the origin of the human body. Agreeing with Zahm's view entirely, he concludes that there is no conflict between the evolutionary origin of Adam's body and the teachings of Thomas Aquinas. The Church Fathers, according to Fleming, say nothing on the matter. There are also no objections on the part of philosophy and physics, whereas based on Genesis alone it is impossible to settle the dispute between creationism and evolutionism. As concerns the creation of Eve, Fleming quotes Cajetan and Origen (who both supported a metaphorical interpretation of Eve's derivation from Adam's side), indicating that they had not been censored by the Church. At the end of the article, he remarks:

> In our humble opinion, and we speak under correction, we are not compelled by any principle of theology or exegesis to insist upon the strictly historical and scientific nature of the account of the creation and formation of Eve.... The practical unanimity of interpreters on the point does not place the matter beyond all respectful and reverent inquiry. We gladly leave the matter to the authority of the Apostolic See.[123]

Having read Fleming's review, one might notice that not only did he agree with *Evolution and Dogma*, but on some issues went even further than the author himself. The general tone of the review was favorable, and the book was advertised as admirable and useful.

However, not all readers of *Evolution and Dogma* reached the same conclusions as David Fleming. A few months later (in January 1897) *La Civiltá Cattolica* printed a review written by Francesco Salis Seewis, who—after expressing his discontent with the "choir of praise" for Zahm's book—indicates that there also were negative opinions, and that the bishops—the rightful guardians of Church doctrine—did not share the same enthusiasm for Zahm's claims. Seewis set the case of evolution on a purely biological plane:

> We have always judged [evolutionary theory] only from scientific perspective. Our question has always been this alone: What value does evolutionism have in the court of positive science and logic?... We have concluded each time that evolutionism can only be deemed a tissue of vulgar analogies, arbi-

122. Ibid., 250.
123. Ibid., 254 (*Negotiating Darwin*, 137).

> trary suppositions, not sustained but proven wrong by the facts, fantastic adages and subterfuges that render indecent the seriousness of science.[124]

According to Salis Seewis, although many Catholics find that there is no conflict between evolution and dogma, the true question is not whether evolution agrees with faith, but whether it is actually founded on empirical science. The holy Doctors have always taught that of the many senses of an inspired text, a Catholic may choose the one most compliant with scientific arguments, to avoid unreliable interpretations. But the situation is different with respect to evolution. According to Seewis:

> When evolutionism has passed its examination in the court of sciences, and emerges with the patent of a system founded on evident principles, logical deductions, and positive facts, only then will it be worthwhile to consider it in the light of Revelation.... But so long as it presents nothing more than the hope of future demonstrations..., while it continues reasoning as if logic had nothing to do with it..., while things are as they are, we hold that it is useless to introduce this scientific failure into the sacristy and it is astonishing that there are Catholics rushing to do so.[125]

According to Seewis, Catholic apology should follow clear lines of defense—first, disputes within the natural sciences should be resolved; and if evolution is thus proved by science, it would then be possible to consider its reconciliation with religion.

Activities of the Congregation of the Index

In early November 1897, Archbishop Otto Zardetti denounced Zahm's work to the Congregation of the Index. In his letter the Archbishop listed ten statements subject to condemnation. They may be summarized as follows:

1. Evolution proposes a nobler concept of God than the classical concept of creation.

2. The book is a defense of how a Catholic can be an evolutionist.

3. By endorsing the evolution of the human body, the author asks if it is in conflict with dogma or metaphysics and gives a negative answer.

4. Analogy and compliance with the broader theory of evolution require the recognition of the evolutionary origin of the human body.

5. The author quotes Mivart, calling him an acclaimed theologian.

124. F. Salis Seewis, "*Evoluzione e Domma* pel Padre J.A. Zahm," *La Civiltá Cattolica*, 16th ser., 9 (1897), 201–4, at 202.

125. Ibid., 203.

6. The evolution of the human body is in complete agreement with the teachings of St. Augustine and St. Thomas Aquinas.

7. The author quotes Dalmace Leroy, even though his ideas had been condemned by competent authority.

8. The last chapter is entirely favorable to evolution as an "ally" to religion. Special creation explains nothing and hampers development.

9. Evolution does not degrade man but rather elevates apes.

10. The author advertises his theses as agreeing with the Bible, the Church Fathers, and prominent Catholic scientists.

In response to the letter, the Congregation appointed Enrico Buonpensiere (known from Leroy's case) to prepare a report. On April 15, 1898, the consultant submitted his text, containing over fifty pages. The report is divided into three parts. The first refers to the scientific layer of Zahm's book. The consultant, quoting extensively from the initial pages of the book, exposes the author's contention that the Church has not yet formulated any theory of the origin of the world and its inhabitants, and thus no Catholic is obliged to support any specific theory until some proofs are given on its behalf. The American clergyman alludes to the examples of Copernicus, Newton, and a few geological theories, suggesting that evolution would experience a similar fate and that it was surprising that some people had not learned anything from the past. According to the consultant, these statements are proof of the author's poor knowledge of metaphysics, theology, and history, thus decreasing his competence.

Furthermore, Buonpensiere accuses the scholar of the mistaken attribution of Empedocles's doctrine to Aristotle. Consequently, in his opinion, one may imagine how much truth there might be in ascribing evolutionist views to Albert the Great and Thomas Aquinas. Referring very concisely to Zahm's hundred-page scientific discussion of evolution, Buonpensiere notes that arguments in favor of evolution are no more than assumptions and arbitrary explanations of biological processes, which can be as easily overturned as they are presented by Zahm; what is more, these arguments are contrary to metaphysics and theology.[126] Criticism is also leveled at Zahm's statement that the fact of evolution "is scarcely any longer a matter for controversy."[127]

In the second part of the report, Buonpensiere approaches more important questions, namely the possibility of harmonizing evolution with theism and the issue of the origin of man. First of all, Buonpensiere notices that the American priest erroneously represents the concept of special creation. No one, he writes,

126. ACDF, Index, *Protocolli*, 1897–1899, 180, 12.
127. Ibid.

would argue that God had created everything at once, directly and out of nothing. The idea of special creation suggests rather that God had created primitive matter, and then formed the other things using passive properties embedded in the previously-created cosmic matter. By presenting a number of distinctions, the consultant defines the arena of dispute between the evolutionists and their opponents in metaphysical categories. The question is whether the potency for developing the first plants, animals, and man from the cosmic matter was active or just passive—or perhaps only partially active with respect to some organisms: "With these distinctions and subdistinctions, and with still others soon to be introduced, problems multiply, and the basic theorems of evolutionism and anti-evolutionism form themselves into two opposing sides, as anyone can observe."[128] The evolutionists speak of the active principle of the potency embedded in the secondary causes, while the anti-evolutionists disagree with this. According to them, the initially-created chaotic matter had instead only had a passive potency—one that was only actualized by substantial forms of plants and animals. That potency was actualized by God's Word during the days of creation—just as Moses describes in Genesis. Thus Buonpensiere attempted to interpret creation in terms of Aristotelian-Thomistic metaphysics, which might provide an adequate response of the Church to the problem of evolutionism.

Next, Rome's consultant addresses the claim that St. Augustine and St. Thomas Aquinas were precursors of evolutionism. Augustine's *rationes seminales* only referred to the passive capacity of matter—embedded in it at the beginning by God—that was subsequently actualized by His power. According to Buonpensiere, to attribute evolutionism to Augustine is to defame a Saint. Though it is not easy to define the exact intention of the Doctor of Grace with reference to the concept of *rationes seminales*, one should easily reject the exaggerated interpretation of this doctrine devised by the American priest who also—and even more strongly—distorted the idea of St. Thomas.

Proceeding to the analysis of the origin of the human body presented by Zahm, Buonpensiere remarks that Zahm does not see any possibility of identifying a link between ape and man. Therefore, in Zahm's own opinion, a scientific proof is unavailable. Nevertheless, Buonpensiere points out, Zahm argues through analogy—quite arbitrarily and deductively—that if evolution occurs in other cases, it should consequently be adopted with reference to man. The consultant also finds Zahm's treatment of Biblical hermeneutics unacceptable. The American priest distinguishes between Revelation and interpretation, attributing absolute value only to the former. However, according to Buonpensiere, this would suggest that there is no difference between the individual

128. Ibid., 15.

opinion of any given person about the holy text and, for instance, a common agreement of the Church Fathers. Therefore, the consultant proposes: "I would deem it opportune to warn the illustrious author about the ambiguity of the expressions he uses in biblical exegesis."[129]

Summarizing Zahm's views, the consultant presents a vision of evolutionism as provided in *Evolution and Dogma*: God created primary matter in a state of chaos but furnished it with primary forces and movements and subjected it to the law of progressive development for the purpose of forming the universe. By the power of these natural forces, plant life emerged, which—under God's Providence—developed step by step until it reached the level of animal life. Next, over a very long period of time, anthropomorphous life appeared. God summoned one of the anthropomorphic individuals and infused him with a rational soul, creating Adam. Adam's body was thus not created directly by God, but indirectly, through the forces embedded by God in matter at the first moment of creation.

In the third part (44–53) the consultant proposes his own thesis, in capital letters:

> I THINK IT IS CATHOLIC DOCTRINE TO STATE THAT GOD HAS MADE ADAM IMMEDIATELY AND DIRECTLY FROM THE MUD OF THE EARTH.[130]

In support of his opinion, the consultant invokes the hermeneutical principle that the natural and obvious sense of Biblical words should not be abandoned as long as it does not lead to absurd conclusions. Such a situation does not apply to this case, as direct creation does not exceed God's power and is well-documented by the Church tradition. Therefore the literal interpretation should be maintained with regard to formation of the first human body. Over the next seven pages the consultant quotes the Church Fathers and theologians—including Peter Lombard, Albert the Great, Thomas Aquinas, Alexander of Hales, Durand, Duns Scotus, Bonaventure, and Suarez, all of whom had supported his thesis. Some of these authorities even regarded it as part of the Catholic faith. "Now then," writes Buonpensiere, "the unanimous agreement of the Church Fathers and Scholastic Theologians in matters of Faith and Customs bears certain witness to Catholic Dogma. . . . The truth of the conclusion presented above is sustained."[131]

Furthermore, Buonpensiere mentions the Thirteenth Canon of the Synod of Braga (613), condemning the Manicheans and Priscillans for claiming that bod-

129. Ibid., 41.

130. Ibid., 45 (*Negotiating Darwin*, 149).

131. Ibid., 51 (*Negotiating Darwin*, 150).

ies had not been created by God but by the evil angels.[132] He also reminds his readers of the decree of the Synod of Cologne (1860) that asserts the direct creation of the first human parents by God. As is evident from the above-quoted statements, Rome's expert believed that Church doctrine about the origin of man was clear. This was the basis for his final evaluation: "Reverend Father Zahm's book, leaving aside other theological ambiguities, is a continuous apology of a doctrine contrary to the truth of the Catholic faith: It does not seem to me susceptible to emendation, for it would have to be done over from the beginning. Therefore, it merits proscription."[133]

At the end of the report, its author presents the Congregation of the Index with one more proposition:

> As it is necessary, once and for all, to let Catholic naturalists know publicly that it is not permitted to teach that Adam's body may not have originated immediately from the mud of the earth but comes from an anthropomorphic brute, I propose that, as was done on other occasions, this Holy Congregation condemn the following proposition, or another like it, that is: God did not make the body of Adam immediately from the mud of the earth, but out of the body of an anthropomorphic brute, which had been prepared to be produced by the forces of natural evolution from lower matter.[134]

The Congregation of the Index took steps against Zahm's book, but it did not have the competence to make the statement demanded by Buonpensiere. The records show no trace of his suggestion having ever been submitted to the Holy Office.

On August 5, 1898, *Evolution and Dogma* was investigated by a preparatory meeting of the Congregation of the Index chaired by the Secretary Marcolino Cicognani, O.P. After a lengthy discussion, the work was subjected to a vote,

132. The information about the Synod of Braga of 613 is provided by the authors of *Negotiating Darwin*, probably after Buonpensiere's report. The date, however, is mistaken, as the canon in question appears in the Records of the First Synod of Braga of 561. Apart from Canon 13, Canons 8 and 12 were also relevant to the topic. They read: "VIII. If anyone believes that the devil made some creatures in the world and by his own authority the devil himself causes thunder and lightning, and storms and spells of dryness, just as Priscillian has asserted, let him be anathema. XII. If anyone says that the formation of the human body is a creation of the devil, and says that conceptions in the wombs of mothers are formed by the works of demons, and for this reason does not believe in the resurrection of the body, just as Manichaeus and Priscillian have said, let him be anathema. XIII. If anyone says that the creation of all flesh is not the work of God, but belongs to the wicked angels, just as Priscillian has said, let him be anathema." Quotation from: http://onetruecatholicfaith.com/Roman-Catholic-Dogma.php?id=18&title=Denzinger+200+-+301&page=1 (2 February 2015). Latin text: Denzin ger–Schönmetzer, *Enchiridion Symbolorum Definitionum et Declarationum*, 34th ed. (Barcelona: Herder, 1967), 158 (DS 231).

133. ACDF, Index, *Protocolli*, 1897–1899, 180:52.

134. Ibid., 53 (*Negotiating Darwin*, 151).

with five of thirteen attendants opting for the condemnation of the book and publication of a decree; three for only giving a warning to the author; and two abstaining from voting. Three of the participants proposed to prohibit the book and submit a question to the Holy Office about transformism—namely, whether it was in agreement with the Church doctrine. This was not done.

The preparatory meeting did not declare that species transformism contradicts any defined dogma of faith, but it did confirm that it disagrees with the Holy Scriptures, tradition, theologians, and the Church's ordinary teaching. Such a resolution indicates that, at the time, transformism did not have the status of an entirely and straightforwardly condemned concept. However, on the issue of the origin of the human body, the certainty of theologians was greater.

The decision of the preparatory meeting was passed forward to the cardinals, who met in a general congregation on September 1, 1898. After a longer debate, the cardinals unanimously decided to proscribe Zahm's book, but also—before a relevant decree was issued—to first ask him to revoke his views. Regardless of his submission to the decision of the Congregation, the decree would be published anyway; but if the author revoked his theses, this fact would be mentioned in the document. Thus the decision of the general meeting (that is, the decision of the Congregation) was even more severe than Buonpensiere's proposal. Yet the decree was not published, because the cardinals waited for Zahm's response. At that moment, influential friends and superiors of the American priest in Rome initiated a campaign against the publication of the decree of the Congregation.

The Campaign Against the Publication of the Decree

At the time when the case of Father Zahm was being considered, the Superior of the Congregation of the Holy Cross was Gilbert Français. As soon as he received a letter from the Congregation of the Index informing him of the condemnation of Zahm's book, he resolved to protest the decision made in Rome. Immediately after consulting his subordinate, he sent two letters to the Prefect of the Congregation, Cardinal Steinhuber, the first reporting that Zahm had submitted to the decision, and the second confirming the withdrawal and asking that the decree remain unpublished. In the second letter, Français writes:

> I can add in my own name and in [Zahm's] that we are wholly disposed to do all that is prescribed for us, to repair that which ought to be repaired in this matter. Again I dare to solicit the great goodness of your Eminence, that you might stop the publication of the decree. Your Eminence knows America well enough, the juxtaposition of the different races found here, and their present state of mind, to be able to think that such publications perhaps could harm the life of Father Zahm, who is a truly worthy priest, and a man of religion

> whose great influence only has need of direction for it to have great utility. Moreover, such publication, besides being for myself and my Congregation certainly a cause of authentic suffering, could create serious difficulties of administration. In these circumstances, Father Zahm has ceased to follow presumptuous and rash ideas. It is also beyond doubt that he possesses real qualities as an administrator, and that, in this area, his cooperation could not be more precious to me.[135]

Evidently the reasons presented by the Superior were of a practical nature—he wished to avoid the degradation of the priest whose help he needed in administering the Congregation. At least this was the official claim. However, months went by and the case remained in suspension. At a personal audience in November 1898, Cardinal Serafino Vannuttelli petitioned Pope Leo XIII to refrain from the publication of the decree. The Pope agreed, but it was not a conclusive decision. During an audience in early February 1899, however, Leo XIII ordered Cardinal Steinhuber to adjourn publication of the decree until the author in question—who was soon to visit Rome—could be heard in person. (Zahm had left Rome in January 1898 upon being made the provincial of the order in the USA.) Thus, by virtue of a papal decision the case was again delayed, this time, as it turned out, indefinitely.[136]

Meanwhile, Jesuits gathered around *La Civiltá Cattolica* had enhanced the negative reception of Zahm's book. At the end of 1898, Salvatore Brandi, S.J. published an article entitled "Evoluzione e domma" in which he harshly criticized the book. Despite these unfavorable circumstances, the Roman Curia approved a decision to reappoint Zahm as a provincial superior of the Ameri-

135. Letter of Gilbert Français to the Prefect of the Congregation of the Index of November 4, 1898. See *Negotiating Darwin*, 157–58.

136. The decision resulted from earlier efforts made by Français and Zahm to stop the publication of the decree. In October 1898, the superior general personally traveled to Rome to negotiate with various individuals in order to form a common front of influential figures. Concurrently to Zahm's case, another book, indirectly connected with it, was also being investigated. After the death of Isaac von Hecker, founder of the Paulist Fathers, Walter Elliott published a book, *The Life of Father Hecker* (1891). Elliott—a follower of Hecker—wrote a biography that largely manifested the views later referred to as "Americanism" (named so by its supporters themselves). The book stirred up a storm of controversy and complaints. The issue of Americanism ended with the *Testem benevolentiae* letter (of January 22, 1899) from Pope Leo XIII to Cardinal Gibbons, in which the Holy Father (introducing some distinctions) condemned Americanism, defined as a doctrine aimed at changing the Church doctrine and loosening morality (cf. note 233). The group of Americanists residing in Rome included Bishop John J. Keane, Cardinals Vincenzo and Serafino Vannuttelli, Rector of the North American College Dennis O'Connell, Rector of the French School in Rome, Louis Duchesne, and consultant to the Sactum Officium David Fleming. During his several-month stay in the Eternal City, Zahm became well acquainted with these figures and actively participated in a kind of "lobby" of Americanists. So when his book was deemed condemnable, and the case of *The Life of Father Hecker* also went "on trial," the whole group decided to use its influence to neutralize the actions of the Congregation and to rescue both Americanism and the theory of evolution.

can Province of the Congregation. The pope's decision of February 3, 1899 about the delay of the publication of the decree was essentially a private statement, thus leaving the case unsettled. Over the following months, various sources published information about the proscription of Zahm's views. This way the case, initially veiled, was becoming public, and despite the absence of an official document, Zahm was losing what he had intended to save—his views on evolution and an influential position among the Americanists. At the same time, the Vatican Secretary of State Cardinal Mariano Rampolla, as well as the pope himself, insisted once more that Zahm come to Rome to present his explanations.

In late April 1899, Cicognani, the Secretary of the Congregation of the Index, ordered the withdrawal of the French edition of the book. This decision was directly prompted by a favorable review published in the French press. In general, withholding the publication of the decree caused Zahm's ideas to spread, which Rome in turn saw as increasing the urgency for announcing the condemnation. After receiving a warning from Cicognani, Zahm was seriously frightened that the issue of condemnation might return with all its force. Therefore, he wrote two letters—one to his French editor, asking to withdraw the book, and another, similar one to the Italian editor. In the letter to the Italian editor, dated May 16, 1899, he writes:

> I have learned from an irreproachable source that the Holy See is opposed to any further distribution of *Evolution and Dogma* and, therefore, I beg you to use all of your influence to withdraw the book from the market. You may well have foreseen this outcome and so it won't surprise you.... As for me, I will not suffer seeing the fruit of so much work consigned to oblivion. God rewards intent and our intentions were good.[137]

However, the case would have still remained unsettled had the Italian editor not attempted to resolve the issue on his own. Unbeknownst to the author, Alfonso Galea published Zahm's letter in *Gazzetta di Malta*. In late June, the thread was taken up by *La Civiltá Cattolica*, where Salvatore Brandi presented Zahm's letter along with a statement by Galea and a short comment. This way, the author's request for the withdrawal of his book from sale became known—and the only public document confirming the investigation of his work in Rome. *Nolens*

137. See *Negotiating Darwin*, 195–96. A few days before the letters were sent, Archbishop Sebastiano Martinelli, the apostolic delegate to the United States, paid an official visit to Notre Dame. During an official dinner given in honor of the Archbishop, Zahm stood up and made a splendid toast to the excellent guest, also full of esteem for the authority of the Pope. According to some historians, this gesture was of key importance in ending the problem of the publication of the decree (*Negotiating Darwin*, 195). A similar claim is made by Ralph Edward Weber in his biography of Zahm. Cf. R.E. Weber, *Notre Dame's John Zahm: American Catholic Apologist and Educator* (Notre Dame: University of Notre Dame Press, 1961).

volens, Zahm abjured his publication, even though the official condemnation demanded by the Congregation of the Index had never been enforced. Until the opening of the archives, the short letter of the priest, publicized in the papers, was the only available proof of the negative reception of Zahm's book by the Magisterium.

Evolutionist Elements in the Publications of Bishops G. Bonomelli and J.C. Hedley

Bishop Geremia Bonomelli and the Repeal of the "Important Appendix"

Geremia Bonomelli was born in Nigoline in 1831. He joined the seminary in Bresci in 1851 and four years later was ordained a priest. Having defended his doctoral thesis at the Gregorian University, he became a lecturer in philosophy and hermeneutics at his diocesan seminary. In 1871 he was appointed Bishop of Cremona, an office he held until his death in 1914. Bonomelli was already a controversial bishop because of his open sympathy for the new Italian state and support for some ideas of the then-emerging modernism. In 1889 he published an article in which he proposed a compromise between the Church and Italy. His solution to the Church/State issue was quite close to the one adopted forty years later in the Lateran Treaty, but at the time Bonomelli presented his ideas, Church authorities were still opposing the unlawful seizure of Rome by the Italian revolutionaries. Bonomelli's article was added to the Index in the same year it was published.

The bishop's activities over the following years almost had him dismissed from office.[138] In 1890, Bonomelli edited an Italian translation of the sermons of the French Dominican Jacques-Marie Monsabré, including his own annotations, which provoked a great deal of controversy. Even Monsabré distanced himself from the Italian edition of his sermons on account of Bonomelli's comments.

In March 1893 an Italian intellectual, Antonio Fogazzaro, gave a few lectures on evolution. Bonomelli, as his trusted friend, advised him to add a clear reservation about the direct Divine origin of the human soul before publishing his lectures as a book. The author followed the bishop's advice. Still, the book faced strong scientific criticism from the Jesuit Francesco Salis Seewis.[139] Fogazzaro,

138. Bonomelli was strongly reprimanded for his political activity by Pope Pius X in 1906. The Vatican records also contain a letter of Bishop Antonio Agliardi (later Cardinal) from 1892, reporting that he had performed his duty and that Bonomelli was ready to surrender the Bishopric of Cremona (cf. *Negotiating Darwin*, 204–5 and 215).

139. One ought to quote a fragment of Seewis's article that accurately represents the standpoint of the Catholic apologetics of the period: "When, through the work of unbelievers around forty years ago this phantom of evolution arose to break and harm Revelation, Catholic apologists displayed

however, was no scientist, and presented his thoughts in the form of poetic and philosophical considerations having little to do with the advanced biological theories of species transformism.

Having read the lectures written by his friend, Bonomelli gradually came to adopt the idea of theistic evolution. In his letter of April 4, he wrote to Fogazzaro: "Creation, as it was understood in the past, by blows, by lightning bolts, by jumps, from day to night, etc., etc., is poetry: now we have science. Science agrees with faith in the original creation out of nothing: but science requires evolution, and faith should not exempt anything."[140] The deeper the Italian bishop studied the philosopher's text, the more convinced he became of the "new idea of creation." Three months later he wrote:

> Rereading your lecture for the third time [I came to the conclusion that] God creates, but he lets things develop in accord with the forces He has placed in them, and here evolution begins. What good work you would do if you developed these two powerful ideas: 1. God always works through secondary causes; 2. And therefore everything is made little by little through evolution, in the three kingdoms, from the atom to man.[141]

In 1897, Fogazzaro came across Zahm's book *Evoluzione e domma*, which fully consolidated his evolutionist views. Soon, he reported his discovery to the Bishop of Cremona, who also purchased and read Zahm's book. At that time, Bonomelli was finishing the first volume of *Seguiamo la ragione* (*Let Us Follow*

unanimity and took the position that the subject required, staying within the compass of science and from there relentlessly unmasking the emptiness of that hypothesis and its ostensible demonstrations. The result was as it should have been and as Fogazzaro himself confesses: the total defeat of the system, which now cannot anymore be sustained because it is demonstrated, but only because someone *wants* to retain it. In this situation, our author proposes the truly poetic and novelesque strategy of abandoning our victorious position and joining the enemy, perhaps for the pleasure of hoisting him on our shoulders, during the proclamation of a Christian evolutionism. I hope the author might excuse us, for we cannot follow him. Science having declared that evolutionism, whether baptized or not, is a myth, has only us believers to sustain it against the crude dogmatism of the unbelievers. We cannot be traitors to her, even if only for the honor and independence of our reason. Then, religious feeling, at least in the way we and most believers experience it, rebels against the idea of denying both science and the doctrines taught by the Church in order to base the concept of Creation upon the dream of minds agitated by incredulity. That would be like erecting some pagan idol on our altars to more worthily represent to us the objects of our sublime Christian cult. To conclude, in this as in any struggle, the false science of unbelief must itself recognize its error. In fact, it is so doing. It certainly is not our role to back the cause [...] and participate in its shame." F. Salis Seewis, "L'origine dell'uomo e il sentimento religioso," *La Civiltá Cattolica* 15, no. 8 (1893), 339. In *Negotiating Darwin*, 208.

140. "A letter from G. Bonomelli to A. Fogazzaro, Cremona, 4 April 1893" in C. Marcora, *Corrispondenza Fogazzaro–Bonomelli* (Milano: Vita e Pensiero, 1968), 146. See *Negotiating Darwin*, 208.

141. "A letter from G. Bonomelli to A. Fogazzaro, Cremona, 9 July 1893," ibid., 149–50. See *Negotiating Darwin*, 209.

Reason), a treatise presenting the essential Catholic truths in the light of reason. At the end of his work he decided to add a thirteen-page text vaguely entitled "Important Appendix." In fact, the "appendix" was a very complimentary opinion of Zahm's book. In the eighth chapter of his work, Bonomelli makes a distinction between evolution as a scientific theory and its materialistic interpretation. He encourages believers to abandon ideology and accept what is possible for them. With reference to the idea of the evolutionary origin of the human body, he states that such an approach had been popular twenty years earlier but was fading.[142] However, in the precipitate "appendix" to the book, he goes further, reiterating Zahm's thesis on the absence of any inconsistency between evolution and the Christian tradition. To him, evolution does not threaten Christianity, and its acceptance agrees with reason and faith:

> Some Catholics . . . , seeing dogma so fiercely attacked, they perhaps launched headlong into their defenses, rejecting that which could be conceded without risk as well: they did not see evolution and transformism except as a formidable machine against the principles of the faith. Now things are better clarified, and it has been recognized that many concessions can be made, while the confines of dogma remain safe. [. . .] We must ease the road for those who are outside the Church, that they might enter, in such a way that no one will find reproachable.[143]

The Italian bishop did not view himself as an expert on scientific matters, but in the book he treats the theory of evolution as valid because it is an expression of modern science. He has no grounds to abandon evolutionism, nor does he have grounds to accept it. Relying on the authority of Zahm, he had apparently decided that the new concept was justified. Still, he was a man open to new solutions in various fields. In consequence, he placed evolution within the realm of science and reason, reiterating that Christianity can oppose neither:

> My cry is this: No fear of science in whatever form it may present itself. If it is true science, it can only come from God and lead us toward God. To fear that science might destroy faith is to err with respect to faith itself, to doubt the divine fundamentals on which it is based. We Catholics should applaud all the new conquests of science, which are conquests of truth, of God himself which is its source.[144]

Undoubtedly, the claim that science is not contrary to faith would have been endorsed by all Bonomelli's opponents, starting from Seewis. However, the Catholic apologists did not say that science was contrary to faith, but that evo-

142. G. Bonomelli, *Seguiamo la ragione* (Milano: 1898), 118.
143. Ibid., 202.
144. Ibid., 202–3.

lutionism was an unfounded hypothesis. As such, evolutionism contradicts science and reason itself, and, next in line, also faith. By identifying evolution with science, Bonomelli shifted the dispute from "evolution vs. creation" to "science vs. religion." In this way he was able to invoke arguments that were very strong and surely correct, but only applicable if his initial assumption was true. The attack on narrow interpretations of the Bible was also only justified if the idea of the separate creation of species and the human body was merely the opinion of some theologians with poor exegetical skills. But the Church experts disagreed with a solely metaphorical interpretation of the Genesis account, for they believed independent creation of species to be the subject of faith, confirmed by Tradition.

Deeper in his "Important Appendix," Bonomelli summarizes Zahm's book, issue by issue, presenting arguments in support of evolution, problems with this theory, and his argument for the compatibility of evolution and Christianity. One might say that the "Important Appendix" became one of the texts which, in Catholic thinking, started to give theistic evolution the status of a view that was not only orthodox, but even best-fitted to the demands of its time.

Nevertheless, when the text was published, the bishop's situation became somewhat complicated. A few controversies around his works—including the circumstance that one of them was listed on the Index, numerous allegations from various parties, and a piece of good advice from Cardinal Agliardi—induced the author to revoke his opinions. In October 1898 the periodical *Lega Lombarda* published Bonomelli's letter recanting his theses from the first volume of *Seguiamo la ragione*:

> I published that appendix with the intent to call attention to possible surprises that modern science holds for us, to motivate both clergy and lay believers to better study the matter, and above all, just as Father Leroy has done in France, as an effort to extend our hands to some intellectuals who vacillate between faith and error. But, right after the publication of my summary and ever since, many kind friends who are reliable both for their knowledge and their authority, have told me in conversation and in writing that this doctrine, even as a simple hypothesis, cannot be made to agree with the common interpretation given by the Church. . . . I deem it appropriate and necessary to ask those readers who take as my own the ideas expressed in the main part of the book, . . . not those which, as a hypothesis, I presented in the appendix, based on Professor Zahm's authority.[145]

This recantation was not well-received by liberal Catholics. However, it was a

145. G. Bonomelli, *Lega Lombarda*, no. 287, Milan, October 25–26, 1898, 1. After *Negotiating Darwin*, op. cit., 214–15.

wise response to the mood in Rome and did much to help save Zahm from the publication of the decree condemning him. Fogazzaro was disappointed, and Duchess Sabina Paraviccino (personally involved in the propagation of evolutionism) wrote in her letter to Rev. Denis O'Connell:

> Bonomelli's letter has left me desolate. He had made up his mind that Zahm was headed for the Index and had no wish to follow him with his famous Appendix. It looks like someone told him that his book *Seguiamo la ragione* had been denounced to the Index on account of the famous appendix, and then he wanted to preempt any action. When I wrote to him, I was not able stop from expressing my shock at his act.[146]

At the same time, Bonomelli justified his decision in his letter to Fogazzaro, saying:

> I must explain: if the theory of evolution were demonstrated and were not just a magnificent hypothesis, but a truth, I too, just like you, would say: even though I might lose my honor and my life, I do not yield, and what I say stands and I affirm it. But as of now it is not a truth, it is a hypothesis, which presents all the characteristics of a future thesis. In this case one can submit to the competent authority. It is known that the opposite of the evolutionist hypothesis is not heresy or even error. Surely condemnation is not infallible, inasmuch as the authority is a respectable Congregation, that is playing an inside game. The time could arrive when the hypothesis becomes a certain thesis, like Galileo's theory: but in the Church, authority must be respected and I respect it: if not, goodbye to discipline and order! All this is reasonable. The whole cosmic order and plan of Providence, not only in the economy of nature but also in the supernatural, require evolutionary theory. . . . But, for now, let us stop here. . . . So let's not worry a lot or a little: truth conquers all and it is necessary to fight so that it does triumph.[147]

Apparently the words of the controversial bishop to the no-less-controversial philosopher were a prophecy of some sort. Without a doubt, Bonomelli believed in evolution and was honestly convinced by the idea of reconciling Catholicism with the theory. Nevertheless, Bonomelli's public statements about evolution ended with the "Important Appendix" and its repeal. Theistic evolution still remained censored in the years that followed.

Press Polemics and the Ideas of Bishop John C. Hedley

John Cuthbert Hedley was born in 1837, in Morpeth, UK. In 1862 he became a

146. "A letter from S. Parravicino to A. Fogazzaro, Cremona, 10 November 1898" in O. Confessore, *L'americanismo cattolico in Italia* (Roma: Studium, 1984), 156. See *Negotiating Darwin*, 216.

147. "A letter from G. Bonomelli to A. Fogazzaro, Cremona, 6 November 1898" in C. Marcora, *Corrispondenza Fogazzaro–Bonomelli*, op. cit., 178–79. See *Negotiating Darwin*, 217.

priest of the Benedictine Order. He worked as a lecturer in philosophy until 1873, when he was appointed auxiliary bishop of the Newport Diocese. He held that office from 1881 until his death in 1915. From 1879 to 1884 he was editor of the *Dublin Review*. Some of his theological works made him a renowned author. The controversy around Hedley's evolutionary sympathies had two phases. The first began in 1898, the second in 1902.

Hedley addresses the views of Zahm in the article "Physical Science and Faith," published in the *Dublin Review* in 1898 (July–October).[148] The article, which is essentially favorable to Zahm's thesis from *Evolution and Dogma*, attracted the attention of the liberal press. As early as October of the same year, the London *Tablet*[149] published an anonymous positive comment about Hedley's paper. The comment found its way into the hands of Duchess Sabina Parravicino, who, though unacquainted with Hedley's original article, decided to translate and publish the text from the *Tablet*, along with her own commentary. It appeared in the Italian paper *La Rassegna Nazionale* under the pseudonym "Theologus," with the title "Le idee di un Vescovo sull'Evoluzione" (The Ideas of One Bishop about Evolution).[150] In reaction to this anonymous text, Salvatore Brandi, S.J. published in *La Civiltá Cattolica* another article of the anti-evolutionary apologetic series, under the same title as Zahm's book (*Evoluzione e domma*).[151] This was the end of the first phase of controversy around Hedley's views.

These articles represent an advanced phase of the dispute during the investigation of Zahm's book by the Congregation of the Index, occurring just when Bishop Bonomelli had decided to revoke his views. First of all, Hedley did not uncritically approve of the ideas of Father Zahm. Although he does state that there is no essential conflict between creation by God and evolution, he also observes that when one penetrates the more detailed aspects of Christianity, some difficulties arise. This point follows the lines of Hedley's much earlier publication, in which he had expressed his reservations against the then-popular theory of Mivart.[152]

Hedley opens his treatment of Zahm by considering the relationship between science and religion. He notices the problem of the possible abuse of science by unbelievers, who may easily be tempted to draw conclusions going beyond what is permitted by the scientific data. There are many ways, he observes, that physical (natural) theories can influence the study of dogmas,

148. J.C. Hedley, "Physical Science and Faith," *Dublin Review* 123 (July–October 1898), 241–61.

149. Anonymous commentary to "Physical Science and Faith," *Tablet* (29 October 1898), 690.

150. Theologus (S. Parravicino), "Le idee di un Vescovo sull'Evoluzione," *La Rassegna Nazionale* 104 (November 16, 1898), 418–20.

151. S.M. Brandi, "Evoluzione e domma," *La Civiltá Cattolica* 17, no. 5 (1898), 34–49.

152. J.C. Hedley, "Dr. Mivart on *Faith and Science*," *Dublin Review* (July–October 1887), 401–19.

the Bible, and even morality. Thus, Catholics may come across theories containing theological or philosophical errors that stem from ignorance of these domains among natural scientists.[153] In consequence, Catholics often reject these new findings as being against faith. Among the examples of such initial "rejection" Hedley names heliocentrism, earth stratification theory, critical analyses of the Bible, and the system of evolution. According to the bishop, condemnation of those doctrines went beyond addressing religious error, and thus was the result of stretching the religious authority beyond its competence. People who did this should have had better advisors. Even though scientific truth, just like any other truth, is a manifestation of the law formulated by God himself, it is of secondary importance in comparison to moral and spiritual truths.

Thus, in the first pages of the article, we learn that the bishop rejects the doctrine of two truths, and sets out a correct hierarchy of statements according to different cognitive levels. However, he also places evolutionism among strict and provable theories of the natural sciences. Therefore, like Bonomelli, he adopts an entirely different perspective than that of Seewis and Brandi, who consistently rejected the possibility of recognizing evolution as reliable science. For Hedley, the dispute was between science and religion; and because there cannot be permanent conflict between science and religion, the problem of evolution and Christianity from his perspective was only apparent. The Catholic apologists, like Seewis and Brandi, also believed in one truth, but for them it was a dispute between false ideology on the one hand and reliable science and religious truth on the other. We can see that the two sides of the dispute, even though both Catholic, entertained different interpretations of the status of evolutionism. As a result, there was no common ground in the debate from the very start.

Later in the article, the English bishop states that, as of that date, the majority of Catholics had accepted the evolutionist view, though not in the version proposed by Haeckel and Spencer. Proceeding to Zahm, the author introduces him as an excellent Catholic scientist who, thanks to independent judgment and clarity of mind, is able to distinguish between acceptable and unacceptable elements in the theory of evolution. Zahm accepts evolution, though he emphasizes that there are many obscurities concerning its mechanisms. In his view the whole universe achieved its present state through evolution, except for the human soul. Evolution, as he understood it, is something different from the "special creation" of various species of living beings by independent acts of God. Hedley emphasizes that most educated Catholics had abandoned the idea of special creation in response to arguments from geology, paleontology, and

153. J.C. Hedley, *Physical Science and Faith*, 242.

embryology. Nonetheless, he further explains, "Still there are amongst us not a few who consider that the theory of evolution leads to atheism and to materialism, that it is equivalent to a denial of Divine Providence, that it leaves God without witness in the world, that it is against Holy Scripture, and that it cannot be reconciled with Catholic philosophy."[154] He then attempts to refute these allegations with the use of Zahm's ideas.

Hedley notes that the ideas of the American priest are sometimes too optimistic, and, unlike Zahm, Hedley imposes certain restrictions on evolutionary explanations: they can tell us nothing about God's actions in the universe. The emergence of the human soul in particular requires special Divine intervention and is not subject to the process of evolution. Moreover, he thinks it more probable that there had been supernatural interventions in the emergence of the first life and the body of man. Taking into account these reservations that, according to Hedley, were outside the jurisdiction of science, a believer can rationally accept the theory of evolution without harm to the faith. "Thus, it may fairly be said that, whatever the assertions and generalizations of unbelieving philosophers, there is nothing in the theory of evolution, or proved by fact, that is really antagonistic to Catholic faith."[155]

Salvatore Brandi noted that, according to Hedley, evolution may be accepted on the condition that divine intervention is recognized with respect to the creation of the soul, and probably also with respect to the formation of the first life and the human body. However, Brandi believes this solution is not credible, and asks how it could be possible that evolution is palatable only if we accept all the reservations that are repugnant to the basic principles of evolution, as defended by Spencer, Haeckel, Darwin, Wallace, Mivart, and others. Catholic writers, eager to agree with scientific "novelties," are not afraid to be illogical and incoherent.[156] Brandi's objection is serious because he points to the fundamental difficulty of "theistic evolution": it disagrees both with the postulates of natural scientists, who seek to dismiss any supernatural causation in the natural world, and with traditional Catholic philosophy, which speaks about the supernatural origin of life, species, and humanity. Over the next ten pages of his article, Brandi outlines a solid critique of Zahm's views; at one point, he writes that the theory of evolution "is a fantastic edifice and there is no better way to describe it than as a tissue of vulgar analogies and arbitrary suppositions that are not supported by the facts."[157]

Brandi analyzes the compatibility of evolution with Catholic theology on

154. Ibid., 246.
155. Ibid., 253.
156. Cf. *Negotiating Darwin*, 228.
157. Ibid., 45.

four different levels: with reference to the Bible, the Catholic Tradition, the Magisterium of the Church, and reason. Having shown the scientific weakness of the theory, he states that it would be careless to abandon the natural and traditional interpretation of the Holy Scriptures on the origin of man:

> The first impediment to accepting evolution for educated Catholics comes not from the fear of contradicting the Bible, but from the scientific insufficiency of that system, that is, the absolute lack of evidence that confirms it, whether as a theory or as a hypothesis. In this situation, it seems to me that whoever stubbornly defends the theory of the human body's descent from a monkey or any other animal, against the traditional views of the Church Fathers, can with good reason be called rash. Besides the respect due to the Bible, it is certainly required that the words of eternal Truth not be interpreted and warped on the basis of gratuitous hypotheses, to make them say today in obedience to one theory, what will be said tomorrow in obedience to another.[158]

Referring to the arguments "from the Church doctrine," Brandi invokes Zahm's suggestion that the Magisterium had never condemned evolution. According to the Italian apologist, the fact that the Church had not condemned evolution is not a sufficient argument for a Catholic to endorse it. In support, Brandi quotes Pope Pius IX:

> A Catholic ought to reject not only the opinions formally condemned by the Church and those that are opposed to the doctrines it has defined or taught through its ordinary Magisterium; he should likewise repudiate ideas that he knows are contrary to the opinions that the common and consistent consensus of Catholics holds as theological truths and conclusions, as certain as the opinions contrary to them, though they cannot be called heretical, still merit theological censure.[159]

Finally, Brandi recalls the case of Leroy as an author who had to recant his evolutionist views in response to Church action taken against his publication.

In January, 1899, two months after the article by Brandi, Bishop Hedley published a sort of correction in the *Tablet*. It was not a retraction of his own views but rather a call for attention to the fact that Leroy—like Mivart—had postulated the evolution of the human body from lower animals. If the ideas of Leroy were rejected by a competent Church authority, he argued, then obviously Mivart's theory, even if it had not been explicitly condemned, could not be maintained by Catholics. However, Hedley himself had never endorsed

158. Ibid., 45–46.

159. Ibid., 46–47. The statement by Pius IX comes from the letter *Tuas libenter* to the Archbishop of Munich of December 21, 1863. See H. Denzinger, A. Schönmetzer, *Enchridion Symbolorum, Definitionum, Declarationum* (Freiburg: Herder, 1966), DS 2875–80.

Mivart's claims and never promoted human evolution from lower animals. Therefore, this paper was not a recantation of his own views, but rather a kind of clarification given to the decisions of the Church authorities regarding Leroy's case and the idea of human evolution. The press polemic ended after this, only to re-emerge for a short time two years later.

In 1902, a statement by Hedley describing his own evolutionist views appeared in the book *England and the Holy See* by a Protestant author, Spencer Jones.[160] Explaining his position, the bishop remarked that none of his writings had been reproached by the Holy See. Recalling the polemic from two years before, Hedley explained that the article from *La Civiltá* by Brandi had not given an accurate account of his case, because it implied that any pro-evolutionary approach was untenable for a Catholic. However, to that point, argued Hedley, evolution had not been condemned by the Roman congregations. The press recantation by Leroy only mentioned "competent authority" as having kept his book from dissemination. But this might have referred just to Leroy's religious superiors, not the higher Church authorities in charge of the doctrinal teaching. Therefore, Hedley argued, Brandi's criticism was unfounded.

In response to this observation by Hedley, Brandi this time limited himself to a three-page text entitled "Evoluzione e domma: Erronee informazioni di un Inglese" ("Evolution and Dogma: Erroneous Information from an Englishman").[161] Brandi argued that Hedley downplayed the Church's negative stance on evolution. As a matter of fact, neither the English bishop nor the Italian Jesuit was fully informed about the decisions on Leroy and Zahm made in Rome. Hedley unquestionably diminished their importance, attributing them merely to religious superiors. Brandi, on the other hand, found himself in a difficult situation, as he probably had some unofficial information about the unpublished decree in Zahm's case. However, he could only mention the official facts; i.e., the press corrections presented by the particular authors. In his reply he invokes Leroy's letter published seven years earlier in *Le Monde* and Zahm's letter made public in *Gazzetta di Malta*. Nevertheless, Brandi erroneously attributed the recantations of both scholars to the actions of the Holy Office, instead of the Congregation of the Index.

The articles written by Brandi—who lived in Rome and published his writings in the official Catholic press—were regarded as a credible source of information both for his contemporaries and the later scholars. The result was that many important facts concerning the early debate about evolution in the Church remained unknown or misinterpreted until 1998. It is also worth not-

160. S. Jones, *England and the Holy See: An Essay towards Reunion* (London: Longmans, 1902).

161. S. Brandi, "*Evoluzione e domma*: Erronee informazioni di un Inglese," *La Civiltá Cattolica* 18, no. 6 (1902), 75–77.

ing that the second Hedley-Brandi polemic concerned not so much the substantial arguments in the evolution-creation debate, but rather the interpretation of the Church's position. It supplanted the question: Does evolution agree with the Catholic faith?—with the question: Does the Church admit evolution? The important problem of the very compatibility between faith and evolution was thus replaced with the secondary issue of the interpretation of the Catholic position, a perspective that still predominates. Looking at the further development of the discussion, it seems that after the year 1900, Catholic apologists less and less frequently referred to arguments based on "Tradition" and "sound philosophy."

5

The Pontifical Biblical Commission Decrees, 1905–1909

Origin and Content of the Decrees

In October 1902 Pope Leo XIII issued the Apostolic Letter *Vigilantiae Studiique*, which established The Pontifical Biblical Commission. The original Commission consisted of cardinals and biblical experts appointed by the Pope, and its structure was similar to that of Roman congregations. Its pronouncements had doctrinal value and were binding. In 1907 Pope Pius X issued a motu proprio *Praestantia Scripturae Sacrae*, in which he announced:

> We do now declare and expressly prescribe, that all are bound in conscience to submit to the decisions of the Biblical Commission, which have been given in the past and which shall be given in the future, in the same way as to the Decrees which appertain to doctrine, issued by the Sacred Congregations and approved by the Sovereign Pontiff.[1]

During the first years of its activity (1905–1915) the Commission issued fourteen documents, titled *Responsum* ("reply"), regarding the interpretation and historicity of the Books of the Bible. The documents included a total of fifty-nine questions. The replies were technical and limited to "yes" and "no," and only occasionally included additional comments. The actual doctrinal content was

1. EB 271. "Quapropter declarandum illud praecipiendumque videmus, quemadmodum declaramus in praesens expresseque praecipimus, universos omnes conscientiae obstringi oficio sententiis Pontificalis Consilii de Re Biblica, sive quae adhuc sunt emissae, sive quae posthac edentur, perinde ac. Decretis Sacrarum Congregationum pertinentibus ad doctrinam probatisque a Pontifice, se subiiciendi." After *Enchiridion Biblicum. Documenta Ecclesiastica Sacram Scripturam Spectantia: Auctoritate Pontificiae Comissionis de Re Biblica edita* (Roma: Apud Librariam Vaticanam, 1927), 87. An interesting historical analysis of the significance of the Pontifical Biblical Commission was proposed by John F. McCarthy in his article *Pontifical Biblical Commission: Yesterday And Today*, available at: http://www.catholicculture.org/culture/library/view.cfm?recnum=4679 (February 2, 2015).

included in the questions themselves, which, although indeed posed by researchers, were carefully edited and precisely defined by the Commission's experts. *Responsa* were later incorporated into *Enchiridion Biblicum*, a collection of the Church's doctrinal pronouncements regarding Holy Scripture.[2]

There were four documents relevant to the questions of evolution: 1. "On the Tacit Quotations Contained in the Holy Scripture" (February 13, 1905); 2. "Decree Concerning the Narratives in the Historical Books Which Have Only the Appearances of Being Historical" (June 23, 1905); 3. "On the Mosaic Authorship of the Pentateuch" (June 27, 1906), and 4. "On the Historical Character of the First Three Chapters of Genesis" (June 30, 1909), all four of which have been cited by pro-evolutionary writers. The implication is that these four were viewed as a potential obstacle in adopting the evolutionary interpretation of the biblical account of the creation of the world.[3]

The first decree addresses the inconsistencies of the Bible's historical narratives. The question was worded as follows:

> Whether it is allowable for a Catholic commentator to solve difficulties occurring in certain texts of Holy Scripture, which apparently relate historical facts, by asserting that we have in such texts tacit or implied quotations from documents written by a non-inspired author, and that the inspired author by no means intends to approve of these statements or make them his own, and that these statements cannot, in consequence, be regarded as free from error.

The Commission replies in the negative, unless it can be proved based on reliable arguments that the inspired author (1) is indeed quoting somebody and (2) that he has no intention to regard the quotation as expressing a viewpoint that he himself shares. The reply was intended to protect the Bible from being freely interpreted by scholars using the critical-historical method. The decree was signed by David Fleming (already known from the Zahm case), who at that time was the Commission's consultant.[4]

The second decree, also signed by Fleming, responds to the following question:

> Whether we may admit as a principle of sound exegesis the opinion which holds that those books of Holy Scripture which are regarded as historical, either wholly or in part, sometimes narrate what is not history properly so-called and objectively true, but only have the appearance of history and are

2. *Enchiridion Biblicum*, 57–122.

3. One of those who referred to the documents was H. Dorlodot—the first scholar promoting theistic evolution whose writings did not encounter any reaction from the Magisterium. H. Dorlodot, *Darwinism and Catholic Thought*.

4. *Enchiridion Biblicum*, 57–58 (EB 160).

> intended to convey a meaning different from the strictly literal or historical sense of the words.

The response, in the negative, contained the following reservation:

> Excepting always the case—not to be easily or rashly admitted, and then only on the supposition that it is not opposed to the teaching of the Church and subject to her decision—that it can be proved by solid arguments that the sacred writer did not intend to give a true and strict history, but proposed rather to set forth, under the guise and form of history, a parable or an allegory or some meaning distinct from the strictly literal or historical signification of the words.[5]

The third decree provides an answer to four questions related to the authorship of the Pentateuch.[6] It is worth quoting them in full:

> (1) Whether the accumulated arguments by critics to impugn the Mosaic authenticity (*authentia Mosaica*) of the sacred books designated by the name Pentateuch are of sufficient weight, notwithstanding the very many evidences to the contrary contained in both Testaments, taken collectively, the persistent agreement of the Jewish people, the constant tradition of the Church, and internal arguments derived from the text itself, to justify the statement that these books have not Moses for their author but have been compiled from sources for the most part posterior to the time of Moses. Answer: "No."

> (2) The Mosaic authenticity of the Pentateuch (*Mosaica authentia Pentateuchi*) necessarily postulates such a redaction of the whole work as to render it absolutely imperative to maintain that Moses wrote with his own hand or dictated to amanuenses all and everything contained in it; or whether it is possible to admit the hypothesis of those who think that he entrusted the composition of the work itself, conceived by himself under the influence of divine inspiration, to some other person or persons, but in such a manner that they render faithfully his own thoughts, wrote nothing contrary to his will, and omitted nothing; and that the work thus produced, approved by Moses as the principal and inspired author, was made public under his name. Answer: "No" to the first part, "yes" to the second part.

According to this reply, a Catholic does not need to maintain that Moses wrote down or dictated the entire Pentateuch himself, but rather that the Pentateuch is compliant with what he preached, thus gaining Moses's approval and in a certain way becoming his own creation. Therefore, the Pentateuch does not contain anything that would be inconsistent with his inspired spirit or intentions.

5. Ibid., 58 (EB 161).
6. Ibid., 62–63 (EB 181–84).

> (3) Whether it may be granted, without prejudice to the Mosaic authenticity of the Pentateuch, that Moses employed sources in the production of his work, i.e., written documents or oral traditions, from which, to suit his special purpose and under the influence of divine inspiration, he selected some things and inserted them in his work, either literally or in substance, summarized or amplified. Answer: "Yes."

Hence, the Commission did not claim the lack of any externally derived narrations, which can be easily recognized even from non-scholarly readings of the text. The decree does, however, rule out the presence of many different, contradictory, or later traditions and issues in the sacred text.

> (4) Whether, granted the substantial Mosaic authenticity (*substantialiter Mosaica authentia*) and the integrity of the Pentateuch, it may be admitted that in the long course of centuries some modifications have been introduced into the work, such as additions after the death of Moses, either appended by an inspired author or inserted into the text as glosses and explanations; certain words and forms translated from the ancient language to a more recent language, and finally, faulty readings to be ascribed to the error of amanuenses, concerning which it is lawful to investigate and judge according to the laws of criticism. Answer: "Yes, subject to the judgment of the Church."

The fourth and the most significant document is the 1909 response on the literal understanding of Genesis.[7] It consists of eight questions. The first three sections constitute a rejection of the critical-exegetical claim that the historical and literal meaning of Genesis 1–3 should not be maintained:

> (1) Whether the various exegetical systems, which, in order to exclude the literal, historical sense of the first three chapters of the book of Genesis, have been devised and put forward under the guise of science, are supported by a solid foundation? Answer: "No."

The statement, formulated in a positive manner, meant that historical criticism or criticism of form (so-called higher criticism) is not a reliable science if it leads to the questioning of the historical meaning of the Bible. In other words, there is no method of analysis that could invalidate the historical and literal meaning. The following questions contain more specific characteristics of the historicity of the first three chapters of the Bible. The second question concerns the general historicity of the events recounted in Genesis 1–3:

> (2) Whether, notwithstanding the historical character and form of the book of Genesis, the specific connections of the first three chapters among themselves and with the following chapters, the manifold witness of the Scriptures from both the Old and New Testaments, the nearly unanimous opinion of the

7. Ibid., 98–100 (EB 324–331).

holy Fathers, and the traditional sense, which, transmitted also by the Israeli people, the Church has always held, it is able to be taught, that the aforesaid three chapters of Genesis contain, not narratives of things that truly occurred; that is, narratives that correspond to objective realities and historical truths; but are either fables drawn from the mythologies and cosmogonies of primitive peoples and, purged of any polytheistic errors, accommodated to monotheistic doctrine by the sacred author; or allegories and symbols, lacking a foundation in objective reality, given under the appearance of history in order to inculcate proposed religious and philosophical truths; or finally legends, partly historical and partly fictitious, freely composed for the instruction and edification of souls? In the negative to every part.

The third question specifies which events in particular must be held as historical:

(3) Whether in particular the literal, historical sense can possibly be called into doubt, where it is treated in the same chapters of the narrated facts that belong to the foundations of the Christian religion: as, among others, the creation of all things by God at the beginning of time; the special creation of man (*peculiaris creatio hominis*); the formation of the first woman out of the first man (*formatio primae mulieris ex primo homine*); the unity of the human race; the original happiness of our first parents in a state of justice, integrity and immortality; the command given by God to man in order to test his obedience; the transgression of the divine command, with the devil under the appearance of a serpent as counselor; the casting out of our first parents from that primæval state of innocence; and the promise of a future Redeemer? Answer: "No."

In subsequent responses the decree pronounced that (4) if a passage of those three chapters had been interpreted by the Church Fathers and Saint Doctors differently, without establishing anything definite, then one could, while remaining compliant with the teachings of the Church and analogy of the faith, interpret them according to one's own prudent convictions; (5) moreover, if in a certain passage a literal interpretation shall be in opposition to reason, one may abandon such interpretation with regard to certain words or phrases;[8] (6) one may also, assuming the literal and historical sense, recognize additional allegorical and prophetic understanding of those texts in compliance with the interpretations of the Church Fathers; (7) a Catholic scholar is not, however, obliged to try to find in every phrase a strictly scientific meaning; (8) for example, the

8. "Are we bound to interpret in their strictly literal sense every single thing, words namely and phrases, in these chapters, so as never to depart from it even when expressions are patently not used in the strict sense but metaphorically or anthropomorphically, and when, too, reason or necessity compels us to give up the literal sense? Negative reply." 99–100 (EB 328).

word *day* (Hebrew *Yôm*), used in the description of the creation, may be understood either in its literal meaning, as a natural day, or in the sense of an unidentified period of time; free discussion on the matter is allowed.[9]

The decree defends the sacred text against the arbitrary interpretations to which Catholic exegesis was more and more often subjected. The time of publication of the decree coincided with the peak of the modernism controversy, at the core of which was the discussion regarding the approach to the Bible. From the evolutionary viewpoint, the decrees issued in the years 1905–1909 pose a great difficulty for the theistic theory of evolution, although, as it turns out, not an insurmountable obstacle. We can now consider what effects the documents had for the accommodation of evolution within the Church.

The Significance of the Decree on the Historical Character of Genesis 1–3 (1909)

The 1909 decree of the Pontifical Biblical Commission claims that Genesis tells a true history of the creation of the world. Thus it shall neither be construed merely as a metaphor, nor as a legal statement, justifying, for example, the necessity of the Sabbath. It is not just a hymn exalting the miracles of God's works. Nor is it just an ancient poem originating in other cultures and later incorporated by some editor into the Pentateuch. All of those interpretations were popular in Catholic circles as early as at the beginning of the 20th century, but the Commission points out that they were reductive and gutted the text of its essential meaning.

While the biblical account is not a scientific report or a history textbook, that does not mean that it does not tell a true history. The decree echoes Tripepi's report, stating that "it is completely different to say that there are metaphors in the first pages of Genesis, and to say that these pages are metaphors."[10]

In line with the literal and historical sense of the text, one may easily note that the description concords the most with the stance nowadays referred to as progressive creationism. God creates at certain intervals. First he creates the heaven and the earth, which Church tradition understands as the world of angels (the invisible universe) and the matter of the physical world (the visible part of creation). The matter is, however, formed in some way, because otherwise it would only be first matter (*materia prima*) and would not exist in an actual manner. Genesis 1:2 defines that state of matter as *tohu vabohu* (chaos, formlessness, and emptiness). Next, the physical universe is gradually formed by the Word, i.e., by God's power. God's Word creates celestial bodies and plan-

9. *Enchiridion Biblicum*, 99 (EB 335–39).

10. Cf. Chapter Four, under "The Intervention of the Congregation of the Index."

etary systems. The waters do not create numerous animals on their own; it all happens due to God's activity of uttering the words of creation. All beings are born by God's Word, as if at one moment and "according to their kinds" (Hebrew *l'mînô*). Thus, we have a few stages in the creation of large groups of different species. The second, subsequent description of creation talks about God molding from clay all land animals and birds (Gen 2:19). This means that the manner in which those beings were created was similar in each case and the same as the manner in which God created man.

Before forming a human body, God seems to stop and say: "Let us make man in our own image, in the likeness of ourselves" (Gen 1:26a). Man, therefore, is a result of a separate idea, of God's design, and is thus endowed with the image of the Creator. Yet his body, as in the case of animals (cf. Gen 2:19) is also formed by God's power from the dust of the earth. Dust is not a living being. The body starts living when God fills it with a spirit. Before that moment it had no life at all. The body itself is created from the dust, something formless, insignificant, albeit belonging to the matter of this world. The material from which God forms man comes from the ground; and such a material is not capable of anything by itself. It is exactly like clay in the hands of a potter: it needs an intelligent, effective power in order to be turned into a useful form.

Next, God creates a woman from the side, that is, the body of Adam, and then God supplements the lack in his body that resulted from the formation of the woman. Hence, Adam does not lack anything when the woman is created; and the woman is fully herself, because she, like Adam, was created by God's infinite power. This is how Genesis reveals the complete humanity and direct descent from God of both parents.

Man's direct descent from God gives him dignity not only because of his immortal soul, but also because of the body. As Saint Paul puts it, "your body is the temple of the Holy Spirit, who is in you and whom you received from God" (1 Cor 6:19). On the other hand, the description of the creation of the first parents establishes a proper relationship between them as well as a proper understanding of their identity. Gender is not just a cultural construct; instead it is embedded in human nature—this is the way the human was created by God. In addition, gender identity presupposes the complementarity of man and woman to the extent that one cannot live without the other, or at least that "it is not good" if one lives in such a way (cf. Gen 2:18).

Thus man's value and dignity are increased not only because man was directly created by God, but also because the manner in which that creation took place is significant. The first man—at the time of creation embodying all of mankind—rises up from the ground in order to make him aware of the fact that he is a part of the world, that he is not an alien here. He is not a stranger from the beyond wandering accidentally on this particular planet, but is intimately connected to the planet at the very basic level of his existence—he rises up from it and returns to it at his death.

Another essential aspect of the account is that Eve was formed from Adam's rib. Not from any other part of the body, but from the rib. There is no other part in Adam's body that could be used and would guarantee both the unity of humankind and equality of both sexes. In any other case, either one sex would be lacking something and the other would be favored, or both would be humiliated. Thus creating the woman from the rib not only does not diminish anything, but benefits both sexes.[11] Since in Adam God complemented what He had taken from him, and in Eve He created far more than He had taken from Adam, thus, she also is a result of God's direct action. Hence, both can enjoy the unity of their origin and equal dignity of their bodies as well as their souls being created directly by God. This is why when Genesis mentions Adam's rib it is not some redundant detail or metaphorical appendix. It constitutes one of the central truths on which the dignity and identity of mankind is based.

So what challenges to the evolutionary interpretation of the origin of species and of man are posed by the literal sense of Genesis? First of all, evolution, even in its limited form, assumes the gradual development of different life-forms from one or a few primordial ones. According to Holy Scripture, however, somewhat suddenly a multitude of individuals appears. It is true that in the case of sea creatures and some land creatures the Bible says, "Let the water teem" (Gen 1:20) and "Let the land produce" (Gen 1:11, 24), but it all happens at God's Word. Rather than a gradual formation of each of them, there is the sudden emergence of an entire group, followed by a break and then again creation of more individuals distinguished immediately according to their kind. Thus instead of natural, secondary causality, we see supernatural, direct activity. The biblical description would accord with a concept of evolution if it explicitly differentiated between the emergence of a primordial organism and the emergence of all subsequent organisms as a result of the ordinary actions of nature. There are, after all, many examples of such a "natural course of nature" in the Old Testament[12]—whereas the description of creation represents something exceptional, something that happened only once, over a specific period of time

11. Thomas Aquinas comments: "It was right for the woman to be made from a rib of man. First, to signify the social union of man and woman. . . . Secondly, for the sacramental signification; for from the side of Christ sleeping on the Cross the Sacraments flowed—namely, blood and water—on which the Church was established." *S.Th.*, I, 92, a. 3, c.

12. Eccl 1:4–7: "A generation goes and a generation comes, But the earth remains forever. Also, the sun rises and the sun sets; And hastening to its place it rises there again. Blowing toward the south, Then turning toward the north, The wind continues swirling along; And on its circular courses the wind returns. All the rivers flow into the sea, Yet the sea is not full. To the place where the rivers flow, There they flow again."

("six days"), the results of which, in the form of diversity of species, are still observable today.

If we adopt the view that God acted with his direct causative power only on the first day—that is, at the moment he created "the heavens and the earth" from nothingness, and then entrusted the rest to the actions of secondary causes—then the "seventh day," the day of God's rest, becomes inexplicable. The Bible says that there was a "time of work," a period described as six days in which God acted in a specific manner. The Biblical Commission's decree allows for an interpretation of a biblical day as not necessarily a "natural day." Thus it should not be ruled out that those six days were a very long period of time in which the world was formed, the traces of which we may find in fossil records. At some point, however, that period of God's creative activity definitively ended and God rested (Gen 2:2). This is why we do not see the emergence of entirely new species in nature. At most we observe some variations, like the formation of races, varieties, or even biological species, but never new genera or families. Thus bare facts, stripped of evolutionary theory, comply with the account in Genesis.

Another difficulty for theistic evolution is the description of the molding of all animals and birds from the soil of the earth (Gen 2:19). Such a description not only does not stand in concord with the evolutionary concept of the emergence of beings, but it flatly contradicts it. The lack of concordance becomes evident when the general meanings seem to point to something else. Thus there is no concordance between God's "Let there be" (which God says on several occasions for each particular group of organisms) and the evolutionary concept of species being created by natural processes. A positive exclusion, in turn, takes place when the Bible talks in a more detailed way about *how* God creates. We can see that the Bible does say *how* God creates, and not only *that* He creates. The entire description is filled with many details regarding the *how*. The Bible, for example, says that God created Eve from Adam's rib, and not Adam's leg or arm.

Further on, Genesis says also that God created animals from clay. At the turn of the 19th century such a literal interpretation was discarded by scholars who based their opinions on scientific claims. In the Catholic tradition, however, abandoning the literal interpretation is only permissible if it contradicts reason. And that is why a Roman consultant asked: "God could create. Could he not have created and acted in the way indicated by the literal sense? Who might dare to say so?"[13] Neither the creation of species nor that of man directly by God using existing material in the form of clay contradicts reason or is beyond

13. Cf. Tripepi's report, Chapter Four, under "The Intervention of the Congregation of the Index."

God's power. Since Holy Scripture expresses these truths clearly and straightforwardly, abandoning them could only be warranted by very serious arguments. Most Catholic theologians at the beginning of the 20th century did not find such arguments. The core of the problem was that the evolutionary theologians abandoned the literal sense, appealing to "scientific achievements," even though the science of the time could offer no evidence either to prove the evolutionary origin of species or to disprove their creation.

According to theistic evolutionists, the first human body is an effect of processes similar to those in connection with which other animal organisms were created—by being gradually formed from a lower form of life. However, in the biblical account we find a kind of leap: as if God stopped for a moment before creating man—the first human body, not just a soul. The words "Let us make man in our image" themselves imply a different nature of the forthcoming being. The Bible goes on to say: "Then the Lord God formed man of dust from the ground, and breathed into his nostrils the breath of life; and man became a living being" (Gen 2:7). The Bible does not say that "God has chosen the most perfect of animals and breathed a spiritual soul into it," but rather that He "shaped man from the soil of the ground." He breathed life into the body, which means that previously the body was not living. God did not breathe the light of intellect or some additional faculty into an already-formed living structure. It was through God's breath that the molded figure gained life, a full life, that is, at all levels—vegetative, sensory, and intellectual. There is no place in Holy Scripture that would indicate or allude to the fact that man is of animal origin.[14] Even greater obstacles face a "metaphorical" interpretation of the origin of the first woman. The origin of Eve was such a great problem for evolutionary interpretation that even Leroy, in dispute with Brucker, ultimately acknowledged her special formation.

14. There are many places in the Scriptures that speak of human origins. All of them, however, point towards God immediately molding man from clay. Job 10:8–9: "Your hands fashioned and made me altogether, And would You destroy me? Remember now, that You have made me as clay; And would You turn me into dust again?" Job 33:4: "The Spirit of God has made me, and the breath of the Almighty gives me life." Job 33:6: "Behold, I belong to God like you; I too have been formed out of the clay." Eccl 3:22: "Both [men and beasts] have the same life-breath, and man has no advantage over the beast; but all is vanity. Both go to the same place; both were made from dust and to the dust they both return." Sir 17:1: "God created man of the earth, and made him after his own image." Wis 7:1: "I myself am a mortal man, like all others, and of the race of him, that was first made of the earth, and in the womb of my mother I was fashioned to be flesh." Ps 119:73: "Your hands have made me and formed me." 2 Macc 7:28: "I beseech you, my son, look upon heaven and earth, and all that is in them, and consider that God made them out of nothing, and mankind also." Especially in the last fragment, the Bible emphasizes that God does not employ any indirect causes, but rather creates Himself, directly from nothing. The genealogy of Jesus also does not put any creature between Adam and God (cf. Lk 3:38).

To summarize the discussion of the decree of the Pontifical Biblical Commission, one should emphasize that it is the literal sense of Genesis (chapters 1–3) that indicates how the world was created. The principle of historical and literal exegesis, applied to the origin of species and mankind, has caused insurmountable obstacles for the theistic theory of evolution, which turned out to contradict the natural sense of the words in Holy Scripture. One may therefore say that the decrees from the years 1905–1909, and especially the last one (on the historical character of Genesis 1–3), have ruled out biological macroevolution, giving Catholic scholars an alternative, positive response to the question about origins.

The Misinterpretation of the Decrees of the Pontifical Biblical Commission

The year 1909 marked the first significant "Darwinian anniversary," as it had been 100 years since the birth of the British researcher and 50 years since the publication of *On the Origin of Species*. Such anniversaries have always provided an opportunity to propagate Darwin's theory. This time, at the invitation of Cambridge University, the celebration included a participant from the Catholic University of Louvain.[15] On its behalf, Fr. Henri de Dorlodot (1855–1929) delivered a lecture in which he claimed that he did not believe there still existed scientists who were not convinced of Darwinian evolution. Dorlodot also compared Darwin's work to the achievements of Newton. What the latter discovered in the inorganic world, he argued, the former extended to the world of living organisms: "Darwin was the interpreter of the organic world, just as Newton was the voice from heaven come to tell us of the glory of the Creator, and to proclaim that the universe is a work truly worthy of His hand."[16] The lecture was a clear manifestation of support for both Darwin's work and its theological implications. The theory of evolution was also propagated by other authors, such as Fr. John O'Brian and the Jesuit Karl Frank, but Dorlodot's lectures are the most representative of that time.

A few years later Dorlodot was asked by the University of Louvain to give

15. Dorlodot himself often emphasized the support that his stance on evolution was given by the authorities of the Catholic University of Louvain. The introduction to his book included the following statement: "If the thesis of the origin of man by way of evolution had been regarded as in substance worthy of condemnation—if Darwin were a heretic on this point, as certain people have declared—then the three Doctors of Divinity in the Rectoral Council [...] would not have insisted as they did that the University should not fail to join in the celebration at Cambridge, and the Rectoral Council would have been obliged to decline the invitation" (H. Dorlodot, *Darwinism and Catholic Thought*, 2–3).

16. Cf. H. Dorlodot, *Darwinism and Catholic Thought*, Appendix V, 177. Por. D. O'Leary, *Roman Catholicism and Modern Science*, 126–27.

lectures to professors on the theory of evolution. Two extensive conferences were later published as the book *Le Darwinisme au point de vue de l'Orthodoxie Catholique* (1921), more widely disseminated in its English translation, titled *Darwinism and Catholic Thought* (1922).[17] The main message was that Christianity is entirely consistent with an evolutionary understanding of the creation of the world.

Dorlodot stands, as he put it, between absolute (that is, including cosmic and chemical) evolution and "creationism" or "fixism." He bases his position on two principles: (1) the beginning of living beings is a result of a special act of God, who breathed life into one or a number of basic organisms; (2) primordial organisms, through evolution over the span of many centuries, gave rise to all other organic species that exist today or that we know existed in the past through fossil evidence.[18]

After a brief account of the encyclical *Providentissimus Deus*, the Belgian priest goes on to discuss the decrees of the Biblical Commission. First he recognizes their formal significance, even recalling Pius X's 1907 motu proprio *Praestantiae Scripturae Sacrae*. Then he introduces principles for understanding these documents: "For instance, if the Biblical Commission declares that we may not affirm with certainty (*affirmare cum certitudo*) an opinion, it does not thereby follow that we may not regard it as a possible view."[19] Having discussed the "Decree on the Mosaic Authorship of the Pentateuch," Dorlodot does not see any reason not to present the documentary hypothesis (Welhausen's hypothesis) and consider Moses merely a compiler of the Pentateuch: "The part of Genesis which specially interests us is thus the work of a compiler, whom we will call Moses if you wish, and who composed it by piecing together two fragments of different literary origin."[20] Finally, the scholar proposes that the first chapter of the Book of Genesis was written to express the fundamental truth that God created everything and to direct people to the true religion.[21] That is, he restricts the biblical message to include only the fact *that* God created, not *how* God created.

Commenting on the 1909 decree "On the Historical Character of the First Three Chapters of Genesis," Dorlodot once again emphasizes the meaning and significance of the document. In reference to the third reply (to whether the literal, historical sense of Scripture can be called into doubt), he states that the decree discusses only a few fundamental Christian truths that should be under-

17. H. Dorlodot, *Darwinism and Catholic Thought.*
18. Ibid., 4.
19. Ibid., 18.
20. Ibid., 20–21.
21. Ibid., 30–31.

stood in their literal sense, but "only one of these has to do with the subject of [evolution]: that of the creation of all things made by God in the beginning of time."[22] Thus the Belgian scholar takes only one out of five truths listed by the Biblical Commission as relevant to a proper understanding of Genesis 1–3. The Commission's list, however, includes two more significant phrases: "special creation of man" and "the creation of the first woman from the first man." The word "special" is used to distinguish this event from "natural events," and "creation" is used to underline that it was not a long-lasting process, but an instant event.[23]

After quoting the fifth reply—that the literal understanding of the biblical account of creation may be abandoned only if doing so is dictated by reason—Dorlodot has no difficulty further interpreting the decree:

> In this Reply the Pontifical Commission makes it sufficiently clear that it considers the style of the first three chapters of Genesis to be fairly figurative. . . . The Commission clearly suggests here that certain too literal interpretations which were held at other times must now necessarily be abandoned. . . .[24] The setting-out of the questions makes it sufficiently evident that the opinion which considers the *Hexameron* as belonging to the class of literature known as figurative and popular history meets with the entire approval of the Commission.[25]

In the 1920s and 1930s Father Dorlodot's views became practically the norm in Catholic academic communities. Invoking the Church Fathers and St. Thomas Aquinas to support the theory of evolution—which just two decades before the Roman consultant Buonpensiere had considered "defaming to the saints"—had become common in theological interpretation. Soon St. Augustine was considered the "father of evolution" and scholars ignored the arguments of apologists as well as the doctrinal statements of the Church. The beginning of the twentieth century undoubtedly witnessed a significant change in the approach to theistic evolution in Catholicism.[26] It is noticeable, however, that while this change occurred within mainstream theology, the Magisterial

22. Ibid., 21.

23. The Scholastic definition of creation which is behind the Papal Commission's decree reads: "*Creatio non est mutatio sed simplex emanatio entis ex nihilo*" (Creation is not a change but simple emanation of being out of nothing).

24. Ibid., 22.

25. Ibid., 23–24.

26. The change of the approach to evolution took place also in Protestantism, and even in Judaism. See more on the development of theistic evolutionism in Judaism in R.G. Olson, *Science and Religion* 1450–1900 (Baltimore: The Johns Hopkins University Press, 2004), 216ff. Cf. H.W. Paul, *The Edge of Contingency. French Catholic Reactions to Scientific Change from Darwin to Duhem* (Gainesville: University Press of Florida, 1979), 101ff.

teaching remained unchanged. Thus in the following decades the discrepancy between an official Church doctrine and the speculations of pro-evolutionary theologians only grew.

Catholic evolutionists, unable to gain open support from the bishops, attempted to influence the Magisterium in a different manner. In the summer of 1925 a group of secular and clerical scholars organized an international session referred to by some as the "synod of Altamira." Over four days the session discussed the issues surrounding evolution. It ended with a memorandum asserting the complete consistency of Christianity with the theories of evolution. Once again the Church Fathers, and especially St. Augustine, were the main focus. The document was presented to Pope Pius XI for his official approval. The Pope did not grant it, but neither did he condemn the Catholic evolutionists, instructing them only to stick to prudence and objectivity.[27]

In 1931 the publication of Rev. John A. O'Brien's *Evolution and Religion* attempted to show the lack of contradiction between Holy Scripture and philosophy on one front and evolution on the other.[28] The following year, in turn, saw the publication of a book entitled *Evolution and Theology* (1932) by Fr. Ernest Messenger, Dorlodot's student, which attempts to reconcile the theory of evolution with all of Catholic teaching, from the Holy Scripture through the Church Fathers, Scholastics, and Christian philosophers to the latest statements of the Magisterium. Whether from revelation, Tradition, or philosophy, Messenger finds only slight inconsistencies that could easily be overcome by contemporary biblical exegesis and the natural sciences.[29]

According to Messenger, the Biblical Commission's *Responsa* could not be considered infallible. The Commission forbade Catholics from abandoning the literal historical sense of Genesis, but it did not give an authoritative indication of what the literal historical sense really is. "Hence," he concludes, "we are left

27. A memorandum sent to Pope Pius XI through a nuncio in Paris contains the following: "This word evolution must be taken in its widest sense, without going into the discussion of the theories of the schools (Darwinism, Lamarckism, transformism, etc.). To state our thought precisely: evolution is after all neither a theory nor a hypothesis. Its principle is the scientific method itself, since it consists of considering beings and things in their normal order of succession. This is done in a way recognizing that they are at least partially the product of beings and events that preceded them and prepared for them and the principle of what follows them. This does not affect at all the ontological cause or the principle of creation by God. The theory of evolution reaches only the exterior surface of what the permanent creative act of God successively materializes in time and space. [...] On the whole evolution is only a condition of knowledge." As cited in: H.W. Paul, *The Edge of Contingency*, 104. More on the subject in: J.C. Greene, *Darwin and the Modern Worldview* (Baton Rouge: Louisiana State University Press, 1961), 25–26.

28. J.A. O'Brien, *Evolution and Religion* (1930, reprt.; New York: The Century Co., 1932).

29. E.C. Messenger, *Evolution and Theology.*

to ourselves to determine this sense as best as we can."[30] The Catholic evolutionists accept Genesis 2:7[31] as literally true, he insists, because they hold that the matter of the human body came ultimately from earth and was formed by Divine Power collaborating with secondary causes. Thus, "There is nothing in Genesis 2:7 which, when rightly understood, disproves the theory of the origin of Adam's body by way of organic evolution."[32] Messenger claims that the phrase "special creation of man" (*peculiaris creatio hominis*) refers first and foremost to the final effect of the creation of man, i.e., the soul, and in doing so does not rule out the evolutionary origin of the body.[33]

Analyzing Messenger's arguments, one notes that in his attempts to reconcile the Church's teaching with the ideas of evolution, he bent the meanings of words and phrases, going beyond the limits of permissible interpretation. Nevertheless, during the first years after the publication of the decrees of the Biblical Commission, the analyses of Dorlodot and Messenger had much more impact on future theology than the decrees themselves. Today those documents are rarely considered by theologians or biblical scholars. Moreover, the measures then taken by the Church are often reported as an obstacle to growth in biblical studies. Joseph A. Fitzmyer, S.J. called the period of the Commission's activity "the dark cloud of reactionism that hung over the Catholic interpreta-

30. Ibid., 114.

31. Gen 2:7 reads as follows: "Then God formed man from the dust of the ground, and breathed into his nostrils the breath of life; and the man became a living being."

32. E.C. Messenger, *Evolution and Theology*, 114–16.

33. The American priest performs hermeneutical contortions to prove that the decree of the Biblical Commission does not rule out man's evolutionary origin. According to Messenger, the only fragment of the Biblical Commission's *Responsa* with any relation to the issue of evolution is a decree that one shall not question the literal and historical sense of the Book of Genesis in reference to the special creation of man. Firstly, he argued, had the Commission wished to condemn evolution, it would have done so directly, using straightforward terms. Secondly, the decree does not talk about the "first man," only a "man", just as it does not mention his body, but rather talks about a man as a whole. Thirdly, the decree used the word *creatio*, and not *formatio*, which in the author's opinion suggests a relationship between this expression and the first description of creation of man (Gen: 1:2). Yet the first description says that God created (*creavit*) man in His image and in His likeness (*Et creavit Deus hominem ad imaginem suam, ad imaginem Dei creavit illum, masculum et feminam creavit eos* Gen: 1:27). God's image and likeness, in turn, according to St. Augustine and St. Thomas, are contained in the soul and not in the body. Therefore, according to Messenger, the decree of the Commission refers first and foremost to the final effect of the creation of man, i.e., the soul, and in doing so does not rule out the evolutionary origin of the body (ibid., 229–31). A broader analysis of Messenger's argumentation lies beyond the framework of this book. One should, however, take notice of the method of relativization of the Church's teaching applied by the authors of that time. It consisted in nominalistic reading of fragments of decrees, in isolation from the text as a whole, and sometimes in subtle changes in the meanings of the words, so that the final conclusions could defend a presupposed thesis. Messenger, like Dorlodot, on the one hand considered the biblical description as essentially metaphorical, but on the other treated the Church's decrees in so juridical and literal way that he could not elicit their true meaning.

tion of the Bible in the first half of the twentieth century." In his opinion, the Commission's *Responsa* caused "fear and suspicion about everything connected with the Bible, so that clergy and faithful alike suspected anyone who tried to interpret it as dangerous and almost unorthodox."[34]

The Alleged Invalidation of the Decrees of the Pontifical Biblical Commission

According to some scholars, the early decrees of the Pontifical Biblical Commission were reinterpreted by the Church within fifty years of their publication.[35] One of the most significant English-language biblical commentaries, under the title "Church Pronouncements," claims:

> Many of these decrees [PBC in the years 1905–1915] now have little more than historic interest, being implicitly revoked by later decrees, by *Divino Afflante Spiritu*, and by Vatican II. The early decrees must be evaluated according to the 1955 clarification issued in Latin and in German by A. Miller and by A. Kleinhaus, secretary and assistant secretary of the Pontifical Biblical Commission.[36]

Joseph A. Fitzmyer also made references to the 1955 text by Miller and Kleinhaus, observing that "This double review, then, proved to be an important clarification, which would affect the future work of all Catholic interpreters."[37]

The 1955 "clarification" mentioned by Fitzmyer appeared in the professional literature several times, first in German in a Biblical periodical, *Benediktinische*

34. J.A. Fitzmyer, Foreword to *The Biblical Commission Document "The Interpretation of the Bible in the Church": Text and Commentary* (Roma: Editrice Pontificio Instituto Biblico, 1995), 19–20.

35. Rev. Sean Kopczynski, C.P.M. points out the problem of teaching in theological seminaries that the decrees of the Pontifical Biblical Commission supposedly ceased to have any influence on Biblical exegesis. The author attempts to answer the question of why the pronouncements of the Pontifical Biblical Commission had been almost completely forgotten. The further analysis of the issue is inspired by his article "Rediscovering the Decrees of the Pontifical Biblical Commission," *Living Tradition*, 94 (July 2001); http://www.rtforum.org/lt/lt94.html (February 3, 2015).

36. T.A. Collins, O.P.; R.E. Brown, S.S., "Church Pronouncements" in *The Jerome Biblical Commentary* (New Jersey: Prentice-Hall, 1968), [72:25], 629.

37. Fitzmyer, op. cit., 21. According to Fitzmyer, the "clarification" was published on the occasion of the appearance of the fourth edition of *Enchiridion Biblicum* in 1954. It was then that the secretary of the Pontifical Commission, Athanasius Miller, O.S.B., included his German text in *Benediktinische Monatschrift*, while the vice-secretary, Arduin Kleinhaus, O.F.M. (Fitzmyer says Kleinhans, which is a typographic error) published an identical review of *Enchiridion* in Latin in *Antonianum*. Fitzmyer claims that the clarifications were issued by two secretaries of the Biblical Commission, who believed that the *Responsa* were obsolete and that contemporary scholars studying the Holy Scripture could conduct their research in "absolute freedom." J.A. Fitzmyer, *To Advance the Gospel: New Testament Studies*, 2nd ed. (Grand Rapids: Wm.B. Eerdmans, 1998), 31. References to the clarification are nowadays common in literature. Another example can be found in the 2008 book: P.M.J. Hess, P.L. Allen, *Catholicism and Science* (Westport: Greenwood Press, 2008), 99.

Monatschrift, then in Latin in *Antonianum*, and later in English in *The Catholic Biblical Quarterly*.[38] This gave rise to a common conviction that there existed an official or semi-official clarification (or revocation) of early decrees of the Biblical Commission.

What was this supposed clarification? A relevant passage can be found in the book *Rome and the Study of Scripture*:

> Inasmuch as it is a collection of documents which show how Sacred Scripture has always been the primary source and foundation of the truths of Catholic faith and of their progress and development, the *Enchiridion* renders great service first of all to the history of dogmas. It reflects clearly, moreover, the fierce battle that the Church at all times has had to fight, though with varying degrees of intensity, to maintain the purity and truth of the Word of God. Especially in this respect the decrees of the Pontifical Biblical Commission have great significance. However, as long as these decrees propose views which are neither immediately nor mediately connected with truths of faith and morals, it goes without saying that the scholar may pursue his research *with complete freedom and may utilize the results of these investigations*,[39] provided always that he respects the teaching authority of the Church. Today we can hardly picture to ourselves the position of Catholic scholars at the turn of the century, or the dangers that threatened Catholic teaching on Scripture and its inspiration on the part of liberal and rationalistic criticism, which like a torrent tried to sweep away the sacred barriers of tradition. At present the battle is considerably less fierce; not a few controversies have been peacefully settled and many problems emerge in an entirely new light, so that it is easy enough for us to smile at the narrowness and constraint which prevailed fifty years ago. Finally, the *Enchiridion* has notable apologetic value, because it bears witness to the Church's untiring vigilance and her perennial solicitude for the Scriptures.[40]

The core of the "clarification" consists in distinguishing in the Church's documents a layer related strictly to faith and morality, which is subject to the Magisterium, and a layer "not related to faith and morality," in regard to which a researcher has "complete freedom." It is unknown, however, what criteria

38. A.M. "Das neue Biblische Handbuch," *Benediktinische Monatschrift* 31 (1955): 49–50; A. Kleinhaus, "De nova Enchiridii Biblicii edition," *Antonianum* 30 (1955), 63–65; E.F. Siegman, "Decrees of the Pontifical Biblical Commission," *The Catholic Biblical Quarterly* 18.1 (1956), 23–29, 24–25.

39. The words in italics are omitted in the English translation of the clarification included in the collection *Rome and the Study of Scripture*. They are, however, present in both the German (*in aller Freiheit*) and the Latin (*plena libertate*) texts. The omission of the key phrase shows that some translators of the clarification attempted to soften its impact, which means that they might have recognized the formal ecclesiastical authority behind them.

40. *Rome and the Study of Scripture: A Collection of Papal Enactments on the Study of Holy Scripture together with the Decisions of the Biblical Commission*, ed. C. Louis, 7th ed. (St. Meinrad, IN: Abbey Press Publishing Division, 1964), 169–70.

would determine in which of those two groups a particular truth should be classified. The 1909 decree of the Pontifical Biblical Commission rules out any interpretation of Genesis that would deny or diminish the special creation of man. For scholars embracing the theory of evolution, however, this was a matter of science that went beyond the competence of the Magisterium. Thus, following the rule established in the "clarification," one could question virtually any truth of the faith simply by removing it from the scope of "faith and morality" and assigning it to the authority of natural science. We shall therefore ask: what was the formal authority of the article?

According to Rev. Edward F. Siegman, who commented on the clarification in his paper in *The Catholic Biblical Quarterly* (1956):

> To date it [the clarification] has not appeared in the *Acta Apostolicæ Sedis* and hence escaped the immediate attention of many scholars. It should not, perhaps, be called official in the strict sense ... because the writer is identified only by the initials 'A.M.' ... though there seems to be no doubt that the reviewer is the Very Reverend Athanasius Miller, O.S.B. Certainly we have here the mind of the Biblical Commission."[41]

Nevertheless, the clarification was not included in any future issue of the Acts of the Apostolic See. Therefore, it is difficult to consider authoritative a text that has never been promulgated pursuant to the Church law, and has only been published in biblical periodicals. For this reason, Fr. Sean Kopczynski claims that "This article is at least potentially dangerous to the faith."[42] The decrees do not have merely "historical and apologetic" value, as the author of the clarification put it, but along with the encyclicals *Providentissimus Deus* and *Divino afflante Spiritu* they present the fundamental principles of Catholic biblical interpretation, effectively protecting it from subjective and arbitrary interpretations by Catholic scholars.

According to Kopczynski, there are some arguments to support the claim that the clarification is not an authentic document. Firstly, in the same year, 1955, Athanasius Miller wrote an instruction of the Biblical Commission, which was signed not only by him, but also by Pope Pius XII, and then published in the Acts of the Apostolic See. Given the style and theological message of the instruction, it seems almost impossible that the "clarification" was written in the same year by the same person.[43] Secondly, as has been pointed out, the decrees had a doctrinal character—they concerned faith—but the Church has

41. Quotation after S. Kopczynski, *Rediscovering the Decrees of the Pontifical Biblical Commission.*

42. Ibid.

43. The instruction contains the following statement: "But it is to be regretted that these activities [meetings of various biblical associations] are not carried out in every area in full accord with the norms just laid down.... The speakers, we are told, are not always those men who are well versed in

never revoked what it teaches regarding faith and morality. Moreover, the decrees do not state anything that had not previously been a subject of the Church's teachings.

The "fraud theory" seems to be confirmed by yet another document of the Pontifical Biblical Commission, a 1948 letter to Cardinal E.C. Suhard, which argues that "these replies [from 1905, 1906, and 1909] are in no way a hindrance to further truly scientific examination of these problems in accordance with the results acquired in these last forty years. *Consequently, the Biblical Commission believes that there is no need, at least for the moment, to promulgate any new decrees regarding these questions.*"[44] It is very unlikely that the position presented in 1948 should be essentially reformulated in the "clarification" published only seven years later (1955). In the 1950s and 1960s the Magisterium was still trying to stop the destruction of Catholic biblical scholarship in the form of so-called "historical criticism," treating Holy Scripture as an ordinary text and based on completely arbitrary and often inconsistent assumptions. The attempts, however, turned out to be futile.[45]

To properly assess the meaning of the "Responsa" we need to consider the fact that the Biblical Commission was established as an organ of a teaching Church, which was expressly confirmed by Pope Pius X. Only later, due to pressure from some hierarchs and academic communities, was the Commission's

the matters of which they treat; some of them are entirely too ready to follow less reliable authors, or rashly and boldly to accept and spread doubtful or false opinions. . . . We have even heard it to have happened that speakers paid little heed to those norms on which the Sovereign Pontiff now happily reigning again gravely insisted in his encyclical letter *Humani Generis*, that they boldly set forth theories condemned by the Magisterium of the Church, or even went so far as to propose in place of the literal sense duly brought out under the Church's watchful eye, some new sense which they called symbolic and spiritual, by which difficulties inherent in the literal sense were supposed to vanish. There is no one who cannot realize how incalculably dangerous all these things are when proposed to hearers not thoroughly skilled in biblical matters." Instruction of PBC from December 15, 1955. On biblical associations, *AAS*, 48 (1956), 61–64 (EB 625).

44. *AAS*, 40 (1948), 46 (EB 579). The English translation of the letter available on the Internet omits the last sentence contained in the quote in italics. The sentence, however, is the core of the letter, which was written as an answer to the question about the validity of the PBC's early decrees. (Emphasis mine.) Cf. http://www.catholicscripture.net/enchiridion/suhard.html (February 3, 2015).

45. What may be considered the last attempt to stop the influence of critical exegesis is the monitum of the Holy Office from the time of Pope John XXIII, issued for the benefit of biblical researchers and warning them to "always keep in mind the teaching of the holy Fathers and the mind and Magisterium of the Church. Otherwise, the consciences of the faithful will be disturbed and harm will come to the truths of the Faith" (Monitum of the Holy Office issued June 20, 1961). In 1988 Cardinal J. Ratzinger talked about the crisis in contemporary biblical studies and pointed out the necessity for "self-criticism of the historical-critical method" (Lecture delivered on January 27, 1988 at Saint Peter's Church in New York). See. J. Ratzinger, "Biblical Interpretation in Crisis: On the Question of the Foundations and Approaches of Exegesis Today," in R. J. Neuhaus, *Biblical Interpretation in Crisis* (Grand Rapids: Wm. Eerdmans, 1989), 1–23.

status changed. In 1971 Pope Paul VI reorganized it and excluded it from the Magisterium. Since then, in the words of Cardinal Joseph Ratzinger, it is no longer "an organ of the teaching office, but rather a commission of scholars who, in their scientific and ecclesial responsibility as believing exegetes, take positions on important problems of Scriptural interpretation and know that for this task they enjoy the confidence of the teaching office."[46] Therefore, in evaluating any Biblical Commission pronouncement, the time of its publication plays a crucial role. The older decrees belong to the Church's Magisterium even if the latter ones do not have doctrinal value.

The Magisterium's authentic pronouncements bear great significance when it comes to the issue of evolution. On the one hand, they pave the way for a proper understanding of the origin of man; on the other, they protect Holy Scripture itself against evolutionary reinterpretation. After the decrees fell into oblivion, the expansion of evolutionism in theology led not only to a redefinition of the origin of the human body, but of the origin of the Bible as well.

Fr. Kopczynski notes that in diocesan and religious seminaries the evolutionary theories of the origin of the Bible are the ones most commonly taught. He gives as an example the authorship of the Pentateuch, referred to in the 1906 decree of the Biblical Commission:

> Today it is held almost universally that Moses could not possibly have written the Pentateuch for various reasons such as his death reported in the last chapter of Deuteronomy. They argue, how can Moses have written a book that recounts his own death? Rejecting Mosaic authorship, modern scholars ([those] studied in the seminaries today) prefer to infer authorship from internal evidence alone. For example, in regard to the Pentateuch they identify at least three or more authors based upon style and content. Then they propose various theories to explain how we got the first five books of the Bible. One very popular modern theory, the Documentary Hypothesis, is evolutionary in nature and holds that the Pentateuch was not written by one author, but by three or four authors or traditions which modern scholars call J, E, P, and D. . . . These three or four authors or traditions sometimes had different stories and sometimes had conflicting versions of the same story. Eventually someone put all the different stories together while preserving their originality as much as possible. As a result, the final product is a patchwork of conflicting traditions, often contradictory, now hopelessly mixed [together] and confused . . . by the final editor. In other words, the Pentateuch evolved over time from who knows how many contributing authors to reach finally the books we have today. The PBC decrees address this prob-

46. See: J. Ratzinger, Introduction to the English-language edition of the Pontifical Biblical Commission's document *The Interpretation of the Bible in the Church* from April 23, 1993. Text available online at http://www.ewtn.com/library/CURIA/PBCINTER.HTM (February 3, 2015).

> lem by narrowing down the possibilities. . . . The Pentateuch could have various sources, but it has only one human author—Moses. Joshua or someone else could easily have added the last chapter recounting Moses' death.[47]

For some, Fr. Kopczynski's opinion is like looking into a mirror; for others it is like looking at an image in a distorting mirror. But even a distorting mirror can sometimes reveal those aspects that are difficult to notice without any type of mirror. The question of critical exegesis and its influence on our understanding of human origins is a separate issue, which would require another comprehensive study.

47. S. Kopczynski, "Rediscovering the Decrees of the Pontifical Biblical Commission."

6

Evolution During the Pontificate of Pius XII

Departure from the Traditional Doctrine of Human Origins in Mainstream Theology

Luigi Tripepi, in his 1894 report on Leroy's book, remarked that some Catholics questioned the accord of a number of theologians regarding the direct creation of man. Tripepi mentioned the writings of Sorbonne Professor Jules Fabre d'Envieu, lecturer in theology Johannes Gmeiner, John A. Zahm, and St. George Mivart. Nevertheless, he said, "they cannot deprecate the complete, solemn, unbroken, and common agreement of theologians on this matter."[1] In his 1933 work *Tractatus de Deo creante et elevante,* Jesuit Charles Boyer warned that the previous two decades had opened the way to the acceptance of evolution.[2] In 1899, Leroy wrote a review of a book by Jean Guibert, who had followed Joseph Brucker in affirming the direct creation of both the soul and the body of man (cf. Chapter Four, under "The Intervention of the Congregation of the Index").[3] In response to Guibert's idea, Leroy proposed that there are two views on this subject within Catholicism: one like Guibert's and the other suggesting that evolution might have prepared the substrate into which God breathed the soul, thus creating the human body. He also noted that Cardinal Zeferino González did not oppose the latter position. As a result,

1. L. Tripepi, ACDF, Index, *Protocolli*, 14, after: *Negotiating Darwin*, 81.

2. Ch. Boyer, *Tractatus de Deo creante et elevante*, 3rd ed. (Roma: Pont. Univ. Gregoriana, 1940), 186. Boyer himself reiterated the classical doctrine distinguishing the three phases of creation by God: "Etenim utraque opinione [i.e., two concepts present in the Church's Tradition—Ambrose's and Augustine's], paucis omissis, eodem fere sensu intelligitur triplex opus quod distingui solet: opus creationis, quo caelum et terram producuntur informia; opus distinctionis, quo caelum et terra fiunt formata; opus ornatus quo caelum et terra in eis habitantia accipiunt." C. Boyer, *Tractatus de Deo creante et elevante* (Roma: Pont. Univ. Gregoriana, 1957), 93.

3. J. Guibert, *Les Origines*.

Leroy's writings began to consolidate the false opinion that both the evolutionary standpoint and direct creation were equally accepted by the Church.

Leroy's texts were soon invoked by another Dominican, Juan González de Arintero (1860–1928), who in 1898 published two (of the planned eight) volumes on evolution.[4] The Spanish theologian argues that evolution is a better manifestation of God's perfection than the separate creation of species:

> The genesis of the organic world through the mediation of natural agents requires infinitely more genius than direct Creation. I have no doubt about the difference between a watchmaker who makes a precision watch, and an inventor who creates a machine capable of producing the same watch by itself; the inventor is 100 yards beyond the bench worker.[5]

Moreover, Arintero cites the French Paleontologist Jean F.A. du Pouget (cf. Chapter Four, under "The Debate about the Book") who, despite being against transformism, had claimed:

> A certain school is accustomed to say that the Catholic Church condemns the transformist doctrine. This is wrong: there are Catholic scholars who have supported it and do so with determination. It is enough to mention Father Leroy, of the Order of Preachers, and Dr. Maisonneuve, professor of the Catholic Institute of Angers.[6]

Du Pouget was not a theologian and probably did not understand the concept of the "universal agreement of theologians." Nevertheless, the French scientist suggests that the supporters of transformism offer a legitimate trend of thought as an alternative to the classical view. In this way, step by step, the recognition of the "universal agreement of theologians" started to be replaced by the opinion that there were "two standpoints within Catholicism." In subsequent years, more and more theologians accepted the idea of the absence of conflict between evolution and Christianity.[7]

By the 1940s, the belief that the evolutionary origin of the human body does not go against the truths of the faith was already quite common among theolo-

4. The remaining planned volumes were never published. J.T. González de Arintero, *La evolución y la filosofía Cristiana: Introducción general y Libro primero, La evolución y la mutabilidad de las especies orgánicas* (Madrid: Librería de Gregorio del Amo, 1898).

5. Ibid., 93.

6. Ibid.

7. In 1912, Étienne Hugueny, O.P. presents the thesis that the Bible and the Church teach that God took the elements of the human body from the earth, but that they do not specify whether this was a direct creation of the body or the elements had previously been prepared by evolution. See E. Hugueny, *Critique et Catholique*, vol. 1 (Paris: Letouzey et Ané, 1912), 241–42. In 1932, the periodical *America* published an article by W.H. McClellan, S.J. in which the author examines the status of the doctrine on the origin of man: "Evolution of non-human organic species offers no point of opposition to Catholic belief, so long as a Supreme Intelligence is admitted as the first cause. Mankind

gians. In Poland, for example, Franciszek Kwiatkowski, S.J. in his 1947 book distinguished between the truth *that* God creates and the truth of *how* He does it. The first question is answered by the Bible; the second, by "rational investigation."[8] Neither did the theologian see any problem in the evolutionary origin of the body: "God might have used the body of an animal when he created man."[9] Stanislaw Bartynowski, S.J. set forth a similar view in the 7th edition of his *Apologetyka podreczna* (*Concise Apologetics*) from 1948.[10] Bartynowski did not accept evolution uncritically. He opted for polyphyletic evolution, i.e., that in which all species developed from many different, previously created types. It was a strongly limited model of evolution, albeit permitting species transformism. The idea had already been developed in the late 19th century by the Austrian Jesuit Erich Wassmann. Wassmann's works never faced any reaction from the Magisterium, as they were written from the scientific point of view (entomology). What is more, Wassmann excludes man from the evolutionary process.[11]

Bartynowski's *Apologetyka* is a good illustration of the standpoint popular to this day among some theologians. On the one hand, he distinguishes the theory of evolution "as such" from particular versions of the theory, showing that the former is not contrary to the truths of the faith, and on the other, presents a number of arguments against specific biological theories. However, if we cannot explain any mechanism of evolution, why would we accept it as "data" in theological studies? As a result, Bartynowski's work is entangled in contradictions characteristic of this approach. At one point, for instance, he states that "Botanists and zoologists have noticed that we can still find traces of the emergence of new, systematic species of plants and animals."[12] However, a few pages further, he remarks that natural selection does not explain the appearance of

forms an exception, as by every right of reason it should. No evolutionary process can account for a rational soul. Of the first human body such an origin is possible without prejudice to faith, but not to be held as positively probable until solid evidence is at hand. This is, in broad lines, the unchanged status of the question for Catholics." Quoted in *Theology and Evolution*, ed. E. C. Messenger (London; Glasgow: Sands & Co. Ltd., 1949), 76.

8. "Biblical experts teach that the inspired writer wanted to emphasize that the whole world comes from God, but he does not explain the way in which individual beings come from Him; he only indicates that previously created beings participate in God's further activity. In what way? That is a matter of rational investigation." F. Kwiatkowski, *Filozofia wieczysta w zarysie*, vol. 2: *Filozofia bytu. Filozofia świata nieorganicznego. Filozofia duszy* (Kraków: WAM 1947), 252–53.

9. Ibid.

10. S. Bartynowski, *Apologetyka podręczna: obrona podstaw wiary katolickiej i odpowiedzi na zarzuty* (1911; reprt. Te Deum, 2001).

11. Such a view (i.e., polyphyletic evolution excluding man) was professed by such Catholic researchers as G.V. Schiaperelli, P. Schanz, and P. Gemelli.

12. S. Bartynowski, *Apologetyka podręczna*, 134.

new features, and that the "variability of organisms has rather narrow limits."[13] On the next page, he writes that "people like Haeckel, Bastian, Bronn, and others, unfavorable towards the religious truth that God had created the first organisms and the first human couple, decided to abuse Darwin's theory for their anti-religious purposes."[14] And immediately after, having demonstrated the weakness of the arguments for man's origination from an animal ancestor, he argues that anyone "who extends the theory of evolution to the origin of man's body, does not oppose a clearly expressed dogma."[15] In fact, the last claim is too obvious to be relevant, as the direct creation of Adam's body was not (and still is not) a separate, clearly defined dogma. If such a dogma did not exist, hardly any view could oppose it.

Another example of such incoherence can be found in *Dogmatyka* (*Dogmatic*) by Rev. Wincenty Granat (1900–1979), published eleven years after the encyclical *Humani Generis*. The author reminds readers that "no being, by virtue of any natural or supernatural properties, can assist the Creator physically in the creation of the world."[16] But at another point he writes: "Acceptance of the theory of abiogenesis, or the theory of evolution in general, is in no conflict with the idea of God the Creator, and even provides a proof of His existence."[17] As in Bartynowski's book, in Granat's *Dogmatyka* even the possibility of the direct creation of the human body is nowhere to be found; instead, there is a robust critique of concordism.[18]

One might thus notice how the accent gradually shifted within Catholic theology, and the truth that in 1870 was to become a solemn teaching was slowly falling into oblivion. Still in 1948, Cardinal Ernesto Ruffini published the book *La Teoria dell'evoluzione secondo la scienza e la fede* (*Theory of Evolution Judged by Reason and Faith*), in which he openly criticizes the new trend in Catholic theology:

> The question, Can transformism be extended, as regards man, at least to his body?, is certainly grave and important, precisely because many Catholics have thought to answer it in the affirmative. Let us state at once that we are of a different opinion. Indeed, we do not see how such an opinion can be reconciled with Biblical testimony, with the explicit teaching of the Fathers and theologians, with the common belief of the faithful, while it is not favored by reason or by true science.[19]

13. Ibid., 140.
14. Ibid., 141.
15. Ibid., 149.
16. W. Granat, *Dogmatyka*, vol. 2, *Bóg Stwórca; Aniołowie—Człowiek* (Lublin: TN KUL, 1961), 89.
17. Ibid., 41–42.
18. Ibid., 47–48.
19. E. Ruffini, *The Theory of Evolution Judged by Reason and Faith*, trans. by F. O'Hanlon (New York: Joseph F. Wagner; London: B. Herder, 1959), 117.

Cardinal Ruffini's book is divided into two parts, the first dealing with the emergence of living beings in general, the second with the origin of man. In part one, the author first refutes arguments proposed by scientists in support of the evolution of species. He consecutively disproves arguments from the fields of paleontology, embryology, comparative anatomy, and physiology, biogeography, parasitology, and genetics. Next, he demonstrates the impossibility or insufficiency of all then-known mechanisms of evolution: Lamarck's environmental influence, Darwin's natural selection, and the theory of mutation defended by Hugo de Vries. Ruffini was aware of the different ways in which the biblical account of creation could be interpreted. In the book he describes the broad and strict senses, the historical and literal senses, the ideal or allegorical sense, and the mythological sense. None of these, however, leads him to deny the supernatural emergence of species.

In the second part, he first indicates the insufficiency of paleontological arguments for the animal origin of man. Then he cites examples of Catholic scholars who accept evolution of species but exempt the human body from an evolutionary origin.[20] Finally, referring to the Bible, the Greek and Latin Fathers, and the Scholastic theologians, he argues that the Church had always viewed the independent and direct creation of the first human body as a truth of the faith.[21] For support, Ruffini also invokes the decree of Cologne and the decrees of the Pontifical Biblical Commission from the years 1905–1909. In the Appendix he separately addresses the claim that St. Augustine and St. Gregory of Nyssa supported species transformism. Analyzing the doctrines of these two Fathers, he shows that such an opinion could not be maintained. This book by an Italian Cardinal was a complete answer to the theses of Catholic evolutionists of his time.

Two years later, however, Pius XII's encyclical *Humani Generis* deprived the Catholic apologists of their main argument—continuous and clear opposition of the Church to the evolutionary origins of all living forms. Perhaps Ruffini's 1948 work would not have even been published had it been written two years

20. Among them, he mentions such individuals as A. Fogazzaro, D. Leroy, J.A. Zahm, G. Bonomelli, St. G. Mivart, Father Hugo Obermaier (†1946), H. Dorlodot, A.D. Sertillanges, and P.M. Périer. Ibid., 111–13.

21. With respect to Dorlodot's claim that St. Augustine supported the evolution of the human body, Ruffini, having invoked a few statements of the Bishop of Hippo indicating quite a different interpretation of the subject by Augustine, writes: "And yet St. Augustine is commonly cited by evolutionists of all shades as their great patron. In our next conferences, wrote Professor de Dorlodot in 1921, we shall see that Saint Augustine holds as certain the theory of absolute natural evolution of living beings from brute matter to the human body inclusively. We shall demonstrate fully . . . how unfounded is such an assertion." Ibid., 129.

later. In 1950, in the pro-evolutionary book *Origines de l'univers et de l'homme d'aprés la Bible*, Rev. Charles Hauret asserts that

> At the beginning of the century the slogan *man comes from an ape* was often an expression of a materialistic perspective. This theorem occupied a prominent place in the antireligious arsenal. But today, more and more Catholics, some of them professors at universities, publicly declare their sympathy for theistic transformism. Their opinion did not remain confined within the circle of initiators, but has gained supporters among their students and among the Catholic elite. It gradually reaches the circles of ordinary people.[22]

After 1950 it is hard to find publications maintaining the truth about the direct creation of Adam's body. The 1992 edition of the *Catechism of the Catholic Church*, referring to the creation of man, declares *that* God did create him, but says nothing of *how* He did so. A quotation from St. Irenaeus stating that "God formed man with His own hands" appears elsewhere—in the discussion of the Holy Spirit.[23] As the quotation can be interpreted figuratively, it is not decisive anyway. Taking into account the number of books and articles alone, it might seem that after 1950 the evolutionary paradigm became the common standpoint in Catholic theology.[24]

One of the few exceptions was the monograph by Rev. Patrick O'Connell, *Science of Today and the Problems of Genesis*. This book, first published in 1959 and subsequently reissued several times (1960, 1969, 1993), exposes the lack of scientific grounds for the acceptance of the evolution of man in Catholic theology.

O'Connell traces the source of evolutionary influence on Catholicism to a small group of French intellectuals and clergymen interested in reconciling Christianity with Darwinism. According to Henri Bégouën, the group constituted an informal movement inside Catholicism, which included "Catholics, Free-thinkers, Evolutionists, and supporters of the theory of spontaneous gen-

22. Ch. Hauret, *Origines de l'univers et de l'homme d'après la Bible* (Paris: J. Gabalda, 1950), 71.

23. CCC n. 704.

24. The opinion is supported by P. Kapusta, pointing to the 1960s as a period when, due to the popularization of the works of Teilhard de Chardin, "systematic theologians in favour of evolutionary approaches constitute the vast majority." P. Kapusta, "Darwinism from Humani Generis to the Present," in *Darwin and Catholicism*, ed. L. Caruana (London, New York: T&T Clark, 2009), 32. From the 1960s to the present, there have appeared dozens of books written by Catholic clergymen from the point of view of theistic evolution. Some works include: F.M. Bergounioux, A. Glory, *Les premiers hommes: précis d'anthropologie préhistorique* (Toulouse: Didier, 1943); M. Grison, *Problemes d'Origines: L'univers Les vivants. L'homme* (Paris: Letouzey et Ané, 1954); A. Hulsbosch, O.S.A., *God in Creation and Evolution*, ed. M. Versfeld (New York: Sheed and Ward, 1965); O.A. Rabut, O.P., *God in an Evolving Universe*, trans. W. Springer (New York: Herder and Herder, 1966); F. Euvé SI, *Darwin et le christianisme: vrais et faux débats* (Paris: Buchet-Chastel, 2009); J. Zycinski, *God and Evolution. Fundamental Questions of Christian Evolutionism* (Washington, DC: The Catholic University of America Press, 2006).

eration against Pasteur."[25] Among them were clergymen such as Dorlodot and Teilhard de Chardin. O'Connell comments on the works of scholars—Messenger, Grison, Abbé Breuil, Bergounioux, and Hauret,[26] to name but a few. Fr. Hauret, for example, was deeply convinced that he was not competent to undermine the "scientific platform of findings by paleontologists, biologists, and anthropologists." According to Hauret, most scholars nowadays affirm the animal origin of human body, so "exegetes and theologians are by no means justified to ignore or belittle those truths."[27] The clear conclusion of Fr. Hauret's book is that the claims of scientists cannot be undermined; therefore, the results of their research must be included in theological considerations.

O'Connell, however, suggests that this *a priori* trust in scientists' claims is not well-founded. Catholic paleoanthropologists advocating human descent from apes, he notes, had employed outdated and inaccurate research, or simply non-scientific assumptions. He argues that the bones found at excavation sites could be classified as belonging either to an ape or one of the human races, who do not differ from the contemporary ones any more than the contemporary ones differ from one another. He also argues that in dubious cases it is highly advisable to wait for further findings instead of adopting hasty conclusions. In his opinion, "each and every priest has at his disposal sufficient knowledge on biology in order to evaluate whether indirect scientific arguments in favor of evolution are well-founded or not."[28]

Summing up the position held by numerous Catholic evolutionists, O'Connell writes:

> The intentions of these men were good. The enemies of the Church had been boasting that modern science had proved that the theory of evolution was no longer a theory but a fact, and that the Mosaic account was therefore wrong, and that Genesis was only a tissue of fables. Men like Dr. Messenger, Fr. Hauret, etc., tried to take the weapon out of the enemies' hands by admitting the very thing they wanted to be believed—the ape origin of man—and even went as far as to say that this was the proper interpretation of the Mosaic account. It was like attempting to put out a fire by throwing kerosene on it. . . . Furthermore, most atheistic propagandists for the theory of human evolution are now aware that the arguments from paleontology based on the

25. H. Bégouën, *Queues souvenirs sure le movement des ideas transformistic dans les milieux catholiques suivi de la mentalité spiritualiste des premiers homes* (Paris: Bloud & Gay, 1945). Quotation after P. O'Connell, *Science of Today and the Problems of Genesis* (Rockford, IL: Tan Books, 1993), 74.

26. See M. Grison, *Problémes d'origines*. H. Breuil, R. Lantier, *Hommes de la pierre anciene* (Paris: Payot, 1951). E.M. Bergounioux, A. Glory, *Les premieres hommes*. Ch. Hauret, *Origines de l'univers et de l'homme d'aprés la Bible*.

27. Quotations after P. O'Connell, *Science of Today*, 80–81.

28. Ibid., 92.

> existence of half-man, half-ape fossils, have collapsed, and men like Sir Julian Huxley have abandoned most of them. These men, therefore, can have nothing but contempt for those Catholic writers who abandon the biblical account of the origin of man for reasons known to them to be worthless.[29]

O'Connell's book is an important testimony to the state of science and theology at the peak of the Darwinists' offensive. It indicates that not all theologians had succumbed to the common opinions presented as "scientific truth" but not always been scientifically well-founded.

Humani Generis: Main Theses

The early 20th century saw a gradual yet consistent reshaping of the Catholic understanding of the origin of man. The influence of culture (and often also mere propaganda by those ill-disposed towards the Church and religion) sparked new beliefs regarding the origin of man among scholars. Two previously uncontested truths were now put on trial: the creation of man from the earth and the creation of Eve from Adam's rib. Disputing these truths led to further questions, already posed by many theologians in the early 20th century: Does humankind come from one couple only, or did it evolve in different places, at different times in history, and from various lower species? Is the human soul in any way a derivative of matter and is its adjunction to the body determined by biological development? Do human beings differ from animals only through different organization of their bodies, or are there other qualities that make humans exceptional? These questions triggered numerous disputes and controversies. The previous discussion—which concerned transformation of species, that is, evolution in biology—was now focused almost exclusively on the question of human origin. It is understandable, then, that Pope Pius XII decided to take the floor.

The first of his utterances appeared during the third year of his pontificate, in a speech to the Pontifical Academy of Sciences on November 30, 1941. Pius XII argued that the *ex nihilo nihil fit* principle (nothing comes from nothing) applies to all beings besides God, at whose command everything began to exist. It was at God's word that heaven and earth were created, and "also man was fashioned out of dust from the soil and God breathed into his nostrils a breath of life and thus man became a living being."[30] Furthermore, the pope states that man comes from man only, and that Eve was created from Adam:

29. Ibid., 90–91.

30. "Address of Pius XII to the Pontifical Academy of Sciences of November 30, 1941," *AAS* 33 (1941), 506. English translation after *Papal Addresses to the Pontifical Academy of Sciences* 1917–2002 (Vatican: The Pontifical Academy of Sciences, 2003), 92.

> Only from man could there come another man who would then call him father and ancestor; and the helpmate given by God to the first man came from man himself and is flesh from his flesh, made into a woman and called such because she came from man.[31]

Thus in the 1941 address Pius XII repeats the classical doctrine of creation of man from the earth as well as the creation of woman from man's side. The principle that "only man could be the ancestor of man" explicitly alludes to evolutionary doctrines. What is innovative in the pope's speech are his deliberations on the role of natural sciences in answering questions regarding origins. "The multiple research," the pope argues,

> be it paleontology or of biology and morphology, on the problems concerning the origins of man have not, as yet, ascertained anything with great clarity and certainty. We must leave it to the future to answer the question, if indeed science will one day be able, enlightened and guided by Revelation, to give certain and definitive results concerning a topic of such importance.[32]

So far church apologists had maintained that science can explain *how* the world functions, how biological organisms function, etc., but not *whence* the world or different natures came. This is why Pius XII, writing about the capacity of science, adds the words "science, enlightened and guided by Revelation," since science alone would be unable to provide a full explanation of the origin of man. The phrase was an indirect rejection of the "theory of two truths" according to which science and religion have their own different (or even incompatible) answers to the question of origins. As the pope adds, "True science never lowers or humiliates man in his origins, rather it exalts and elevates him since it sees, compares and admires in each member of the human family the traces of the Divine Image."[33]

Yet again Pius XII alludes to the thesis of the animal origin of man, and he implicitly rejects such a belief. He refers to "true science," i.e., to what had been really discovered and not to mere speculation often heavily burdened with prejudice. According to the pope, such a science—one based on empirical facts—can never lead to the idea of a low human origin. He also warns that, in the hands of men, science may become a double-edged sword that can bring either health or death.[34] Thus Pius XII ascribes to science limited competences, though he does not exclude the possibility of the natural sciences being able to shed some light on the origin of man. He only remarks that science had not then established anything certain regarding this matter and that, if science were

31. *AAS* 33 (1941), 506.
32. Ibid.
33. Ibid., 507.
34. Ibid., 512.

to establish anything in the future, it would be on condition that it is enlightened by revelation.[35]

Nine years later (August 12, 1950) Pius XII announced the encyclical *Humani Generis: On Some False Opinions Threatening to Undermine the Foundations of Catholic Doctrine.* The encyclical is composed of three parts, corresponding to questions regarding faith, philosophy, and science. The pope touches upon the problem of evolution at the very beginning:

> If anyone examines the state of affairs outside the Christian fold, he will easily discover the principal trends that not a few learned men are following. Some imprudently and indiscreetly hold that evolution, which has not been fully proved even in the domain of natural sciences, explains the origin of all things, and audaciously supports the monistic and pantheistic opinion that the world is in continual evolution. Communists gladly subscribe to this opinion so that, when the souls of men have been deprived of every idea of a personal God, they may the more efficaciously defend and propagate their dialectical materialism.[36]

The document reviews various errors being made in theology and philosophy at the time. Pius XII points to the important role of the Church in the interpretation of Holy Scripture and recommends resorting to classical (Thomistic) philosophy when interpreting the truths of faith. In the end, the pope describes the issues concerning the relation between faith and natural sciences.

The third part of the encyclical consists of two paragraphs: the first concerning the relationship between biology and anthropology, the second concerning the relationship between history and Holy Scripture. Only the first paragraph of the third part refers to issues of interest to us here. This fragment does not exceed 5% of the total extent of the document. One can note, therefore, that we are not speaking about a comprehensive and authoritative treatise but rather about several papal remarks regarding the origin of man. This short paragraph is the most complete statement on evolution expressed by the Magisterium to date:

> It remains for Us now to speak about those questions which, although they pertain to the positive sciences, are nevertheless more or less connected with the truths of the Christian faith. In fact, not a few insistently demand that the

35. The First Vatican Council had expressed its opinion on the subject of the competence of science: "Nor does the Church forbid these studies to employ, each within its own area, its own proper principles and method: but while she admits this just freedom, she takes particular care that they do not become infected with errors by conflicting with divine teaching, or, by going beyond their proper limits, intrude upon what belongs to faith and engender confusion." *Dogmatic Constitution on the Catholic Faith: Dei Filius* IV, 12; http://www.ewtn.com/library/COUNCILS/V1.htm#4 (February 10, 2015).

36. Pius XII, *Humani Generis* in *AAS*, 42 (1950), 562.

> Catholic religion take these sciences into account as much as possible. This certainly would be praiseworthy in the case of clearly proved facts; but caution must be used when there is rather question of hypotheses, having some sort of scientific foundation, in which the doctrine contained in Sacred Scripture or in Tradition is involved. If such conjectural opinions are directly or indirectly opposed to the doctrine revealed by God, then the demand that they be recognized can in no way be admitted. For these reasons the Teaching Authority of the Church does not forbid that, in conformity with the present state of human sciences and sacred theology, research and discussions, on the part of men experienced in both fields, take place with regard to the doctrine of evolution, in as far as it inquires into the origin of the human body as coming from pre-existent and living matter—for the Catholic faith obliges us to hold that souls are immediately created by God. However, this must be done in such a way that the reasons for both opinions, that is, those favorable and those unfavorable to evolution, be weighed and judged with the necessary seriousness, moderation and measure, and provided that all are prepared to submit to the judgment of the Church, to whom Christ has given the mission of interpreting authentically the Sacred Scriptures and of defending the dogmas of faith. Some however, rashly transgress this liberty of discussion, when they act as if the origin of the human body from pre-existing and living matter were already completely certain and proved by the facts which have been discovered up to now and by reasoning on those facts, and as if there were nothing in the sources of divine revelation which demands the greatest moderation and caution in this question.
>
> When, however, there is question of another conjectural opinion, namely polygenism, the children of the Church by no means enjoy such liberty. For the faithful cannot embrace that opinion which maintains that either after Adam there existed on this earth true men who did not take their origin through natural generation from him as from the first parent of all, or that Adam represents a certain number of first parents. Now it is in no way apparent how such an opinion can be reconciled with that which the sources of revealed truth and the documents of the Teaching Authority of the Church propose with regard to original sin, which proceeds from a sin actually committed by an individual Adam and which, through generation, is passed on to all and is in everyone as his own.[37]

At the beginning the pope claims that scientific issues can be combined with truths of faith to different degrees. However, the achievements of positive sciences should be taken into account only if they are clearly proven facts. Pius XII suggests that the positive sciences may provide the answer to the question about the origin of the human body. His approach therefore converges with the traditional teaching of the Fathers and Scholastics. In the Catholic tradition, if

37. Ibid., 576–77.

a truth of natural knowledge is duly proven, it has to be accepted as a criterion of interpretation of Holy Scripture. If, for instance, Holy Scripture mentioned the movement of the sun across the sky,[38] it did not mean that the sun moved but was simply the way of describing natural phenomena from the point of view of an earthly observer. However, before heliocentric theory was demonstrated,[39] biblical passages speaking about the movement of the sun were necessarily interpreted according to the closest and the most natural sense of the wording, i.e., as implying that the sun really goes around the Earth. In this case, a well-established scientific theory became a criterion by which the Bible is to be interpreted.

The question for Pius XII is whether the origin of man's body also may be subject to the competence of science. Before him, most Catholic theologians believed that that truth, unlike the question of the movement of the sun or the shape of the earth, is not subject to substantial modifications in the light of scientific research, since it belongs to the realm of faith. Science is unable to positively confirm direct acts of God, although it is able to, and ultimately should, arrive at conclusions consistent with God's actions and attain such results that would not contradict them. Thus science, with respect to the origin of man, could constitute only a negative background.

It is a similar situation with other truths of the faith. For instance, when it comes to Christ's resurrection, historical research may prove that Jesus's tomb was empty, that no cult of the dead Jesus has ever been confirmed, that the apostles believed they had encountered the risen Christ, that most of them died for that belief, and so on. If, however, a scholar argues or assumes that Christ's resurrection was impossible, it would have to be stated *de fide* that he or she cannot be right. Such a scholar could, for instance, claim to have found the remains of Jesus or his re-burial place. Yet all these "discoveries" would be rejected by the Church *a priori* by virtue of faith itself. Pius XII affirms this approach as well: "One should not favor hypothetical assumptions that directly contradict the doctrine revealed by God."

In the late 19th and early 20th centuries, the belief that God directly formed the first human body enjoyed the status of ordinary Church teaching. Apologists not only argued science had failed to prove that humans evolved from animals, but also altogether excluded the possibility of proving it at any point in the future. Science as such, they claimed, could only discover, for example, that

38. ". . . Father who is in heaven, who makes his sun to rise upon the good, and bad, and rains upon the just and the unjust" (Mt 5:45). "The sun rises, and goes down, and returns to his place: and there rising again, makes his round by the south, and turns again to the north" (Eccl 1:5–6a).

39. Of course, heliocentric theory makes sense assuming that the solar system constitutes a reference point.

we all come from one couple or that a sudden appearance of humankind took place. These truths would not contradict faith, but rather indirectly support it.

Pius XII stood in the same line of teaching, but there was a subtle shift in his approach to the origin of man. Despite his assertion that science had not proven anything certain about the origin of man, the pope admitted the feasibility of this happening in the future. However, if science is said to be capable of explaining the origin of the human body, it implies that it is no longer a matter of faith. This follows from the simple fact that the truths of faith cannot be the subject of science. So in Pius XII's teaching, the direct creation of the first man is no longer protected as a matter of faith, and in consequence science is deemed competent to ultimately solve the issue.

The idea articulated in *Humani Generis* is depicted even more clearly in the pope's 1953 address to the First International Congress on Medical Genetics.[40] Thus Pius XII's views were influenced by theories that scientists had been presenting for almost a hundred years. As a result, the pope sanctioned a new way of thinking about human origin. It implied that science can give a positive answer and, in a way, may judge theological doctrine, an idea previously not acceptable to Catholic apologists.

The most significant thesis of *Humani Generis* reads as follows:

> Teaching Authority of the Church does not forbid that, in conformity with the present state of human sciences and sacred theology, research and discussions, on the part of men experienced in both fields, take place with regard to the doctrine of evolution, in as far as it inquires into the origin of the human body as coming from pre-existent and living matter.[41]

Pius XII does not state that evolution led to the emergence of man or that the natural sciences confirm such a hypothesis. He affirms only that research

40. An address to the participants of the First International Congress on Medical Genetics: "Genetics, Heredity, Evolution" (September 7, 1953). Referring to research on the origins of man, the pope mentioned again that no proofs whatsoever had been shown thereof by scientists, and that is why the issue requires wise and reasonable treatment. Pius XII confirmed that the answer to the question about the origin of man may be found by science; however, any such results should be balanced by theology. "If you consider—taught the pope—what we have said about research and scientific knowledge, it should be evident that neither from reason nor from a Christian way of thinking does one meet obstacles to investigations, to understanding, to confirmation of the truth. Their goal is to prevent that unproven hypotheses are accepted as established facts, to not forget that one source of knowledge must be complemented by another so that the scale of value and the level of certainty of one source of knowledge is not interpreted incorrectly." *AAS*, 20 (1953), 604.

41. "Ecclesiae Magisterium non prohibet quominus 'evolutionismi' doctrina, quatenus nempe de humani corporis origine inquirit ex iam exsistente ac vivente materia oriundi—animas enim a Deo immediate creari catholica fides non retinere iubet—pro hodierno humanarum disciplinarum et sacrae theologiae statu, investigationibus ac disputationibus peritorum in utroque campo hominum pertractetur." Ibid., 575.

"within the evolutionary paradigm" is not forbidden. What does that mean? We should take into account three possible interpretations.

According to the first (now commonly recognized among Catholic theologians), Pius XII means that evolutionary research may reveal the true origin of man. In other words, it is possible that man, regarding his body, came into existence through long evolution, and that science might prove this in the future. This interpretation deprives the origin of the human body of the status of a truth of faith, shifting it to a matter of biological research. The change introduced by the Pope is fine in words, then, but fraught with consequences.

According to the second interpretation, the Church knows the truth about the origin of man, yet will listen with interest to what scientists have to say on this matter. If evolutionary scientists search for evidence supporting the animal origin of man, the Church will not stand in their way. In order to respect academic freedom as such, it will not hinder such research. This interpretation, however, implies a "double-truth theory," which means that science and religion each possess their own truth. These two truths may convey contradictory messages because they belong to completely different and "non-overlapping" realms.[42] But double-truth theory has been condemned by the Fifth Lateran Council;[43] therefore, this interpretation should not be accepted by Catholics.

The third possible interpretation is that Pius XII allows the evolutionary origin of man to be discussed only in order to make evident the grave error of this idea. Similarly, Paul VI allowed for discussion about birth control, not to support contraception, but to reinforce Catholic teaching with the final outcome of the debate.

It is hard to decide which of the three interpretations is closest to the mind of Pius XII, but only the third could be harmonized with Christian tradition and documents like the decision of the Council of Cologne (1860), the wording from the encyclical *Arcanum* by Leo XIII (1880), and the decree of the Pontifical Biblical Commission of 1909. Just two months before the publication of *Humani Generis*, Cardinal Ernesto Ruffini wrote in *L'Osservatore Romano* (June 3, 1950):

> Evolution has been discussed in schools and in books for several decades; nevertheless, Catholics have never thought that they should call into doubt

42. S.J. Gould, who developed this idea, spoke about NOMA—non-overlapping magisteria. Cf. S.J. Gould, *Rocks of Ages: Science and Religion in the Fullness of Life* (New York: Ballantine Books, 1999).

43. "Since truth cannot contradict truth, we define that every statement contrary to the enlightened truth of the faith is totally false and we strictly forbid teaching otherwise to be permitted." (Fifth Lateran Council, Session 8, Dec 19, 1513.) Cf. http://www.ewtn.com/library/COUNCILS/LATERAN5.HTM (February 10, 2015).

> the teaching of the catechism, that man was created immediately by God, even as regards his body.[44]

These words should provide the proper theological and historical context for interpreting the words of Pius XII. Apparently, at the time of *Humani Generis* there were still high-ranking Church officials who unambiguously defended the immediate creation of Adam.

Having stated that the Church does not forbid discussion of evolution, Pius XII describes conditions to which scientific debate should adhere:

> 1) It is necessary to consider and respect the arguments of both parties.
>
> 2) The evolution hypothesis must not be presented as a certain doctrine, since it has not been proven by science.
>
> 3) The Church's decrees are always to be taken into consideration.
>
> 4) The evolution hypothesis must not be treated as if revelation contains nothing that would require considerable moderation and caution.

It seems that none of the Catholic supporters of the evolution hypothesis met all these conditions simultaneously. The first was simply a reasonable call for honest debate. In contrast, evolution scholars have usually disregarded arguments opposing their beliefs. The second condition—that human evolution has not been proven by science—stands in stark contrast to the views of almost all supporters of the theory of evolution. And finally, conditions three and four directly challenge Dorlodot, Messenger, and others, who claimed that nothing in Church Tradition had ever contradicted the evolutionary hypotheses. All in all, the pope's statement is a notably explicit warning against evolutionists, both atheistic and theistic.

Church pronouncements regarding evolution have rarely met with due respect, and, in like manner, *Humani Generis* failed to produce the desired effect. Among Catholics the general impression arose that Pius XII accepted evolution as the explanation of the origin of the human body. However, the document contains no such statement. The pope had merely allowed scientific research and debate in this matter. The encyclical also reveals the reasons for making such a decision. "Catholic theologians and philosophers," wrote the pope,

> whose grave duty it is to defend natural and supernatural truth and instill it in the hearts of men, cannot afford to ignore or neglect these more or less erroneous opinions. Rather they must come to understand these same theories well, both because diseases are not properly treated unless they are

44. Quotation after: *The Theory of Evolution Judged by Reason and Faith*, 160.

> rightly diagnosed, and because sometimes even in these false theories a certain amount of truth is contained, and, finally, because these theories provoke more subtle discussion and evaluation of philosophical and theological truths.[45]

The last concept mentioned by Pius XII is polygenism, the idea that humans come from more than one original couple. This theory appeared in theology alongside the emergence of the evolutionary hypothesis.[46] If humans, regarding the body, emerged according to natural biological laws, why would it happen only once? Laws of nature operate consistently over billions of years. If something occurred once in the past, there is no reason to assume it would not occur many times in the past and be repeated in the future. Nevertheless, in this area the pope did not allow for academic freedom. He rejected polygenism since it was incompatible with the doctrine of original sin. If there had been any other people than Adam and Eve at the beginning, or if they represented a certain number of parents, then the sin of one couple would not affect every man. Yet it is a tenet of faith that each human is burdened with this sin transferred through sexual generation. By this, Pius XII confirms that truths of the faith are not subject to the judgments of natural sciences. Scientific truths cannot contradict truths of the faith. However, science could theoretically prove something contrary to polygenism, namely, that at the beginning there was only one couple and that all humans are their descendants. If this were the case, then believers would gain additional certainty that such a scientific conclusion is true because it is congruent with knowledge provided by faith.[47]

45. *AAS*, 42 (1950), 563.

46. The doctrine of polygenism, outside of the area of theology, was discussed even before the appearance of the theory of evolution. From Antiquity, many scholars and researchers have proposed different ideas on this matter. J. Kulisz, S.J. points to Isaac de la Peyrère (†1676), who was the first to contest the belief in monogenism. See his *Teilhardowskie rozumienie grzechu* (Warsaw: ATK, 1986), 59. Supporters of this doctrine were, *inter alios*, G. Bruno and Voltaire. A French ethnologist, William Edwards (†1842), presented his version of polygenism in *Des Caractères physiologiques des races humaines considérés dans leurs rapports avec l'histoire, lettre á M. Amédée Thierry* (Paris: Compère Jeune, 1829). Ch.H. Smith (†1859) believed that the three main human races could not share one ancestor. See his *The Natural History of the Human Species* (Edinburgh, 1848). One of the first modern Catholic authors to allow the doctrine of polygenism was E. Messenger. In his commentary on Genesis 1:26–28 he writes: "To anyone carefully studying the Hebrew text of this passage, it is evident that Adam here is used collectively rather than singularly, and signifies not so much a particular individual, but rather the race as such, i.e., Adam and Eve with their descendants. . . . From an examination of this passage alone, then, we cannot tell whether or not the sacred author knew that the human race had descended from one common ancestor, though he is certainly describing the origin of the whole human race." *Evolution and Theology*, 100–01.

47. In 1987, A.C. Wilson and colleagues published a paper based on mitochondrial lineages, claiming that all women could trace their ancestry to a single woman in Africa 160,000 years ago. This matrilineal ancestor was dubbed "mitochondrial Eve" by the popular press. In the mid-1990s the mitochondrial Eve hypothesis became fashionable for a time. Some theologians considered it almost

Note that for Pius XII the only clear reason for rejecting polygenism is the impossibility of reconciling it with the doctrine of original sin. Thus he applies the functional rather than the substantial criterion. Consequently, some Catholic scholars have concluded that if polygenism could be harmonized with the doctrine of original sin, Church teaching would allow polygenism. That is why, after *Humani Generis*, various theories arose aimed at reconciling the Catholic understanding of original sin with polygenism. All that debate came, however, to a dead end, for even if a theoretical solution had been found, polygenism would still have been unacceptable. According to classical Christian teaching, people descend from one couple not only because such a doctrine best explains the propagation of original sin, but because this is the positive teaching of the Holy Bible and Tradition.[48] But a clear objection to polygenism in the Church never consolidated, and so this doctrine periodically returns in writings of theologians.[49]

---

a scientific confirmation of monogenism. However, in 1995 biochemist F. Ayala challenged the idea of mitochondrial Eve, trying to show that in a given time of human history (about 2 million years) one cannot reduce the human genome to one single couple. Since then "mitochondrial Eve" has meant not one person, but a population in which the alleged divergence of human and apes took place. Thus the mitochondrial Eve hypothesis is now used to challenge the traditional belief in one historical human couple as the origin to all humans. Setting aside all the problems with this hypothesis, it should be noted that it says nothing about monogenism. Even in its original form it merely stated that contemporary people derived from one woman. It did not prove that before, after, or simultaneously, there existed no other human races that exist no longer today. The weak scientific points of this hypothesis are: 1) assumption concerning a constant mutation rate; 2) assumptions of no strong selection for genetic change and no gene conversion; and 3) assumptions of random breeding among individuals and no migrations into or out of the breeding population. All of this results in huge discrepancies between different research findings on the alleged divergence between human and apes, which vary between tens of thousands and millions of years. Thus, this hypothesis—as M. Behe put it—"is tricky and depends on many assumptions" (Cf. M. Behe, *The Edge of Evolution*, 70).

48. Since Pius XII, Catholic theology has usually treated polygenism and original sin together, but this had not always been the case. There are a few Magisterial documents stating that the whole of humankind comes from one human couple, or from Adam, regardless of the problem of original sin. There are two documents in particular worth mentioning: first, the solemn profession of faith by Pope Pelagius I (see Appendix); and second, the 1459 decree of Pope Pius II condemning errors of Canon Zaninus. One of the condemned ideas states that "God created also another world than this, and in its time many other men and women existed, and as a consequence, Adam was not the first man." ("Deum quoque alium mundum ab isto creasse, et in eius tempore multos alios viros et mulieres exstitisse, et per consequens Adam primum hominem non fuisse.") (DS 1363).

49. The debate on polygenism was raging in the Church in the post-conciliar period. The Sixties were marked with multifarious attempts to explain the origin of the human being and the propagation of original sin. Even Pope Paul VI was drawn into the debate. In 1966 he addressed the audience at a symposium: "It is evident that you will not consider as reconcilable with the authentic Catholic doctrine those explanations of original sin, given by some modern authors, that start from the presupposition of polygenism, which is not proved" (*AAS*, 58 [1966], 654). Nevertheless, this short statement in a speech of minimal importance did not halt the invasion of polygenism in theology.

Three years after *Humani Generis*, Pius XII reiterated the central theses of his encyclical in a speech to the participants of the First Medical Genetics Congress in Rome. Drawing on the results of research on genetic inheritance, he underlines the fact that science proves the fundamental laws of inheritance, which display no substantial innovations and no transfer of acquired traits. Nevertheless, some scholars allowed for the possibility of a significant alteration to genetic inheritance due to mutations. Referring to the common descent of all living creatures, the pope adds:

> In recent works, geneticists say that nothing better explains the connection of all living beings, than a common family tree. However from time to time it is indicated that it is just a picture, a hypothesis and not a proven fact.[50]

Pius XII adds that other hypotheses are possible and had indeed been formulated by some renowned scholars. He points to several additional difficulties, such as a number of discrepancies among scientists in the defining of terms employed in the debate, the impossibility of experimentally deriving one species from another, and the inability to clearly define at which stage of evolution the humanoid abruptly crossed over into humanity. Following these reservations, Pius XII claims that, depending on the future findings of the natural sciences, either the presently adopted image of the evolution of man will be validated or there will be a need to replace it and elaborate a completely new one.[51]

In sum, *Humani Generis* failed to resolve the debate on the origin of man. Much as the Holy Father allows the possibility of a scientific solution to this issue, he never states whether science will in fact satisfactorily solve it. He does argue, though, that science had not yet arrived at any clear-cut answer.

It is important to note that the Church speaks authoritatively on matters of faith and morals, but does not enjoy a supernatural gift of infallibility guaranteed by the Holy Spirit when it comes to scientific issues. Thus, when Pius XII shifted the question of the origin of man from theology to the realm of scientific research, and spoke about the abilities or achievements of natural science, he did not entertain the authority of infallibility. Furthermore, when touching upon an issue as pivotal as the origin of man, theologians would expect a state-

50. The address *Genetics, Heredity, Evolution*, from September 7, 1953, *AAS*, 20 (1953), 599.

51. "The definite conclusion stemming from this is as follows: depending on whether in future the former or the latter interpretation finds its firm validation, the accepted picture of human evolution will be confirmed or replaced by a brand new one. It would be a proper thing to state that deliberations on the origins of human being are only fledgling, and so the image emerging from them cannot be treated as definite. This is the conclusion on relations between the theory of inheritance and the theory of evolution" (*AAS*, 20 [1953], 600).

ment of a higher doctrinal rank. Thus, as much as the encyclical elucidates, it fails to resolve the dispute conclusively since it does not define whether man came into existence through evolution or through direct creation.

Four Scientific Assumptions in the Dispute over the Origin of Man

The Church Fathers, followed by numerous theologians and the Magisterium itself, invariably maintained that the natural and literal sense of the Bible should be abandoned only when it would contradict reason or self-evident truths.[52] For instance, when the Bible mentions "the right hand of God," it is an obvious anthropomorphism that should be interpreted non-literally. In modernity it appeared that the Church might abandon the literal interpretation of certain biblical texts due to new scientific discoveries. Natural science can prove irrefutably that certain truths are well-founded to such a degree that maintaining the opposite would be contrary to facts and reason. Undoubtedly such scientific discoveries include the spherical shape of the earth;[53] the Earth's revolution around the Sun (assuming the proper point of reference); the existence of multiple galaxies instead of one spherical firmament of stars; and the great age of the universe, significantly exceeding the several thousand years suggested by Holy Scripture. Thus, a number of scientific truths surfaced in modern times that altered the Christian understanding of the Bible.

Some theologians have assumed that the Darwinian theory of evolution—the evolution of the human body in particular—should be ranked among the truths altering Christian faith. However, Catholics believe that the Holy Spirit has preserved doctrinal truth unchanged across the centuries. Neither the belief in the heliocentric model of the solar system nor the belief in billions of years of the earth's existence have affected in any way the articles of faith. It is different with the evolutionary hypothesis, which resulted in abandoning the truth about the origin of the human body. The creation of the human body by the power of God directly from the dust of the earth is not at odds with reason; there is no *logical* obstacle to God's creation of man in this manner. So the question to be asked—bearing in mind the Church debates of the 1940s and 1950s—is this: are arguments in favor of the evolutionary origin of man strong

52. *Providentissimus Deus* (*AAS*, 26 [1893–1894], 282). See Chapter Four, under "The Intervention of the Congregation of the Index."

53. It is noteworthy that the spherical shape of the Earth was already commonly known to the ancient peoples. It is not true that modernity came up with this discovery. There existed a number of cosmogonies, including the biblical version, offering different interpretations. The Bible itself never yields evidence that the Earth is flat. On the contrary—the expressions "the circle of Earth" and "the heavenly circle" are used several times (Is 40:22; Sir 24:5).

enough to allow the Church to abandon the natural and historical sense of the Genesis account?

In the 1950s (though this is still common now), the evolutionary origin of man was typically illustrated with an image of different stages, an ordinary ape gradually and smoothly transforming into a modern man. This image, cropping up both in textbooks and in scholarly writings, appeals strongly to readers' imaginations. This "icon of evolution" (drawing on the expression used by J. Wells[54]) first appeared in the writings of Haeckel and Huxley in the mid-nineteenth century. A critical analysis of the evidence, however, indicates that the gradual transformations portrayed in the popular image are merely a speculative gloss on the actual findings. The majority of actual findings can be unequivocally classified as either ape or human fossils. Considering that at least 90% of apes went extinct, one would expect to unearth far more potential candidates for hypothetical "missing links," because every single ape species possessed a distinctive set of features that could be used to place it at one of the presupposed stages of evolution. Neither can we exclude that there were different human races in the past. This would mean that the variety of the human population was even greater than we observe today. If one assumes that there must have been transitional forms, then the fossilized re mains of those different races, even though all truly human, would provide a fair amount of material to construct the alleged evolutionary paths. Still, the picture of the gradual evolution of an ape ancestor into a human form raises several fundamental scientific problems.[55]

1. Bipedalism. Bipedalism is a form of movement unique to human beings. Among all contemporary mammals only human beings routinely move around in the vertical position, using only their two lower limbs. The two upper limbs

54. In 2000, Jonathan Wells published his book *Icons of Evolution,* in which he criticizes ten well-known images commonly presented in many textbooks and in popular science literature as evidence for evolution. Wells shows their hypothetical and often misleading or even deceitful messages.

55. My grounds are to be found mainly in works by P. Lenartowicz. In his article "O starożytności człowieczeństwa" [On the Antiquity of Mankind], *Kwartalnik Filozoficzny* 33 (2005), 35–59, he distinguishes between four major mystifications surrounding the origin of man present in the contemporary literature: 1) Fossil findings indicate the common origin of apes and humans. 2) According to research, early human stages were equipped with evolutionary intelligence at some point between apes and Homo sapiens. 3) The shape and the size at early human stages testifies to their "pre-rationality." 4) The outer appearance of early humanoids bore more resemblance to apes than to modern human races. Biochemist M. Giertych presents a concise criticism of the evolutionary icon: "For me, it is a tremendous fallacy to depict an image showing in one sequence a chimpanzee, a gorilla, a Neanderthal man, an Aborigine, and a Scandinavian. What is to be seen? The first features that are particularly eye-catching are the change of color from black to white, the hair reduction and the increasingly upright position of the spine. After all, we are unable to obtain any useful information on the skin color or hair from fossilized bone remnants. . . . In the middle there is a slightly bent figure of a Neanderthal; the image is derived from the first unearthed specimen of this race, found in the vicinity of the Neander Valley, and it happened to be an arthritis-stricken, ailing

are not used when moving, which seemingly makes bipedalism the least efficient form of locomotion among the higher mammals.[56] This is a problem for evolutionary theory. From a Darwinian point of view, natural selection preserves beneficial changes and eliminates disadvantageous ones, so there would be no evolutionary justification for bipedalism in an animal that can already move faster and more efficiently using all four limbs. If anything, evolution would be expected to move in the opposite direction, from bipedal to quadrupedal locomotion.[57]

The problem of bipedalism is related to a more general issue, namely human defenselessness and the lack of defensive features such as fangs, claws, thick furry skin, etc. Humans can survive without those "survival" features thanks to their capacity for reason, which enables them to supplement lack of natural protection by producing clothes, tools, and shelters. This evolutionary scenario, however, ends with the problem: which came first—human reason or the human body? If the predecessor of man had lost the survival features before it acquired the faculty of thinking, it would have been eliminated by natural selection. In order to lose the animal features, the human predecessor would need to have possessed reason, so that thanks to rational activity the animal features would no longer have been necessary for survival. But to possess reason (according to Christian anthropology) means to have a spiritual soul. However, a human soul can only animate a human body, so the non-human body of man's predecessor could not have had reason. Therefore, neither human body nor human soul can be brought about first, but both must come into existence simultaneously.

---

old man. Subsequently discovered specimens are devoid of the bending posture. Even if all unearthed Neanderthals were stooped, could their remains testify to evolution from apes to human beings or perhaps just in the opposite direction? Moreover, in the presented sequence, it is only the Neanderthal that is a genuine fossil, the remaining figures being living creatures. So what constitutes the scientific element in the image—an image familiar to all of us? The message it strives to convey is not grounded in science." See M. Giertych, *O ewolucji w Parlamencie Europejskim* [On Evolution in the European Parliament] (Kórnik, 2007), 8–9.

56. Indeed, hand movements while marching or running help to balance the center of mass; nevertheless, this function of upper limbs is merely auxiliary in nature. Comparing the relative speeds of different species of animals, it follows that the human being is "the slowest of animals." See P. Lenartowicz, *Ludy czy małpoludy: problem genealogii człowieka* [Men or Man-apes: The Problem of Human Genealogy] (Kraków: Wyższa Szkoła Filozoficzno-Pedagogiczna Ignatianum, 2010), 100.

57. See R. Henke, "Aufrecht aus den Baumen," *Focus* 39 (1996): 178; P. Lenartowicz, "O wczesnych stadiach ewolucji człowieka," *Człowiek i świat: Szkice filozoficzne*, ed. R. Darowski (Kraków: WAM, 1972), 161. The proponents of evolution assume a possible loss of said features in the course of development of the species, which gradually emerged, successfully, without those auxiliary attributes. Nevertheless, such an argument contains a *petitio principii*, since its conclusion that higher skills appeared first and auxiliary features were lost later is actually a starting assumption. This stands in contradiction to the gradual acquisition of increasingly higher and more developed skills, culminating in reason, in the alleged evolutionary process.

There is also a logical problem, because if man's predecessor had acquired reason before its body became human, it would have been an animal with reason, which is nothing less than a human. Thus the evolution of man from a lower animal has the logical problem of *petitio principii.*

2. Brain size. A popular argument supporting the gradual evolution of man is based on the gradual development of the size of the brain in different animals. As Piotr Lenartowicz has put it,

> In a nutshell, it seems that there is a rule established in biology: big brain = high intelligence, small brain = low intelligence. As a result, since the skulls of our early Pleistocene or Pliocene ancestors indicate their relatively small brain size, it is presumed that the level of their intelligence remained low.[58]

If this rule were true, the most intelligent creatures should be elephants and whales. But we do not observe a correlation between brain size and the abilities of an individual among either humans or animals. Lenartowicz also distinguishes between sensory abilities observed in the animal kingdom and mental abilities observed only in human beings. The former are dependent, at least to some degree, on the construction of the brain. In animals, parts of the brain are developed at different levels, depending on which abilities they find most useful. But when it comes to intellectual abilities, this rule no longer holds; the basic structure of the brain in higher mammals is the same, but human intellectual faculties exceed those of other animals dramatically. This means that the size of the brain cannot be the sole or main basis for assessing intellectual abilities.[59]

The Nazis, besotted by Darwinism, used to assess human mental abilities by measuring the volume of the head, the proportions of the face, etc. In their view, a man lacking "appropriate" proportions did not deserve to be called fully

58. P. Lenartowicz, "O starożytności człowieczeństwa" [On the Antiquity of Mankind], 47. Lenartowicz also draws attention to the fact that scholars regularly ignore the brain size/brain mass ratio vs. body size/body mass ratio. It is an established fact that Australopithecus had a brain mass amounting to 450–700 cm^3. However, when considering their average height (between 100–120 cm), the ratio resembles that of a contemporary man.

59. The average brain size of the modern human population amounts to approximately 1250–1350 cm^3. However, the scientific literature reports instances of healthy, mentally sound beings equipped with a brain below 700 cm^3. On the other hand, mentally healthy humans with a brain size exceeding 2000 cm^3 are known (Lenartowicz, *On the Antiquity*, 49–51). McHenry strove to evaluate the number of neurons in East African Australopithecus. He stipulated their level at 4.3×10^9. In modern man this number amounts to 8.2×10^9. For McHenry this constituted clear evidence for a relatively low level of intelligence in humanoids. Later on it appeared that the difference between the number of neurons in contemporary human specimens can be as high as 4.5×10^9. See M. Hennenberg, "Brain Size/Body Weight Variability in *Homo Sapiens*: Consequences for Interpreting Hominid Evolution," *Homo* 39 (1990), 121–30.

human, but belonged instead to a lower stage of development. Today the same principle leads to a denial of the humanity of the ancient ancestors of contemporary man. The Darwinian approach in both cases fails, for it is beyond the scope of natural science to judge, on the basis of the natural features of a specimen alone, whether it is a rational being or not. Perhaps the only efficient way to evaluate the presence of rational abilities in extinct creatures is by their activities when they were alive. If we have at our disposal products of culture and art, such as tools or paintings (which animals do not produce), then we are warranted to conclude that rationality is involved.

On the other hand, philosophy teaches us that rationality is linked with freedom (free will understood as a faculty of soul), consciousness, and conscience. Rationality is thus connected with multifaceted personhood, even if in fossils only fragmentary displays are to be found. In fact, philosophical truths are confirmed by archaeological discoveries. Wherever we find rudimentary displays of rational actions, such as basic tools, we also discover clear indications of cultural expression. Consequently, the presence of rationality implies the parallel existence of the other forms of human intellectual activity (technology, art, religion, laws), even if each is in a very primitive form. If there happen to be only remnants of one activity (e.g., tools, but no paintings), it would be fair to assume that it was not because those creatures could not exercise any other kind of intellectual activity, but because the relics of such activity were not preserved. It is also possible that some human races became at a certain point in time so morally corrupt that they were incapable of appreciating any beauty, were unable to obey any laws, entered into incestuous relationships, and perhaps resorted to eating each other or even their own offspring. From the perspective of biological anthropology, they would have reached an animalistic level of existence. Such a state, however, would mean the loss of only moral faculties, not ontological ones. As a result, it would not constitute a stage in evolution towards humanity but rather a dramatic moral and cultural regress.

3. The problem of reconstructions. The assumption underlying the whole evolutionary scheme of man's origin is that all evolutionary stages can be classified, from the most apelike to the most humanlike. Until about the middle of the twentieth century, proponents of evolution claimed that humans descended from apes. In the course of time, however, this statement was replaced with a seemingly more conciliatory one—that humans and apes share a common ancestor. But when we think of those two formulas we immediately realize that the change was merely rhetorical, because the common ancestor of an ape and a man was *at best* an ape. And this is the same as to say that man descended from apes. But the problem is that no one knows what the alleged common ancestor was, or when the evolutionary paths of humans and modern apes diverged. In textbooks on evolution, fossils supposedly representing the first stage of human evolution are reconstructed to bear a striking resemblance to a contemporary chimpanzee; but if a chimpanzee is a by-product of human evolution, constituting another evolutionary end, it cannot be at the same time the starting point of human evolution. Therefore, the most common "icon of evolution" is burdened with striking inconsistency.

Moreover, the general public is not aware of the fact that reconstructions based on fossils have their limits in providing sound knowledge about the past. Most parts of dead organisms are so decomposed that scientists making reconstructions have at their disposal only bones and teeth. This poses a serious limitation. As Lenartowicz points out,

> Basically speaking only two biological dynamics characteristic to man can be reconstructed thanks to the remains. One is the locomotion dynamics and the other is the mastication dynamics, connected with the preliminary processing of foodstuffs by means of teeth, jaws, muscles. . . . In both cases the excavated remains dating back to four or even more million years ago proved that ancient human forms were as different from ape forms as are the modern ones.[60]

But paleoanthropologists' claims rarely stop at the locomotion and mastication of alleged "hominids." They also attempt to reconstruct facial characteristics, external appearance, skin, hair, or even customs. And then the element of interpretation is richly colored by preconceived assumptions. Not surprisingly, such interpretations often prove to be contradictory.[61] The problem is that most people do not know what belongs to positive knowledge and what stems from nothing more than evolutionary assumptions.

When the first ancient human skeleton was discovered in 1856 in Neander Valley (Germany), its reconstruction was distinctively ape-like.[62] After unearthing several hundred related skeletons, scientists decided to abandon the hypothesis of Neanderthals being an early stage in human evolution. Among other things, Neanderthals had brains similar in size to modern man, and they were of the similar height to us. Many now regard Neanderthals as just representatives of an extinct human race. But since some Neanderthal specimens have been dated to 400,000 years ago, no form younger than 400,000 years can be a missing link in the human evolutionary story.

60. P. Lenartowicz, *O starożytności człowieczeństwa* [On the Antiquity of Mankind], 39.

61. For instance, in *National Geographic* (197, March 2000, 140) four very different images of *Homo habilis* were based on the same fossil evidence. There is another example of reconstruction: http://ngm.nationalgeographic.com/ngm/0504/feature2/multimedia.html.

62. The first unearthed Neanderthal skeleton belonged to an elderly arthritis-stricken man. For this reason the first depictions of this stooped, bent figure were at least partly justified.

We can divide the inaccuracies in reconstructing ancient human remains into two categories. The first includes obvious deceptions such as Piltdown Man or Beijing Man, which are discussed further on in this book. The second consists of unjustified assumptions used in reconstructions.

When it comes to the historical sciences, interpretation is an important part of research, the interpretation being what a scholar adds to the existing evidence. Such additions need independent justification; however, that justification cannot simply be the assumption that evolutionary theory is true, for this would be circular reasoning and thus of no scientific value. An example of an inaccurate interpretation is Nebraska Man.[63] Some scientists consider it only an inevitable mistake in the pursuit of scientific truth. But it was not just an isolated case. The story of Nebraska Man, first of all, clearly indicates the importance of the initial assumptions that scholars rely on to interpret facts. According to Piotr Lenartowicz,

> For over 100 years now, paleoanthropologists have taken for granted the scenario of the evolution of human locomotion derived from the anthropoid ape (Pongidae). What does it mean? It means that in scientific terms an unfounded hypothesis is taken for granted, claiming that the human system of locomotion supposedly stems from a gradual transformation of locomotion typical of anthropoid apes. This is the reason why the fossilized remains that today rank among the *Homo* group were formerly referred to as *Pithecanthropus* (from Greek: "ape-man"). Thus the remains of hominid species from two and more million years ago were called Australopithecus (southern ape) although some widely accomplished paleoanthropologists would classify them in the *Homo* group, Day (1969) even dubbing them *Homo sapiens*.[64]

63. In 1922 Henry F. Osborn, the head of the American Museum of Natural History, announced that in western Nebraska he had found a fossilized molar from the Pliocene period. The tooth combined apelike and humanlike features. A heated debate raged on, supported by scientific arguments put forward by both parties, regarding the origin of the tooth in question. Did it belong to Pithecanthropus erectus or to human beings? Soon it was granted the scientific status *Hesperopithecus haroldcooki* (the Nebraska Man). Many recognized experts supported Osborn in his claims. On the basis of the find, the whole head and body of the specimen were painstakingly reconstructed. In July of the same year the *Illustrated London News* magazine published a drawing of the Nebraska Man accompanied by his similar-looking wife and children busy with their household chores. When the popular speaker and politician William Jennings Bryan, expressed doubts about the reconstruction, he was met with widespread criticism. Five years later, other parts of the skeleton were discovered. Then it appeared that together with the tooth they belonged to an extinct species of wild American pigs (*Prosthenops xiphodens*) and had no links whatsoever with either apes or human beings. All the drawings, eagerly popularized in American literature, were removed. See: http://creation.com/fresh-look-at-nebraska-man (1 June 2015).

64. P. Lenartowicz, *Ludy czy małpoludy*, 113.

When searching for the cradle of mankind, there is a common tendency to regard ancient peoples as very primitive ones. One of the most persuasive demonstrations in support of this would be the use of very basic tools. Although simple tools such as stone axes and arrowheads are indeed what have remained, this does not mean that the communities in question were incapable of "producing" law, religion, and art. We don't know what artifacts they made of soft materials or what works of art (whether music or painting) might have been present in those societies. We can only draw conclusions by analogy with uncivilized communities of the present. No one doubts that contemporary primitive peoples belong to the species *Homo sapiens*, and that their intellectual capacity does not differ from that of people in highly advanced societies. Furthermore, although the communities in question use relatively basic tools and unsophisticated technology, there is a difference between the simplicity of a tool and the artistry of using it. Even communities with primitive tools generally use them in highly skilled and dexterous ways. As ethnographers have shown, such communities often also exhibit intricate, complex networks of social relations, worldviews, religion, and other crucial elements of spiritual culture. Perhaps in a million years' time all that will remain of such communities will be a handful of chipped stones, and all other manifestations of their activity will be lost. Therefore, such extant evidence from ancient primitive homesteads does little or nothing to further the hypothesis that humans evolved from animals through many stages of non-rational ancestors.

4. Structural similarity (homology). One assumption central to evolutionary theory is that structural similarity points to common descent. Darwin found similarities in the bones of a horse's leg, a bat's wing, a porpoise's fin, and a human hand. Based on this he concluded that all those organisms must have a common ancestor.[65] The same approach is used by the scientists who pursue human evolution. But the question arises: Is similarity a certain evidence for common ancestry?

Similarities are noticed everywhere in nature. For instance, we can know two or more similar people, but that does not force us to conclude they are siblings. Similarity could be due to common design rather than common biological ancestry. One way to demonstrate the latter would be to show that biological similarities are due to genetic ones, with differences arising through unguided mutations. Indeed, this was a prediction of Darwinian theory. But there is no general correspondence between anatomical and genetic similarities; homologous features can be due to non-homologous genes, and non-homologous fea-

65. Ch. Darwin, *The Descent of Man and Selection in Relation to Sex* (London: J. Murray, 1871), 401.

tures can be due to homologous genes.[66] Therefore, as evidence for common ancestry, homology is most likely false, and at best inconclusive.[67]

Last but not least, a question arises regarding the epistemological status of the concept of common descent. Biological macroevolution (Darwinism) is a broad term defining a historical theory and touches upon multiple events, each of which happened only once in the past. But the scientific demonstration of a one-time event from the past and that of an event that can be repeated many times in the laboratory are quite different things. If the theory of human evolution is historical in nature, it cannot be tested in the same way as theories put forward in the experimental sciences. Karl Popper, for instance, once described Darwinism as intrinsically untestable and hence non-scientific, granting it merely the status of a "metaphysical research program."[68] Some scholars have attempted to salvage the situation by distinguishing between "the fact of evolution" and "the theory of evolution." In this view, evolution becomes "the fact" that cannot be questioned. As Phillip E. Johnson has pointed out, however, the "fact" is merely the theory insulated from empirical challenge.[69]

Considering the many evolutionary stages that would be needed between ape-like creatures and human beings (or between any other two groups of organisms), we would expect to find (in Darwin's words) innumerable intermediate and transitional links. Yet all that scientists actually have at their disposal are a few remnants that are difficult to classify unequivocally. As a result, speculations must play a key role in evolutionary stories of *Homo sapiens*.[70] But even if

66. Gavin de Beer, *Homology: An Unsolved Problem* (Oxford: Oxford University Press, 1971).

67. See Jonathan Wells, *Icons of Evolution*, Chapter Four.

68. In the early stage of his career, Popper did not consider the Darwinian theory to be scientific. "I have come to the conclusion"—he wrote—"that Darwinism is not a testable scientific theory, but a metaphysical research programme—a possible framework for testable scientific theories." See K. Popper, *Unended Quest* (La Salle: Open Court, 1976), 168, cf. 151. "[R]eally severe tests of the theory of natural selection are hard to come by, much more so than tests of otherwise comparable theories in physics or chemistry" ("Natural Selection and the Emergence of Mind," *Dialectica* 32, 3–4 [1978]: 339–355, at 344). Later on, after being severely criticized for his claim, Popper was convinced to change his outlook and give Darwin more credit in the field of science; nevertheless, he continued to distinguish Darwinism from what he considered truly scientific theories.

69. *Darwin on Trial*, 184 n.

70. In 1991 a book was published by Misia Landau, *Narratives on Human Evolution* (New Haven, London: Yale University Press, 1991), in which the author embarks on the strenuous task of tackling the interpretative factor in the analysis of the fossil material of archaic peoples. It appears that a number of those "scientific" interpretations can be compared to fairy tales in their particular structure. The book strives to classify these in terms of certain types. The reader gains the impression that contemporary stories about ancient creatures told by scientists closely resemble archaic cosmogonies or the founding myths of ancient civilizations. According to Landau: "Of all the stories paleoanthropologists have told, only Darwin's *The Descent of Man* (1871) approaches the status of an authorized version. Like the Bible, it can be read from many points of view" (19).

the empirical material were so fantastically complete as to show in chronological order dozens of mediatory forms between ancient apes and modern humans, this would still prove no more than that there were many mediatory forms over time. To establish the evolution of one form into another would require showing not just their successive existence in the past, but the causes that made one evolve into the other and the biological mechanism sufficient to accomplish it.

Undoubtedly, philosophical assumptions of materialism and atheism have also played some role in shaping the idea of an animal origin of man. It seems that contemporary culture embraces various concepts of the origin of man that were present in pagan belief.[71] If we were to rely only on substantiated facts, the concept of the evolutionary origin of man would be pre-scientific in nature and would still need to be formulated as a testable hypothesis. Instead, it seems to persist simply because the traditional Christian alternative has been *a priori* ruled out. In the course of the long-running debate on evolution, the idea of an animal origin of man has been disseminated in textbooks, culture, and social consciousness. Nevertheless, the level of dissemination of a certain idea does not make it more scientific or true. Pagan myths of antiquity, now commonly discarded, were also widely embraced centuries ago. Their popularity, however, did not make them true.

Many modern Christian theologians took for granted the alleged evidence of human evolution and incorporated it as the "starting point" for their theological investigations. According to the classical Christian standpoint, however, should a conflict arise between science (or rather an idea presented as a scientific theory) and the Bible, a Christian is obliged to follow the Bible.[72] Clearly, evolutionary theory contradicts the most natural sense of Genesis. Catholic

71. For example, the main part of St. Irenaeus's *Contra haereses* constitutes a polemic against all kinds of fallacious concepts about the creation of the world from the pagan point of view, as well as of a number of early Christian heresies. Among dozens of mistaken views on the origin of man there appear the ones contradicting his direct formation from mud. According to one pagan concept, at the onset man came into being as a defective creature who had difficulty walking and keeping an upright position, but later on God inserted into him a spark of His divine light in order to perfect him. Irenaeus decisively rejects various views on the gradual emergence of the human body from lower stages.

72. This principle was first stated by Saint Augustine in his commentary to the Book of Genesis, *De Genesi ad litteram* I, 21, 41. His position was substantiated by Leo XIII, who writes in the encyclical *Providentissimus Deus*: "If dissension should arise between them [science and faith], here is the rule also laid down by St. Augustine for the theologian: Whatever they can really demonstrate to be true of physical nature, we must show to be capable of reconciliation with our Scriptures; and whatever they assert in their treatises that is contrary to these Scriptures of ours, that is to Catholic faith, we must either prove it as well as we can to be entirely false, or at all events we must, without the least hesitation, believe it to be so" (*Enchiridion Biblicum*, 40).

apologists at the turn of the nineteenth century referred to the concept of evolution as "merely a hypothesis." Pius XII even prohibited claiming that the evolution of the human body was already completely certain and proved by the facts. Watching the contemporary debate over human evolution, one may easily conclude that modern biology has not provided sufficient evidence to substantially modify Pius XII's position.

7

The Evolutionary Vision of Teilhard de Chardin

Pierre Teilhard de Chardin, S.J. (1881–1955) was more of a naturalist and philosopher than a theologian. Nevertheless, the thinker's significant influence on Church thought and the ubiquitous association of his name with Christian evolutionism requires that we present at least the main tenets of "Teilhardism" and juxtapose them with the position of the Church. This is not an easy task, since his literary legacy exceeds the confines of a short study. In order to present Teilhard's main ideas I will touch upon his concepts from three different perspectives: natural sciences (paleoanthropology), philosophy, and theology.

Science

Teilhard de Chardin, dubbed the "Catholic Darwin," joined the Society of Jesus in 1899. A year after his priestly ordination (1911) he embarked on studies in paleontology and geology in Paris. In 1922 he received his Ph.D. and began lecturing at the Catholic Institute. After his religious superior banned him from teaching (W. Ledóchowski was Jesuit General at that time), in 1926 he traveled to China, where he participated in numerous international scientific expeditions. He lived in China intermittently until 1947. At that time he returned to France and in 1951 left his country again, this time for the USA. Four years later he passed away in New York, where he was buried.

To better understand Teilhard's early engagement in excavations, we need to remember that at the beginning of the 20th century, naturalists carried out an extensive search for any human remnants that could fill in the huge gap between the theory and the facts.[1] Regardless of this fundamental problem, the

1. Neanderthal bones were discovered as early as 1856, but they were not regarded as one of the evolutionary stages. It was only when more fossilized remains were unearthed that Marcelin Boule included them (several dozen years later) in the evolutionary scheme. For more on how Neanderthal man became an icon of evolution, see J. Wells, *Icons of Evolution*, 214–17.

purely deductive concept of human evolution was spreading and increasingly winning supporters. As the theory gained support, researchers were naturally ever more eager to find the missing evidence.

This context sheds some light on the work of two paleontologists, Charles Dawson and Arthur S. Woodward, the latter an employee at the British Museum. Teilhard met them while living in Hastings, England, between 1908 and 1912. In 1908 Dawson claimed that he had found some remains of an ancient evolutionary form between a human and an ape. In 1912 Dawson and Woodward announced to an audience of the Geological Society of London that during four years of work in the quarry in Piltdown, they had unearthed fossilized bone remains consisting of a humanoid skull and an apelike jaw with humanlike teeth. Initially the findings raised some doubts among scholars; however, as S.J. Gould puts it, "Over the next three years, Dawson and Woodward countered with a series of further discoveries that, in retrospect, could not have been better programmed to dispel doubt."[2] A year later Dawson, Woodward, and Teilhard returned to Piltdown, where Teilhard stumbled upon another pivotal remnant—a lower canine tooth. The tooth was apish in form but greatly worn, in accord with the human manner of mastication. Based on this discovery, it was determined that half a million years ago the area had been inhabited by creatures that had distinctively human- and ape-like features. As predicted by the theory, the specimen was equipped with a sizeable brain and apelike jaws. The discovery fit the theory so well that skeptically-minded anthropologists had no other option but to surrender. The long-awaited unearthing gave the group of researchers widespread national and international recognition. The French Jesuit's reputation grew. The Piltdown Man ended up being exhibited in the British Museum and became an object of the most advanced research, and the subject of over 500 doctoral dissertations.[3]

Over time, other fossils were found, and it became increasingly difficult to fit the Piltdown skull into the evolutionary scheme. It was then that the British Museum decided to reveal the truth. In 1953 three experts, Kenneth Oakley, Wilfrid Le Gros Clark, and Joseph Weiner, in a series of tests, demonstrated that the skull in question was not half a million but merely several hundred years old and had been colored with potassium dichromate to make it appear more antique. The jaw belonged to a contemporary orangutan, whereas the teeth happened to be just ordinary ape fangs filed to suit the needs of the finding and glued inside the jaw. Following this revelation, the exhibit was immediately

2. S.J. Gould, "Smith Woodward's Folly," in *New Scientist* (April 5, 1979), 42–44.

3. See M. Muggeridge, *The End of Christendom* (Grand Rapids, MI: Eerdmans, 1980), 59. In 1938 the Piltdown site was even honored with a commemorative obelisk.

removed from the display and gradually sank into oblivion.[4] To date, we have no unequivocal answer as to the perpetrators of this serious fraud. A number of hypotheses circulated and at least five people were mentioned as possible candidates for the fraud. Stephen Jay Gould speculates that the hoax was a joint initiative of Teilhard and Woodward.[5]

The second significant discovery by Teilhard was closely connected with his stay in China.[6] Dr. Davidson Black played the main role there. Black's vivid interest in human evolution was sparked by his visit to Piltdown in 1914, where he assisted in the reconstruction of the skull. After World War I ended he went to China, where he was appointed professor at the Beijing Medical Union College. This institution, generously supported by the Rockefeller Foundation, was aimed at finding other missing links between humans and their supposed evolutionary ancestors.

In 1926 Teilhard joined Black's research group. A year later they hit upon a molar in the vicinity of Zhoukoudian, 30 miles southwest of Beijing. Black claimed that the tooth possessed both apelike and humanlike features, and based on this one find he established the new genus *Sinanthropus pekinensis* (Beijing Man).[7] The next year (1929), the explorers unearthed the remains of a skullcap. According to Teilhard and three other experts, it had a relatively small brain—a clear display of apelike origin. Meanwhile Black made a model of a skull and filed a report. According to Black, the skull represented a completely new species—an evolutionary form between an ape and a modern man, though

4. J. Wells comments on the case of the Piltdown man: "Most modern biology textbooks do not even mention Piltdown. When critics of Darwinism bring it up, they are usually told that the incident merely proves that science is self-correcting. And so it was, in this case—though the self-correcting took over forty years. But the more interesting lesson to be learned from Piltdown is that scientists, like everyone else, can be fooled into seeing what they want to see" (*Icons of Evolution*, 218). Le Gros Clark, a scholar of evolutionary views, expresses his surprise on making his remarkable discovery: "The evidences of artificial abrasion immediately sprang to the eye. Indeed so obvious did they seem that it may well be asked—how was it that they had escaped notice before." Quoted by S.J. Gould in his paper "Smith Woodward's Folly" in *New Scientist*, 43.

5. Cf. S.J. Gould, "Smith Woodward's Folly," 43. Gould even suggests that the Piltdown skull was so clearly made up that initially it could have been just a joke of the two scholars (de Chardin and Woodward). However, due to different circumstances, the skull turned into serious evidence for human evolution, whose credibility Teilhard couldn't have revoked without destroying his career. Besides the two, Arthur Keith, Martin A.C. Hinton, Horace de Vere Cole, and Arthur C. Doyle were also suspected of the fraud. In 1970, Hinton's suitcase was found in the Museum of Natural History in London, containing filed teeth similar to the ones from Piltdown as well as colored bones. In 1978 professor William J. Sollas also came under suspicion. See P. O'Connell, *Science of Today*, 153; J.W.G Johnson, *The Crumbling Theory of Evolution* (Brisbane: Queensland Binding Service, 1982), 113.

6. A detailed history of the discovery is to be found in the book by Chinese scholars J. Lanpo and H. Weiwen, *The Story of Peking Man: From Archeology to Mystery*, transl. Y. Zhiqi (Oxford, New York, Hong Kong: Oxford University Press, 1990).

7. Cf. J. Lanpo, H. Weiwen, *The Story of Peking Man*, 50–51.

the brain capacity was comparable to the average size encountered in human beings in contemporary times.

During further excavation two huge mounds of ashes were discovered, one of them several dozen meters in diameter and reaching the height of two floors. Buried in the ashes were broken bones of numerous animals, as well as pieces of apelike skulls that Black designated as further fragments of *Sinanthropus pekinensis*. No other pieces of apelike skeletons were found there, which indicates that the ape skulls must have been brought to the site. Thanks to Teilhard, the news of a new hominid walking in an upright position was publicized. Moreover, Teilhard claimed that early human beings had lived in the cave and were able to use basic tools and fire.

In 1931 another well-known paleontologist, Henri Breuil, visited the site, and after conducting his own research concluded that the traces of use of fire were simply the result of the industrial furnaces probably used for burning limestone in the construction of the nearby city of Cambuluc. In the vicinity he also stumbled across numerous quartz stones, which later turned out to be different kinds of tools, some of them representing a high degree of sophistication and technique. Breuil expressed doubt that creatures with clearly apelike skulls could have developed such advanced industry. He published the findings of his research the following year in France.

Soon Black, Teilhard, and Pei Wenzhong published a book summarizing their work and compiling all the existing articles on the matter.[8] They did not, however, include Breuil's reservations in their publication. When another paleontologist, Marcellin Boule, visited the excavation site, he instantly concluded that the advanced industry was the work of genuine humans and that the skulls found belonged to ordinary apes. He also determined that the broken bones of various animals were just food leftovers thrown into the ash by men who had prepared meals using fire.

A few years later (1934), more than ten skeletons of modern people were discovered in the same vicinity. Along with the bones were found perforated marine shells, fox canines, and pieces of hematite—all of this evidence of art and funeral ceremonies. Teilhard recognized them as much-later remains that did not have anything to do with *Sinanthropus*. After Black's death, Teilhard took charge of the work for a short time until Franz Weidenreich replaced him.

In 1936–1937, another four skullcaps of *Sinanthropus*, a few teeth, and a female mandible were unearthed. By the time of the outbreak of the Sino-Japanese war, about 70,000 artifacts and a large number of mammalian fossils were

8. D. Black, P.T. de Chardin, C.C. Young, W.C. Pei, *Fossil Man in China: The Choukoutien Cave Deposits with a Synopsis of Our Present Knowledge of the Late Cenozoic in China* (Peiping: Geological Survey of China and Section of Geology of the National Academy of Peiping, 1933).

retrieved. Human fossils, however, were both scarce and incomplete. Facing the upcoming war, Chinese scientists made the decision to move the remains of *Sinanthropus pekinensis* to the United States. Unfortunately, the fossils vanished under mysterious circumstances along the way, and as a result scientists have since had at their disposal only Black's casts.[9] After the disappearance of the original skulls, it became impossible to verify the authenticity of Beijing Man. Nevertheless, the legend of the Beijing Man lived on, and even at present it is sometimes invoked as evidence for human evolution from a lower animal.

Later, in the 1950s and 60s, a debate emerged among scientists who had worked in Zhoukoudian regarding *Sinanthropus*' cultural advancement. Teilhard—and after his death his closest colleague, Pei Wenzhong—argued extensively against Jia Lanpo and others in order to downplay the role of the artifacts produced by Beijing Man. The underlying assumption was that if *Sinanthropus* was a missing link between ape-like and human-like creatures, his skills should be less advanced. Man possessing technical skills and a brain case of over 1000 ccm could not have been the first or most primitive human species. If it had been proven that it was not the "first man," then the overall meaning of the find would dramatically decrease. Now, we know that Beijing Man lived 0.7–0.2 million years ago,[10] used fire in a controlled way, and produced different types of stone and bone tools. All of this should be enough to include him in the human family rather than as a "transitional link" between man and lower animals. Speculations about the inability of *Sinanthropus* to make tools ultimately ceased after human fossils and large quantities of processed animal bones and antlers, dating back 1–1.8 million years, were discovered elsewhere in China.[11] The history of the discovery in Zhoukoudian is another example of how much scientists' conclusions depend on previously adopted assumptions to interpret fragmentary fossils.

As we see, Teilhard's name appears in the scientific literature mainly on the occasion of the two most unreliable "discoveries" regarding human origins ever. Piltdown Man turned out to be a hoax, whereas Beijing Man was just a very ancient man whose skills and culture did not differ substantially from today's primitive peoples. Today, even the proponents of human evolution

9. Jim Foley, in a polemic with young Earth creationist Duane Gish, points out that besides the casts there is other extensive documentation of the Zhoukoudian fossils. According to Foley, "Gish's statement that *All we have available are the models fashioned by Weidenreich* is totally untrue. It ignores not only the difference between models and casts, but also the other extensive documentation available. Weidenreich produced hundreds of pages of detailed monographs on the fossils, with photos, measurements, descriptions, drawings, and even X-rays." See: http://www.talkorigins.org/faqs/homs/a_peking.html (February 14, 2015).

10. See J. Lanpo, H. Weiwen, *The Story of Peking Man*, 197.

11. Ibid., 206, 209–10.

from lower animals admit that *Sinanthropus* cannot be considered the missing link between man and a lower animal.[12]

Teilhard's achievements in the field of paleontology were never highly regarded among professional researchers, but surprisingly he was admired by clergymen and theologians.[13] In a sense, Teilhard was looking at the fossil material only to confirm his presupposed imaginary scenarios. When he could not find it, he supplied the missing data with a strong "scientific faith" rather than scientific arguments. At the same time, his works fully met expectations of Catholics awaiting an easy reconciliation of evolution with Christianity. In this way all parties were satisfied, experiencing the benefits of a scientific worldview combined with a fantastic view of the world evolving throughout history.

Philosophy

At the time Teilhard embarked on his basic theological studies, a book was published that significantly influenced his thinking. It was *L'Évolution créatrice* (1907) by Henri Bergson (1859–1941). According to the young Jesuit, that brilliant book gave fuel to his mind and heart that ultimately helped him to step into an "evolutive" universe and realize the dualism of matter and spirit in which he had previously been enclosed.[14] Matter and Spirit, claims Teilhard, "were no longer two things, but two states or two aspects of one and the same cosmic Stuff."[15] Teilhard's philosophical standpoint was represented by two books: *Le milieu Divin* in 1927 (*The Divine Milieu*) and *Le phénomène humain* in 1942 (*The Phenomenon of Man*). The Church halted the dissemination of both publications.

Teilhard proposes an evolutionary vision of the cosmos in which the central place is occupied by man as a product of natural biological evolution. In his system, alongside the Infinity of Greatness and the Infinity of Insignificance

12. For example, Colin Groves, in his article criticizing Patrick O'Connell's account of the Beijing-man story, admits that he himself does not consider *Sinanthropus* an ancestral form of *Homo sapiens*. http://www.talkorigins.org/faqs/homs/oconnell_cg.html (February 13, 2015).

13. Teilhard's discoveries served mainly to justify theologians in their admission of the evolutionary paradigm into theological considerations. For instance, Rev. B. Halaczek recently claimed that: "The success of excavations of the Twenties and Thirties of our century does not allow theologians to persist in ignoring the fact of the existence in the past of human forms distinctively different from that of modern man." In Fr. Halaczek's opinion, Teilhard was a coryphée in this realm. (See B, Halaczek, "Ewolucja pogladów teologicznych na ewolucje," *Slaskie Studia Historyczno-Teologiczne* 31 [1998]: 17–25, 20.)

14. P. Teilhard de Chardin, *The Heart of the Matter*, transl. R. Hague (San Diego: Harcourt Brace Jovanovich, 1978), 25. Cf. J. Grim, M.E. Tucker, Biography: http://teilharddechardin.org/index.php/biography (February 14, 2015).

15. P. Teilhard de Chardin, *The Heart of Matter*, 26.

there exists a third force—the Infinity of Complexity, the human being. According to Teilhard's ontology, the world is evolving towards increasingly perfected forms in the grand process of evolution, which never ceases and never reverses. The universe undergoes subsequent stages, from the shaping of cosmic space, through the emergence of the biological world, to the crowning achievement of the form of a human being, which in turn initiates the "noosphere"—the space embracing the universal and all-encompassing world of ideas and minds. The French Jesuit regarded evolution as an irrevocable fact to be used as the interpretive criterion for all theories. Future development of the world, he suggests, would be focused on higher human consciousness and the strengthening of our spiritual powers. According to him, the world is being transformed from chaotic variety to sophisticated simplicity, which is supposed to be an organized variety. This process is taking place spontaneously, guided by obscure laws and principles, which Teilhard seems to find within the domain of science.[16] The progress of the noosphere is reflected in closer contact among people. Science and technology make it possible for people to be present in every corner of the world at the same time. This phenomenon was described by the French Jesuit as a "gigantic psycho-biological operation, a sort of mega-synthesis, the super-arrangement, to which all the thinking elements of the earth find themselves today individually and collectively subject."[17] The aim of evolution is to achieve the culminating Omega Point, which is a state of higher consciousness. All layers of consciousness will ultimately converge in Omega, melting and mingling together, although each and every individual aspect of consciousness remains fully aware of itself at the end of the process.[18]

Teilhard's vision is undeniably attractive, because it is holistic and coherent in nature. Within the framework of his philosophy every single phenomenon

16. Trying to provide a plausible explanation of his thesis on the spontaneously increasing complexity in nature, Teilhard referred to (among other things): a "vast, universal phenomenon of complexification of matter," "molecules' capability of appearing, of germinating, anywhere, without exception, in the world of atoms," to "major currents that affect the universe in its totality," "unfettered moleculization," "glow of life," "cosmic movement of corpusculization," "hidden laws of biogenesis," "fundamental law of complexity-consciousness," "compressive socialization," "latent germinal powers of the earth," etc. Teilhard imagines the existence of some radial and tangential energies, the interaction of which was supposed to result in the preservation of life and emergence of higher orders of complexity. All those esoteric concepts and laws seem to have been created *ad hoc* in order to justify a scientifically unfounded cosmology rather than express an unbiased phenomenology. See *Man's Place in Nature: The Human Zoological Group* [Le Groupe Zoologique Humain] (London: Fontana Books, 1971), 19, 28, 31, 32, 56, 60, 98, 109; *The Phenomenon of Man*, transl. B. Wall (New York: Harper, 1959), 48, 77.

17. See Teilhard, *The Phenomenon of Man*, 244.

18. Ibid., 258–62.

gains a new meaning and explanation. But the question remains unanswered: Does this coherent vision have anything to do with reality? Or is it just an enchanting dream?

Popes have repeatedly spoken out about the role of philosophy in theology, often pointing to the value of Thomistic philosophy as the realistic and objective one. Teilhard's proposals display the characteristics of H. Bergson, V. Cousin, and other representatives of spiritualism and early-20th-century vitalism. Bergson's main work and the one that briefly inspired Teilhard, *L'Évolution créatrice*, was included in the papal Index of Prohibited Books. Pius XII, highly conversant with the view of the French Jesuit, vehemently opposed philosophical idealism in his speech addressed to the Papal Academy of Sciences (November 30, 1941). The Pope asks:

> Does philosophy seek to be an ideal dream which confuses God and nature, which gazes longingly upon visions and illusions of idols drawn from the imagination? Is not philosophy rather the very discipline which keeps us firmly rooted in the reality of the things that we see and touch, and the search for the deepest and highest causes of nature and of the universe?[19]

Pope Pius XII implicitly rejected Teilhard's style of philosophy, which he believed was illusory. Nevertheless, criticism did not come only from "conservative Roman circles," as the situation is customarily depicted. Peter Medawar, professor at Oxford University, a scientist and winner of the Nobel Prize (1960) was not a Christian and believed in evolution. Nevertheless, after reading *Le Phénomène Humain* he wrote a devastating critique of the book:

> The greater part of it, I shall show, is nonsense, tricked out with a variety of metaphysical conceits, and its author can be excused of dishonesty only on the grounds that before deceiving others he has taken great pains to deceive himself.[20]

Medawar's strong dislike does not seem to stem exclusively from the underlying antagonism between the British and French communities. Medawar was a scientist of high stature, a genuine proponent of scientism in the Anglo-Saxon

19. *AAS*, 33 (1941), English translation after *Papal Addresses to the Pontifical Academy of Sciences*, 97.

20. P.B. Medawar, "Critical Notice," *Mind* 70 (January 1961), 99–106. Medawar opened his article with, as he put it, a "little bouquet of aphorisms" taken from Teilhard's works: "Everything does not happen continuously at any one moment in the universe. Neither does everything happen everywhere in it; There are no summits without abysses; When the end of the world is mentioned, the idea that leaps into our minds is always one of catastrophe; Life is born and propagates itself on the earth as a solitary pulsation; In the last analysis the best guarantee that a thing should happen is that it appears to us as vitally necessary."

style, and apparently he found it infuriating to tolerate a scholar embellishing his philosophical endeavor with scientific garnish. The British Nobel laureate was perfectly acquainted with the way the world and nature function and he knew that there was no known reality that could account for the laws and powers imagined by Teilhard.

But even some representatives of extremely heterodox theological schools recognized the devastating influence of Teilhard's philosophy on Christianity. Thomas J.J. Altizer, a proponent of the Nietzschean idea of the death of God, summarized one of Teilhard's works as follows:

> It is true that Teilhard occasionally and inconsistently introduces traditional Christian language into the pages of *The Phenomenon of Man*, but this fact scarcely obviates the truth that virtually the whole body of Christian belief either disappears or is transformed in Teilhard's evolutionary vision of the cosmos.[21]

In the real world, nothing takes place spontaneously—there are no phenomena that just "happen," propelled by some indefinite vital forces or evolutionary laws. In the real world every effect must have a cause and no effect can be greater than its cause. This is the fundamental problem with Teilhard's vision. Does the world really constitute a self-propelling organism? Is the energy of the total system on the increase? Do we experience a spontaneous proliferation of complexity and organization of structures in the world around us?

Thanks to Edwin Hubble's discoveries and to Einstein's theoretical account of those discoveries, at the time Teilhard's works appeared physicists knew that the more accurate theoretical model of the universe does not disclose an ever-growing complexity or the unceasing emergence of new physical structures. Actually, science yields evidence to the contrary. In the middle of the last century, scientists finally rejected the model of a stationary universe, which had predominated at least from the time of Aristotle. The universe bears strong evidence that it had a beginning and that it is continually expanding. Within it, the large distribution of matter decreases, stars burn out and cool off, clusters of galaxies become more dispersed. Similar processes occur in matter at the atomic level. Protons decay, and atoms dissipate into radiation. So far as we can tell, this process is irreversible in nature. According to physics, the universe as a whole is slowly "burning out," not "heating up," and will inevitably submit to heat death.

Similarly, in the biological world what we experience regularly is extinction, not the creation of new species. This phenomenon, known by empirical obser-

21. Quotation in D.H. Lane, *The Phenomenon of Teilhard: Prophet for a New Age* (Macon, GA: Mercer University Press, 1996), 75.

vation, is referred to as the law of increased entropy (or the Second Law of Thermodynamics). According to this general principle, every isolated physical system undergoes spontaneous decomposition if not supplied with energy from the outside. There can be local spikes in energy, and, where intelligent agents are involved, increase in information and functional complexity. But due to standard physical laws, the universe as a whole is moving toward less organization. We see the same idea confirmed in the Bible, which mentions the passing away or even "wearing out" of the world.[22] Pope Pius XII took the problem of entropy and its philosophical implications into consideration in his speech addressed to the Papal Academy of Sciences on November 22, 1951. The pope said that knowledge about this "fatal destiny" is the tangible result of positive scientific research and renders completely unfounded hypotheses of the spontaneous renewal of creation.[23]

22. One of the Psalms reads: "In the beginning, O Lord, you founded the earth: and the heavens are the works of your hands. They shall perish but you remain: and all of them shall grow old like a garment: And as a vesture you shall change them, and they shall be changed" (Ps 102:26–27).

23. "Modern science has not only enlarged and deepened our knowledge of the reality and magnitude of the mutability of the cosmos; it has also offered us valuable indications concerning the direction according to which the processes of nature are carried out. While a hundred years ago, especially after the discovery of the law of constants, it was thought that the natural processes were reversible, and therefore, according to the principles of strict causality—or, rather, determination—an ever-recurring renewal and rejuvenation of the cosmos was considered possible. With the law of entropy, discovered by Rudolf Clausius, it became known that the spontaneous natural processes are always related to a diminution of the free and utilizable energy, which in a closed material system must finally lead to a cessation of the processes on the macroscopic scale. This fatal destiny, which only hypotheses, sometimes far too gratuitous ones such as that of the continuous renewal of creation, forcibly try to deny, but which instead comes from positive scientific experience, eloquently postulates the existence of a necessary Being.... [Also] in the narrow confines of the microcosm itself, we meet with a law which indicates the direction of evolution and which is analogous to the law of entropy in the macrocosm. The direction of spontaneous evolution is determined by means of the diminution of the energy utilizable in the structure and the nucleus of the atom, and up to now no processes have been noted which could compensate or cancel this diminution by means of spontaneous formation of nuclei of high energetic value." Speech of Pius XII to the Pontifical Academy of Sciences of November 22, 1951, *AAS*, 44 (1952), 37–38.

For some unknown reason, the last sentence quoted above was distorted in the official English translation published in 2003. As a result, the content as rendered in the translation is opposite that in the original document. In the Italian original published in the *Acts of the Apostolic See* in 1952, the sentence reads as follows: "La direzione dell'evoluzione spontanea e determinata mediante la diminuzione dell'energia utilizzabile nella compagine e nel nucleo dell'atomo, e finora *non sono noti processi*, che potrebbero compensare o annullare tale sfruttamento per mezzo della formazione spontanea di nuclei di alto valore energetico" [my emphasis]. The translation reads: "The direction of spontaneous evolution is determined by means of the diminution of the energy utilizable in the structure and the nucleus of the atom, and up to now processes have been noted which could compensate or cancel this diminution by means of spontaneous formation of nuclei of high energetic value" (see *Papal Addresses to the Pontifical Academy of Sciences*, 137).

In the physical world, we do not observe evolution understood as the emergence of fundamentally new ordered structures due to the capacities of nature alone. What happens instead is reduction (devolution), or an increase in disorder. Therefore, Teilhard's vision, in which so many Catholics sought the synthesis of philosophy, science, and theology, may have been internally consistent, but had nothing to do with scientific knowledge. His vision actually contradicts both science and experience.

A complicating factor in the interpretation of the French Jesuit's idea is that he did not articulate a definite line between the material and the spiritual worlds. In the material world we can observe processes that are different from those about which he writes (entropy, rather than emergence). However, in the spiritual world, such as in the realm of culture (noosphere), his thesis could be partially justified. Matter is not productive, but mind can give rise to all sorts of novelties. In this sense we can actually talk about evolution in different spheres of human activity—in art, technology, the economy, law, or science. These fields show advance and the growth of complexity. But in these fields as well, neither the creative power of evolution nor unilinear progress is completely apparent. Teilhard, for instance, speaks about streams of consciousness that converge into one Omega Point. This vision seems quite attractive, but in reality the reverse movement—the divergence and diversification of ideas—can be observed as well. For instance, when it comes to science, we may observe the increasingly more detailed areas of knowledge that are increasingly less related to one another. That is why, although the idea of the noosphere shows an increase of complexity and a general cultural advancement, it happens rather according to St. Augustine's paradigm of rational reasons (*logoi spermatikoi*), which means that nothing substantially new can appear unless it had previously existed, if only in its most primitive form.[24] Generally speaking, the philosophical vision of Teilhard de Chardin is coherent, which many Catholics found attractive; however, a coherent idea is not necessarily a true idea.

Theology

The theological doctrine of Teilhard is the consequence of his various scientific and philosophical assertions. Its author was not strictly a theologian, and theol-

24. When it comes to the development of religious doctrine in Christianity, its basic model was described by St. Vincent of Lerins as early as the 5th century. It was not, however, an evolutionary model after Teilhard's fashion. As St. Vincent writes: "Shall there, then, be no progress in Christ's Church? Certainly; all possible progress. For what being is there, so envious of men, so full of hatred to God, who would seek to forbid it? Yet on condition that it be real progress, not alteration of the faith. For progress requires that the subject be enlarged in itself, alteration, that it be transformed into something else" (*The Commonitory*, ch. 23, n. 54).

ogy (specifically dogmatics) was not a key interest of his. On the other hand, Church authorities, according to their nature and vocation, drew attention above all to the theological implications of his theses. Therefore, I will focus primarily on the decisions of Church authorities concerning Teilhard, which will give us an overall view of his doctrine.[25]

The first official intervention was undertaken by Teilhard's provincial superior after his lecture on original sin, delivered in Belgium in 1922. Teilhard questioned the very possibility of the historical existence of Adam and the reality of Eden. As a consequence he postulated also a redefinition of original sin.[26] The superior ordered the professor to deny the presented thesis. After the French Jesuit signed a declaration withdrawing the theses, the superior sent the corrected version of the lecture to Rome, enclosing Teilhard's statement. While waiting for the official response, Teilhard kept developing his controversial theses on original sin in his publications and lectures. As a result, in 1925 a Jesuit general superior, Włodzimierz Ledóchowski (1866–1942), ordered him to sign a declaration renouncing the theories he was spreading, and forbade him from delivering further lectures at the Catholic Institute.[27] Two years later, the Holy See denied him an *Imprimatur* for the book *Le Milieu Divin*. Further problems appeared in 1933, when the religious authority ordered Teilhard to resign from his post in Paris. Six years later, *L'Energie Humaine* (1939) was added to the Index of Prohibited Books. In 1941, Teilhard submitted for approval his main work, *Le Phénomène Humain*. The case ended three years later with a refusal of permission for publication. In 1947, Teilhard was forbidden to lecture on the subject of philosophy. The following year the Jesuit repeated his request to publish *Le Phénomène Humain*. In consequence, he was summoned by his religious authorities to Rome, where again he was banned from publishing his work, and also denied an office at the Collège de France. The next year he was forbidden to publish *Le Groupe Zoologique* (1949). The last act of the Holy See during the

25. A complete criticism of Teilhard's theologico-philosophical system can be found in the book *Theistic Evolution: The Teilhardian Heresy*, by Wolfgang Smith (Tacoma, WA: Angelico Press, 2012).

26. Teilhard claimed, among other things, that "The more we bring the past to life again by means of science, the less we can accommodate either Adam or the earthly paradise." P. Teilhard de Chardin, "Note on Some Possible Historical Representations of Original Sin," in *Christianity and Evolution*, transl. R. Hague (NY: Harcourt Brace Jovanovich, 1971), 45–46.

27. In the middle of 1925 there occurred an interesting coincidence of various events connected with evolution. In the USA, the Scopes trial was underway (its aim being to repeal the ban on teaching evolution in Tennessee, which eventually was achieved; cf. H.W. House, "Darwinism and the Law," in *Intelligent Design 101: Leading Experts Explain the Key Issues* [Grand Rapids: Kregel Publications, 2008], 177–214). In Europe, there was a meeting of Catholic evolutionists in Altamira, held for the purpose of introducing evolutionism into theology (cf. ch. II, 7, c). And at the same time (in July 1925), Teilhard de Chardin was subjected to his first teaching ban.

life of the French Jesuit was to deny him participation in the International Paleontological Congress of 1955.

Based on these facts, we can conclude that the Church, represented by the religious authorities and the Roman congregations, never doubted the destructive influence of Teilhard's publications and activities. During his life, by issuing consistent proscriptions and reprimands, Church authorities intended to stop Teilhard's ideas from spreading. In our context, it is important that his works were written according to the evolutionary paradigm, and that evolution constituted the core of his doctrine. None of the adduced disciplinary acts pertained directly and exclusively to evolution. The issue did recur in numerous discussions with Teilhard, but it was never the primary object of controversy. Therefore, the Church did not condemn Teilhard for evolutionism as such, but for the theological implications stemming from his ideas. It may be asserted that the actions taken against Teilhard demonstrate the overall opposition of the Church to the theological paradigm represented in his writings. This attitude was expressed in the encyclical *Humani Generis*, which may be interpreted as a denunciation of the views of the French Jesuit, though it does not mention him by name.[28]

After Teilhard's death, all his proscribed works were disseminated by private publishers without the permission of Church authority.[29] From this moment on, Teilhard's ideas began to gain popularity in the Church, and this provoked

28. In his private correspondence, Teilhard left a testimony of his extreme dislike for the encyclical of Pius XII. He claimed that a good psychoanalyst would have revealed "the clear traces of a specific religious perversion" in the Encyclical and "the masochism and sadism of orthodoxy; the pleasure of swallowing, and making others swallow, the truth under its crudest and stupidest forms." In the same letter he declares: "I'm resolved to continue quite simply along my own way in a direction which seems to me to point exactly towards the dogmatic realism that Rome wants." See R. Speaight, *Teilhard de Chardin: A Biography* (London: Collins, 1967), 298–99.

29. In 1971, John W. Flanagan, in a brochure of the British Catholic Priests Association ("CPA Newsletter") published the article "A Periscope on Teilhard de Chardin," in which he provides information about the circumstances of the publication of Teilhard's works. Before his death, he made a last will in which he bequeathed the copyrights to his books to private publishing houses. It was an act contrary to the dictates of the vow of poverty, according to which all goods of a deceased member of the order should be passed to the order. However, as Teilhard's will was subject to state law, the order lost the rights to his works. The article by Father Flanagan can be found on the Internet at: http://www.traditioninaction.org/Questions/WebSources/B_303_Periscope%20on%20Teilhard.pdf (February 17, 2015). In the same article, Flanagan reports that on November 15, 1957, the Holy Office issued a decree prohibiting the distribution, archivization in libraries, and translation into other languages of Teilhard's works. (The decree is not included in the *AAS*; thus, even if it was really published, it cannot be treated as an official decision of the Holy Office.) In addition, in 1958, all Jesuit publications in Spain included a note from the local provincial stating that any works of Teilhard in that country had appeared without the permission of the Church authorities and in violation of the previous decrees of the Holy See.

further reactions from the Magisterium. In 1962, the Congregation of the Holy Office issued a warning (*monitum*) noting the increasing influence of Teilhard's writings, recommending Church authorities to protect the minds, especially of young people, from the danger of these works. The document reads:

> Prescinding from a judgment about those points that concern the positive sciences, it is sufficiently clear that the above-mentioned works abound in such ambiguities and indeed even serious errors, as to offend Catholic doctrine.[30]

What ambiguities could the Congregation have had in mind? Teilhard writes about Christ:

> "Christ has a cosmic body that extends throughout the whole universe." "Christ coincides with the universe, as the universal center common to cosmic progress and gratuitous sanctification." "Christ is still the only cosmic element capable . . . of embodying modern hopes of spiritual organization of the world." "Between the Word on the one hand and the Man Jesus on the other a sort of christic third nature (if I dare say so) emerges—found everywhere in the writings of St Paul: the total and totalizing Christ in whom, by the transforming effect of the resurrection, the individual human element born of Mary finds itself carried not only to a state of cosmic element (or milieu or curve) but also of final psychic center of universal concentration." "Christianity can only survive (and super-live) . . . by sub-distinguishing in the human nature of the Word Incarnate between a terrestrial nature and cosmic nature."[31]

These few sentences are quite representative of the Christology of the French Jesuit. Unfortunately, other dogmatic issues were presented no less ambiguously. It should be noted that the *monitum* of the Congregation does not mention the issue of evolution. On the other hand, neither does it mention any specific truth of the faith which Teilhard's writings would oppose. The problem, as defined by the Congregation, is that his texts were "ambiguous and containing serious errors." Because of the ambiguity, they were hard to argue with, and because they abounded in multiple errors, they were incorrigible. On the other hand, the coherence, and a certain totalism, of Teilhard's concepts might have easily deceived the minds of theology students. Therefore, Catholic theologians were not instructed to look for the seeds of truth in the doctrine of the French Jesuit, but to reject his concepts as a whole.

From the beginning, Catholic intellectual circles had different opinions on the teaching of Teilhard de Chardin. His ideas were supported, for instance, by

30. AAS, 54 (1962), 526.

31. All quotations taken from S. Cowell, *The Teilhard Lexicon* (Brighton, Portland: Sussex Academic Press, 2001), 27–29.

Henri de Lubac,[32] but opposed by Dietrich von Hildebrand,[33] Jacques Maritain,[34] and Étienne Gilson. Gilson, for one, thought that the basic problem of Teilhard's doctrine lies in the very method of his philosophy. In a letter to de Lubac, he writes:

> What worries me is that while our Christian theologians developed their theologies from meditations on the Scriptures, Teilhard, grounded in his evolutionist consciousness, built his theology on a meditation on science.... Myself, I'd a hundred times rather be a Lutheran than a Teilhardian.[35]

Gilson indicated a different starting point and criterion in Teilhard's theology. It was not supernatural revelation, but natural knowledge. In consequence, nature became the criterion of revelation and Christian truth. True science could not be in conflict with revelation, so it does not constitute any threat to Christianity. But Teilhard's scientific views often step away from scientific data and constitute some other source of knowledge. This is why his approach led to various "reductionisms," such as naturalism or spiritualism. Regardless which reductionism was implied by his method, evolution as the principle of all real-

32. Henri de Lubac popularized Teilhard's ideas in several publications: *La pensée religieuse du Pére Teilhard de Chardin* (Paris: Aubier, 1962); *Teilhard et notre temps* (Paris: Aubier, 1971); *Teilhard de Chardin: The Man and his Meaning* (New York: Hawthorn Books, 1965).

33. Hildebrand called Teilhard a "false prophet." In one of his books he conducted a critical analysis of basic theological notions, demonstrating how they were distorted in the writings of the French Jesuit. See D. von Hildebrand, *Trojan Horse in the City of God* (Manchester, NH: Sophia Institute Press, 1993), 273–303. In his later book, *The Devastated Vineyard*, von Hildebrand described Teilhard's theories as "absolutely incompatible . . . with the teaching of the holy Church." D. von Hildebrand, *The Devastated Vineyard*, trans. J. Crosby and F. Teichert (Chicago: Franciscan Herald Press, 1973), 80.

34. It was Maritain who dubbed Teilhard's writings "theological fiction." In one of the papers entirely devoted to criticism of Teilhard, Maritain wrote: "[Teilhard has] turned Christianity upside down, so that [is it] no longer rooted in the Trinity and Redemption but in the evolving Cosmos. No theologian, mystic, or meditative scholar, no matter how hard he tries, is equal to that—nor even a wonder-worker." J. Maritain, "Teilhard de Chardin and Teilhardism," *U.S. Catholic* 33 (1967), 9–10; quotation in D.H. Lane, *The Phenomenon of Teilhard: Prophet for a New Age*, (Macon, GA: Mercer University Press, 1996), 74.

35. Gilson also writes: "You can't get any benefit or enlightenment from thinking about Teilhard. The ravages that he has wrought that I have witnessed are horrifying. I do everything I can to avoid having to talk about him. People are not content with just teaching him, they preach him. They use him like a siege engine to undermine the Church from within (I am not kidding) and I, for one, want no part of this destructive scheme." See "Teilhard de Chardin: False Prophet," *Christian Order* (May 1992). Quotation in http://www.theotokos.org.uk/pages/creation/misc/teilhard.html (February 18, 2015).

In another place Gilson expressed the feeling a Christian has after reading Teilhard: "We feel as though we were before an empty tomb: they have taken away Our Lord, and we don't know where they have laid him." Quotation in D.H. Lane, *The Phenomenon of Teilhard: Prophet for a New Age* (Macon, GA: Mercer University Press, 1996), 74.

ity made it impossible to preserve in his discourse the objective and permanent nature of the truth.

The dispute about Teilhard had one more episode in the Church, namely in 1981, on the occasion of the 100th anniversary of his birth. The celebration took place at the Catholic Institute in Paris, headed by its rector, Archbishop Paul Poupard. On that occasion the Vatican Secretary of State, Card. Augostino Casaroli, on behalf of Pope John Paul II, sent a letter to the Archbishop, which was commonly interpreted as a rehabilitation of Teilhard. Casaroli wrote of

> "the astonishing resonance of his research" and "the brilliance of his personality and richness of his thinking [which] have profoundly marked our epoch. . . . In him, a powerful poetic intuition of nature's profound value, a sharp perception of creation's dynamism, and a broad vision of the world's future join together with an incontestable religious fervor."[36]

Casaroli noted that the complexity of problems and diversity of approaches adopted by Teilhard raise "difficulties that understandably called for a calm, critical study."[37] The celebration of the 100th anniversary of Teilhard's birth, he suggested, would certainly be an opportunity for "encouraging evaluation [of his work] using a just methodological distinction of procedures in order to achieve a rigorous epistemological study."[38] At the end of the letter, Casaroli writes:

> What our contemporaries will undoubtedly remember, beyond the difficulties of conception and deficiencies of expression in this audacious attempt to reach a synthesis, is the testimony of the coherent life of a man possessed by Christ in the depths of his soul. He was concerned with honoring both faith and reason, and anticipated the response to John Paul II's appeal: Be not afraid, open, open wide to Christ the doors of the immense domains of culture, civilization, and progress.[39]

These unquestionably warm opinions about Teilhard say nothing definite about his doctrine. The letter mentioned both the greatness of his personage, and the methodological and interpretative difficulties of his concepts.

The anniversary celebration was mostly attended by Teilhard's sympathizers, among them not a few non-believers or opponents of the Catholic tradition. His problems with the Magisterium were usually presented as a form of perse-

36. "Lettera del Card. Casaroli al. Rettore dell'Istituto Cattolico di Parigi," *L'Osservatore Romano* (June 10, 1981), 1. The letter is dated May 12, 1981.

37. Ibid. Text also available on the Internet:
http://www.traditioninaction.org/ProgressivistDoc/A_020_CasaroliTeilhard.htm (February 18, 2015).

38. Ibid.

39. Ibid.

cution of a prominent and independent thinker by the conservative elements in Rome.[40] Thus, it was to be expected that the participants in the celebration would be particularly sensitive to the "voice from the Vatican." In this context, the pope decided to appeal to the good will of the celebrators. Casaroli presented the most favorable interpretation the Church hierarchy could afford to offer at the time. The effects were quick to come. The international press instantly announced a "change in the Vatican policy" and "rehabilitation of Teilhard." In reply, a few days later, *L'Osservatore Romano* printed the following statement of the Holy See Press Office:

> The letter sent by the Cardinal Secretary of State to His Excellency Mons. Poupard . . . has been interpreted in a certain section of the press as a revision of previous stands taken by the Holy See in regard to this author, and in particular of the *Monitum of the Holy Office* of 30 June 1962. . . . The question has been asked whether such an interpretation is well founded. After having consulted the Cardinal Secretary of State and the Cardinal Prefect of the Sacred Congregation for the Doctrine of the Faith, which, by order of the Holy Father, had been duly consulted beforehand, about the letter in question, we are in a position to reply in the negative. Far from being a revision of the previous stands of the Holy See, Cardinal Casaroli's letter expresses reservation in various passages—and these reservations have been passed over in silence by certain newspapers—reservations which refer precisely to the judgment given in the Monitum of June 1962, even though this document is not explicitly mentioned.[41]

This response was straightforward and provided further confirmation of the lack of Church acceptance of Teilhard's doctrine.

In the following decades, interest in Teilhard's ideas diminished considerably, though the interest in the Church's assessment of his doctrine did not diminish. In 1986, Cardinal J. Ratzinger wrote about the French Jesuit:

> No doubt many and various fruitful ideas came out of Teilhard's intuitions, which enriched the philosophical and theological dialogue with the natural sciences. They could not provide a definitive answer, because his foundations in the natural sciences were limited essentially to the fields of anatomy and morphology (excluding the genetic processes), and his development of philosophical and theological concepts remained unsatisfactory as well.[42]

40. See, for example, D. O'Leary, *Roman Catholicism and Modern Science*, 132–33.

41. English edition of *L'Osservatore Romano* (July 20, 1981). After http://www.catholicculture.org/culture/library/view.cfm?id=3160 (February 18, 2015).

42. *Creation and Evolution: A Conference with Pope Benedict XVI in Castel Gandolfo*, ed. S.O. Horn, S. Wiedenhofer (San Francisco: Ignatius Press, 2008), 9.

A statement that provoked some repercussions was the one voiced by Benedict XVI in July 2009, during ceremonial vespers at the Aosta cathedral:

> It's the great vision that later Teilhard de Chardin also had: At the end we will have a true cosmic liturgy, where the cosmos becomes a living host.[43]

These words, already susceptible to overinterpretation, were further enhanced by the comment of the papal spokesman, Fr. Luigi Lombardi, who stated: "By now, no one would dream of saying that [Teilhard] is a heterodox author who shouldn't be studied."[44] John L. Allen observed a certain ambivalence of Joseph Ratzinger towards the heritage of the French scholar.[45]

The doctrine of Teilhard de Chardin was summarized in a longer discourse by Cardinal Christoph Schönborn in the catecheses he delivered at the Vienna Cathedral in late 2005 and early 2006. The cardinal stated that:

> Hardly anyone else has tried to bring together the knowledge of Christ and the idea of evolution as Fr. Teilhard de Chardin, S.J., has done. His fascinating vision has remained controversial, and yet for many it has represented a great hope, the hope that faith in Christ and a scientific approach to the world can be brought together under one head, under Christ the evolutor.[46]

Having outlined the ascending evolutionary vision of the philosopher, the Viennese cardinal notes:

> The fascination which Teilhard exercised for an entire generation stemmed from his radical manner of looking at science and Christian faith together. This unity of vision, in which he intended to unite natural science and Christian faith, was of course also problematical. Critics have shown that he could not do complete justice to both sides. His vision of evolution as an upward movement that ceaselessly produces higher and ever higher forms is more of a philosophical speculation than a scientific theory. On the other hand, his

43. See J.L. Allen, "Pope Cites Teilhardian Vision of the Cosmos as a 'Living Host,'" *National Catholic Reporter* (July 28, 2009); http://ncronline.org/print/14207 (February 18, 2015).

44. Ibid.

45. J.L. Allen mentions that J. Ratzinger spoke of Teilhard in favorable terms in his book *Introduction to Christianity* (1968), in which Ratzinger remarks that the works of the French Jesuit had stimulated the restoration of the cosmic and metaphysical dimension in Western Christianity. Moreover, according to Allen, Ratzinger regarded Teilhard as an authentic exponent of St. Paul's Christology. On another occasion, however, commenting upon the Constitution *Gaudium et Spes*, he claimed that its typically "French" and particularly "Teilhardian" influences led it to reduce the role of sin. In his 2006 Easter homily, Pope Benedict XVI, referring to the theory of evolution, spoke of resurrection in Teilhardian terms, as "the greatest mutation, absolutely the most crucial leap into a totally new dimension that there has ever been in the long history of life and its development." See J.L. Allen, "Pope Cites Teilhardian Vision of the Cosmos as a 'Living Host.'"

46. C. Schönborn, *Chance or Purpose? Creation, Evolution and a Rational Faith* (San Francisco: Ignatius, 2007), 141.

> naturalization of Christ as the driving force of evolution inevitably ran up against contradiction in theological terms. Despite the criticism from both sides, many people have come to feel his concerns and have valued them. . . . Teilhard de Chardin dared a venture that was at the same time full of risks and yet necessary. . . . It is true that faith and science should be distinguished from each other. Yet it is also true that they ought not to be separated. Through his work, Teilhard de Chardin helped many scientists to overcome the prejudice that faith cramps science.[47]

Cardinal Schönborn primarily commends the methodology of Teilhard's research, leading to the connection of theology and empirical sciences. Thanks to such an approach, according to Schönborn, many scientists regained belief in the possibility of a friendly coexistence of faith and science. The cardinal does not evaluate the content of Teilhard's conception in full, though he takes note of some of its problems, as well as valuable elements. In the latter category he includes the notion of finality, rejected by radical evolutionary naturalists. Evolution, according to Teilhard, is driven to some kind of fulfillment, and is headed for development towards higher forms of consciousness. By calling Teilhard's conception "necessary," the Viennese cardinal most probably means the historical necessity of synthesizing evolutionism—which was already present in science and theology—within a uniform system involving science, philosophy, and theology. However, in the cardinal's view this does not mean that Teilhard's synthesis is actually in agreement with science and theology, or that it is the only possible synthesis of this kind.

Taking into account all the pronouncements regarding Teilhard de Chardin, we see that the official Church stance has not changed since the 1962 *monitum* by the Holy Office. More recent comments by Pope Benedict and higher Church officials evince a somewhat more positive attitude towards the philosophical endeavor of the French Jesuit. None of them, however, changes the meaning of the *monitum*. Its validity was explicitly confirmed under John Paul II. Therefore, we should conclude that even though the overall climate has changed, Teilhard's writings should still be considered erroneous.

47. Ibid., 142–43.

8

The Standpoint of Pope John Paul II

There is a gap of several decades in the development of Church doctrine on evolution. Indeed, during the pontificates of John XXIII, Paul VI, and John Paul I, we will not find any statements addressing this issue, particularly with reference to biological evolution and the origin of man. As mentioned, the pontificate of Paul VI coincided with a timely theological discussion about polygenism. The entire debate made sense only if theologians embraced a different concept of the origin of man than the one maintained within classical theology. Most Catholic theologians of the 19th and early 20th centuries did not trouble themselves with polygenism, as this idea was *a fortiori* excluded by the historical understanding of Genesis and belief in direct creation.

The period from 1950 to 1985 was marked with a kind of triumph of evolutionism in mass culture. During the same period Catholic theology was more absorbed by the reception of the reforms introduced by the Second Vatican Council than by other issues. Different problems came to the foreground of Church life, such as a new form of ecumenism, liturgical reform, dialogue with other religions or the contemporary culture, and all that was called *aggiornamento*. The conciliar constitution *Gaudium et Spes* included the motif of "evolving culture," which some linked to the influence of Teilhard de Chardin. Undoubtedly the conciliar constitution revalorized the category of historicity in the doctrine of the Church and demonstrated the theological aspect of the growth of human society and civilization over ages.[1]

In the 1950s and 1960s, science introduced the so-called "synthetic theory of evolution" (neo-Darwinism), which combined classic Darwinism with new genetic discoveries. In the 1970s, the dominant view in mass culture was that

1. See *Gaudium et Spes*, no. 4, 42, 54.

the whole world, all living beings, including man—and even culture, law, ethics, and the family—are products of evolutionary mechanisms. Earlier, we demonstrated how an opposite initiative—so-called "scientific creationism"—developed in American Protestant circles.[2] For many decades this movement imposed an interpretative scheme on the creation-vs.-evolution controversy which to this day casts a shadow on the correct understanding of the entire issue. Too often science was countered directly with the Bible, and different levels of discourse (scientific, philosophical, theological) were confused. At this point we only remark that scientific creationism was based on the *sola scriptura* principle, and that for this "methodological" reason alone it had little in common with traditional Catholic creationism based on the Church Fathers and Scholastic philosophy. Nevertheless, Catholic theology nearly lost the classic idea of creation, and in consequence a Catholic voice defending creation was virtually non-existent in the public debate over several decades.

We shall emphasize that all Church statements concerning evolution that appeared after the encyclical *Humani Generis* (1950) were relatively low in rank. For this reason we will only indicate here certain directions of Catholic thinking, rather than present any definite doctrine. Moreover, even though John Paul II's pontificate produced countless comments on many moral and theological issues,[3] all of his statements about evolution can be confined to a single typescript page. The long pontificate of John Paul II (1978–2005), then, was not a homogenous period in terms of teaching about evolution. All papal statements on this topic were issued in the years 1985–1986, with the exception of one in 1996. Therefore, we will discuss the early comments in the first section, and then devote the two following sections to the statement of 1996.

Early Statements

John Paul II's earlier statements were issued on two separate occasions. The first was a symposium under the title "Christian Faith and the Theory of Evolution," held in Rome. On April 26, 1985, the pope delivered a speech in which, after quoting *Humani Generis*, he stated:

> Rightly comprehended, faith in creation or a correctly understood teaching of evolution does not create obstacles: Evolution in fact presupposes creation; creation situates itself in the light of evolution as an event which

2. See Chapter Two, under "From Biblical Creationism to Scientific Creationism."

3. The legacy of John Paul II, published in *Acta Apostolic Sedis*, accounts for over 40% of all Church teachings in the 20th century, which shows that this pontificate was twice as productive as the previous pontificates of the last century.

> extends itself through time—as a continual creation—in which God becomes visible to the eyes of the believers as Creator of heaven and earth.[4]

In this short passage, John Paul II makes a few reservations that are quite important in understanding what kind of compatibility between creation and evolution he endorsed. First of all, he mentions that the teaching of evolution must be correctly understood. However, without a more precise definition of evolution itself it is hard to say what its correct understanding would be. The opponents of biological macroevolution might claim that evolution here refers just to microevolution, which according to them is the correct understanding of the very idea of evolution. In such a case, evolution would not constitute any challenge to even the most traditional faith in creation understood as the special and separate creation of natural species of different living beings. Moreover, the pope claims that evolution presupposes creation. In this phrase, the lack of a precise definition of creation poses an interpretative difficulty. If evolution means just microevolution, then creation in this context would mean a separate creation of different living beings. Only after they are created may they evolve within their definite limits. Therefore, the papal statement may be interpreted in such a way as to be compatible with progressive creationism, theistic evolution, or even Young Earth Creationism, as long as the latter does not exclude some kind of evolution. The only type of evolution excluded by the pope would be a purely materialistic process accounting for all biodiversity. This kind of evolution could not reveal God as the creator of heaven and earth and thus would not meet the papal definition.

The second occasion to refer to the topic of evolution was a series of General Audiences (Wednesday Catecheses) about God the Father, mainly during the discussion of creation (1985–1986). The first reference to the theory of evolution occurred in the catechesis of July 10, 1985, when the pope discussed the rational arguments supporting the existence of God. In the talk, he refers to the long Christian tradition which, following the words of St. Paul (Rom 1:20), indicates the possibility of knowing the invisible God through his visible works:

> All the observations concerning the development of life lead to a similar conclusion. The evolution of living beings, of which science seeks to determine the stages and to discern the mechanism, presents an internal finality which arouses admiration. This finality which directs beings in a direction for

4. John Paul II, address to the participants of the symposium "Christian Faith and the Theory of Evolution," April 26, 1985. English text found at http://www.ignatiusinsight.com/features2006/print2006/mbrumley_origins_aug06.html (February 26, 2015). This address, however, is not included in the *Acata Apostolicae Sedis*.

> which they are not responsible or in charge, obliges one to suppose a Mind which is its inventor, its creator.[5]

This passage only indirectly demonstrates part of John Paul II's attitude towards biological evolution. He says two things: (1) evolution is a subject of scientific research; (2) evolution reveals a "surprising internal finality." What he does not say is (3) that evolution is an adequate subject of scientific studies; (i.e., that evolutionary research is a fully justified part of natural science) or (4) how he understands evolution. Thus the quoted fragment may only serve as indirect support for evolution, in the sense that the pope adopted the "occurrence of evolution" as a beginning premise for developing an argument for the existence of God. If the beginning premise (the occurrence of evolution) were untrue, the argument for the existence of God would also be unreal. However, it was the intention of John Paul II to present a real, not just an apparent, argument in favor of the existence of God; so he must implicitly have assumed the reality of evolution. At the same time, the association of evolution with "surprising finality"—which should be understood as finality transcending the natural order—indicates that we are speaking of evolution exclusively in the theistic sense. The implicit support contained in the statement essentially refers to the philosophical and theological aspects of the biological theory.[6]

Reservations (3) and (4) show that the possible exclusion (by science or the future Magisterium of the Church) of the actual occurrence of biological macroevolution would not stand in conflict with this assertion by the pope. After all, the quoted declaration may be interpreted in a conditional sense: if evolution really occurs according to the idea that living beings tend towards one goal, then it reveals the internal finality of nature. As such, evolution would constitute an additional argument for the existence of God.

At the end of the same catechesis, John Paul II tells his audience:

> To all these "indications" of the existence of God the Creator, some oppose the power of chance or of the proper mechanisms of matter. To speak of chance for a universe which presents such a complex organization in its elements, and such a marvelous finality in its life would be equivalent to giving up the search for an explanation of the world as it appears to us. In fact, this would be equivalent to admitting effects without a cause. It would be to abdicate human intelligence, which would thus refuse to think, and to seek a solution for its problems.[7]

The full meaning of these words was revealed only twenty years later, when,

5. Catechesis: *The Proofs for God's Existence* (July 10, 1985); http://inters.org/John-Paul-II-Science-Proofs-God (February 26, 2015).

6. Ibid.

7. Ibid.

shortly after the pope's death, the debate over the role of chance in evolution raged in the Church. Many scholars maintained that Catholic theology finds no difficulty in adopting Darwinian explanations, because God could have used chance to bring about all that we see in the universe. However, this position is not in harmony with John Paul II's statement, which clearly says that neither chance events nor "mechanism of matter" can account for the formation of the universe.

John Paul II also mentions evolution a second time in his catechesis of January 8, 1986:

> In our own day the mutual relationship between scientific and religious truth is better understood. Many scientists have assumed an attitude of increasing respect for the Christian view of creation, while legitimately raising serious problems. These problems concern the evolution of living forms, and of human beings in particular, as well as the immanent finality of the cosmos itself in coming into being. This field allows for the possibility of fruitful dialogue concerning the different ways of approaching the reality of the world and of the human person. These ways are sincerely recognized as different, though they converge at the deepest level in favor of man, who is unique. Man was created in the image of God and therefore as the intelligent and wise master of the world, as the first page of the Bible states. . . . The Biblical-Christian view of the origins of the cosmos and of history, and of humanity in particular has had an important influence on the spiritual, moral and cultural formation of entire peoples for more than twenty centuries. This view is so undeniably outstanding, inspiring and original, that to speak of it explicitly, even if synthetically, is a duty which no pastor or catechist can omit.[8]

Here the pope only mentions the theory of evolution in passing by invoking the theory of biological evolution as one of the examples of harmonious relations between science and faith, and the fact that science does not have to lead to a departure from faith. Such an approach is similar to the previous one; i.e., it implicitly assumes that the theory of evolution is an example of true science. Furthermore, if evolution as adopted in science is to agree with revelation, the pope must have meant theistic evolution, that is, evolution somehow guided by God. However, the pope points to the "serious problems" concerning the evolution of living forms, and of human beings in particular. These words may be interpreted as a reminder that the widespread acceptance of evolution in science is not proportional to its scientific justification. In the history of science one finds many examples of commonly accepted theories being completely refuted later. As the Holy Father was speaking of the evolution of "living forms, and of human beings in particular," we should assume he was referring to biological macroevolution, especially the formation of man, instead of microevo-

8. Catechesis: *The Mystery of Creation* (Jan 8, 1986); http://inters.org/John-Paul-II-Catechesis-Mystery-Creation (February 26, 2015).

lution, which is a change within natural species.[9] Virtually no contemporary scientist denies the occurrence of changes within lower taxonomic categories. Such changes are observed both in nature and in the laboratory. What is disputed by some scientists is a far-reaching extrapolation of these results in which it is claimed that all diversity of life is derived from a single primitive cell, or from inanimate matter. And this idea, according to the pope, "raises serious problems" when we adopt and respect the Christian view of creation.

In this catechesis, John Paul II says three things about the interdependence of science and religion: (1) the relation between science and religion is now better understood than at any previous time; (2) many scientists share and respect what the Christian faith says about creation; (3) a productive dialogue about the origin of man is possible despite the legitimate differences between the two discourses. The three statements, of which only the third is normative rather than descriptive, may be completely true regardless of any opinions about evolution—its scientific value, actual occurrence, or absence. The dialogue between science and religion stems from basic Christian premises such as the belief that both books, the book of nature and the book of Bible, have one divine source. This dialogue is independent of any particular scientific discoveries and is possible in any paradigm, not only the evolutionary one. The pope mentions here the theory of evolution only as an example of fruitful dialogue. But that does not mean he lends any support to Christian evolutionism.

On the other hand, the pope emphasizes the pastor's and catechist's duty of providing reliable education about the "Biblical-Christian view of the origins of the cosmos and of history." This seems to run counter to the presently popular claim (especially among Bible scholars) that the Genesis account is purely figurative and does not convey any message about the manner in which the world was formed.

John Paul II developed this theme further three weeks later, in his catechesis of January 29, 1986. Here, the pope speaks more directly of the biblical text:

> The account of the work of creation deserves to be read and meditated upon frequently in the liturgy and outside of it. As regards the individual days, one detects between one account and the other a strict continuity and a clear analogy. The account begins with the words: In the beginning God created the heavens and the earth, that is, the entire visible world. Then, in the description of the individual days, the expression recurs: God said: Let there be. . . . Through the power of this word of the Creator's fiat, let there be, the visible world gradually arises. In the beginning the earth is without form and void. Later, under the action of God's creative word, it becomes suitable for life and is filled with living beings, with plants and animals, in the midst of

9. More on the terms "species" and "evolution," see Chapter One.

> which God finally created man in his own image (Gen 1:27). Above all, this text has a religious and theological importance. It doesn't contain significant elements from the point of view of the natural sciences. Research on the origin and development of the individual species in nature does not find in this description any definitive norm or positive contributions of substantial interest. Indeed, the theory of natural evolution, understood in a sense that does not exclude divine causality, is not in principle opposed to [*non contrasta, in linea di principio*] the truth about the creation of the visible world, as presented in the Book of Genesis.[10]

This utterance addresses, and in a way responds to, the two long-recognized problems in the discussion about evolution: (1) the competence of the biblical message to judge scientific achievements, and (2) the possibility of harmonizing the biblical account with the theory of evolution.

As regards the first issue, the pope indicates the importance of separating science from the biblical message: "It [the text of Genesis] doesn't contain significant elements from the point of view of the natural sciences." But the pope does not indicate what elements lack significance from the point of view of natural sciences. Obviously, there are certain truths in the Holy Scriptures that have been confirmed by science. There are also truths which are somewhat in-between science and faith, thus belonging to the competence of both. And, there are truths that exceed the capacity of natural sciences, such as the doctrine of *creatio ex nihilo*.[11] Moreover, there are many truths in the Bible which scientists have tried to dismiss but which have always been defended by the

10. Catechesis: *In Creation God Calls the World into Existence from Nothingness* (Jan 29, 1986). http://inters.org/John-Paul-II-Catechesis-Creation-Nothingness (February 26, 2015). John Paul II spoke in a similar manner in his address to the Pontifical Academy of Sciences on October 3, 1981: "The Bible itself speaks to us of the origin of the universe and its make-up, not in order to provide us with a scientific treatise, but in order to state the correct relationships of man with God and with the universe. Sacred Scripture wishes simply to declare that the world was created by God, and in order to teach this truth it expresses itself in the terms of the cosmology in use at the time of the writer. The Sacred Book likewise wishes to tell men that the world was not created as the seat of the gods, as was taught by other cosmogonies and cosmologies, but was rather created for the service of man and the glory of God. Any other teaching about the origin and make-up of the universe is alien to the intentions of the Bible, which does not wish to teach how heaven was made but how one goes to heaven." After *Papal Addresses to the Pontifical Academy of Sciences* 1917–2002 (Vatican: The Pontifical Academy of Sciences, 2003), 250.

11. A good example of the complementary character of science and Genesis is the question of the very beginning of the material universe. Science can go only as far as the "Big Bang" theory, which implies that the universe began in some distant past from an infinitely small point with infinite temperature and density. The Bible, on the other hand, says that the world was begun by God, who made heaven and earth. The Biblical account does not mention any previously existing creation. As long as the "Big Bang" theory is not understood as a blind self-formation of the whole universe, both approaches are compatible and complementary, even though they are derived from different disciplines using different methods.

Church for the sake of the Holy Scriptures. For instance, many times in history, miracles were subjected to trial, and many scientists tried to explain them in purely natural terms. In spite of these various theories, the Church has maintained the authenticity of such miracles as the revival of the dead, the transformation of water into wine, and the resurrection of Jesus.

Thus the papal statement encounters a problem: should the origin of the first man regarding his body be placed in the category of miracles that the Bible defends against the alleged scientific theories, or should it be classified among the works of nature whose details are not to be found in the Bible? By adopting the latter solution, we implicitly reject the belief in the direct creation of the human body. Then, also, the belief in monogenism (one human couple at the beginning of all humanity) is virtually untenable. Moreover, the very notion of human nature as a defined and unchanging concept of humanity, providing the basis for moral standards, is challenged here. This is because, if evolution is some kind of a universal law operating in nature at all times, there is no reason to suspect that its mechanisms worked to establish one unchangeable reality at a specific point in history. On the contrary, from time to time (measured in millions of years), different species of man should come into being, and the ones that already exist should develop into different, probably super-human forms. Therefore, the claim that Genesis does not contain any elements significant from the point of view of science cannot be accepted without any reservations. There are at least a few elements in the Biblical account of creation that do influence the understanding of science, or at least impose limits on scientific explanations.

Nevertheless, the fundamental message of the pope is clear: the Genesis account as such is not a criterion for scientific theories. This means the history of the deluge tells us nothing, or very little, about the movement of tectonic plates or the formation of continents, river courses, or oceanic trenches. Similarly, the description of creation provides no information about interstellar distances, forces of gravity, or the temperature of the stars. Analysis of individual days of creation will not teach us about the number of planets in the solar system, or the existence of dinosaurs. In this sense, the Bible does not contain "any elements"—as the pope writes—significant to science. Still, there remains the question of whether the theory of the evolutionary origin of species is the kind of science that is in no way verifiable by the Bible. Or, perhaps, does the Bible shed some light on the origin of species?

An implicit answer to this question is found in the second assertion. In the catechesis, the pope states that "the theory of natural evolution, understood in a sense that does not exclude divine causality, is not in principle opposed to the truth about the creation of the visible world as presented in the Book of Genesis." The pope does not claim that the Bible simply does not oppose the theory of natural evolution. Instead, the statement is accompanied by two reservations: (a) the addition of the phrase "in principle" and (b) the stipulation that the theory be understood "in a sense that does not exclude divine causality." The first reservation is a plain mitigation of the sentence, which implies that in some circumstances—perhaps using some more advanced exegesis—it might be proved that the Bible is opposed to evolution even if in principle it is not. On the other hand, the second condition is much more rigorous towards evolutionism. Of course, it rules out all atheistic interpretations of evolution at once, but what about the theistic form of evolution? Does this claim exclude theistic evolution?

This question cannot be answered on the basis of the quoted sentence alone. Theistic evolution assumes that God acted in a direct manner at the moment of the first creation, when, as the Bible tells us, "God created the heavens and the earth." After that, God acted in natural history only through so-called "secondary causes." Different versions of theistic evolution might introduce various degrees of limitations of God's activity. For example, Charles Darwin, like many Catholic evolutionists, claimed that God had to create one or a few living organisms.[12] However, it was only a non-substantial appendix to his theory, required for the time before the evolutionary paradigm was popularized in the wider culture. That limitation on evolutionary history was removed very quickly, and currently most theistic evolutionists do not need a "special act of creation" to obtain the first living being. It has been replaced by chemical and biochemical evolution. According to theistic evolution, the world and all species, including the first human body, emerge by virtue of presumed natural laws (such as the alleged potency of matter for self-organization), whereas the direct causality of God is limited to the first creative act alone. This "self-organization" of the world occurs under some sort of general divine providence, but never through direct divine acts. This contrasts with the classic Christian view, wherein direct causality was necessary to create fundamentally new natures, such as, for instance, completely new species of living organisms. This means that theistic evolution preserves God's primary causation only with respect to the first creative act (*creatio ex nihilo*), and excludes it from the subsequent "six days" of creation, replacing it with secondary causation. Therefore, theistic evolution in some sense excludes divine causality from the original formation of the universe. It follows that if the phrase "divine causality" signifies a direct operation in the formation of the universe, then theistic evolution is disqualified.

The pope's statement should be interpreted according to its most natural

12. Cf. Ch. Darwin, *The Origin of Species*, 483–84 and 488.

meaning. In our times the most popular version of theistic evolution is based on neo-Darwinian mechanism, which according to the common scientific understanding excludes divine causality of any sort, and even any kind of teleology. Thus if the pope wished to assert the essential absence of opposition between the Bible and evolution, it would be some form of evolution different from the one commonly acknowledged in contemporary science. The best candidate is the theistic variety, in which the vestiges of God's causality are not detectable on an empirical level, but the whole process is somehow immersed in Divine providence. Thanks to God's more general guidance and intimate presence in creation, the random and necessary processes of evolution bring about the pre-planned effects. Only this kind of evolution would be acceptable on the Pope's terms. If the catechesis had been a solemn and definite statement, Catholics could not claim anymore that Genesis disqualifies theistic evolution. Such an assertion would nearly settle the debate Catholic creationists and evolutionists fought over past century. Nevertheless, the low status of this statement and its conditional nature make it unable to solve the problem.

As this papal utterance is not decisive, it certainly leaves room for Catholic theologians to claim that the biblical account cannot be reconciled with evolution, even in its theistic form. Moreover, even if the Bible did not contradict evolution, that would not mean it supports it with any positive claims. One may imagine that, even if *in principle* there is no conflict between Genesis and theistic evolution, the sacred text is still more in accordance with the concept of special creation. Indeed, the pope inclines to the opinion that there is no inconsistency between revelation and evolution, but he does not put it forward as a binding decision.

The catechesis of January 29, 1986, may be regarded as the most "pro-evolutionary" of all John Paul II's statements. Surprisingly, it remains relatively unknown and has never been used in the media in the same way the much less "pro-evolutionary" statement of 1996 has been. Even in the works of proponents of theistic evolution, it is hard to find references to this excerpt from the papal catecheses.

Another important reference to evolution occurred in the catechesis of March 5, 1986, in which John Paul II says:

> God the Creator is he who accomplishes all things according to the counsel of his will (Eph 1:11). The whole work of creation belongs to the plan of salvation, the mystery hidden for ages in God who created all things (Eph 3:9). Through the act of the creation of the world, and especially of man, the plan of salvation begins to be realized. Creation is the work of a loving Wisdom, as Sacred Scripture mentions on several occasions (cf. e.g., Prov 8:22–36). It is clear that the truth of faith about creation is radically opposed to the theories

of materialistic philosophy which view the cosmos as the result of an evolution of matter reducible to pure chance and necessity.[13]

John Paul II clearly distinguishes the Catholic understanding of creation from evolution understood as purely material and blind process. Nominally, theistic evolutionists recognize the existence of a divine plan in the universe; but in practice, two theses accepted by them seem to contradict the quoted words.

First of all, contemporary theistic evolution employs neo-Darwinism as an explanation of biodiversity. But the driving forces of neo-Darwinian evolution are random genetic mutations and natural selection. In philosophical terms, it is nothing more than a play of chance and necessity. This idea, according to the pope, "is radically opposed" to the truth of faith about creation.

Secondly, this pope's statement places supporters of theistic evolution in a difficult position. Theistic evolutionists often radically and uncompromisingly dismiss the theory of intelligent design.[14] But the only alternatives to intelligent design are precisely those "materialistic philosophies" that the pope called contrary to the Catholic faith about creation. Thus, theistic evolutionists encounter two serious problems: On the one hand they are unable to clearly define the reason for their rejection of intelligent design, while on the other they must accept the existence of a divine plan in nature to remain orthodox Christians. At best, this leads to an inherent conflict or inconsistency within theistic evolution.

John Paul II rejects "pure chance and necessity" as the only explanation of the origin of the universe. If it were not pure chance and necessity, there must have been some other factor involved in the origination of nature in its different forms. The only remaining factor, besides chance and necessity, is intelligence. Therefore the pope's words necessarily imply the need for intelligent causation in the formation of the universe, which is the core claim of the mod-

13. Catechesis: *Creation Is the Work of the Trinity* (March 5, 1986); http://inters.org/John-Paul-II-Catechesis-Creation-Trinity (February 26, 2015).

14. A survey of contemporary literature promoting theistic evolution reveals considerable criticism of the ID theory. Catholic authors expressing disapproval for ID from the position of theistic evolution include the late J. Zycinski, who wrote, for instance: "[promoting theories based on intelligent design] leads to anti-intellectual interpretations, ignoring the standpoint of theistic evolutionism, and instead regarding a pathetic mix of ideology and apologetics as representative of Christian thought. In consequence of such practice, there arises an intellectual conflict in which emotions prevail over arguments" (*Wszechswiat emergentny*, 111). In fact, however, throughout his discussion of ID, J. Zycinski misinterpreted this concept and presented it in a derisive manner, while overlooking important scientific arguments (cf. ibid., 151–55). Other Catholic authors who have criticized intelligent design include: Kenneth R. Miller, *Only a Theory: Evolution and the Battle for America's Soul* (New York: Penguin, 2008); François Euvé, S.J., *Darwin et le christianisme: Vrais et faux débats* (Paris: Buchet Chastel, 2009); John F. Haught, *God after Darwin: A Theology of Evolution* (Boulder: Westview Press, 2000), and others.

ern intelligent design theory. If these words had been spoken fifteen years later, commentators might have interpreted them as overt support for intelligent design. But in 1986 intelligent design was not yet part of the debate. Should the pope's words be therefore viewed as an inspiration to pursue a new theory that could overcome the hegemony of "chance and necessity" in contemporary science? Regardless of any specific answer to this question, it is true that the pope not only rejected atheistic evolution but also set a difficult task before theistic evolutionists: now they would need to explain how to harmonize the idea of a divine plan embedded in natural world with the blind processes that are the only forces operative in the Darwinian evolutionary theories.

John Paul II's last declaration on evolution in this series of catecheses took place on April 16, 1986. On that occasion, the Pope summarized his previous statements on the relationship between the Church doctrine and evolution:

> In modern times the theory of evolution has raised a special difficulty against the revealed doctrine about the creation of man as a being composed of soul and body. With their own methods, many natural scientists study the problem of the origin of human life on earth. Some maintain, contrary to other colleagues of theirs, not only the existence of a link between man and the ensemble of nature, but also his derivation from the higher animal species. This problem has occupied scientists since the last century and involves vast layers of public opinion. The reply of the Magisterium was offered in the encyclical *Humani Generis* of Pius XII in 1950. In it we read: "The Magisterium of the Church is not opposed to the theory of evolution being the object of investigation and discussion among experts. Here the theory of evolution is understood as an investigation of the origin of the human body from pre-existing living matter, for the Catholic faith obliges us to hold firmly that souls are created immediately by God. . . ." (DS 3896). It can therefore be said that, from the viewpoint of the doctrine of the faith, there are no difficulties in explaining the origin of man in regard to the body, by means of the theory of evolution. But it must be added that this hypothesis proposes only a probability, not a scientific certainty. However, the doctrine of faith invariably affirms that man's spiritual soul is created directly by God. According to the hypothesis mentioned, it is possible that the human body, following the order impressed by the Creator on the energies of life, could have been gradually prepared in the forms of antecedent living beings. However, the human soul, on which man's humanity definitively depends, cannot emerge from matter, since the soul is of a spiritual nature.[15]

There are two important points in this passage.

The first concerns the diversity of opinions among scientists on the animal

15. Catechesis: *Man Is a Spiritual and Corporeal Being* (April 16, 1986); http://inters.org/John-Paul-II-Catechesis-Spiritual-Corporeal (February 26, 2015).

origin of man. It should be noted that the pope calls evolution a theory and not a hypothesis, and indicates the existence of two positions—some scientists recognize the evolutionary origin of man, while others do not. In this way the pope seems to moderate the popular claim that since *Humani Generis* science has made such huge progress that evolution, previously a mere hypothesis, has gained the status of an incontestable fact. Actually, already in the time of Darwin there were scientists who treated evolution as a completely proven concept, as well as those who refused to grant it scientific status at all, consigning it rather to the sphere of philosophy, or even imagination.[16] This situation has not substantially changed for 150 years, since all the new scientific discoveries that were assumed to support biological evolution usually revealed unconquerable difficulties as well. Thus the scientific debate has not been won by either side, even if victory has been declared many times on both sides. Perhaps this perennial debate is due to the fact that biological macroevolution, being a historical science, cannot be tested in the same way as strictly scientific theories. Moreover, John Paul II indirectly confirms the requirement imposed by his predecessor Pius XII to approach the issue of evolution objectively, taking into account the arguments of both sides.

The other thesis concerns the relationship between *Humani Generis* and the teachings of John Paul II. Pope Pius XII allowed the possibility of discussing the evolution of man from lower "living matter." Such permission implicitly assumed that evolution may be reconcilable with Catholic doctrine. John Paul II presents this truth explicitly, stating that "from the viewpoint of the doctrine of the faith, there are no difficulties in explaining the origin of man in regard to the body, by means of the theory of evolution." This sentence complements his assertion of January 29, 1986, when he noted that *in principle* there is no contradiction between the Book of Genesis and natural evolution. Now he adds that there is no conflict between evolution and the "doctrine of the faith," i.e., virtually all that is taught by the Church. It is hard to tell if this includes (and if so, to what extent) the Catholic tradition, including Church Fathers, Holy Doctors, and Scholastic theologians. It is certainly impossible to harmonize evolution, even the theistic variety, with the doctrine of St. Thomas Aquinas.[17] Neverthe-

16. Cf., e.g., Tripepi's report discussed in Chapter Four, under "The Intervention of the Congregation of the Index."

17. One of the last authors to defend this thesis at the time of *Humani Generis* was Cardinal E. Ruffini. For many years the doctrine of St. Thomas was not mentioned in the context of evolution, as in the post-*Vatican II* period theologians essentially abandoned the teachings of Thomas Aquinas. In the 1990s, theistic evolutionists (as Dorlodot and Messenger eighty years earlier) attempted to prove the full compatibility of Aquinas's doctrine with biological macroevolution. See e.g., W. E. Carroll, "Creation, Evolution, and Thomas Aquinas," *Revue des Questions Scientifiques* 171, no. 4 (2000), 319–47. Other Thomists who see harmony between Aquinas's doctrine and biological macroevolution are

less, these two utterances, of January 29 and April 16, 1986, constitute the most "pro-evolutionary" statements in all the teaching of John Paul II.

Address to the Pontifical Academy of Sciences (1996)

The Pontifical Academy of Sciences (Pontificia Academia Scientiarum, or PAS) gained its current constitution after a reform instituted by Pius XI in 1936. The aim of this Vatican body, nominally subject directly to the pope, is to promote "the progress of the mathematical, physical, and natural sciences, and the study of related epistemological questions and issues."[18] Members of the Academy do not have to be believers, but they should be recognized in the world of science and enjoy a good reputation for morals. At the beginning of his pontificate, John Paul II expressed his confidence in the research conducted by members of this pontifical academy. In a speech given in 1981, he said:

> I have firm confidence in the world scientific community, and in a very special way in the Pontifical Academy of Sciences, and I am certain that thanks to them biological progress and research, as also all other forms of scientific research and its technological application, will be carried out in full respect for the norms of morality, safeguarding human dignity, freedom and equality.[19]

On October 22–26, 1996, a plenary session of the PAS was held in Rome. The meeting concerned issues regarding the origin and evolution of life. On this occasion the meeting's participants asked the pope to give an address on the

Edward Feser and Michael W. Tkacz, among others. Only in 2010 did other scholars begin to point out that this interpretation contained numerous errors and imprecisions concerning Aquinas's thought. See L.P. Gage, "Darwin, Design and Thomas Aquinas: The Mythical Conflict between Thomism and Intelligent Design," *Touchstone* 23, no. 6 (November/December 2010), 23. Article available online at: http://www.touchstonemag.com/archives/print.php?id=23-06-037-f (February 26, 2015). L.P. Gage, "Can a Thomist Be a Darwinist?" in *God and Evolution* (Seattle: Discovery Institute Press, 2010), 187–202; L.P. Gage, R.C. Koons, "St. Thomas Aquinas on Intelligent Design," in *Proceedings of the American Catholic Philosophical Association*, vol. 85 (2011), 79–97; M. Chaberek, Swiety, "Tomasz z Akwinu a ewolucjonizm: Polemika z tezami P. Lichacza i W.E. Carrolla" [Thomas Aquinas and Evolutionism. A Polemic with P. Lichacz's and W.E. Carroll's Theses], *Filozoficzne Aspekty Genezy* (2012); online at http://www.nauka-a-religia.uz.zgora.pl/index. php?action=tekst&id =228 (February 26, 2015). V. Torley published a series of five articles aimed at disproving Tkacz's claims: http://www.angelfire.com/linux/vjtorley/thomas1.html (February 26, 2015).

18. Cf. Statute of PAS 1, 2: http://www.casinapioiv.va/content/accademia/en/about/goals.html (February 26, 2015).

19. "Address to the members of the plenary session of the Pontifical Academy of Sciences and participants of the study week Cosmology and Fundamental Physics of 3 October 1981" in *Papal Addresses to the Pontifical Academy of Sciences, 1917–2002* (Vatican: The Pontifical Academy of Sciences, 2003), 251.

Church's approach to evolution. The speech, given on October 22, 1996, is by far the most recent papal document on the subject; although, unlike the encyclical of Pius XII, it does not have doctrinal rank.

The Holy Father begins his address by reminding his audience that the Academy was established because Pius XI wished to be surrounded by scientists who would "inform the Holy See in complete freedom about developments in scientific research." From his "scientific senate," Pius XI demanded "service to the truth."

Next, the Pope observes that at first sight there are apparent contradictions between scientific research and the message of Revelation, but that in fact these cannot be real, because "truth cannot contradict truth." Referring directly to the topic of evolution, John Paul II remarks that the Magisterium has already expressed its opinion on this issue, and invokes two statements: (1) the encyclical *Humani Generis*, and (2) his own speech from 1992, when he addressed the Academy at a session devoted to Galileo.

From *Humani Generis*, John Paul II extracted the following theses:

> 1) that there is no conflict between evolution and the doctrine of faith about man and his vocation, provided that certain fixed truths are preserved;
>
> 2) that Pius XII had regarded the doctrine of evolutionism as a serious hypothesis, worthy of consideration and deep reflection equal to those given to the opposite hypothesis; he had also formulated two methodological prescriptions: (a) evolution should not be accepted as if it were already proven; and (b) the message of revelation on the subject should not be ignored.

In his speech on Galileo given in 1992, John Paul II had reminded his audience that

> for the correct interpretation of the inspired word a rigorous hermeneutic is needed. It is necessary to determine the proper sense of Scripture, while avoiding any unwarranted interpretations that make it say what it does not intend to say. In order to delineate the field of their own study, the exegete and the theologian must keep informed about the results achieved by the natural sciences.[20]

Next, the pope expressed his view concerning the doctrine of the Church up until then, as presented in the encyclical *Humani Generis*. In this context, he pronounced a claim that would later be widely publicized:

20. Cf. "Speech given on 31 October 1992," *AAS* 85 (1993), 764–72. Quotation after *Papal Addresses to the Pontifical Academy of Sciences* 1917–2002, 370–74.

> Today, almost half a century after the publication of the encyclical, new knowledge has led to the recognition of the theory of evolution as more than a hypothesis.[21]

At least two versions of the statement appeared in different languages. First of all, some confusion was caused by the first English translation published in *L'Osservatore Romano*. The original text of the speech was in French and the sentence in question read as follows:

> Aujourd'hui, près d'un demi-siècle après la parution de l'Encyclique, de nouvelles connaissances conduisent á reconnaître dans la théorie de l'évolution plus qu'une hypothèse.[22]

Relying on a certain ambiguity of the French "une," which can be both an indefinite article and a numeral, the English translation read:

> Today, more than a half-century after the appearance of that encyclical, some new findings lead us toward the recognition of more than one hypothesis within the theory of evolution.

However, this translation was deemed unnatural and insufficient. In the corrected version the sentence proposed that the theory of evolution should be regarded as something more than just a hypothesis.[23] Interestingly, the official 2003 English edition of the pontifical addresses to the PAS, officially authorized by this institution, preserves the first translation, speaking of the multiplicity of hypotheses within the theory.[24] Nevertheless, the texts that have effective force in the Church are those published in *AAS*, where the address is given in its French text.[25] French grammar does not allow a numerical translation of the expression "plus q'un";[26] so, after all, the correct wording is "more than a hypothesis." This interpretation is additionally confirmed by the context—both the preceding and the following sentences.[27]

Most Catholic evolutionists derive the clause "evolution is more than a

21. "Address to the members of the Pontifical Academy of Sciences of 22 October 1996 in relation to the session 'The origin and evolution of life,'" *AAS*, 89 (1997), 186–90.

22. *AAS*, 89 (1997), 188.

23. "Today, almost half a century after the publication of the encyclical, new knowledge has led to the recognition of the theory of evolution as more than a hypothesis." Another version of the English translation conveys the same meaning: "Today, almost half a century after the publication of the encyclical, new knowledge has led us to realize that the theory of evolution is no longer a mere hypothesis" (O'Leary, *Roman Catholicism and Modern Science*, 207).

24. Papal Addresses to the Pontifical Academy of Sciences, 1917–2002, 372.

25. *AAS*, 89 (1997), 186–90.

26. Cf. *Le Bon Usage*, M. Grevisse, ed., 11th ed., rev. (Duculot, 1980), 956.

27. In spite of this, the Polish translation does not offer the correct meaning of papal words, as it states directly: "nowe zdobycze nauki każą nam uznać, że teoria ewolucji jest czymś więxcej niż hipotezą [new scientific findings make us agree that the theory of evolution is something more than

hypothesis" from the context and consider it some kind of validation of the idea of evolution and an increase in its significance. But is it always the case that raising the rank of some concept makes it more convincing or acceptable?

To answer this question we need to go back to the broader context. In 1986, the then-Prefect of the Congregation of the Doctrine of Faith, Cardinal J. Ratzinger, wrote that in our time, "evolution has been exalted above and beyond its scientific content and made into an intellectual model that claims to explain the whole of reality and thus has become a sort of first philosophy. Whereas the Middle Ages had attempted a derivation of all science from theology (Bonaventure), we can speak here about a derivation of all reality from evolution."[28] No doubt for many evolutionists the theory greatly exceeds the framework of just a scientific theory, or even a philosophy. It has become a program for life, a worldview, even a religion. As Michael Ruse, a philosopher and one of the renowned proponents of evolution, has claimed: "certainly, there's no doubt about it, that in the past, and I think also in the present, for many evolutionists, evolution has functioned as something with elements which are, let us say, akin to being a secular religion."[29] According to Richard Dawkins, it was only Darwin's theory that made it possible to be an intellectually fulfilled atheist.[30] In its extreme form, then, evolution has become the religion of atheists; and in this sense it is certainly something more than just a scientific hypothesis. Perhaps the most accurate interpretation of what the pope actually meant was given by Alison Abbott, who wrote in *Nature* that "Pope John Paul II has now indicated

just a hypothesis]"; while a more accurate translation should say: "nowa wiedza prowadzi do rozpoznania w niej czegoś więcej niz hipotezy [new knowledge leads us to recognize in it something more than a hypothesis]". "To make one agree" means that there is no other option, as the new scientific findings proved evolution true. On the other hand, "to lead one to recognize" suggests that the process is not over yet, and might change its course. In the first case, the recognition has occurred; in the other, it is in the process of occurring. Therefore, the Polish translation compels the reader to accept evolution as a theory, while the original only states the fact that the new knowledge (rather than "new scientific findings") leads to the recognition of a theory of evolution. The Polish translator arbitrarily gave the papal statement a normative meaning, while in the original it is merely descriptive. The French text, i.e., what the pope actually said, is only a description of the current situation, without an assessment or evaluation, and without determining whether the described state of knowledge is a fact or just a common opinion.

28. See *Creation and Evolution: A Conference with Pope Benedict XVI in Castel Gandolfo*, 9.

29. The 1993 speech *Nonliteralist Antievolution* given during a symposium held by the American Association for the Advancement of Science (AAAS), Symposium on "The New Antievolutionism" (February 13, 1993).

30. "An atheist before Darwin could have said, following Hume: I have no explanation for complex biological design. All I know is that God isn't a good explanation, so we must wait and hope that somebody comes up with a better one. I can't help feeling that such a position, though logically sound, would have left one feeling pretty unsatisfied, and that although atheism might have been logically tenable before Darwin, Darwin made it possible to be an intellectually fulfilled atheist." R. Dawkins, *The Blind Watchmaker* (New York: Norton, 1986), 6.

that the Catholic Church is ready formally to accept scientific evidence that evolution is more than just a hypothesis."[31]

The papal address contains a few other important messages. John Paul II speaks of science's progressive recognition of this theory and the "convergence of neither sought nor fabricated" studies that constitute an important argument in its favor. He further defines what a theory is and what conditions it must meet:

> A theory is a metascientific elaboration, distinct from the results of observation but consistent with them. . . . A theory's validity depends on whether or not it can be verified; it is constantly tested against the facts; wherever it can no longer explain the latter, it shows its limitations and unsuitability. It must then be rethought. Furthermore, while the formulation of a theory like that of evolution complies with the need for consistency with the observed data, it borrows certain notions from natural philosophy. And, to tell the truth, rather than the theory of evolution, we should speak of several theories of evolution. On the one hand, this plurality has to do with the different explanations advanced for the mechanism of evolution, and on the other, with the various philosophies on which it is based.[32]

The pope seems to have defined here what this "more" is that makes evolution not just a hypothesis. The context suggests (though it is not stated explicitly) that evolution is a theory. But the pope had already called evolution a theory a decade earlier. Moreover, in everyday language these two terms are generally used interchangeably, and both of them—"hypothesis" and "theory"—may suggest that some thesis has not been proven. Thus, there is no great novelty in this particular phrase.

Still, it is significant that right after calling evolution a theory, the pope reminds his audience of the fundamental requirements that every scientific theory must meet. He mentions compliance with facts, and asserts that if a theory does not account for the facts, it should be rethought. Contemporary critics of Darwinism provide strictly scientific evidence (e.g., in biochemistry) that the neo-Darwinian mechanism is not an adequate explanation of the emergence of molecular structures in living organisms. The reason is that biochemical structures reveal two features: extraordinary precision of operation and an irreducible system of connections between their elements. The synthetic theory of evolution assumes that minor errors in the copying of genetic information accumulate over long periods of time, leading after many generations to large beneficial changes in organisms. R. Dawkins even wrote a book, *Climbing*

31. A. Abbott, "Papal Confession: Darwin Was Right about Evolution," *Nature* (October 31, 1996), 393(6603), 753.

32. *AAS*, 89 (1997), 188.

Mount Improbable,[33] in which he explained how any given organ can be developed through small steps. However, Dawkins uses metaphors rather than real research, so he does not present a strictly scientific way of reasoning. The first person to draw attention to the problem of irreducible complexity was the biochemist Michael Behe. In contrast to Dawkins, Behe describes real organic structures and actual cellular processes. It is an interesting coincidence that his book *Darwin's Black Box* was released in the same year as the aforementioned book by Dawkins and the papal address (1996). We know that John Paul II received a copy of Behe's book in August 1996, though we do not know if the pope knew the content of Behe's publication at the time he delivered his address to the PAS.

Over the next fifteen years, the theory of evolution confronted the problem that, as a metascientific elaboration, it has failed to explain facts and account for newly recognized biological phenomena. According to the theory of evolution, living organisms should bear numerous traces of genetic errors. Based on this assumption, evolutionists willingly talked about "junk DNA," that is, non-functional, superfluous genetic material, which was supposed to constitute most of human genome. However, it turned out that although deleterious and non-functional mutations do occur, the vast majority of DNA actually encodes important information and plays a role in the process of life.[34] Therefore, genetic junk does not constitute a major part of living organisms' DNA. In this case neo-Darwinism proved to be rather a hindrance in research, and only its "suspension" has led to further discoveries. As John Paul II has written, "Wherever [theory] can no longer explain the facts, it shows its limitations and unsuitability. It must then be rethought."

In the concluding sections of the address, John Paul II also touches upon the issue of the origin of man. He repeats the statement of Pius XII in the conditional clause: "If the origin of the human body comes through living matter that previously existed, the spiritual soul is created directly by God."[35] He also slightly develops the teaching of Pius XII:

> With man, we find ourselves facing a different ontological order—an ontological leap, we could say. But in posing such a great ontological discontinuity, are we not breaking up the physical continuity which seems to be the main line of research about evolution in the fields of physics and chemistry? An appreciation for the different methods used in different fields of scholar-

33. R. Dawkins, *Climbing Mount Improbable* (New York: Norton, 1996).

34. Cf. J. Wells, *The Myth of Junk DNA* (Seattle: Discovery Institute Press, 2011). Different examples of how neo-Darwinian theory cannot explain some of the latest observations can be found in books by Stephen C. Meyer and Michael Behe.

35. *AAS*, 89 (1997), 189.

> ship allows us to bring together two points of view which at first might seem irreconcilable.[36]

The problem addressed here is linked to an old dispute about the hominization of "pre-existing living matter." As we might remember (Chapter Four), theologians of the early 20th century questioned whether it is at all possible to speak of the evolutionary emergence of the body, and indicated that the infusion of the soul must, by its very nature, involve the transformation of animated matter. For this reason most of them rejected the physical continuity of evolutionary generation of the first human body. Instead, they spoke about the necessity of a Divine act and supernatural transformation of an animal body into a human one, even if this physical transformation could hardly be observed by science. This reasoning was only abandoned in the post-conciliar period, when theologians either did not know the principles of classical philosophy or rejected them altogether. This more "naturalistic" solution was adopted in the papal address that embraced the "ontological leap" (special infusion of the soul), but questioned the "physical leap" (special transformation of the body). The reason for not adopting the "physical leap" was a desire to maintain the compatibility of the Catholic position with "the main thread of research into evolution in the field of physics and chemistry." According to this concept, the human body was developed through purely natural evolution from start to finish (no physical leap). In fact, however, such a solution is untenable for philosophical reasons. If the soul is an individual form of the body (which is the solemn Catholic teaching), then infusion of a new soul must be accompanied by transformation of the matter that constitutes the body. Thus any "ontological leap" in hominization necessitates a "physical leap." All other solutions would ultimately boil down either to materialism or spiritualism, or would raise the problem of the psycho-physical unity of man. In any event, they are not compatible with traditional Christian anthropology. This can explain why John Paul II concluded his considerations only very generally and vaguely, stating that "An appreciation for the different methods used in different fields of scholarship allows us to bring together two points of view which at first might seem irreconcilable."

It is difficult to understand what the "appreciation for the different methods used in different fields of scholarship" might mean. Is it a problem of the method of various studies, or rather of their substantial content and conclusions? What are these studies that allow us to reconcile theological, philosophical, and biological premises altogether within the concept of the evolution of the human body from the lower animals? Neither of these questions was answered. Finally, the very statement about "two points of view which at first

36. Ibid.

might seem irreconcilable" is quite meaningful. Perhaps the "irreconcilability" is not only apparent if at least some researchers, using various methods of analyses, come to the conclusion that man did not originate from animals.[37]

Reception of the Papal Address

The media reactions to John Paul II's address were quite predictable. For instance, *Il Giornale* announced that the pope said we may have been descended from apes, and *La Repubblica* reported that the "pope had made peace with Darwin." *Time* announced that "the pope blessed natural selection," and a *The Washington Post* headline read "Pope backs acceptance of evolution." An article in *Nature* was entitled "Papal confession: Darwin was right about evolution." The analysis of the cultural reception of Darwinism is not the subject of this work. Instead, we are focusing here on the interpretations drawn by theologians and scientists. Following the instruction of Pius XII to present the arguments of both sides, we will analyze the reception of the pontifical message by both critics and proponents of evolution. For example, in Poland, the address was widely commented upon by Archbishop Jozef Zycinski and Rev. Marek Slomka on one side, and by Rev. Professor Piotr Lenartowicz, S.J. and professor of biology Maciej Giertych on the other.

According to Giertych, the address of John Paul II was misinterpreted, as most commentators saw it primarily as expressing support for the Darwinian theory of evolution in biology. However, according to Giertych, the main message of this address was to recall the ancient truth that the human soul was created directly by God. John Paul II rejected the theory of the emergence of specifically human properties in the evolutionary process.[38] Professor Giertych notes also that the defense of emergentism, initiated by Archbishop J. Zycinski after the papal speech, went directly against the pope's words. Second, Giertych comments on the statement that "New knowledge leads to recognition in the theory of evolution of something more than a hypothesis," writing:

> The Pope states that the matter is thus presented by the scientific community, which does not necessarily mean it is his own opinion. He also asserts that the convergence of research in many disciplines independent of each other is an argument in its favor. Such convergence is obviously a consequence of specific interpretations, not the voice of empirical evidence. The letter of the Holy Father permits such interpretation, which is nothing new.[39]

37. See, for instance: A. Gauger, D. Axe, C. Luskin, *Science and Human Origins* (Seattle: Discovery Institute Press, 2012).

38. M. Giertych, "Papież o ewolucji," *Opoka w Kraju*, No. 20(41), (December 1996): 1–2. "Wokół ewolucji," *Opoka w Kraju*, No. 22(43), (May 1997): 3–5. http://opoka.giertych.pl/ (February 26, 2015).

39. M. Giertych, "Papież o ewolucji," 1.

Third, Giertych notes that the papal address met with extreme reactions all over the world. On the one hand, the liberal and leftist circles were "delighted that the Pope had said that the theory of evolution is more than a hypothesis"; while on the other hand "the orthodox circles . . . regret that the Holy Father had not mentioned the increasing criticism of the evolution theory, based on new empirical data and the scientific disqualification of its previous evidence."[40] Giertych indicates that the value of the message lies in the very fact that the pope opened the discussion about evolution—which its supporters would rather consider closed. The debate of whether evolution is a theory or a hypothesis by no means allows one to call it a "proven fact." Finally, Giertych observes that

> the Pontifical Academy of Sciences is composed exclusively of evolutionists, both among the natural scientists and among philosophers and theologians. The Academy recruits its members through co-optation, so the Holy Father is effectively separated from new scientific information denying the theory of evolution.[41]

This opinion was shared by Professor Lenartowicz, who wrote:

> One needs to notice an interesting fact, namely that the Pope—who was acquainted with the significance of some biological discoveries—was presumably not informed about other important results which cause considerable difficulties in maintaining the fundamental and traditional theses of the theory of evolution.[42]

Giertych and Lenartowicz independently point out the same problem with the information John Paul II received from scientists. In his 1981 address the pope had declared his full confidence in the Pontifical Academy of Science, but apparently the Academy did not respond in accordance with his expectations; i.e., by truthfully and freely informing the Holy See about the actual state of science. If virtually all members of the Academy were supporters of Darwinian views, it was quite improbable that any of them would fairly present the pope with arguments of the opposing side. This commonsense requirement for any fruitful debate was probably unmet in this case.

40. M. Giertych, *Wokól ewolucji.*

41. Ibid. Giertych took part in the session of the PAS in 2008 as a guest without the right to speak. The session was entirely devoted to evolution. In his memoirs he wrote: "I was sitting silently. During the breaks I tried to debate the participants in private. In the program of the session there was not even one lecture critical of evolution, critical from the scientific standpoint. Those people, mostly retirees, have never heard of scientific research questioning the theory of evolution. With such a selection of speakers, neither will the Church hear about them." "O ewolucji w Rzymie," *Opoka w Kraju,*" no. 68(89) (December 2008), 1–6, 5.

42. P. Lenartowicz, "Czy Papież uznał wiarygodność teorii ewolucji?" *Na początku. . . .* (1/82) (1997), 7–11.

In his further commentary on the address, Lenartowicz observes that the main message of the pope's statement concerned not evolution but other issues, such as the question of the nature of man, the conviction of the Church about man's destiny of eternal life, the biologically inexpressible value of human life, and the necessity of going beyond matter in reflections about human life. Lenartowicz presented the major contemporary scientific problems for evolutionary theory stemming from genetics and paleontology. Next, he reminded his readers that only microevolution has been proven; i.e., changes of individuals within narrower taxonomic groups; such changes have never been observed beyond the biological level of families. He also wrote that the pope not only strengthened the importance of evolution by calling it a theory (instead of just a hypothesis), but also presented it with demands that are difficult to fulfill. The pope defined the theory in modern categories, that is, as an "intellectual construct independent from the results of observations," rather than—as it used to be defined—an in-depth view of the very nature of biological phenomena. In order for an "evolution theory" to be established, it needs not only to agree with facts, but also to borrow some concepts from natural philosophy:

> This further complicates our image of the theory of evolution. We might ask, where does natural philosophy draw its concepts from? Can they be safely borrowed? Does this philosophy guarantee that those notions have anything to do with reality? . . . John Paul II is perfectly aware that evolutionism is an expression of many different concepts, not necessarily biological ones, and a result of tendencies that might have little in common with the content of biological discoveries.[43]

In sum, the two opponents of evolution indicated: (1) the necessity for a balanced interpretation of the papal address, without making the pope a supporter of Darwinism; (2) scientific problems with the theory of evolution that were not adequately taken into account in the address; and (3) the need to restore the substantial content of the papal address; i.e., the search for true human nature and the insufficiency of biology to fully explain the origin of man.

John Paul II's speech was read rather differently by the supporters of theistic evolution. According to Zycinski: "In his document, John Paul II reminds us that a Christian has no reason to treat the natural theories of evolution as merely speculative hypotheses."[44] Moreover, Zycinski believed that John Paul II introduced an "evolutionary perspective," and that the papal statement was

43. Ibid., 10–11.

44. J. Zycinski, *Bóg i ewolucja* (Lublin: TN KUL 2002), 9.

"thorough and competent."[45] In an article about the papal address published in 1997 the hierarch notes that the pope

> dismissed the possibility of adopting the philosophical concept of so-called ontological emergentism, according to which the development of the rich world of the human psyche is just an inevitable necessity in the process of the emergence of increasingly complex biological structures.[46]

Nevertheless, he adds:

> The presented limitations do not suggest that every form of emergentism should be deemed as opposing Christian thought. . . . If a scientist . . . in scientific discourse spoke of the emergence of human psychism, this would not stand in conflict with Christian thought.[47]

There is little doubt that Zycinski's view on the emergence of human consciousness deviated from the opinion of John Paul II, who explicitly rejected the possibility of matter being transformed into consciousness by any natural processes.

Rev. Dr. Marek Slomka believed that "John Paul II rejected only atheistic evolution."[48] This, however, was not a faithful paraphrase of the Pope's statement. The pope did not say that he dismisses only atheistic interpretations of evolution, but those which are materialistic and fail to respect the dignity and spiritual nature of man: at least these two conditions must be met simultaneously. As is evident in the statements by Zycinski, not every theistic version of evolution fully recognizes the truth that, for instance, the human psyche is neither a product nor an epiphenomenon of matter.

Furthermore, according to Slomka, "The whole address greatly surpasses the views of Pius XII from his encyclical *Humani Generis* and is an affirmation of the theory of evolution by declaring that the theory of evolution is more than a hypothesis."[49] In fact, it is clear that the address was far from being an affirmation of the theory of evolution. It is also uncertain whether a document of such low rank as an address (*nuntium*) may be regarded as "greatly surpassing" a

45. Por. J. Zycinski, *Bóg i stworzenie: Zarys teorii ewolucji* (Lublin: Wydawnictwo Archidiecezji Lubelskiej Gaudium 2011), 10–11.

46. J. Zycinski, "Bóg i ewolucja," *Tygodnik Powszechny* 2478, no. 10 (January 5, 1997): 1, 10.

47. Ibid. In a 2009 interview Zycinski adopted an agnostic position regarding the emergence of human psychism. See: "Zaplanowani i ukochani wciąż ewoluujemy," *Tygodnik Powszechny,* March 17, 2009, no. 3115; http://tygodnik.onet.pl/cywilizacja/zaplanowani-i-ukochani-wciaz-ewoluujemy/kf5n7 (February 26, 2015).

48. M. Slomka, "Straszenie Darwinem," *Tygodnik Powszechny,* no. 2905 (March 13, 2005); http://apologetyka.com/ptkr/groups/ptkrmember/spor/pl/document.2005-03-10.5957624946 (February 26, 2015).

49. Ibid.

doctrinal document like the encyclical *Humani Generis*. However, one may agree with the suggestion that the pope wished to express an increased degree of credibility for the evolutionary hypothesis.

Moreover, according to Slomka, the 1996 address is a "particularly important document pertaining to the Church stance on the theory of natural selection."[50] But the phrase "natural selection" does not even appear in the document. Apparently, for Slomka, the terms "natural selection" and "evolution" are interchangeable, and thus he interprets the address as supporting neo-Darwinism based on the mechanism of random mutations and natural selection. Yet, the document asserts that there are actually many different theories of evolution, which also include borrowings from philosophy. Thus, we cannot know exactly how far the pope's appreciation of evolution as a theory may be extended to the Darwinian mechanism of natural selection.

The supporters of theistic evolution generally ignored the pope's statements about the multiplicity of different theories of evolution and imputed to him support for one particular theory, namely neo-Darwinian macroevolution. Besides, they usually overlooked the important message of the document, which was the insufficiency of biology to explain the mystery of man, specifically human origins. It is worth mentioning that in Poland the Darwinian interpretation of the papal statement was contested mainly by scientists, while it was defended mostly by philosophers and theologians.

The pontificate of John Paul II was not homogenous in terms of teaching on evolution. All statements but one were made in the years 1985–1986, and after the address in 1996, there were no more. It is very unlikely that in a low-rank address in 1996 the pope said everything he wanted to say. This suggests that the pope intentionally ceased to express his opinions on the matter.

In fact, the topic of evolution began to reemerge in the public debate in full force just after 1996. Around that time, the Discovery Institute opened the Center for Science and Culture and proposed an explanation of biodiversity alternative to the Darwinian one. This initiated a fierce debate around intelligent design theory, regularly fueled with new publications by Behe, Meyer, Dembski, and Wells. Thus, we can observe two different shifts after 1996: on the one hand, an increased interest in evolution in the public sphere; on the other, a diminished involvement of Pope John Paul II.

50. Ibid.

What was the reason for the peculiar silence of the Holy Father? There was likely some pressure from the Pontifical Academy of Sciences for the condemnation of intelligent design, if all its members were indeed either theistic or atheistic evolutionists. If the pro-evolutionary stance of Pope John Paul II was as unambiguous as some Catholic scholars believed it to be,[51] then during the next nine years of his pontificate he certainly would have expressed a negative opinion about intelligent design. Instead, the Pope remained silent. He did not speak on this matter after 1996, even though both in scientific circles and in the media the issue received increased publicity. Are these valid grounds to formulate a thesis that John Paul II diminished his trust in the PAS and decided to refrain from speaking until he obtained more independent information?[52]

Surely, overcoming the evolutionary paradigm would not be a task for just one pontificate, but rather for the whole Church, and it would require many years of debates. One possible interpretation of John Paul II's silence is that he, being aware of the size of the challenge and seeing the complete lack of willingness on the part of the PAS and Catholic scholars, decided to hand the case down to future popes and future generations of Catholics. Indeed, the matter was heated up again in July 2005, only three months after the death of John Paul II, when Cardinal Christoph Schönborn voiced his opinion in *The New York Times.*

In order to properly assess the meaning of papal pronouncements, we need to consider two factors: first, the rank of the document and the formulas it employed; second, whether or not a given teaching concerns faith and morals. This double condition was articulated by the First Vatican Council when it defined papal infallibility as a dogma. According to the council, papal teaching is infallible when it is pronounced *ex cathedra* (in special manner and wording) and when it concerns faith or morality.[53] It is obvious that truths taught by

51. Cf. K.R. Miller, "Darwin, Design, and the Catholic Faith." http://www.millerandlevine.com/km/evol/catholic/op-ed-krm.html (February 27, 2015); J. Zycinski, *Bóg i ewolucja*, 53; idem, *Bóg i stworzenie. Zarys teorii ewolucji*, 10–11; M. Slomka, "Straszenie Darwinem" [Threatening with Darwin], *Tygodnik Powszechny* (March 13, 2005). B. Halaczek, "Ewolucja pogladów teologicznych na ewolucje," *Slaskie studia historyczno-teologiczne* 31 (1998), 23. G.M. Verschuuren, *God and Evolution? Science Meets Faith* (Boston: Pauline Books & Media, 2012), 5, 9–11.

52. As we mentioned before, the book *Darwin's Black Box* was given to the pope in the summer of 1996. Knowing the pope's passion for reading new publications from different disciplines, one might suspect that he did become acquainted with its content. Could this book have influenced the views of the Holy Father? Perhaps some more advanced research would enable us to answer this question.

53. "When the Roman Pontiff speaks EX CATHEDRA, that is, when, in the exercise of his office as shepherd and teacher of all Christians, in virtue of his supreme apostolic authority, he defines a doctrine concerning faith or morals to be held by the whole Church, he possesses, by the divine assistance promised to him in blessed Peter, that infallibility which the divine Redeemer willed his Church

popes do not always directly concern faith and morals, so we may speak of different degrees of connection to faith, and thus of different degrees of the certainty of statements. John Paul II's teaching on evolution also needs to be considered from these two perspectives.

According to T. Płonka, all the papal documents from the pontificate of John Paul II can be divided into 23 degrees of importance.[54] Among them, catecheses are listed at rank 18, whereas addresses (*nuntii*), which according to the *Acts of the Apostolic See* include the declaration of 1996, rank 14. Thus both of these documents are relatively low in rank. The most important expressions used in the 1986 catecheses are: the "theory of natural evolution is not in principle opposed to the truth about the creation of the visible world, as presented in the Book of Genesis," and: "[F]rom the viewpoint of the doctrine of the faith, there are no difficulties in explaining the origin of man in regard to the body, by means of the theory of evolution." In contrast, the 1996 address does not contain such expressions of "higher theological rank"; instead, it is full of remarks regarding scientific and methodological issues. What does this mean? In the most important matters—that is, those concerning the compatibility of evolutionary theory with Catholic teaching—the statements had very low rank, whereas when the rank was slightly higher, the theological significance was reduced, because the subject did not concern the faith. In the 1996 address, John Paul II does not repeat his strongest "pro-evolutionary" theses from a decade earlier, though he also fails to mention the need for finality in evolution, which recurred in the catecheses.

Don O'Leary, summarizing the doctrine of John Paul II, concludes: "The pope had, notwithstanding some outstanding difficulties, made peace with Galileo, but he did not completely come to terms with Darwin."[55] This opinion, though accurate, adopts a popular but questionable assumption, that it is the Church which needs to make concessions in order to reconcile with Darwin. Darwinian evolution is *a priori* regarded as infallible and unchangeable; therefore, changes are possible only on the part of the Church and theology. Perhaps this assumption about theories presented in science proved correct in the argument over geocentrism. But how can we know that the same expectation must

to enjoy in defining doctrine concerning faith or morals. Therefore, such definitions of the Roman Pontiff are of themselves, and not by the consent of the Church, irreformable." *Dogmatic Constitution on Christ's Church Pastor Aeternus*, ch. IV, no. 9 (Denzinger, 1839). English text after: https://www.ewtn.com/library/councils/v1.htm#6 (February 27, 2015).

54. Cf. T. Płonka, *Stopniowalność orzeczeń Magisterium Kościoła w nauczaniu Stolicy Apostolskiej podczas pontyfikatu Jana Pawla II* [Gradation of Church Pronouncements in the Teaching of the Holy See during John Paul II's Pontificate] (Warszawa: Instytut Papieża Jana Pawła II, 2011).

55. D. O'Leary, *Roman Catholicism and Modern Science*, 207.

apply to Darwinian evolution? In fact, there is no simple analogy between Galileo and Darwin. Galileo tried to explain *how* the elements of the universe work, while Darwin wanted to explain *where* they came from. It is the prerogative of science to settle the first issue, but the second belongs to theology.[56]

56. The difference between these two questions was accurately described by Isaac Newton when he wrote: "Though these bodies may, indeed, continue in their orbits by the mere laws of gravity, yet they could by no means have at first derived the regular position of the orbits themselves from those laws. . . . [Thus] this most beautiful system of the sun, planets, and comets could only proceed from the counsel and dominion of an intelligent and powerful Being." Isaac Newton, *Mathematical Principles of Natural Philosophy and His System of the World* (1686), trans. A. Motte, ed. F. Cajori, R.T. Crawford (Berkeley: University of California Press, 1934), 543–44.

9

The Current Theological Debate

Recent years have not produced any official document of the Magisterium regarding evolution. Essentially, we have at our disposal only one substantial statement by Pope Benedict XVI, a short comment by Pope Francis, and a few insights from Cardinal Christoph Schönborn. There is also an opinion delivered by the International Theological Commission and the proceedings of a few scientific sessions held in Rome, which were organized by such institutions as the Pontifical Academy of Sciences, the Pontifical Council for Culture, and the Roman universities. Strictly speaking, the Magisterium of the Church includes only the pope and individual bishops. Thus the utterances that we will discuss are mostly outside of the doctrine of the Church, and usually express only the opinions of various bodies or individuals. The Second Vatican Council affirms that "Although the individual bishops do not enjoy the prerogative of infallibility, they nevertheless proclaim Christ's doctrine infallibly whenever . . . they are in agreement on one position as definitively to be held."[1] As we shall see, bishops today have not reached a common agreement on evolution.

A Document of the International Theological Commission: Communion and Stewardship (2004)

In the years 2000–2002, the International Theological Commission held a number of meetings in order to prepare a document on the subject of the nature, dignity, and origin of man in the context of the theological truth of man's creation in the image of God (*imago Dei*). July 23, 2004 saw the publication of the document *Communion and Stewardship: Human Persons Created in*

1. Dogmatic Constitution on the Church *Lumen Gentium*, no. 25, http://www.vatican.va/archive/hist_councils/ii_vatican_council/documents/vat-ii_const_19641121_lumen-gentium_en.html (February 27, 2015).

the Image of God.[2] The document does not discuss the credibility of the evolutionary origin of man, nor does it attempt to solve the theological or metaphysical problems that might arise from that idea. The evolutionary worldview is simply taken as the starting point for any theological considerations.

The text consists of three chapters: (1) "Human Persons Created in the Image of God," (2) "In the Image of God: Persons in Communion," and (3) "In the Image of God: Stewards of Visible Creation." The section treating the issue of creation is found in the third chapter, in the section entitled "Science and the Stewardship of Knowledge." The Commission did not limit itself to reflections on the origin of man, but extended its considerations to the origin of the entire material universe. At the beginning of the text, for example, "discredited concordism" is rejected because "Christians have the responsibility to locate the modern scientific understanding of the universe within the context of the theology of creation."[3] The authors of the document presuppose that the contemporary scientific paradigm must be true; therefore, it is not the role of Christians to examine its value, but to incorporate its conclusions into theology.

After these general methodological remarks, the Theological Commission proceeds to a concise interpretation of the beginning of the world. The world is about 15 billion years old, and it started with the Big Bang.[4] Since that moment, it has been expanding and cooling down. To this is it added that "Later there gradually emerged the conditions necessary for the formation of atoms, still later the condensation of galaxies and stars, and about 10 billion years later the formation of planets."[5] Thus the Commission accepts the vision of the purely natural formation of matter, planetary systems, and the Earth. However, it does not address how the Big Bang, by itself, could have caused the formation of evidently ordered structures. In the cosmogony presented by the Commission, the universe simply emerges and develops. The scientifically well-established theory of fine-tuning is not even mentioned.

The theologians then remark that, with respect to the first life, scientists have not yet reached agreement; they write, "While there is little consensus among scientists about how the origin of this first microscopic life is to be explained,

2. International Theological Commission, *Communion and Stewardship: Human Persons Created in the Image of God*; http://www.vatican.va/roman_curia/congregations/cfaith/cti_documents/rc_con_cfaith_doc_20040723_communion-stewardship_en.html (February 27, 2015).

3. Ibid., no. 62.

4. Section 67 of the document concerned the attitude of theology towards the Big Bang theory: "With respect to the *creatio ex nihilo*, theologians can note that the Big Bang theory does not contradict this doctrine insofar as it can be said that the supposition of an absolute beginning is not scientifically inadmissible. Since the Big Bang theory does not in fact exclude the possibility of an antecedent stage of matter, it can be noted that the theory appears to provide merely indirect support for the doctrine of *creatio ex nihilo*, which as such can only be known by faith."

5. Ibid., no. 63.

there is general agreement among them that the first organism dwelt on this planet about 3.5–4 billion years ago."[6] Thus, these theologians show themselves as essentially certain about the common origin of life from a single ancestor, though they do not know how this first organism originated, or what it was. In their opinion, "Since it has been demonstrated that all living organisms on earth are genetically related, it is virtually certain that all living organisms have descended from this first organism."

However, not all scientists agree on this assumption, and the Commission fails to mention this fact. The problem with the argument presented in the document lies in the ambiguity of the expression "be related." What kind of relation did the theologians mean? Biology has shown that there are similar genes in many organisms. Therefore, the relation that joins these organisms is one of similarity but not necessarily of affinity—which common ancestry would require. Moreover, common ancestry may explain genetic similarities; but what we actually observe are astonishing differences between organisms that, according to the theory, should be very closely related.[7] However, even if we assume that all organisms share a common ancestry, this assumption provides a plausible explanation of the genetic similarities. Organisms are genetically similar because they are related. But how do we know they are related? Because they are genetically similar. In this reasoning, the assumption is identical with the conclusion, so that the argument ends up as circular. Theologians accept this obvious error in scientific argumentation, not because they are unable to see the problem due to the lack of biological knowledge, but because they uncritically trust the authority of evolutionary biology and do not even consider the possibility that some conclusions reached within this discipline could be wrong.

In further evaluation of the scientific picture of the origin of the universe, the International Theological Commission endorses the idea of evolution regardless of the evidence supporting any particular theory: "Converging evidence from many studies in the physical and biological sciences furnishes mounting support for some theory of evolution to account for the development and diversification of life on earth, while controversy continues over the

6. *Communion and Stewardship*, no. 63.

7. For decades evolutionary biologists expected that the "trees of life" built upon fossil data would be confirmed by trees built upon genetic similarities. However, nothing like this has happened. In fact, certain organisms that should be closely related based on their anatomy have been shown vary significantly in their genetic material. Conversely, certain organisms that are very similar genetically have been determined to be only remotely related based on their anatomy or fossil record. Moreover, even organisms belonging to one family may have very different genomes, whereas some staggering similarities occur between taxonomically highly distant organisms. Cf. S.C. Meyer, P.A. Nelson, J. Moneymaker, S. Minnich, R. Seelke, *Explore Evolution: The Arguments for and Against Neo-Darwinism* (Melbourne and London: Hill House Publisher, 2013), 57–58.

pace and mechanisms of evolution."[8] The authors thus assume that macroevolution takes place, though its mechanism remains unknown. From the perspective taken by the Commission, evolution is deemed a "fact" and distinguished from a mechanism of evolution, which is to be explained by a "theory." Facts are undeniable, although theories can change. Nevertheless, many biologists (and not only ID proponents) maintain that no evidence of macroevolutionary transitions has ever been found, and that if the mechanism of these alleged transitions is not known, we are not justified in speaking of macroevolution as a "fact." Moreover, if the scientific debate is unresolved, there is no sufficient reason to incorporate the naturalistic theory of biological macroevolution into Christian teaching.

Discussing the origin of man, the authors embrace arguments in favor of the emergence of human species in Africa, about 150,000 years ago. In their words,

> However it is to be explained, the decisive factor in human origins was a continually increasing brain size, culminating in that of *Homo sapiens*. With the development of the human brain, the nature and rate of evolution were permanently altered: with the introduction of the uniquely human factors of consciousness, intentionality, freedom and creativity, biological evolution was recast as social and cultural evolution.[9]

Again, the theologians admit that the gradual development of the brain remains unexplained, but this lack of knowledge is no hindrance to determining that it was the decisive factor in the emergence of man. Unfortunately, they unreservedly adopt the scientifically unproven and historically discredited claim that the size of the brain determines the intellectual properties of an individual (cf. Chapter Six, under "Four Scientific Assumptions in the Dispute over the Origin of Man").

In the next section, the Commission refers to the 1996 address of John Paul II. The theologians note that it cannot be perceived as a blanket approbation for all theories of evolution, as the pope dismissed materialistic interpretations. The Holy Father had also indicated the "ontological leap" with reference to the emergence of man. Therefore, evolution is of interest to the Church particularly because of the concept of man.[10]

Further analyzing human nature, the theologians assert that "the common ancestry and natural unity of the human race are the basis for a unity in grace

8. Ibid.

9. *Communion and Stewardship*, no. 63.

10. "[T]heories of evolution and of the origin of the universe possess particular theological interest when they touch on the doctrines of the creation *ex nihilo* and the creation of man in the image of God." Ibid., no. 64.

of redeemed human persons under the headship of the New Adam."[11] This formulation touches upon the deepest truths connected to the theology of humanity. Unfortunately, their wording appears in the context of common ancestry as it is understood in biological evolution. As a result it is difficult to avoid the impression of a confusion between the two meanings of the term "common ancestry." If the natural basis for grace is the common descent of all people from Adam, as the document correctly states, one may ask if this alleged common decent from a single unknown microorganism should not extend this unity headed by Adam to all living beings. If yes, how could we argue for the special dignity of humans and their unique call to life in grace? The stark acceptance of the evolutionary story on the one hand, and on the other the attempt to present humans as completely exceeding other beings in the order of grace and dignity, leaves the reader with an impression of inconsistency in the document. In classical Christian theology the fundamental "lack of unity" between man and the world of animals is explained by the separate act of creation of the human body and supernatural creation of the soul—not just by attaching something invisible (a soul) to the visible animal.

In sections 68–70, the authors refer to the central problem of the evolutionary paradigm in the theology of creation, namely, divine causality and the role of contingency. First, they offer as their point of view the "standard" version of theistic evolution:

> God is the cause not only of existence but also the cause of causes. God's action does not displace or supplant the activity of creaturely causes, but enables them to act according to their natures and, nonetheless, to bring about the ends he intends. In freely willing to create and conserve the universe, God wills to activate and to sustain in act all those secondary causes whose activity contributes to the unfolding of the natural order which he intends to produce. Through the activity of natural causes, God causes to arise those conditions required for the emergence and support of living organisms, and, furthermore, for their reproduction and differentiation.[12]

The vision of God's causality presented here leaves no room for special (i.e., immediate) acts of creation. God, even when forming completely new natures of living beings, acts through the agency of secondary causes. The authors assert that there is a scientific debate regarding the finality of neo-Darwinian evolution, but admit that theologians cannot determine whether design can be identified at the level of scientific research:

11. Ibid., no. 65.
12. Ibid., no. 68.

> Many neo-Darwinian scientists, as well as some of their critics, have concluded that, if evolution is a radically contingent materialistic process driven by natural selection and random genetic variation, then there can be no place in it for divine providential causality. A growing body of scientific critics of neo-Darwinism point to evidence of design (e.g., biological structures that exhibit specified complexity) that, in their view, cannot be explained in terms of a purely contingent process and that neo-Darwinians have ignored or misinterpreted. The nub of this currently lively disagreement involves scientific observation and generalization concerning whether the available data support inferences of design or chance, and cannot be settled by theology.[13]

This passage asserts that theologians cannot judge the scientific debate regarding chance and design. But if that were true, only the suspension of theological judgment could be justified. However, the Commission itself did not suspend the judgment. Instead, it put much effort into combining Catholic theology with the scientific idea of randomness as it is accepted in Darwinism. Therefore, we see here a significant inconsistency in the Theological Commission's approach to the debate over chance and purpose.

Further on in the document the Commission tries to explain how Divine causality is compatible with the randomness of the evolutionary process. If this were presented successfully, Catholics could indeed believe that neo-Darwinism and the Christian understanding of Providence are fully compatible. The document continues:

> It is important to note that, according to the Catholic understanding of divine causality, true contingency in the created order is not incompatible with a purposeful divine providence. Divine causality and created causality radically differ in kind and not only in degree. Thus, even the outcome of a truly contingent natural process can nonetheless fall within God's providential plan for creation.[14]

Apparently the theologians are referring here to the classical Catholic notion of God's providence, which stretches over planned as well as chance events. If the Commission members had stopped at this point, their conclusions might not have raised objections. However, in support of their claims, they cite St. Thomas Aquinas:

> The effect of divine providence is not only that things should happen somehow, but that they should happen either by necessity or by contingency. Therefore, whatsoever divine providence ordains to happen infallibly and of

13. Ibid., no. 69.
14. Ibid.

> necessity, happens infallibly and of necessity; and that happens from contingency, which the divine providence conceives to happen from contingency.[15]

According to the authors, Aquinas's words justify the opinion that God used contingent events in bringing about the universe, and in particular all species of living beings. This statement is quite distant from the actual view of St. Thomas, and thus it requires further explanation.

First of all, in the cited passage Aquinas only says that regardless of whether something happens by chance or by design, it is nonetheless subject to God's providence. However, this principle is not applicable to the situation described in the document. Aquinas does not refer to the emergence of things, but to their current administration by God. (The quotation is taken from the question about divine providence.) The contemporary theory of evolution, as the Commission observes, claims that chance (and necessity in the form of natural selection) is the main driver for the generation of species. Thus the important question is not whether Aquinas allows chance within divine providence or not, but rather whether he allows the possibility of chance in the generation of completely new species of living beings. To evaluate the neo-Darwinian mechanism in the light of Aquinas' doctrine, we need to find the answer to the latter question. In the *Summa Theologiae*, St. Thomas, having presented the view of Avicenna, according to whom some created beings produce other beings, comments:

> This opinion cannot stand, for two reasons. First, because . . . to create belongs to God alone, and hence what can be caused only by creation is produced by God alone. . . . Secondly, because, according to this opinion, the universality of things would not proceed from the intention of the first agent, but from the concurrence of many active causes; and such an effect we can describe only as being produced by chance. Therefore, the perfection of the universe, which consists of the diversity of things, would thus be a thing of chance, which is impossible.[16]

In the *Summa Contra Gentiles* Aquinas presents the same teaching from a different perspective:

> Things whose distinction from one another is derived from their forms [and these are different species of plants and animals] are not distinct by chance, although this is perhaps the case with things whose distinction stems from matter. Now, the distinction of species is derived from the form, and the distinction of singulars of the same species is from matter. Therefore, the dis-

15. *S.Th.*, I, 22, 4, ad 1.

16. *S.Th.*, I, q. 47, 1, c.

> tinction of things in terms of species cannot be the result of chance; but perhaps the distinction of certain individuals can be the result of chance.[17]

Finally, St. Thomas maintains that it is not chance but a plan present in the world that demonstrates the operation of God for the sake of a purpose: "That God acts for an end can also be evident from the fact that the universe is not the result of chance, but is ordered to a good."[18] This and other statements clearly demonstrate that Aquinas excludes chance from the formation of the world, though he does not exclude real chance in the operation of the universe once it is already formed. Thus, the doctrine presented by the International Theological Commission distorts Aquinas's teaching on chance and purpose. The Commission's endorsement of evolution as a "secondary cause of creation" seems to be closer to Erasmus Darwin's *Zoonomia* by than to the teachings of Aquinas (cf. Chapter One).

The last relevant passage of *Communion and Stewardship* is concerned with the emergence of man. The authors endorse a fully evolutionary account of the emergence of the human body. No alternative concept is even mentioned. According to the authors:

> Catholic theology affirms that the emergence of the first members of the human species (whether as individuals or in populations) represents an event that is not susceptible of a purely natural explanation and which can appropriately be attributed to divine intervention. Acting indirectly through causal chains . . . , God prepared the way for what Pope John Paul II has called an ontological leap . . . the moment of transition to the spiritual. While science can study these causal chains, it falls to theology to locate this account of the special creation of the human soul.[19]

As we observed when commenting on John Paul II's distinction between "physical continuity" and "ontological leap," this approach raises serious difficulties regarding the substantial unity of the human being. If the soul is considered the one and complete form of the human body, then infusion of the soul necessarily entails transformation of the material element. The "physical leap" must follow the ontological one. Otherwise, human souls could be attached to different bodies, which would go even beyond Cartesian dualism. The Commission claims that regardless of how man came to be, the event should be attributed to "divine intervention." However, the supernatural infusion of the soul is not, properly speaking, "divine intervention." Intervention (from Latin *inter-venio*) implies that some order of natural causes and effects is destroyed by God's "entering between" the natural events. Creation is not this type of

17. *Summa Contra Gentiles*, II, cap. 39, n. 3. My insertion.
18. *Summa Contra Gentiles*, II, c. 23, n. 6.
19. *Communion and Stewardship*, no. 70.

event, because in the creative act some new being is added to the order of nature without destroying anything that already exists. It is more like adding a new layer of being over the previously created ones. Therefore, even the very idea of God's creative action is not accurately depicted in the document. The concept of the origin of man presented by the Theological Commission is not new. As we already know, very similar ideas were adopted by the first Catholic evolutionists during the late 19th century. At that time, however, these ideas met proscriptions by the Congregation of the Index, and the majority of Catholic theologians dismissed them as contrary to reason and faith. The lack of any assessment of the previous Catholic teaching is a serious downside of the document. When the Theological Commission decided to adopt those views, one would have expected an explanation of why theologians rejected them a hundred years earlier and why theological positions now should be changed. The document is clearly detached from Catholic tradition and presents the matter as if nothing had ever been said about the origin of the human body by the Church Fathers and Holy Doctors.

The document employs the term "special creation" with reference to the human soul. According to theistic evolutionists, special creation leads to the "god of the gaps"—an error consisting in filling gaps in people's knowledge by appealing to supernatural causation wherever a natural cause is lacking. So the question arises, how can theology employ "special creation" with regard to the human soul while simultaneously abandoning the "special creation" of the human body? According to the authors of the document, the "god of the gaps" is not present in the case of direct creation of the soul because "The appeal to divine causality to account for genuinely causal, as distinct from merely explanatory, gaps does not insert divine agency to fill in the 'gaps' in human scientific understanding."[20] Thus, the theologians distinguish two kinds of gaps: "causal" and "explanatory." The first kind of gap can be filled by direct creative acts of God, while the second cannot. But what are the criteria for assigning individual gaps to either category? This question the document left unanswered. A theologian rejecting the evolutionary origin of species might say that the origin of completely new species requires special divine creative acts, and that this is not "filling gaps" because these are merely "causal gaps" and not "explanatory" ones. Again we see in the document an arbitrary solution that, at best, leaves the reader with an impression of inconsistency in the Commission's theological speculations.

In summary, *Communion and Stewardship* is the first Church document written entirely from the perspective of theistic evolution. As such, on the one hand, it reveals all contradictions and aporias inevitably accompanying this

20. Ibid.

standpoint; and on the other it shows how far the theological community has departed from the tradition of the Church Fathers and Holy Doctors regarding the origin of the universe and man. The purpose of the document was to demonstrate the value of a human person as the image of God (*imago Dei*). Unquestionably, the document includes many valuable remarks and theological observations concerning relations between man and the Holy Trinity, as well as within human community. Yet when it comes to the doctrine of creation it imposes schemes and notions foreign to Catholic tradition, introduces false interpretations of classical theological issues, and very often relies on untenable claims allegedly adopted from natural science.

The Views of Joseph Ratzinger/Pope Benedict XVI

Benedict XVI's teachings may be divided into two periods. The first one covers the time before his pontificate (until 2005), and the other concerns the time of his papacy. While Benedict XVI did not promulgate any documents on evolution, Joseph Ratzinger was the author of a few quite comprehensive lectures on the topic.

In 1968, as a professor of theology at Tübingen, Joseph Ratzinger took part in a series of radio interviews broadcasted by *Süddeutscher Rundfunk*, in which he discussed the issue of evolution and Christianity.[21]

First, Ratzinger observes that in the evolutionary framework, the essential component enters a fixed relationship with time so deeply that eventually being becomes time. Being is realized through becoming and change. However, as this framework does not include a neutral standard that could determine what is better or worse, it is unknown whether evolution is connected to progress or not.[22] Nevertheless, the special relationship man has with the rest of reality entitles him to view himself as a point of reference. This leads to discovering the direction of evolution and its ultimately progressive nature. Even if some of the side-roads of evolution are dead ends, the main road leads to a purpose demonstrated by evolution itself.[23] Having asserted the purposefulness of evolution, the German theologian asks: What does belief in creation mean in the context of the evolutionary understanding of the world? The answer to this question cannot be given by the theory of evolution itself:

21. J. Ratzinger, "Schöpfungsglaube und Evolutionstheorie" in H. J. Schulz, *Wer ist das eigentlich —Gott?* (Wien: Buchgemeinschaft "Welt und Heimat," 1969), 232–45. Also in: J. Ratzinger, *Dogma und Verkündigung* (München: Erich Wewel Verlag, 1973), 147–60.

22. J. Ratzinger, *Dogma und Verkündigung*, 156.

23. Ibid.

> [Belief in creation means] that the world as a whole, as the Bible says, comes from the Logos, that is, from creative mind, and represents the temporal form of its self-actuation. . . . [T]emporal being as a whole is encompassed by the one creative act of God, which, in its division, gives it its unity, in which at the same time its meaning consists, a meaning that is unfathomable to us because we do not see the whole but are ourselves only parts of it. Belief in creation does not tell us what the meaning of the world is, but only that there is one.[24]

Due to this all-encompassing act of creation, the theologian rejects the model of the Creator as a craftsman manufacturing all kinds of things separately, and proposes to replace it with a model of the creative thought working in the universe. He also offers a definition of belief in creation: "To believe in creation means to understand, in faith, the world of becoming revealed by science as a meaningful world that comes from a creative mind."[25] Obviously, this kind of "belief" in a "creative mind" faces the problem of distinction between the mind and the universe. Ratzinger found an "ingenious comment" in the works of Teilhard de Chardin. He quotes Teilhard's solution:

> What distinguishes a materialist from a spiritualist is no longer by any means . . . the fact that he admits a transition between the physical infrastructure and the psychic superstructure of things, but *only* the fact that he incorrectly sets the *definitive* point of equilibrium in the cosmic movement on the side of the infrastructure, that is, on the side of disintegration.[26]

According to the German theologian, one might wonder about the details of this formulation; but the key point seems "quite accurate" to him. Following Teilhard, Ratzinger decides that:

> spirit is not a random product of material developments, but rather that matter signifies a moment in the history of spirit. This, however, is just

24. Ibid., 157. The original text reads "[D]as zeitliche Sein ist als ganzes umspannt von dem einen schöpferichen Akt Gottes, der ihm in seiner Zerteilung seine Einheit gibt, in der zugleich sein Sinn besteht, der uns nicht nachrechenbar ist, weil wir nicht das Ganze sehen, sondern selbst nur Teile sind. Der Schöpfungsglaube sagt uns nicht das Was des Weltsinnes, sondern nur sein Dass." This uneasy sentence is surely an attempt to express something that is inexpressible in human language—the simultaneous unity and multiplicity of creative acts. Such statements by Ratzinger seem to suggest that he professed the currently popular belief that the universe may have been created and, at the same time, it may be the product of evolution. In this approach, evolution becomes "a manner of creation by God." In effect, however, the belief in creation tells us nothing about the manner of its emergence. It is only manifested as some kind of external interpretative principle that helps harmonize the biblical account with the essentially naturalistic viewpoint dominating contemporary science and philosophy.

25. Ibid., 158 (all English quotations taken from *Creation and Evolution*, 13–16).

26. Ibid.

> another way of saying that spirit is created and not the mere product of development, even though it comes to light by way of development.[27]

We see that Ratzinger rejects the idea of spirit being a product of the evolution of matter, but at the same time he also seems to reject the idea of God working in the formation of the universe through direct activity.

The second issue concerns the reconciliation of creation with the evolution of man. According to Ratzinger, the creation of man does not refer to a distant beginning, but rather a view of each person alongside Adam: "The faith declares no more about the first man than it does about each one of us, and, conversely, it declares no less about us than it does about the first man."[28] Furthermore, the spirit does not appear as something foreign, as another substance added to matter. The appearance of the spirit means, rather, that the progressive movement achieved the goal to which it had been directed. Therefore, the theologian assumes that "If creation means dependence of being, then special creation is nothing other than special dependence of being."[29] The claim that man was created in a more special manner, more directly by God, taken somewhat less metaphorically, means that man is specially wanted by God, as a being that knows God and is able to think of him. From this perspective, one may immediately define the essence of anthropogenesis:

> The clay became man at that moment in which a being for the first time was capable of forming, however dimly, the thought *God*. The first Thou that—however stammeringly—was said by human lips to God marks the moment in which spirit arose in the world. Here the Rubicon of anthropogenesis was crossed.[30]

The beginning of humanity is not determined by the use of weapons or fire, or new methods of cruelty, but by the possibility of entering into a relationship with God. According to Ratzinger, "this holds fast to the doctrine of the special creation of man."[31] At the end of the broadcast, he stresses once more:

> The theory of evolution does not invalidate the faith, nor does it corroborate it. But it does challenge the faith to understand itself more profoundly and thus to help man to understand himself and to become increasingly what he is: the being who is supposed to say Thou to God in eternity.[32]

27. Ibid., 158–59.
28. Ibid., 159.
29. Ibid.
30. Ibid., 160.
31. Ibid.
32. Ibid.

These first opinions on evolution expressed by Ratzinger in the 1960s clearly fold into theistic evolution the idea that God used evolutionary processes in order to bring about the diversity of things and reveal the spirit. Human origins are explained by materialistic processes of smooth and gradual development continuing until the human spirit can be revealed. Special creation of man means merely "special dependence in being."

During Lent of 1981, J. Ratzinger, as a Cardinal and Archbishop of Munich, gave four sermons on creation.[33] The German hierarch opened his first sermon by asking whether the Genesis account of creation is still valid in the context of modern science. The answer known to everyone is that one needs to distinguish between the form and content of the biblical message. There is a defined set of religious truths that the Bible conveys; the rest is to be delineated by science. In the sermon, Ratzinger regards this answer as essentially correct, but insufficient. "For when," he says, "we are told that we have to distinguish between the images themselves and what those images mean, then we can ask in turn: Why wasn't that said earlier?"[34] The cardinal argues that, by surrendering successive truths to the competence of science, "we will gradually end up in emptiness, and that the time will come when there will be nothing left to defend and hide behind," because "the whole landscape of Scripture and of the faith will be overrun by a kind of reason."[35] How can we thus define the limits of *reason*? According to Ratzinger, Jesus is the guide who shows us what is an image and what is the proper, permanent substance of biblical statements. The belief in creation is rational, and Christocentrism is its measure.

In the second sermon, Ratzinger observes that the 19th-century vision of a stationary world, eternally governed by unchangeable laws, was destroyed in the 20th century. It was replaced by the principle of entropy: the world is not constant anymore, but is subject to the law of changing and passing away. All this reality, however, is not random in nature, but reveals a design.[36]

The third sermon is the most important to our topic. There the German theologian favors a figurative interpretation of the Biblical account of the origin of man. When the Bible speaks about creating man from the dust of the earth, it suggests that we are all made from the same clay; i.e., that all people constitute a unity. "There are not," explains Ratzinger, "different kinds of blood and soil, to use a Nazi slogan. There are not fundamentally different kinds of human beings, as the myths of numerous religions used to say and as some

33. J. Ratzinger, *In the Beginning: A Catholic Understanding of the Story of Creation and the Fall*, trans. B. Ramsey (Grand Rapids, MI: William B. Eerdmans Publishing Company, 1995).

34. Ibid., 6.

35. Ibid., 7.

36. Ibid., 22–25.

worldviews of our own day also assert."[37] The essential message of Genesis, indeed, is that every man is wanted by God, and every man is made in His image. The fact that man is an image of God shows that he is something more than "dust of the earth." Man as an image cannot remain closed in himself, he refers beyond himself. Next, Ratzinger asks:

> But is it not ultimately disproved by our scientific knowledge of how the human being evolved from the animal kingdom? Now, more reflective spirits have long been aware that there is no either-or here. We cannot say: creation or evolution, inasmuch as these two things respond to two different realities. The story of the dust of the earth and the breath of God, which we just heard, does not in fact explain how human persons come to be but rather what they are. It explains their inmost origin and casts light on the project that they are. And, vice versa, the theory of evolution seeks to understand and describe biological developments. But in so doing it cannot explain where the project of human persons comes from, nor their inner origin, nor their particular nature."[38]

And furthermore:

> It is the affair of the natural sciences to explain how the tree of life in particular continues to grow and how new branches shoot out from it. This is not a matter for faith. But we must have the audacity to say that the great projects of the living creation are not the products of chance and error. Nor are they the products of a selective process to which divine predicates can be attributed in illogical, unscientific, and even mythic fashion. The great projects of the living creation point to a creating Reason and show us a creating Intelligence, and they do so more luminously and radiantly today than before. Thus we can say today with a new certitude and joyousness that the human being is indeed a divine project, which only the creating Intelligence was strong and great and audacious enough to conceive of. Human beings are not a mistake but something willed; they are the fruit of love.[39]

These statements by the future pope demonstrate that he accepted evolution as a premise coming from science, and that he evaluated the biblical account within its paradigm. He saw the possibility of reconciling evolving reality with the Catholic faith, provided one recognizes in the world the clear traces of the Divine project.

Four years later, the Congregation of the Doctrine of Faith under the prefecture of Cardinal Joseph Ratzinger hosted a symposium entitled "Evolutionism and Christianity." The views of the then-Prefect of the Congregation of the

37. Ibid., 43.
38. Ibid., 50.
39. Ibid., 56–57.

Doctrine of Faith were presented later in materials from the symposium published in 1986.[40] At the beginning, Ratzinger evaluates the current status of Church doctrine regarding evolution. Pius XII in *Humani Generis* had handed the issue of the origin of individual species over to the competence of natural sciences. The origins of man, however, cannot be explained exclusively in biological terms, because each human soul is created through a separate act of God. Nevertheless, according to the Prefect, even that classical anthropological model could not be easily reconciled with the entirely different starting point assumed in the theory of evolution.[41] Having identified a fruitful though insufficient contribution of Teilhard de Chardin to the dialogue between theology and metaphysics on one side and the sciences on the other, Ratzinger remarks that "evolution" had been elevated above and beyond its scientific meaning, becoming a sort of first philosophy from which natural, ethical, and religious concepts are derived. Because evolution is endorsed by scientists, it elicits an almost irrefutable obedience, made all the more possible because philosophical thought itself is in crisis. For Ratzinger, the current debate surrounding evolution is much different from the one carried on in the 19th century. Today, according to the cardinal, the extrapolation from scientific knowledge to philosophy leads to a situation wherein evolutionary philosophy attempts to explain even the very emergence of being, all the way to its deepest foundations:

> The derivation of all reality from matter thus attains a totality that in the nineteenth century was still scarcely imaginable. Whereas faith today no longer has any difficulty in allowing the scientific hypothesis of evolution to develop in peace according to its own methods, the absolute claim of the philosophical explanatory model of evolution is an all the more radical challenge to faith and theology. It is obvious that reinterpretations, retoolings, are often far more dangerous than flat denials.[42]

Ratzinger suggests that philosophy should reclaim its competences, because only then can the debate remain rational and not turn into a protest of faith against reason. To sum up, Ratzinger's symposial text indicates the markedly excessive influence of the scientific idea of evolution in contemporary culture, and stresses the need to restore the proper levels of the discussion. The threat, for him, lies not in the dominance of evolutionism in science, but in its extrapolation to and dominance within the field of philosophy.

40. *Evolutionismus und Christentum*, ed. R. Spaemann, R. Löw, P. Koslowski (Weinheim: Acta Humaniora, VCH, 1986), vii–ix. The text is also included in the book *Creation and Evolution: A Conference with Pope Benedict XVI in Castel Gandolfo.*

41. *Creation and Evolution. A Conference with Pope Benedict XVI in Castel Gandolfo*, 8–9.

42. Ibid., 10.

In 1999 (November 27), Cardinal Ratzinger gave a lecture at the Sorbonne on the topic of evolution. According to Cardinal Schönborn, this speech is the most detailed discussion of the topic in the whole output of the pope to-be. Ratzinger begins with an analysis of the current intellectual situation in Western thought. The lecture's main focus is a clarification of the interdependence between two disciplines—physics and metaphysics. The confusion of the two is most detrimental for metaphysics. According to Ratzinger, "The theory of evolution has increasingly emerged as the way to make metaphysics disappear, to make 'the hypothesis of God' (Laplace) superfluous, and to formulate a strictly 'scientific' explanation of the world."[43]

Ratzinger repeats that the general theory of evolution has become a sort of first philosophy of our time, attempting to represent the very foundations of the deeper understanding of the universe. In consequence, *theologia physica* has disappeared completely, replaced by a doctrine of evolution that plays the role of a new *theologia naturalis* unfamiliar with God or Creator in the Christian sense. "Has the last word been said?" asks the cardinal. In his opinion, the debate on the effective scope of the doctrine of evolution must be approached objectively, with an intention to hear both sides. This has been done only to a limited extent so far.

Ratzinger also notes that no one has any serious doubts about scientific evidence for microevolution, or the modifications of organisms within their species, but what needs to be questioned is the promotion of evolution as *philosophia universalis*—a universal explanation of reality that excludes all other levels of thinking.[44] He indicates also that the problem arises at the transition from micro- to macroevolution. Ratzinger refers to two contemporary scholars, Eörs Szathmáry and John Maynard Smith, both evolutionists, who claim that "There is no theoretical basis for believing that evolutionary lines become more complex with time; and there is also no empirical evidence that this happens."[45]

At this point, the then-Prefect of the Congregation of the Doctrine of Faith spoke against biological macroevolution. As we already argued, the rank of this and similar utterances was negligible, both for formal reasons (a lecture given by one bishop) and due to the content (the assessment of biological theories is not directly a matter of faith). Nonetheless, this statement by Ratzinger shows that in the late 1990s a high-ranking Church official doubted the existence of

43. Ibid., 17.

44. "It is not toward that point [microevolution] that a believer will direct the question that he puts to modern rationality, but rather toward the development of evolutionary theory into a generalized *philosophia universalis*, which claims to constitute a universal explanation of reality and is unwilling to allow the continuing existence of any other level of thinking." Ibid., 19.

45. Ibid.

scientific evidence for macroevolution. This implies that the classic interpretation of the origin of species is not excluded even in the contemporary declarations of hierarchs and, more importantly, that there is a plurality of views on the matter within the Church.

Next, the cardinal again questions the limits of evolutionary theory—can it be presented as a universal explanation of everything? Do those ultimate questions not go beyond scientific data? Having quoted Karl Popper, according to whom life consists of "problem-solving physical structures," and species emerged through "reproduction and variability," the cardinal again states that he does not share this opinion: "The question is whether reason, or rationality, stands at the beginning of all things and upon their foundation, or not."[46] If Christianity is to choose between chance and reason (rationality), then, inspired by the Evangelical statement, "In the beginning there was the Word (Logos)," it opts for reason. Ultimately, in Ratzinger's opinion, the answer to the riddle of life cannot be based exclusively on scientific or even philosophical grounds. There is great need of reason in reflection about reality. Christianity is enlightened by reason; therefore, the denial of reason "must, contrary to all appearances, mean, not an evolution, but an involution, a shrinking of enlightenment."[47]

In the final part of the lecture, Ratzinger defines the relationship between evolution and ethics. For him, an explanation of reality that cannot provide a meaningful and comprehensible foundation for ethics necessarily remains inadequate. The theory of evolution, extended to universal philosophy, has even become the foundation of a new ethos:

> Yet this evolutionary ethic that inevitably takes as its key concept the model of selectivity, that is, the struggle for survival, the victory of the fittest, successful adaptation, has little comfort to offer. Even when people try to make it more attractive in various ways, it ultimately remains a cruel ethic.[48]

Thus, according to the cardinal, the evolutionary paradigm is of little use for a Christian understanding of ethics. However, a true religion must be based equally on orthodoxy and orthopraxy. Love and reason are two pillars of reality; true reason is love, and love is true reason.

The Paris lecture was the last reflection of Joseph Ratzinger on evolution before he became pope. Undoubtedly, it was much more critical of evolution than his 1968 radio talks, which were clearly influenced by Teilhardism and the evolutionary paradigm. The main message of the 1999 lecture includes two

46. Ibid.
47. Ibid., 20.
48. Ibid., 21.

points: (1) biological macroevolution is now meeting a challenge from science; (2) Christianity opposes purely materialistic explanations that employ chance and necessity as the primary forces working in the universe. At the same time, Christianity opts for a foundational role of rationality in explaining the origin of biology. It might seem surprising that five years later the same hierarch, as the Prefect of the Congregation of the Doctrine of Faith, signed the document *Communion and Stewardship*, which, with few reservations, promoted an essentially materialistic account of the origin of the universe. The Paris lecture is the most "anti-evolutionary" speech Cardinal Ratzinger ever made.

The first statement of Pope Benedict XVI to refer to the issue of evolution appeared in the homily inaugurating his pontificate. On April 24, 2005, the new pope said: "We are not some casual and meaningless product of evolution. Each of us is the result of a thought of God. Each of us is willed, each of us is loved, each of us is necessary."[49] These words represent a strong and, in a way, exemplary objection of Benedict XVI to the evolutionary ideas that embrace natural and random processes as the only factors responsible for the origin of man. The declaration firmly opposes materialistic evolutionists of the 20th century such as Jacques Monod or George Gaylord Simpson.[50] We can see, therefore, that the Pope opposed the purely materialistic interpretation of the origin of man. However, opposition to radical evolutionary thought was quite obvious for any theist, and it doesn't tell us much about the Papal assessment of the sophisticated details of theistic evolution.

Benedict XVI followed a somewhat different direction when he gave a homily on Easter Sunday the following year (April 15, 2006). Having quoted a German theologian who had asserted that the resurrection would be meaningless if it only represented a one-time return of the body to life, the pope said:

> But the point is that Christ's resurrection is something more, something different. If we may borrow the language of the theory of evolution, it is the greatest mutation, absolutely the most crucial leap into a totally new dimension that there has ever been in the long history of life and its development: a

49. All statements by Benedict XVI are quoted from *Zenit* (the global news service of the Holy See); http://www.zenit.org/article-12826?l=english (February 27, 2015).

50. Simpson's dossier includes such statements as, "Man is the result of a purposeless and natural process that did not have him in mind." G.G. Simpson, *The Meaning of Evolution*, 345. J. Monod writes in the same vein: "Even today a good many distinguished minds seem unable to accept or even to understand that from a source of noise natural selection could quite unaided have drawn all the music of the biosphere." J. Monod, *Chance and Necessity: Essay on the Natural Philosophy of Modern Biology*, trans. A. Wainhouse (New York: Vintage, 1971), 112. And again: "The ancient covenant is in pieces; man knows at last that he is alone in the universe's unfeeling immensity, out of which he emerged only by chance. His destiny is nowhere spelled out, nor is his duty." Ibid., 180.

> leap into a completely new order which does concern us, and concerns the whole of history.[51]

Calling the Resurrection the "greatest mutation in history" shows some attraction towards evolutionary language, though it does not express any attitude to the theory itself.

On November 9, 2005, when the article by Cardinal Schönborn in *The New York Times* was still under lively discussion, and while the balanced teaching of the issue of evolution was being tried in court in the USA,[52] Benedict XVI, during a general audience, commented on Psalm 135. At the end, he put down his papers and referred to the words of St. Basil:

> *Some, deceived by the atheism they bear within them, imagined the universe deprived of a guide and order, at the mercy of chance. . . .* I believe the words of this fourth-century Father are of amazing timeliness. . . . How many are these some today? Deceived by atheism, they believe and try to demonstrate that it is scientific to think that everything lacks a guide and order. . . . The Lord, with sacred Scripture, awakens the drowsy reason and says to us: In the beginning is the creative Word. In the beginning the creative Word—this Word that has created everything, which has created this intelligent plan,[53] the cosmos—is also Love.[54]

The pontiff concludes by exhorting his listeners to allow themselves "to be awakened by this Word of God" and inviting them to pray that God "clear our minds so that we will be able to perceive the message of creation, inscribed also in our hearts: The beginning of everything is creative Wisdom and this Wisdom is love and goodness."[55] This spontaneous statement by Benedict XVI is certainly among the most explicit protests against the hegemony of materialistic theories, including atheistic evolutionism, which seek to explain the origin and the activity of the universe in purely atheistic terms.

51. http://www.zenit.org/article-15817?l=english (February 27, 2015).

52. *Kitzmiller vs. Dover School District* was aimed at the abolition of the law that required teachers to read a short statement in biology classes informing students that the theory of evolution is not the only theory explaining the origin of life and species. The process ended on December 20 with the defeat of the school district, which meant the statement was no longer to be read.

53. Benedict XVI used the Italian words *intelligente progetto*, which can be translated as "intelligent design/project" or "plan." The papal utterance in November 2005 coincided with the visit to Rome of the Austrian bishops, led by Cardinal Schönborn, who recently had been under attack for his *New York Times* article. Some saw the remarks of the pope as support for the position of Cardinal Schönborn's, who at that time supported the theory of intelligent design. In fact, in the first translation into English, the phrase "intelligent design" was used. However, it was changed to "intelligent plan" immediately after the first translation was reported by the media.

54. General Audience, November 9, 2005; http://www.zenit.org/en/articles/creation-reveals-god-and-his-love-says-benedict-xvi (February 27, 2015).

55. Ibid.

At the end of the summer of 2006 (September 1–3), the pope attended a meeting, known as *Schülerkreis*, at Castel Gandolfo with former students of his. The tradition of such academic colloquia reached back to earlier times when Ratzinger was still a lecturer in theology at the university. This time, in a small group, speeches were given by Peter Schuster, Robert Spaemann, Paul Erbrich, S.J., and Cardinal Schönborn. At the time it was expected that the pope would reevaluate his position on evolution and more or less explicitly support intelligent design theory.[56] However, no such thing happened. The proceedings from the meeting were published in 2007. They include only four papers by the participants and the later appendix by Siegfried Wiedenhofer concerning the relationship between belief in creation and evolution.

All speeches, save for the one given by Cardinal Schönborn, express an evolutionary perspective. Schuster, an Austrian biochemist, presents the status of the current scientific arguments in favor of evolution. Spaemann, a Catholic philosopher and ethicist, questions the presence of intelligent design within the framework of biological evolutionary theories and common ancestry. At the conclusion of his speech, he claims that once someone accepts the existence of the Creator, the scientific search for the natural origin of species cannot frighten him.[57] In turn, Erbrich considers the possibility of reconciling creation and evolution. In his view, the latter is a "fact"; therefore, one needs to distinguish the "fact of evolution" from its mechanisms. The mechanism can change,

56. Cf. J. L. Allen, "Benedict's Thinking on Creation and Evolution," *National Catholic Reporter* 6 no. 1 (September 2006); http://www.nationalcatholicreporter.org/word/word090106.htm#one (February 27, 2015). Some columnists even speculated that "the Pope prepares to embrace [the] theory of intelligent design." See J. Hooper, "The Pope Prepares to Embrace Theory of Intelligent Design," in *The Guardian* (August 27, 2006); http://www.theguardian.com/science/2006/aug/28/religion.pope (May 9, 2015). Bruce Chapman, president of the Discovery Institute, was expecting a balanced debate on the theories of evolution and intelligent design. See: W. Cloyd, "Vatican Scholars to Include Intelligent-Design Theory in Meeting," *Citizen-Link* (August 30, 2006); http://www.discovery.org/a/3724 (February 27, 2015). After the meeting, one of its participants, Rev. J. Fessio, commented that the debate produced no change in the views of the Church and that little was said about intelligent design theory (T. Heneghan, "Pope to Debate Evolution with Former Students," *Reuters* [August 30, 2006]). http://www.redorbit.com/news/science/638226/pope_to_debate_evolution_with_former_st udents/ (May 9, 2015).

57. "[O]nce someone has the dimensions of the unconditional at his disposal, and the old rumor about the Creator God keeps haunting him, he will not be intimidated if natural science hopes to find in functionality for survival the sufficient cause for the development of the natural species, including man, and to some extent has already found it." R. Spaemann, "Common Descent and Intelligent Design" in *Creation and Evolution: A Conference with Pope Benedict XVI in Castel Gandolfo*, 69. One should, however, note that Spaemann's position comes close to the opinion condemned by Pius X in the motu proprio *Doctoris Angelici*: "The opinion of certain ancients is to be rejected which maintains that it makes no difference to the truth of the Faith what any man thinks about the nature of creation, provided his opinions on the nature of God be sound, because error with regard to the nature of creation begets a false knowledge of God," in *AAS*, 6 (1914): 337.

but the "fact" of evolution is unquestionable. Having discussed a few attempts to explain the mechanism of evolution, he proceeds to the philosophical implications of the randomness of the evolutionary process and reflects on the possibility of understanding the self-organization of matter into organisms. Finally, he decides that "the beginning of an original totality with its active potencies would be a moment of the creation of the world from nothing, a moment in the one creative act of God. Creation would be something that is still happening all the time and more than just an act of maintaining things in existence."[58] Erbrich needed the notion of incomplete creation in order to justify the alleged "fact" of evolution understood as constant emergence of new orders of creatures. According to his vision, God not only constantly maintains the world in existence but also works somehow within creation to make the blind processes of evolution effective.

All speakers at the meeting represented the viewpoint of theistic evolution, except for Schuster, the featured voice of science, who believed in atheistic evolution.[59] In this context, however, one might raise the same doubt that we mentioned when discussing the teaching of John Paul II—namely, the problem of the access of the pope and Church hierarchs to genuine criticism of modern evolution. There was nobody at the seminar to inform the Holy Father competently and thoroughly about the growing scientific difficulties with the theory of evolution. Cardinal Christoph Schönborn addressed mainly the philosophical and methodological difficulties of the subject, leaving aside the strictly scientific debate. The absence of the "other side" made it virtually impossible for the participants to come to balanced conclusions about faith and evolution.

The proceedings also include transcripts of discussions held by the participants. On the second day, the meeting was joined by Benedict XVI, who became an active speaker. His longest statement was a commentary on the declarations of Schönborn and Schuster. The pope recalled the article written by Cardinal Schönborn for *The New York Times*, calling it a "providential" event, thanks to which the question of creation and evolution reentered debate in the Church. According to Benedict, the article demonstrates the true status of the issue:

> It is not a question of deciding either for a creationism that is closed off from science, as matter of principle, or else for a theory of evolution that has its

58. P. Erbrich, "The Problem of Creation and Evolution" in *Creation and Evolution: A Conference with Pope Benedict XVI in Castel Gandolfo*, 83.

59. Schuster, a leader of the scientific academy in Austria, was invited by Cardinal Schönborn, and when Schuster asked about the reason for this choice, Schönborn supposedly said that "the Pope wanted to have among the participants a scholar who can by no means be suspected of creationism." Cf. D. Sagan, "Debata Benedykta XVI i jego uczniów nad stworzeniem i ewolucją," in *Filozoficzne Aspekty Genezy* 2005/2006, vol. 2/3, 7–17, 11.

> own gaps and yet overplays its hand and is unwilling to look at the questions that go beyond the methodological possibilities of the natural sciences. Rather, it is a question precisely of this interplay of the various dimensions of reason, in which the path to faith opens up as well.[60]

Referring to Schuster's lecture, the pope explains that it made him realize the following four issues: (1) that the theory of evolution cannot be proved by way of experiment; (2) that the probability of the occurrence of evolutionary events is more than zero, but at the same time less than one—which provokes a question about the actual probability of evolutionary events;[61] (3) that there are still "leaps" within this theory and we should examine them thoroughly to find out what they might conceal; (4) that positive mutations are rare, and thus the corridor for spontaneous development of life is narrow. These four points illustrate that Benedict XVI recognized considerable problems that science has not managed to solve within biological evolution.

Next, the pope points out one more problem with evolution, this time a "linguistic" one:

> Not only popular writing about science, but also scholarly scientific texts about evolution often say that nature or evolution did this or that. Here the question arises: Who in fact is Nature or Evolution as an acting subject? There is no such person! If someone says that Nature does this or that, this can only be an attempt to summarize a series of processes in a subject that, however, does not exist as such. It seems obvious to me that this (perhaps indispensable) linguistic expedient contains within it momentous question.[62]

Finally, Benedict XVI notices that the findings of contemporary science lead to questions exceeding its methodological principles, and that these questions cannot be answered within the framework of science alone.

Altogether, the *Schülerkreis* of 2006 did not introduce much novelty to the ecclesiastical debate on evolution. The invited scientists were convinced evolutionists and simply defended their positions, while the clergy asked for moderation in extending the evolutionary paradigm beyond the scientific realm. As Cardinal Schönborn observed: "We have to release Darwin from Darwinism, free him from ideological fetters."[63]

60. *Creation and Evolution: A Conference with Pope Benedict XVI in Castel Gandolfo*, 161.

61. In this context, Benedict XVI alluded to one of the statements by John Paul II, asking: "How high is the probability now? This is important especially if we want to interpret correctly the remark by Pope John Paul II: The theory of evolution is more than a hypothesis. When the Pope said that, he had his reasons. But at the same time it is true that the theory of evolution is still not a complete, scientifically verified theory." Ibid., 162.

62. Ibid., 162–63.

63. Ibid., 90.

Next year, the pope spent his summer vacation in Auronzo di Cadore, in northern Italy. At the end of his time there (July 26, 2007), he held a question-and-answer session with a gathering of 400 local priests. When asked about the controversy around evolution, the pope explained that the debaters wrongly present the two ideas

> as if they were alternatives that are exclusive—whoever believes in the creator could not believe in evolution, and whoever asserts belief in evolution would have to disbelieve in God. . . . This contrast is an absurdity, because there are many scientific tests in favor of evolution, which appears as a reality that we must see and [which] enriches our understanding of life and being. But the doctrine of evolution does not answer all questions, and it does not answer above all the great philosophical question: From where does everything come?[64]

Benedict XVI referred to evolution again during the plenary session of the Pontifical Academy of Sciences, which took place from October 31 to November 4, 2008. In his short address presented on the first day of the session, the pope pointed out a few issues. First, he mentions Pius XII and John Paul II, who had already asserted that "there is no opposition between faith's understanding of creation and the evidence of the empirical sciences."[65] To properly understand this sentence we should note that the Holy Father is not speaking about evolution, but "the evidence of empirical sciences." This means that the pope excludes permanent conflict between scientific facts and faith; however, he does not exclude the possibility of a conflict between faith and theories built upon facts, such as biological macroevolution. It is also meaningful that Benedict XVI does not make a single reference here to the widely publicized statement of John Paul II from 1996. Instead, he quotes John Paul II's address to the PAS from 2003: "Scientific truth, which is itself a participation in divine Truth, can help philosophy and theology to understand ever more fully the human person and God's Revelation about man."[66] The pope reminds his audience here of the Christian principle that reliable science cannot oppose religion, but rather is helpful in pursuing true philosophy and attaining deeper faith.

Nevertheless, Benedict's speech assumes a somewhat evolutionist point of view. For instance, the pope states that the Creator not only created the uni-

64. Quotation after G.M. Verschuuren, *God and Evolution? Science Meets Faith* (Boston: Pauline Books & Media 2012), 12–13. Cf. http://ncse.com/news/2007/07/pope-evolution-again-001199 (March 1, 2015).

65. "Scientific Insights into the Evolution of the Universe and of Life" in *Pontificiae Academiae Scientiarum Acta* 20, ed. W. Arber, N. Cabibbo, M.S. Sorondo (Ex Aedibus Academicis in Civitate Vaticana, 2009), 33.

66. http://www.vatican.va/holy_father/john_paul_ii/speeches/2003/november/documents/hf_jp-ii_spe_20031110_academy-sciences_en.html (February 27, 2015).

verse in the past, but also caused it to develop, and sustains it continually. Even Thomas Aquinas, according to the pope, considered creation "the foundational and continuing relationship that links the creature to the Creator." Clearly, the Holy Father embraces here the idea of creation not as the production of things out of nothing or a supernatural immediate formation, but rather as an unceasing action of God within the world, which unfolds over time through the powers granted it by God. The evolution of the universe can be compared to a book that is unrolled while read:

> This image also helps us to understand that the world, far from originating out of chaos, resembles an ordered book; it is a cosmos. Notwithstanding elements of the irrational, chaotic and the destructive in the long processes of change in the cosmos, matter as such is legible. It has an inbuilt mathematics. The human mind therefore can engage not only in a cosmography studying measurable phenomena but also in a cosmology discerning the visible inner logic of the cosmos.[67]

The pope indicates the presence of order on each step of observed reality. This general order contradicts the idea that chaos and chance are the main forces at work in the universe. The pope does not use the word "evolution," but instead refers to the "long process of change in the cosmos." The idea of change, however, was not controversial to any scholar. Everybody would agree that the visible universe changes over time. Instead, the controversy concerned the spontaneous emergence of the diversity of species in biology. Similarly, the idea of some general plan and order in the universe does not oppose theistic evolution or even some atheistic worldviews, since even atheists usually agree that the universe is not completely devoid of order. What incited the debate over Darwinism and intelligent design was the question of whether science can recognize the presence of true intelligent design in biology or not. Thus we can see that Benedict's statements do not address the "hot" issues in the debate over evolution and intelligent design.

Finally, the pope also reaffirms that man has a soul and—as the Church teaches—that the soul is created directly by God. At this point it is worth noting that the Holy Father did not invoke the thesis about the possibility of the body being generated through evolution, even though he did previously appeal to *Humani Generis*.

Undoubtedly, the 2008 address to the PAS did not go as far as both participants of the session and outside commentators might have expected. In fact, Benedict XVI presented a much more moderate view than did the active participants of the session, all of whom were evolutionists (including an influential

67. "Scientific Insights into the Evolution of the Universe and of Life," 34.

group of atheists). The pope did speak from the evolutionary point of view, but whenever he mentioned evolution, he always emphasized its limitations. When in March of 2009 (a Darwinian anniversary) another session on evolution was held in Rome, Benedict neither attended nor addressed any statement to the participants.

Benedict XVI's last direct reference to evolution was made in his homily delivered on Easter Eve of 2011 (April 23). This time, the whole text was formulated from the "creationist" point of view:

> We relate to God as Creator and so we have a responsibility for creation. Our responsibility extends as far as creation because it comes from the Creator. Only because God created everything can he give us life and direct our lives. . . . The world is a product of the Word, of the Logos, as Saint John expresses it, using a key term from the Greek language. "Logos" means "reason," "sense," "word." It is not reason pure and simple, but creative Reason, that speaks and communicates itself. It is Reason that both is and creates sense. The creation account tells us, then, that the world is a product of creative Reason. Hence it tells us that, far from there being an absence of reason and freedom at the origin of all things, the source of everything is creative Reason, love, and freedom. Here we are faced with the ultimate alternative that is at stake in the dispute between faith and unbelief: are irrationality, lack of freedom, and pure chance the origin of everything, or are reason, freedom, and love at the origin of being? Does the primacy belong to unreason or to reason? This is what everything hinges upon in the final analysis. As believers we answer, with the creation account and with John, that in the beginning is reason. In the beginning is freedom. Hence it is good to be a human person. It is not the case that in the expanding universe, at a late stage, in some tiny corner of the cosmos, there evolved randomly some species of living being capable of reasoning and of trying to find rationality within creation, or to bring rationality into it. If man were merely a random product of evolution in some place on the margins of the universe, then his life would make no sense or might even be a chance of nature. But no, Reason is there at the beginning: creative, divine Reason. And because it is Reason, it also created freedom; and because freedom can be abused, there also exist forces harmful to creation.[68]

It is obvious that it would be hard to reconcile the contemporary Darwinian standpoint with the pope's words. Benedict XVI directly opposes the hegemony of chance, which so clearly dominates the evolutionary perspective. In place of chance he points to Logos as the source and foundation of all things. Moreover, he developed his inaugural homily by emphasizing that man as a species is not

68. Text of the homily taken from http://www.zenit.org/article-32406?l=english (February 27, 2015).

a product of chance. Although the pope does not mention the idea of design in the speech we are now considering, he refers to Reason as the source of everything. Reason is a higher Intelligence that creates according to its own idea; i.e., design. Nevertheless, this claim is too general to reveal the pope's stance in the controversy over Darwinism and biological macroevolution. Benedict's speech could be read as a support for either theistic evolution or intelligent design, or even for creationism.

A year later, in his homily given on Holy Saturday (April 7, 2012), the pope talked about the creation of light on the first day and the creation of the Sun and Moon on the fourth day in the Book of Genesis. There is no mention of evolution, nor any allusion to the literal meaning of the biblical text, which the pope interprets symbolically: "To say that God created light means that God created the world as a space for knowledge and truth, as a space for encounter and freedom, as a space for good and for love." The pope also compares the creation of light to Christ's resurrection.[69]

Summarizing Pope Benedict XVI's attitude toward evolution, John L. Allen concluded that

> Benedict XVI's views on evolution . . . can't be condensed into a simple slogan, such as whether he's "for" or "against" it. He has a deep respect for science, but at the same time he insists that empirical science by itself must not set the "frame" within which we think about the meaning and purpose of existence. He worries that an uncritical embrace of the theory of evolution has been dangerous, but he also has steered clear of identifying himself with its fundamentalist and Luddite critics."[70]

According to Allen, Benedict XVI is neither a creationist nor a supporter of intelligent design. Based on the statements quoted so far, one may agree with Allen that his teaching on evolution is not easily summarized. One might even argue that the pluralism of Benedict's assertions is as broad as the divergence of views currently held in the Church. Many of his pronouncements were written from the evolutionary viewpoint; that is, based on the assumption that species develop from a single ancestor in the course of natural processes. However, in a 1999 lecture at the Sorbonne, Ratzinger, relying on scientific premises, explicitly rejected macroevolution. Yet one might ask: what is the point of speaking about evolution in a theological context, if it is only limited to biological microevolution? Moreover, if one consistently rejects macroevolution, one also needs to reject the evolutionary origin of the human body. This latter idea, however, was unreservedly endorsed by Joseph Ratzinger in the 1968 radio broadcasts. Did he

69. Cf. http://www.zenit.org/article-34598?l=english (February 27, 2015).

70. J.L. Allen, "Benedict's Thinking on Creation and Evolution," http://nationalcatholicreporter.org/word/pfw090106.htm (February 27, 2015).

radically change his views on macroevolution by the time of the Sorbonne presentation in 1999?

According to Allen, the German cardinal dismissed macroevolution after attending a series of lectures in the 1980s at the Gustav Siewarth Academy, a small private school that had been established with considerable support from Ratzinger. In 2004, however, as the Chairman of the International Theological Commission, he signed *Communion and Stewardship*, a document accepting biological macroevolution as a starting point for theological considerations. Allen attributes this inconsistency to the fact that, in Ratzinger's view, determining the value of scientific theories is not the responsibility of the Church. If we accept this explanation, a question arises: Why would the Church, without determining the scientific value of biological macroevolution, favor an evolutionary rather than a creationist origin of species? Surely, the rejection of the separate creation of species would be nearly as theologically relevant as its acceptance.

In 2006 (two years after the publication of *Communion and Stewardship*), Benedict XVI spoke of gaps and leaps in biological evolution. At that time he concluded his pronouncement with the rather obscure remark that "The question of what this [evolutionary gaps] involves has to be examined in greater detail." Was it an allusion to the divine immediate acts that might be necessary to explain evolution? Regrettably, the pope did not provide those "greater details" himself, which again made his statement inconclusive.

In *Communion and Stewardship*, theologians from the International Theological Commission state that scientific research cannot determine the presence of intelligent design in nature. Aside from the fact that in making this claim they exceed their competences (as these kind of judgments belong primarily to scientists or philosophers of science), it is clear that their statement is aimed against the central claim of intelligent design theory. Joseph Ratzinger would not have signed a document to which he had some crucial objections. On the other hand, the papal statements are full of references to rationality and protests against the belief in chance as the sole factor shaping the world. Allen solves this apparent contradiction by postulating that the pope never refers to design on a scientific level, but to a higher Intelligence, Reason, or Logos, understood in the metaphysical and religious sense.[71] However, such a distinction seems too abstract to be adequate. It also implies double truth theory, that is, the idea that philosophy and theology have their own truth while science has its own. In fact, in both fields we are speaking of the same reality of the visible world and how it was formed. Moreover, in 2006, Benedict XVI stated that "There is, in the first place, a rationality of matter itself. One can read it. It has

71. J.L. Allen, "Benedict's Thinking on Creation and Evolution."

mathematical properties; matter itself is rational, even though there is much that is irrational, chaotic, and destructive on the long path of evolution. But matter *per se* is legible."[72] And again in 2008: "[M]atter as such is legible. It has an inbuilt mathematics. The human mind therefore can engage not only in a cosmography studying measurable phenomena but also in a cosmology discerning the visible inner logic of the cosmos."[73] Do these words pronounced two years after his implicit rejection of the central claim of intelligent design theory concern metaphysical reason? Or are they rather an imitation of the arguments of empirical sciences? Are they compatible with the claim in *Communion and Stewardship* that science cannot discern design in material structures? In analyzing such diverse formulations, one cannot avoid the impression of a certain incoherence in the pope's statements.

In the entire doctrine of Benedict XVI, only two ideas reappear consistently. First, he argues that the theory of evolution has become a present-day *philosophia prima*, and a paradigm not only in science and philosophy but in culture as a whole. Thus it has definitely exceeded its competences to explain reality and, in this sense, it has become "more than a hypothesis." However, the pope never defined the limits of the theory. Second, Benedict XVI repeatedly remarked upon the rationality of reality: What is at the foundation of all things? Reason (Logos), or chaos and chance? He rejects the second option, openly opposing the dictate of chance. Reason is the main principle of the Christian interpretation of evolution. The diversity of papal dictums demonstrates the fact that the Holy Father listened to both sides of the dispute. Perhaps his approach is best described (as Allen suggests) by the statement pronounced in 1999: "This dispute has to be approached objectively and with a willingness to listen, by both sides—something that has hitherto been undertaken only to a limited extent."

The Article "Finding Design in Nature" by Cardinal Christoph Schönborn (2005)

The op-ed by Cardinal Christoph Schönborn, Archbishop of Vienna, published in *The New York Times* in the summer of 2005 had a large impact, and even evoked the official protest of a number of scientists. In order to understand the nature of the debate surrounding the editorial, we must first observe that the theory of intelligent design introduced a new feature into the argument over evolution. Before ID came along, evolutionists and creationists confronted var-

72. *Creation and Evolution: A Conference with Pope Benedict XVI in Castel Gandolfo*, 163.

73. http://www.vatican.va/holy_father/benedict_xvi/speeches/2008/october/documents/hf_ben-xvi_spe_20081031_academy-sciences_en.html (June 1, 2015).

ious theories of evolution with religious beliefs. Biblical creationism opposed evolution by citing the Genesis account of creation, whereas scientific creationism tried to prove the baselessness of evolution by looking for evidence of the short history of the earth and applying an unnaturally strict reading of the first chapters of Genesis.[74]

The result of this debate, which lasted for several decades, was the reinforcement of the false opinion that there is an inherent conflict between faith and reason, religion and science. Many theologians, trying to escape this conflict, accepted the theory of evolution only because "faith cannot contradict reason." This classical Christian adage has been used as justification for some theologians to accept macroevolution without careful examination of scientific evidence. In effect, many theologians would argue for theistic evolution precisely because "there cannot be conflict between science and faith." This position, however, is based on a confusion of terms, because the simple statement that "faith does not contradict science" does not mean that "faith does not contradict evolution." Only after the introduction of intelligent design was Darwinism confronted with an adequate answer—adequate, because derived not from religious revelation but from scientific data. Because the two theories—Darwinism and intelligent design—occupy the same epistemic level, they can be legitimately opposed to one another without confusing religious and scientific argumentation.

The theory of intelligent design does not exclude evolution in the sense of universal common descent or transformation of species; what it does exclude is the central claim of Darwinism that the formation of all biological life could be the result of random mutations and natural selection alone. This is why the crux of the new controversy became not transformation of species or common descent but the notion of chance and what blind processes can accomplish. The opponents of intelligent design attempted to reduce it to another religious view, which—as they claimed—was "creationism merely dressed in scientific garments." If their claim were true, they could fight intelligent design without any effort, just employing old arguments developed in the dispute with creationism. What they missed, however, was the fact that Catholics were in a minority among the advocates of ID. Christians were not the only religious group represented, and there were agnostics as well. This strongly suggests that the new theory is at best loosely related to any religious beliefs, and results from critical scientific research rather than philosophical or religious convictions. Its advocates claim that in an empirical world, by using the scientific method one can discover structures that have been intelligently designed, i.e., that are the products of a mind and not of chance and necessity.

74. The issue has been discussed more broadly in Chapter Two.

At the end of the 1990s a small group of Catholic theologians realized that the arguments from intelligent design could not be ignored. One who took up the issue was Cardinal Christoph Schönborn. He claimed that, even passing over the question of evolution, one cannot agree that the world is the result of a purposeless process. The article caused outrage among both atheistic evolutionists and many theistic evolutionists. In the op-ed, the cardinal challenges them:

> Evolution in the sense of common ancestry might be true, but evolution in the neo-Darwinian sense—an unguided, unplanned process of random variation and natural selection—is not. Any system of thought that denies or seeks to explain away the overwhelming evidence for design in biology is ideology, not science.[75]

For the theologian from Vienna, it was clear that design in nature could not be just a metaphysical, abstract concept, a trace of some unspecified "logos," "reason," or "sense." Even some atheists could agree that the universe in its general nature is not completely senseless. But the design that contemporary science (ID) is discussing is discovered in real terms—by rigorous scientific study and on the basic level of biological and physical structures. Hence, design is the reality of the concrete world and not just a general principle of reality.

Schönborn's editorial was brief, of course, but it appeared in the world's largest daily newspaper. As a private comment, the article is not a part of the Church's teaching office. Nevertheless, it revealed the opinion of one of the leading hierarchs of the Catholic Church. Certainly, the cultural impact of this article has been greater than that of most Church documents.

The article presents two main theses. First, the cardinal opposes the belief of numerous researchers that the Catholic Church supports neo-Darwinism; he also rejects a "pro-Darwinian" interpretation of the 1996 statement by John Paul II.[76] Most of the article, in fact, is an attempt to prove that John Paul II, Benedict XVI, and the International Theological Commission all argue for a purpose and a plan in nature. Second, Schönborn maintains that by using his reason man is capable of recognizing this purpose and plan. The cardinal refers

75. Ch. Schönborn, "Finding Design in Nature," *The New York Times* (July 7, 2005); http://www.nytimes.com/2005/07/07/opinion/07schonborn.html?_r=0 (February 27, 2015).

76. At the beginning, Schönborn writes: "Ever since 1996, when Pope John Paul II said that evolution (a term he did not define) was more than just a hypothesis, defenders of neo-Darwinian dogma have often invoked the supposed acceptance—or at least acquiescence—of the Roman Catholic Church when they defend their theory as somehow compatible with Christian faith. But this is not true. The Catholic Church, while leaving to science many details about the history of life on earth, proclaims that by the light of reason the human intellect can readily and clearly discern purpose and design in the natural world, including the world of living things." See "Finding Design in Nature." The following quotations come from the same article.

to the classical idea in Catholic theology that the reasonable structure of the physical world informs us about God as its Creator. In Schönborn's approach, however, the emphasis is placed on the first premise of the classical argument for God's existence; namely, that the world does not present itself as chaotic and random. Not only believers but also atheists should agree with this, as the purpose and plan are too clear and too well confirmed by observations to question them on the level of reason. Thus the article disputes not only with atheists but also with those Christian theologians and scholars who seek the support of the Church for theistic evolution based on the Darwinian model. The cardinal observes that "Throughout history the Church has defended the truths of faith given by Jesus Christ. But in the modern era, the Catholic Church is in the odd position of standing in firm defense of reason as well." Schönborn also comments on recent teachings of the Church that touch upon evolution. He attempts to show the incompatibility of those statements with the prevailing Darwinian paradigm in science. Referring to John Paul II, the cardinal notes that "While his rather vague and unimportant 1996 letter about evolution is always and everywhere cited, we see no one discussing these comments from a 1985 general audience that represents his robust teaching on nature." Then, the hierarch quotes John Paul II's words from the 1985–1986 catecheses concerning the purpose to be discovered in the world, words that oblige us to accept Mind as its inventor and creator. In relation to Benedict XVI, Cardinal Schönborn had at his disposal only one utterance from the homily inaugurating his pontificate. When referring to the *Communion and Stewardship*, he quotes the qualification made by the International Theological Commission: "The [1996] letter [of John Paul II] cannot be read as a blanket approbation of all theories of evolution, including those of a neo-Darwinian provenance that explicitly deny to divine providence any truly causal role in the development of life in the universe." Moreover, continues Schönborn, the Commission stated that "an unguided evolutionary process—one that falls outside the bounds of divine providence—simply cannot exist." At the end, the author once again reminds the reader that "Scientific theories that try to explain away the appearance of design as the result of chance and necessity are not scientific at all, but, as John Paul put it, an abdication of human intelligence."

Within less than a week after the op-ed's publication, three prominent representatives of the scientific community—including atheist evolutionist Lawrence Krauss, Catholic evolutionist Kenneth Miller, and Francisco Ayala—addressed an open letter to Pope Benedict XVI, Cardinal Christoph Schönborn, and the Prefect of the Congregation for the Doctrine of the Faith, Archbishop William J. Levada. In the letter, the three biologists contrast Schönborn's paper with the words of John Paul II from 1996 and the document *Communion and Stewardship*. They call the papal address "great and wonderful," whereas the recent words of the hierarch from Vienna seem to them to "dangerously redefine the Church's view on evolution."[77] According to the scholars, the cardinal had claimed that

> Evolution in the neo-Darwinian sense . . . is not true. Moreover, he argued that if divine design was not overwhelmingly evident, then the associated claims must be viewed as ideology, and not science. He attacked not only neo-Darwinism, but also the multiverse hypothesis of modern cosmology, both of which he claimed were invented to avoid the overwhelming evidence for purpose and design found in modern science.

The scholars warn against the possibility of renewing the conflict between the scientific method and religious faith. At the end, they appeal to Pope Benedict XVI to "clarify once again the Church's position on Evolution and Science," asking that he might also "reaffirm the remarkable statements of Pope John Paul II and the International Theological Commission, so that it will be clear that Cardinal Schönborn's remarks do not reflect the views of the Holy See."

The letter received no response from the Holy Father. It is known, however, that although the article published in *The New York Times* was not officially approved by the Vatican, even before its publication the cardinal had spoken to Benedict XVI to express his doubts concerning evolution, and that the pope had encouraged him to explain them.[78]

Critical comments on Schönborn's text were offered by other Catholic scholars as well. For example, a philosopher from Georgetown University, John F. Haught, described the words of Schönborn as "fearful and defensive, in contrast to John Paul's pronouncements, which were confident and supportive of science."[79] A professor of biology and philosophy at the University of Notre Dame, Philip Reid Sloan, claimed that the rejection of neo-Darwinism by the cardinal had no grounds in Catholic teaching.[80] Critical remarks were also expressed by Archbishop Jozef Zycinski, the long-time head of the Pontifical Academy of Sciences Nicola Cabbibo,[81] and the Director of the Vatican Observatory, George V. Coyne, S.J. In August 2005, the latter published an article in *The Tablet* in which he suggests that the cardinal was afraid of science, and

77. L.M. Krauss, F. Ayala, K. Miller, "Open Letter to Pope Benedict XVI," July 12, 2005; http://academic.regis.edu/mghedott/lettertobenedict.htm (February 27, 2015). The following quotations come from the same letter.

78. See: M. Hilbert, "Darwin's Divisions: The Pope, the Cardinal, the Jesuit and the Evolving Debate about Origins," http://www.touchstonemag.com/archives/article.php?id=19-05-028-f (February 27, 2015).

79. See: D. O'Leary, *Roman Catholicism and Modern Science*, 214.

80. Ibid.

81. See: J.L. Allen, "Schönborn and Science vs. Theology," *National Catholic Reporter* 41 (July 22, 2005); http://www.nationalcatholicreporter.org/word/pfw072205.htm (February 27, 2015).

ruining the positive dialogue between the Church and the scientific community. In his opinion, the cardinal had rejected the breakthrough declaration of John Paul II from 1996. As Coyne saw it:

> In the universe, as known by science, there are essentially three processes at work: chance, necessity and the fertility of the universe. The classical question as to whether the human being came about by chance, and so has no need of God, or by necessity, and so through the action of a designer God, is no longer valid. And so any attempt to answer it is doomed to failure. The fertility of the universe, now well established by science, is an essential ingredient, and the meaning of chance and necessity must be seen in light of that fertility. . . . We are all literally born of stardust.[82]

In an interview, Coyne even insinuates that the cardinal was being used by the Discovery Institute in such a way that it was someone else who wrote and submitted the text for publication in *The New York Times*. It is not unusual, however, for hierarchs to employ experts to help them express certain matters with greater accuracy. The text was signed by the hierarch and he never revoked its theses.[83] Some commentators noticed the connection between Coyne's criticism of Cardinal Schönborn and his later removal from his position as director of the Vatican Observatory.[84]

The debate over Schönborn's article, however, also had a less political and more scholarly dimension. The author of one important critical text was a molecular physicist and member of the editorial board of *First Things*, Stephen M. Barr. In "The Design of Evolution"[85] Barr accuses the cardinal of confusing two different notions of randomness. According to him, Schönborn employs the theological understanding of the word "randomness" (speaking about the random process of evolution), which means "uncaused," "meaningless," "inexplicable," or "pointless," whereas in science, he asserts, the word has a slightly different meaning: it is a technical term equivalent to "uncorrelated." Following other critics, Barr refers to the document *Communion and Stewardship* in order to support the thesis that God can use contingent processes in the technical and scientific sense of contingency. He also cites St. Thomas Aquinas's discussion of chance events occurring within the physical universe. Hence, Barr makes the same mistake as the International Theological Commission: he fails to distin-

82. G. Coyne, "God's Chance Creation," *The Tablet* (August 6, 2005); http://www.thetablet. co.uk/article/1027 (September 20, 2011).

83. The next section presents the cardinal's catecheses, whose general tenor slightly modifies the energetic criticism of Darwinism that appears in the *New York Times* article.

84. S. Caldwell, "Pope Sacks Astronomer over Evolution Debate," *Daily Mail* (August 23, 2006). http://www.dailymail.co.uk/news/article-401950/Pope-sacks-astronomer-evolution-debate.html (February 27, 2015).

85. S.M. Barr, "The Design of Evolution," *First Things* 156 (October 2005), 9–12.

guish between the occurrence of random events in the already-formed world and the role of contingency in the formation of the world at its origins. While Saint Thomas recognizes the occurrence of chance events within God's providence, he does not allow for chance events in the production of the world, especially different kinds of living beings: that is, precisely what the theory of biological macroevolution claims.

Three months later, Cardinal Schönborn published a rejoinder, in which he pointed out that Steven Barr treated Darwinism with great delicacy, not citing a single word from the numerous pro-Darwinian scientists who make bold theological statements about evolution as an unguided and unplanned process.[86] Schönborn's reply may be summarized in three points. First, the cardinal provides a clear explanation of how the term "random" is used in evolutionary biology. It is quite different from its use in other natural sciences, such as thermodynamics or quantum theory. In those sciences randomness is in fact embedded and constrained by a deeply mathematical and conceptual structure that makes the overall behavior of the system intelligible; whereas in neo-Darwinian biology, according to Schönborn, variations and mutations are random in a straightforward sense. Neither natural selection nor the properties of the environment are correlated to anything. "Yet," writes the cardinal, "out of all that unconstrained, unintelligible mess emerges, *deus ex machina*, the precisely ordered and extraordinarily intelligible world of living organisms. And this is the heart of the neo-Darwinian science of biology." Secondly, the cardinal rejects Barr's claim that if "random" means simply "uncorrelated," then it can be freely used to describe evolutionary processes in biology. In other words, even this "weaker" version of randomness is not justified, because in biology we see the correlation of elements and parts working for a single purpose.

Finally, the Austrian hierarch points out that

> Many Catholics seem to be saying that, so far as we can determine with our unaided human intellects, according to even the *metaphysically modest* version of neo-Darwinism, there is no real plan, purpose, or design in living things, and absolutely no directionality to evolution; yet we know those things to be true *by faith*. In other words, a "metaphysically modest" neo-Darwinism is not so modest after all. It means a Darwinism that does not conflict with knowledge about reality known through faith alone. In the debate about design in nature, *sola fides* takes on an entirely new meaning.

Hence, the author shows that there is a problem with Darwinism beyond the mere definition of randomness. It is a problem of rational foundations of faith.

86. C. Schönborn, "The Designs of Science," *First Things* 159 (January 2006), 34–38. http://www.firstthings.com/article/2006/01/the-designs-of-science (March 1, 2015). The following quotations come from the same paper.

Finality and rationality in nature are not just theological premises; indeed, they can be observed by reason alone, which is what evolutionists deny. In effect, faith necessarily ends up as fideism.

Schönborn's *New York Times* article stands as a straightforward protest against two phenomena in particular: first, against the kind of evolutionism that excludes design from the development of nature; second, against the claim that the Church in her recent statements embraces or somehow supports neo-Darwinian evolution. The cardinal does not mention special creation of species or any kind of divine "interventions" in the natural order of biology. His text is definitely not "creationist." So, what is there in Schönborn's text that caused so much stir among Catholic evolutionists? Most of them declared that they do not exclude some kind of design, or even divine activity, from the universe. It seems, therefore, that the bone of contention was not whether design is present in biology. Instead, it was a question of what the nature of design is and whether it can be identified by the scientific method.

The entire context of the debate over the article shows that there are serious questions regarding Darwinism that must be raised by contemporary Christians. In fact, the more confidently scientists proclaim the "overwhelming evidence" for neo-Darwinian evolution in biology, the more difficult it is to remain faithful to a Christian understanding of the origins of the universe and of life on Earth. The article proves that, in contrast to what theologians generally say, the debate about evolution in the Church is not over. It has not ended with the acceptance of neo-Darwinian explanations in biology. Rather, it has entered a new phase, one in which the role of science in explaining the origins is discussed. The issues at stake certainly go beyond the dispute over the role of chance. In fact, the Viennese cardinal challenged the whole naturalistic paradigm that had been adopted by the majority of theologians and Catholic scientists.

Catecheses of Cardinal Christoph Schönborn, 2005–2006

Cardinal Schönborn first began to grapple with the issue of evolution in 1985, when as a lecturer in theology at Freiburg he was invited to Rome for a symposium on Christian Faith and the Theory of Evolution. Schönborn's lecture was entitled "Catecheses on Creation and the Theory of Evolution: From Truce to Constructive Conflict."[87] After the symposium, a German magazine published an article under the title "The Truce is Over," which clearly referred to Schönborn's speech, suggesting that he wanted to break the alleged consensus. Years

87. C. Schönborn, "Schöpfungskatechese und Evolutionstheorie: Vom Burgfrieden zum konstruktiven Konflikt," *Internationale Katholische Zeitschrift* 17, no. 3 (1988), 213–26.

later the cardinal explained his intentions: "Nothing is more damaging, to both sides, than when nothing is happening. *What affects everyone should be dealt with by everyone,* runs an old adage."[88]

In reply to numerous polemics and comments on the article in *The New York Times*, Cardinal Schönborn decided to address the topic of creation in a cycle of nine catecheses, given in the cathedral church in Vienna during the academic year 2005–2006.[89] These catecheses are, to date, the widest-ranging discussion of the current Catholic teaching on creation provided by a prominent Church hierarch. They belong to the local Church Magisterium, as they were given by an archbishop, in his cathedral church, with the intention of clarifying various difficult issues.

Some commentators have expressed the opinion that the Vienna catecheses mitigated the archbishop's views. When interviewed by Richard Dawkins, George Coyne, one of the most radical critics of the *New York Times* article, described the catecheses as "excellent."[90] Coyne's shift was somewhat surprising, given the cardinal's criticism of him by name in one of the catecheses. However, Coyne expressed this opinion only after he had been dismissed from his position as director of the Vatican Observatory. Obviously, a concise article in *The New York Times* needed to be rather pointed in order to convey the message intended by the author. We know from Schönborn himself that his purpose was to "awaken Catholics from their dogmatic slumber about positivism in general and evolutionism in particular."[91] In the catecheses, many issues are formulated in more detail, new issues are introduced, and some theses are shown in a different perspective. Apparently, the article proved to be a kind of test aimed at disclosing the condition and sensitivity of Catholic minds in terms of the teaching on creation. As can be guessed, in Schönborn's eyes the probe gave no satisfactory results, and revealed a profound misunderstanding of the teaching on creation among Catholic scholars in general and philosophers of nature in particular. There was but one answer the bishop could make—a deeper catechesis, but also a more subtle one, with the potential to reach not only those who had already been persuaded, but also those who had criticized the *New York Times* piece.

The article "Finding Design in Nature" reminded Catholics that the world by

88. Ch. Schönborn, *Chance or Purpose?*, 163.

89. Later published as a book *Chance or Purpose? Creation, Evolution and a Rational Faith*. Original: *Ziel oder Zufall? Schöpfung und Evolution aus der Sicht eines vernünftigen Glaubens* (Freiburg im Br.: Herder, 2007).

90. http://www.youtube.com/watch?v=pooZMfkSNxc [5:10] (March 2, 2015). Coyne commented on a pre-published version of the Catecheses, but there is no reason to suspect that they essentially differed from the final text.

91. Ch. Schönborn, "The Designs of Science."

itself—and not only through the mediation of religious beliefs—reveals plan and purposefulness. This is why critics read this text as an unambiguous statement of support for a group of intelligent design advocates at the Discovery Institute. Undoubtedly, Schönborn had private connections to this group. Nevertheless, his text was based on quotations from the popes, the Catechism, and the First Vatican Council; and as such, it cannot be reduced exclusively to support for a particular lobby within the American scientific community.

In the Viennese catecheses Schönborn refers to the intelligent design movement twice. At one point he criticizes the idea that God must create perfect beings only. In his opinion, the current debate concerning the idea of design cannot move on, because God is perceived in it as an omnipotent technician who manufactures only perfect machines. "Here, in my view," the cardinal argues, "lies the most profound cause of many misunderstandings—even on the part of the intelligent design school in the USA. God is no clock-maker; he is not a constructor of machines, but a Creator of natures."[92] At another point the author conducts a sort of practical defense of this group against unjust attacks:

> The aggressive way in which many oppose the group of American scientists who are devoting themselves to investigating intelligent design does not have much to do with science. One may criticize their methodological approach. Yet the question as to the origins of the obvious intelligent design in living things is an entirely legitimate one; indeed it is a question bound up with man and his human reason. An answer to this question is not to be expected from research working along strictly scientific methodological lines, yet the question is set before man as a being who questions things, wonders at them, and thinks about them.[93]

Later the Viennese hierarch addressed the more general problem of the freedom to question evolutionary theories:

> Many people today are very sensitive and act as if hurt—even aggressive—whenever anyone doubts the theory of evolution. The debate has proven, however, that there is still a good deal of room for questions, and that we do need to leave that place for questions. People who are questioning and inquiring do a good service, for nothing is worse for science than forbidding questions and inquiries.[94]

It can be observed that Cardinal Schönborn keeps his distance from specific methods and ideas of ID proponents; but at the same time he clearly supports

92. Ch. Schönborn, *Chance or Purpose?*, 98.
93. Ibid., 165.
94. Ibid., 53–54.

their right to conduct scientific research in a paradigm that differs from the Darwinian one. A separate question is whether the cardinal is correct in supposing that the theory of intelligent design implies the presence of only perfect designs in nature, and whether employing an analogy between organism and machine is identical to reducing organisms to machines. Answers to these questions can be found in the works of leading ID scientists. They show that scientists working within the framework of ID are aware of restrictions suggested by the cardinal (and other critics) and themselves reject mechanism as a reductive approach to biology.[95]

In the first catechesis, Schönborn reminds his audience that the world was created out of nothing. In contrast, all non-biblical myths and epics begin with a divine being forming the world from something that already existed. Creation *ex nihilo*, a sovereign act of creation, is a unique and independent act described only in the Bible, a vision contradicting both mythology and gnosis. Modern science, however, attempts to explain everything in such a manner as to oust God from the universe. Examples of similar thinking can be found in the works of Laplace and Darwin. Contemporary evolutionists (J. Huxley, W. Provine, P. Atkins) step out far beyond the competence of science, using it as a justification for their philosophical opinions, which are nearly like a materialistic "profession of faith." The cardinal can "see no difficulty in combining faith in a Creator with the theory of evolution, subject to one condition: that the boundaries of scientific theory are adhered to."[96] In support of this thesis, he cites the Roman symposium of 1985 and John Paul II's statement of April 26, 1985.

The second catechesis raises the issue of fanaticism in the belief in creation. The question asked here is: does belief in creation truly indicate religious fanaticism? As Schönborn argues,

> a great deal of aggressive polemic was directed against those who assert that God created them. . . . People who assert these things are called fanatics—and perhaps there really are a few among them, or some of them behave like fanatics; but the fact that someone believes God has created them still does not justify running down such a belief in that way.[97]

95. This matter was systematically discussed by W. Dembski in his book *The Design Revolution*, 57–63. Dembski clearly states that intelligent design in nature does not have to be optimal to remain true intelligent design. Dembski's book was published two years before Schönborn's catecheses. Similarly, in a university debate held in July 2009 between F. Ayala and W.L. Craig, the latter spoke in defense of intelligent design, claiming among other things that God does not have to create only perfect things. Craig used an analogy from everyday life: Trabant and Mercedes—two cars. The first displayed signs of many structural defects and oversights. Yet, it doesn't follow that Mercedes was designed, and Trabant emerged at random. See http://apologetics315.blogspot.com/2009/11/william-lane-craig-vs.-francisco-j-ayala.html (March 2, 2015).

96. Ch. Schönborn, *Chance or Purpose?*, 29–30.

97. Ibid., 36.

In the current polemics, the belief in creation is confused with creationism as understood by some Christian groups in the USA who maintain the young earth view. The cardinal points out that according to St. Thomas Aquinas, Christian faith should not be defended with the use of arguments that ridicule it. Therefore, it is nonsensical to argue that the world is only 6000 years old. Having discussed the concept of creation, the hierarch remarks that God creates things on His own, without the mediation of creatures. Emanationism, pantheism, and monism are three solutions that seem pious, and this is why they may easily be delusive. They seem to elevate creation to a divine rank, but in fact they do the opposite—they lower the divine to the level of the created.

The topic of biological evolution was directly approached in the third catechesis, which had the following motto: "He created everything according to its kinds" (Gen 1:11; 12:24). The speaker reminds the audience that it is not the purpose of the biblical account to inform us about the way the universe came into being, as it is not a text on natural science. Nevertheless, he also notes that one cannot completely separate science and faith and leave all the questions of *how* exclusively to natural science. "The Bible," says Schönborn, "does not offer any theory about the origin of the world and the development of the species. Yet natural science's way of looking at the origin of species is not the only approach to reality."[98] Next, the cardinal observes that the question of "self-organization" is broadly discussed today among scientists, but nothing, according to him, possesses the power of existence and action in itself. According to Schönborn, evolutionism imposed a view that the variety of creatures in nature is simply an effect of a game of chance and necessity. The richness of different biological forms of life is no longer an incentive for discovering in the universe the organizing influence of reason. Moreover, the existence of different species in biology should be viewed as a certainty arising from experience. They are intended by God, and each of them reflects God's goodness and perfection in its own way. Thus, different species are not mere "snapshots," as evolutionism suggests. At this point the cardinal arrives at an important question: "What constitutes the various species? Did God create each one individually?"[99] In response, the author indicates gaps in evolutionary explanations: "Darwin was trying to show that the origin of species is to be understood as a development from a first seed. This fascinating view has become popular, yet it is still full of great questions."[100] Among these questions, the speaker includes missing links in the fossil record, the problem of ascending movement in evolution (whereas the principles of the struggle for life and adaptation should rather lead to the sur-

98. Ibid., 56.
99. Ibid., 61.
100. Ibid., 63.

vival solely of viruses and bacteria), and the existence of unselfish beauty in nature.

In spite of these problems "What Darwin called secondary causes can perfectly well be reconciled with belief in creation."[101] In other words, the cardinal does not see incompatibility between Darwinian mechanisms ("secondary causes") producing new species and belief in creation. Obviously, the cardinal's statement can be true only if creation is understood, not as a direct and supernatural act of God, but as a kind of divine "cooperation" with creatures.

The leading thread of the fourth catechesis is the concept of *creatio continua*. The cardinal observes that it is a phenomenon of our time that evolution is being sacralized. "How does this strange sacralization of a scientific theory come about?," asks Schönborn. [102] In his opinion, this theory is the only scientific theory that has become an "-ism." Nowadays we have to make sure it does not become an ideology. The hierarch reminds his audience that *creation continua* does not signify the emergence of something new, but only the preservation in being of what already exists. In this context, the most important words of all the catecheses were spoken:

> Can the greater thing have arisen from the less? Can lower things bring forth, of their own power, higher and more complex things? Nothing in our experience suggests that something lower can give rise to something higher, simply of itself, without some directive and organizing activity and, still less, do so quite by chance. Are there, then, individual acts of creation after all? Yet how could we establish their existence? Here we need to refer to a perfectly simple distinction that people prefer to overlook. This is the distinction between a precondition and a cause. In order for life to come into being on our planet, a whole series of preconditions were needed, without which there would be no life. . . . Yet these preconditions . . . do not constitute the creative cause of life. They all play a part in life's coming to be; yet the new element in the development of the world, which we call life, cannot be derived from them. For it to come about, it truly needs the creative act of God, the divine spark, in order to come into being. . . . Much the same is true of evolution. The great leaps by which the stages of evolution ascended each had their necessary preconditions, which cannot however be the things that created these new realities. They are genuine contributory causes, but not the actual creative cause.[103]

Although these words remain within the evolutionary paradigm, they are still the best expression of the classical Christian doctrine of creation that has been presented in recent teachings of the ecclesiastical authorities. The essence of the dictum was the explicit statement that a greater complexity in nature cannot

101. Ibid., 65.
102. Ibid., 77.
103. Ibid., 81–83.

"develop by itself" but requires a divine creative act. Implicitly, the Viennese cardinal accepts the multiplicity of creative acts, thus indirectly rejecting theistic evolution.[104]

The fifth catechesis is concerned with the existence of evil in the world. Schönborn presents questions that are very often asked today in light of people's experiences with different kinds of evil:

> Where is intelligent design there? Where is the kind and loving Creator who can say of his creation that it is good? What ought we to think about the never-ending concentration of human suffering?... How can a rational plan of creation be found in a world full of absurd chance happenings?[105]

In the cardinal's opinion, one should not give a hasty response to the question regarding the origin of suffering. This question itself leads to another problem, namely, the problem of the design and finality of the world. According to Schönborn, however, the world does not have to be perfect to reflect God's beauty and goodness. The world is good but finite, and no created beauty and design will ever be able to fully express the glory of the Creator.[106]

The sixth catechesis treats of man's place in creation. Schönborn starts with a reminder of "three great insults" that humanity has suffered at the hands of three scientists: Copernicus, Darwin, and Freud. Under the influence of these scholars, man came to be considered merely a part of nature. But on the other hand the Church reminds us that man is the only creature God wanted for himself, and is thus something exceptional. Next, the hierarch repeats that there is no contradiction between the biblical message and the evolutionary emergence of mankind: "To be immersed in the stream of things coming into existence is entirely compatible with the biblical view of man. It is one of the marvelous aspects of our earthly life that as men we are related to all creatures."[107] Having presented a view in which the universe and "the stream of things" are in the "process of coming into existence," the cardinal once more comes back to the problem of the origin of man. This time, however, he expresses some reservations, and questions the evolutionary story of humankind:

> It is likewise no humiliation when it becomes clear that man's entry on the stage of the earth entails a long history. The long road of hominization is the subject of intensive research, and the more we know about it the less certain our reconstructions of a genealogical tree have become. Is there a common

104. Nevertheless, immediately after making this claim, Schönborn quotes from Leo Scheffczyk words representative of a nearly classical version of theistic evolution, in which evolution is viewed as creation, and creation is the cooperation between God and nature.

105. Ch. Schönborn, *Chance or Purpose?*, 91–92.

106. Ibid., 93–98.

107. Ibid., 116.

line of descent? . . . From what chronological point can we talk about man? Can there be a gradual transition from animal to man?[108]

In response to these doubts, Schönborn recalls the teaching of Pope Pius XII regarding the possibility of reconciling the animal origin of man with faith, provided that one recognizes the creation of the soul. Finally, he points out that the small biological difference between a man and an animal does not denote a small existential difference—there is an important ontological difference between a man and an animal. Despite the "three great insults to humanity," man remains the crown of creation.

The problem of the origin of man, as presented in the sixth catechesis, seems not to harmonize with the lecturer's previous statements. According to Schönborn there is a possibility that the human being, in terms of his body, came into existence as a result of a purely natural process, and this does not contradict faith. But in the fourth catechesis he speaks about the "great leaps of evolution," which could have been overcome only by special divine power. Therefore the question arises: If those "evolutionary leaps" required some additional action on God's part, would not the emergence of the human body have required such action even more? The lack of an explicit statement on the matter leaves the reader with an impression that Schönborn's utterances regarding the origin of man are unclear or even inconsistent.

The seventh catechesis examines the idea that everything comes from God. The author also quotes Hoimar von Ditfurth, who claimed that the evolutionary view of the world did not allow him to accept the objective meaning of the person of Jesus Christ.[109]

The eighth catechesis, in turn, once again touches upon the relationship between faith and science. The Viennese cardinal makes a distinction between evolutionism as an ideology and evolution as a scientific theory. Unfortunately, due to the influence of René Descartes, knowledge in modernity ceased to be perceived as a selfless quest for the very nature of things. Instead, it became a "power knowledge" (original *Machtwissen*), a practical knowledge rejecting the concept of the Creator and eliminating the language of creation. This kind of "knowledge" was employed in practice by two great ideologies: Darwinism and Marxism. According to the cardinal, the alternative of a "theory of evolution *or* creation" is too simplistic, but the dispute on "creation and evolution" is a real challenge that touches upon important ethical issues, as well as the question of what a man is.[110]

108. Ibid., 118.
109. Ibid., 129–43.
110. Ibid., 147–60 (especially 158–59).

The ninth catechesis is a summary of previous considerations. Schönborn begins by recalling the Roman symposium of 1985, for which reason his speech would be interpreted by some as "the end of a truce" in the creation and evolution debate. He points out that the dispute goes as deep as our understanding of the place of reason in thinking about reality. In the cardinal's opinion, the relationship between evolution and creation might be illustrated with the metaphor of two ladders—Jacob's ladder, representing the descendent movement from God to Earth; and Darwin's ladder, illustrating the ascendant movement present in evolution: "These are two movements in two different directions, which offer something like an overall view only when both are seen together."[111] The hierarch notes that in the theory of evolution so many questions remain open that the degree of confidence and emphasis with which it is being proclaimed is surprising. Despite those reservations, he deems the evolutionary history of nature credible: "There is a great deal to support the view that life has developed through a long process, a gradual ascent from the simplest beginnings up to the complexity of man."[112]

It is not completely clear how to reconcile this opinion with the statements made in the fourth catechesis. Most likely, Cardinal Schönborn does not reject the possibility of evolution in general, but only of evolution understood as a purely natural process. Then, we may accept the long process of the ascending development of, as long as a teleology of evolution is also acknowledged by scholars. He adds with regard to such a process that a completely random event would go against reason. In this context the cardinal makes a critical reference to George Coyne: "When an astronomer, who is also a priest and theologian, even has the presumption to say that God himself could not know for certain that man would be the product of evolution, then nonsense has taken over completely."[113] According to the Viennese hierarch, chance (understood as something unplanned) is a real factor in nature, though it is not a great creative principle. The cardinal rejects both complete chance and absolute determinism as ways of formation of the universe. The "third way" is some cooperation of the divine spirit with natural processes.

The final discussion of the catechesis is concerned with the relationship of culture and ethics with Darwinism. Schönborn addresses the problem of freedom in discussing evolution. According to him, resistance to ideological pressure on the part of evolutionism is one of today's forms of living in freedom, and it should be pursued, even if it has its price. Regarding ethical issues, he

111. Ibid., 166.

112. Ibid., 169.

113. This was a reference to a statement by G. Coyne in *Der Spiegel* 52 (Dec 22, 2000). *Chance or Purpose?*, 169.

observes that the Darwinist mentality leads people to take over the role of the Creator. As a result, they think they can freely manipulate the "course of evolution," making decisions about the survival of the fittest in the human world.

In sum, Cardinal Schönborn's Viennese catecheses reflect the current status of Church thought, with all its advantages and defects. His teaching is based on the distinction between Darwinism as an ideology and Darwinian scientific theory. No one has drawn Catholic attention to the threats arising from the Darwinian ideology as clearly as the Viennese cardinal has. He does believe that evolution in the scientific sense may co-exist with the Christian faith; although he also notes that in addition to the rebellious, atheistic Darwinism, we must also be wary of the influence of "bad Darwinian philosophy" on ecclesiastical thought on creation. He demonstrates that many theologians in their "admiration of science" have accepted not only the "scientific theses" of Darwinian evolution, but also its philosophical implications, of which the one most distant from the Christian worldview is the rejection of design in nature. The cardinal reminds us that God created the whole variety of creatures primarily so that they might direct people's minds to His beauty and wisdom. A single created being would by no means be able to reflect this beauty, so the almighty God made a great variety of creatures. However, this does not mean that, collectively, creatures fully depict the nature of God. Creatures are perfect according to the measure of perfection allotted to them by the Creator. Nevertheless, the trace of design and plan in the universe is simply overwhelming. To reject it is to deny the common sense of humanity.

The overall approach in the Vienna catecheses is reconciliatory toward evolution. One can notice a certain discrepancy between, on the one hand, severely critical objections regarding use of the scientific method and the "evidence" for evolution, and on the other hand a broad acceptance of its actual occurrence, and even the possibility of harmonizing evolution with faith. However, if the evidence for evolution is as weak as the cardinal suggests, perhaps the very idea of universal common descent should not be accepted in theology. Otherwise, Catholics could end up reinterpreting the traditional doctrine of creation merely in order to reconcile it with a particular scientific theory ultimately proved wrong. In the fourth catechesis, Schönborn points to the necessity of creative Divine action at the "big leaps" of evolution, but with respect to the formation of the human body (discussed in the sixth catechesis) such a suggestion is not made. One might thus say that the teaching of Cardinal Schönborn is here in considerable harmony with the various statements by Benedict XVI. In both cases, however, the teaching leaves many open questions, and at some points is even more ambiguous than it might seem at first glance.

The Conferences in Rome and the Current Lack of Consensus

Scientific conferences organized in Rome have made important contributions to the understanding of science and its relationship to Christianity. The first of these was the aforementioned 1985 symposium in 1985, at which Pope John Paul II presented his thoughts on evolution. The second occasion, held a number of years later, was the International Catholic Symposium on Creation, organized by the Washington Kolbe Center (October 24–25, 2002). The event had a decisively creationist tone, and it criticized the theory of evolution from the point of view of science, philosophy, and theology.[114]

The year 2009 marked the 150th anniversary of the publication of Darwin's *Origin of Species* and the 200th anniversary of Darwin's birth, as well as the 200th anniversary of the publication of Lamarck's *Philosophie Zoologique*. On this occasion the Pontifical Academy of Sciences joined in the large-scale celebrations by organizing a scientific conference devoted to the issue of evolution. The meeting was entitled "Scientific Insights into the Evolution of the Universe and of Life" (October 31–November 4, 2008).[115] None of the thirty speeches given during the meeting challenged Darwinian evolution from either a scientific or a theological perspective. One of the speakers, however, was Cardinal Schönborn, who spoke on the teaching of Benedict XVI on this topic. Held simultaneously with the conference of the Pontifical Academy of Sciences was a one-day conference (November 3) at the Sapienza University of Rome, during which several scientists, proponents of young earth creationism, presented criticisms of the theory of evolution. The meeting, organized as if in opposition to the PAS session, did not attract the attention of the mainstream media.

The next relevant conference took place during "Darwin's year" (on March 3–7, 2009). This event was widely discussed in the media. The organizers were the Pontifical Council for Culture, the University of Notre Dame, and Gregorian University, and the sponsor was the Templeton Foundation. At all previous events of this rank the pope had been present, or at least prepared some remarks to be delivered on his behalf to the participants. This time, however, neither Benedict XVI nor Cardinal Schönborn was present, and no address to

114. More than 450 pages of conference materials were published by the Kolbe Center, under the title *International Catholic Symposium on Creation. Symposium held in Rome, Italy on October* 24–25, 2002. The speakers included Bishop Andreas Laun; Rev. Victor Warkulwiz; Rev. Brian Harrison; Rev. Johannes Grun; Josef Seifert, PhD; Dominique Tassot, PhD; Guy Berthault; Robert Gentry, PhD; Robert Sungenis; Robert Bennett, PhD; Maciej Giertych, PhD; Robin Bernhoft, PhD; Christian Bizouard, PhD; and Arthur Gohin, PhD.

115. *Scientific Insights into the Evolution of the Universe and of Life*, in *Pontificiae Academiae Scientiarum Acta* 20, ed. W. Arber, N. Cabibbo, M.S. Sorondo (Ex Aedibus Academicis: Civitate Vaticana, 2009).

the participants on behalf of the pope was delivered.[116] The conference was opened with a short speech by Cardinal William Levada—Prefect of the Congregation for the Doctrine of the Faith. His text, however, did not contain any statements relevant to the topic of evolution and faith. All these circumstances strongly suggest that Church officials, including the pope, intended to keep their distance, or, at least, did not wish to add to the publicity of an event that was deliberately designed to dismiss intelligent design and promote theistic evolutionism.

The title of the conference was "Biological Evolution: Facts and Theory: A Critical Approach 150 Years after *The Origin of Species*." During the five days, representatives of the world of science and philosophy, mainly Americans, delivered 34 lectures. Scientists spoke on contemporary aspects of evolution (essentially neo-Darwinian ones) and the directions in which the theory had developed over recent years. Some mentioned certain difficulties associated with the theory and possible solutions to those difficulties.[117] Once again, among more than 30 speakers, not a single serious critic of neo-Darwinian theory was present. Proponents of intelligent design applied, via the Discovery Institute, to attend the session, but they were refused. A 150-page text, containing explanations and a defense of their position, was sent to the organizers before the conference started; however, it was not taken into consideration. This decision, which resulted in a lack of balance in the conference, was attributed by the president of the Discovery Institute, Bruce Chapman, to the explicit instructions of the Templeton Foundation.[118] On the other hand, the agenda included presentations that explicitly disavowed the theory of intelligent design (talks by R. Numbers, J. Arnould, and S.F. Gilbert). Thus, it is doubtful that the organizers followed the common-sense rule, confirmed independently by Pius XII and Benedict XVI, that debates on evolution should take into account the arguments of both sides.

116. Michael Gilchrist states in his article that on March 6, 2009, Benedict XVI addressed a letter to the participants of the conference in which he asserts that the "world did not arise from chaos, but was purposefully created by the First Being." However, this letter cannot be found either on the Vatican's website or on the Zenit portal. It has not been published in *AAS*, either. In fact, the only place where it is mentioned is Gilchrist's article. See M. Gilchrist, "Benedict XVI Addresses a Vatican Conference on Evolution and Christianity," *AD* 2000, 22, no. 3 (April 2009), 3. The article is available online at http://www.ad2000.com.au/articles/2009/apr2009p3_3004.html (December 20, 2013).

117. See *Biological Evolution: Facts and Theories: A Critical Appraisal* 150 *Years after* The Origin of Species *March* 3–7, 2009, ed. G. Auletta, M. Leclerc, R.A. Martínez (Roma: Gregorian & Biblical Press, 2011).

118. See: "Darwin conference does not speak for Vatican, says theorist," *Christian Today*; http://www.christiantoday.com/article/darwin.conference.does.not.speak.for.vatican.says.theorist/22707.htm (March 3, 2015).

Archbishop Gianfranco Ravasi, who as head of the Pontifical Council for Culture was the formal host of the conference, said during a press briefing announcing the event (September 16, 2008) that "there is no incompatibility *a priori* between the theories of evolution and the message of the Bible."[119] Ravasi spoke of theories in the plural, meaning in particular biological theories. However, he did not specify which particular theories he had in mind. The archbishop also failed to mention that, according to recent popes, only those theories are compliant with Christianity that do not exclude God's actions in the world, and acknowledge both inherent finality in nature and the independent creation of the soul. Moreover, Ravasi observed that Darwin had never been condemned by the Catholic Church, and that his main book, *On the Origin of Species*, had never been listed on the Index of Prohibited Books. The latter argument was raised a number of times in recent discussions and was supposed to prove that the Church had never questioned Darwinism. However, this argument is not historically accurate. After the Council of Trent, all books about religious issues written by non-Catholic authors were considered "heretical" by the Church and *a priori* prohibited. This rule was confirmed by Leo XIII when reforming the rules of the Papal Index of Prohibited Books in 1897.[120] Accordingly, a book about religion written by a non-Catholic could be considered free of errors only if positively evaluated. Neither *The Origin of Species* nor any other work by Darwin was approved by such means.[121]

When analyzing the Vatican conferences on evolution, we see that the ecclesiastical academic circles never initiated a real debate. The sessions were organized either from the perspective of young earth creationism or, as was more often the case, in order to promote evolutionism. This fact itself shows that Catholics are far from reaching a full consensus on this matter. So far the Church has not hosted a real discussion between supporters and critics of evolution, involving the natural sciences, philosophy, and theology.

Andreas Laun, Auxiliary Bishop of Salzburg, having reviewed the history of

119. Quotation dated September 16, 2008. See video interview: http://www.youtube.com/watch?v=OmIwEhG-QpI (5:30) (March 3, 2015). See also press release "Evoluzione: Ravasi, 'Non è incompatibile col messaggio della Bibbia.'" http://www.srmedia.org/Home/Newsprecedenti/MonsRavasiEvoluzioneereligionecompatibili/tabid/151/Default.aspx (March 3, 2015).

120. "Books written by non-Catholics that treat religion *ex professo* are prohibited, unless it is ascertained that there is nothing in them contrary to the Catholic faith." Cf. *Negotiating Darwin*, 14.

121. The Index, however, included *Zoonomia* by Erasmus Darwin, who spoke of the evolutionary development of species more than fifty years before Charles Darwin. The fact that *Zoonomia* was specifically condemned did not abolish the general rule (i.e., not adding non-Catholic authors to the Index), but rather confirmed that the Church considered such opinions as those expressed in *Zoonomia* particularly dangerous. The question could be raised whether *The Origin of Species* was a book "treating religion." In fact, Darwin referred numerous times to creation and the manner of God's activity in nature. He explicitly challenged the doctrines "held until now by Christians." One of many

evolutionism, has asked: "And today? Is the battle over, and if so, who has won and who has lost?"[122] Bishop Laun gave a speech during the symposium held in Rome in October 2002. In his opinion, three meanings of evolution should be distinguished:

> (1) *Materialistic theory of evolution*, according to which all differentiation of matter, including man, has arisen simply through evolution.
>
> (2) *Theistic theory of evolution*, according to which God has called the world into being and has endowed it with a potentiality from which everything has developed, including Man.
>
> (3) *A theory of evolution "acceptable to Catholics,"* according to which everything has developed from matter, which God has created, or from the primeval cell created by God, except for the immortal human soul, which is created by God.

According to Bishop Laun, Darwin proposed his theory mainly to exclude any supernatural acts of God from the world. A theologian is competent to answer only those questions the answers to which are somehow contained in divine revelation. Thus, a theologian cannot judge "whether an elephant would climb out of a pond containing frogs, if one only stood for long enough—for millions of years—at the water's edge and waited."[123] But theologians do have the right to consider the stringency of the proofs for the theory of evolution and to question them.

Laun observes that John Paul II had indeed described the theory of evolution as "more than a hypothesis." Yet it does not follow that Catholics are now

examples of a theological statement in his book reads as follows: "I can entertain no doubt, . . . that the view which most naturalists entertain, and which I formerly entertained—namely, that each species has been independently created—is erroneous" (*On the Origin of Species*, 7). In *The Descent of Man* (1871) Darwin explained that he had two reasons to write *The Origin of Species*: one was to present the theory of natural selection, another was to disprove the belief in separate creation of species: "In the earlier editions of my 'Origin of Species' I probably attributed too much to the action of natural selection or the survival of the fittest. . . . I may be permitted to say as some excuse, that I had two distinct objects in view, firstly, to shew that species had not been separately created, and secondly, that natural selection had been the chief agent of change. . . . Nevertheless I was not able to annul the influence of my former belief, then widely prevalent, that each species had been purposely created; . . . Some . . . , seem to forget, when criticising my book, that I had the above two objects in view; hence if I have erred [about natural selection] . . . , I have at least, as I hope, done good service in aiding to overthrow the dogma of separate creations" (*The Descent of Man*, 152–153). Obviously, a book whose main purpose is to change or destroy the Christian understanding of creation should be considered theological, even if theology is not its main topic. Consequently, it is quite probable that the book fell under papal condemnation.

122. See A. Laun, "Evolution and Creationism: Theological Considerations," *Daylight* 34 (April 2004), 5–11, 7. The following quotations come from this paper.

123. Ibid., 5.

obliged to believe in it and may not put it to doubt. First of all, the pope had spoken only in a very general way of "new knowledge" that supports the idea of evolution, but did not say what "knowledge" he meant. Moreover, widespread acceptance of any theory is but a weak argument in its support, indeed—according to Thomas Aquinas—the weakest of all arguments. Secondly, the pope had assigned the theory of evolution to the realm of epistemology and thereby *ipso facto* declined to be responsible for its evaluation. Finally, John Paul II had also allowed the possibility that this theory would prove to be unsuitable and that it would then have to be "reconsidered." In Laun's opinion, merely considering the theological possibility of evolution does not mean to suggest that the proposition is either true or false. It can be "theologically possible" and nevertheless turn out to be a gigantic scientific or philosophical error. The belief that the earth is a disc, and a thousand other scientific theories, once were and still are compatible with faith—and were nevertheless entirely false.

In his discussion of the need for impartiality in evaluating the theory of evolution, the bishop makes an important observation:

> The atheist and the materialist are necessarily in a bad position, which actually forces them into subjectivity. For, if God does not exist, they have to assert that everything has evolved. That means that their atheistic prejudice takes away their scientific freedom. They must assert the truth of evolution in the face of all the evidence and without any real proofs.

Furthermore, he is convinced that:

> Theologians should take up the criticism which has been recently formulated and proved and which shows that evolution really is impossible. Darwin himself said, *If it could be proved that some kind of complex organ exists, which could not possibly have come into existence through many small changes following on one another, then my theory would completely collapse*. But since then it has long been shown that not just one but many such organs exist, which, according to Darwin's own conviction, refute his theory.

Laun concludes his speech with a call for the renewal of the Catholic viewpoint:

> Theologians should take leave of the theory of evolution acceptable to Catholics and in consequence write a new presentation of the teaching of creation—without being caught up in an antiquated theory and without philosophically untenable fantasies.

In his book published in 2009, Archbishop Joseph Zycinski (1948–2011) claimed that "what is worrying are not evolutionary theories but attempts to support anti-evolution interpretations made by circles drawing on Christian traditions."[124] Zycinski openly expresses his anxiety that such a tendency

124. J. Zycinski, *Wszechswiat emergentny* (Lublin: Wyd. KUL 2009), 29.

increased after the death of John Paul II, and admits that "they could do no harm to evolution itself, instead harming the image of the Church and creating an illusory conflict between science and faith."[125] As an example of such "harmful opinions" he mentions the 2005 article by Cardinal Schönborn. According to Zycinski, the value of that utterance was accurately expressed by Francisco Ayala, who had stated that

> the famous text, inspired by non-scientific arguments, published in *The New York Times*, is an insult to the memory of John Paul II. Such evaluation is the more significant in that religious motivations are used also to justify institutional measures aimed against the theory of evolution.[126]

When one archbishop criticized another archbishop as well as a cardinal, and did so by quoting a former Dominican priest, it was certainly not a sign of unity in the Church's views. It is hard to agree with Zycinski that the views of John Paul II and Schönborn diverged considerably. The cardinal had quoted John Paul II's teaching in his article, while the pope many years earlier had appointed Schönborn to edit the *Catechism of the Catholic Church*, which is the fullest expression of the Catholic faith. These facts point to a convergence of the opinions of the pope and the cardinal rather than at the conflict suggested by Zycinski. Nevertheless, dissention within the Church hierarchy is visible. When Bishop Laun had asked theologians to reconsider the entire "Treatise on Creation" in the context of contemporary scientific achievements and reject the outdated theory, Zycinski thought that undermining the theory of evolution was a dangerous anti-intellectual attitude that would inevitably lead to ridicule of the Church. The differences are even more obvious if we consider the various attitudes to John Paul II's address to the PAS in 1996. Even though it may be surprising that Schönborn called it "vague and unimportant," it would certainly be an exaggeration to say, following Zycinski, that it was "one of the most important documents of the previous pontificate."[127]

Disagreements over Darwinian theory do not occur only in Catholic circles. For several years Michael Zimmerman, an evolutionary biologist and member of American Association for the Advancement of Science, has led a campaign among clergy of different denominations in support of evolutionary theory, called *The Clergy Letter Project*. The letter contained the following statement:

125. Ibid.

126. Ibid.

127. J. Zycinski, "Dlaczego ma mi ubliżać ta wspólnota w genealogii z braćmi, którymi są zwierzęta niższe?" [Why should I feel insulted by a genealogical community with our brothers who are animals of a lower order?], *Tygodnik Powszechny* (12) March 17, 2009. Article available at: http://tygodnik.onet.pl/cywilizacja/zaplanowani-i-ukochani-wciaz-ewoluujemy/kf5n7 (March 3, 2015).

> We . . . believe that the timeless truths of the Bible and the discoveries of modern science may comfortably coexist. We believe that the theory of evolution is a foundational scientific truth, one that has stood up to rigorous scrutiny and upon which much of human knowledge and achievement rests. To reject this truth or to treat it as one theory among others is to deliberately embrace scientific ignorance and transmit such ignorance to our children.[128]

Since 2004, the letter has been signed by more than twelve thousand clerics, mainly of Protestant denominations.

In 2001, the Discovery Institute published an online document entitled "Scientific Dissent from Darwinism," which includes the following brief statement: "We are skeptical of claims for the ability of random mutation and natural selection to account for the complexity of life. Careful examination of the evidence for Darwinian theory should be encouraged."[129]

More than eight hundred scientists from all over the world put their names under the statement. And since, in order to sign the letter, one had to possess a doctorate in one of the natural sciences or in the philosophy of science, most of the signatories were active lecturers in their respective fields of study, representing all the famous universities in the world, from Israel to Moscow and from Beijing to California. In this context, it is hard to claim today that scientific community is in full agreement about neo-Darwinism.

Moreover, it seems that nowadays the theory of evolution is more eagerly defended by some theologians than it is by biologists. Indeed, the latter are used to making continual revisions as a result of their research and the rendering invalid of earlier hypotheses. The theory of evolution is irrelevant to how most scientists work in their narrow fields of research. They deal with what exists now—how biochemical systems work, how to classify organisms, and so forth; but the question of where it all comes from has very little to do with their work. They do not even need to know the answer to it, nor do they have to be interested in it more than any other person. Truly scientific endeavor in biology remains valid regardless of acceptance or refusal of the neo-Darwinian paradigm. The case is different with theologians, however. A number of them have taken evolution for granted in their scholarship on creation and tried to make divine revelation fit their naturalistic assumptions. Yet if naturalistic assumptions proved false, not only would an abstract theory uniting evolution and creation fall apart, but the foundations of their worldview would collapse as well. For theologians, Darwinism is never a merely scientific theory, but entails an

128. http://theclergyletterproject.org/Christian_Clergy/ChrClergyLtr.htm (March 3, 2015).

129. "A Scientific Dissent from Darwinism," http://www.dissentfromdarwin.org/ (March 3, 2015).

array of philosophical and theological concepts, such as a particular understanding of God's nature, attitude towards creation, and interpretation of the Bible. Theologians know that once a theological doctrine is true it remains true forever. Sometimes they import the same idea into the natural sciences, forgetting that conclusions reached in the natural sciences are always provisional, always subject to further revisions. That is why theologians usually resist questioning the evolutionary paradigm in science. Therefore, in the entire dispute, the key issue concerns the starting point—whether the question about the origins of the universe, species, and human beings should be first answered by divine revelation and only supplemented with the results of scientific research, or whether the answer should be established by scientific research and only supplemented with general suggestions derived from divine revelation. For Bishop Laun, the point of reference is the Bible and the tradition of Christian philosophy, whereas Archbishop Zycinski openly refers to the philosophy of emergent evolution proposed by F. Ayala.[130]

Christianity has always maintained that science may not contradict faith because nature was made by the same God who reveals himself in the Bible, and God would not contradict himself. The secondary object of faith is creation considered in its relation to God. On the other hand, the object of science is the world with its immanent laws. In both fields of thought it is the same world and the same creation. Because the truth is some kind of equation between reality and the intellect (*adaequatio rei et intellectus*),[131] and since there is only one reality, different levels of knowledge may not be in contradiction. Scholastic theologians used to talk about a dynamic movement: "faith seeking understanding" and "reason seeking faith." The disagreement regarding the theory of evolution in the Church is a fact, even if many theologians would rather not acknowledge it. However, if "truth cannot contradict truth," this means that either evolution or creation has been misunderstood. And as Bishop Laun has observed, the controversy cannot be solved simply by moving the creative act back in time and removing it from the origin of species. If species were not created by a direct act of God but rather developed through natural evolution (by means of secondary causes), there still remains the question of whether God created the first life. If not, then what did he create? Stars and planetary systems? Or perhaps those complex systems also came into being on their own? By withdrawing the creative act, we arrive at the creation of matter; but according to the theory of cosmic evolution, matter also shaped itself as a

130. See Zycinski, *Wszechświat emergentny*, 38. In a book published posthumously, *Bóg i stworzenie*, Zycinski quotes M. Ruse, who called Ayala "one of the most outstanding evolutionists of our times." *Bóg i stworzenie: Zarys teorii ewolucji*, 8.

131. Thomas Aquinas, *S.Th.*, I, q. 16, a. 1.

result of some nuclear processes. Thus, all that God had to do was create a "singular point" from which the world simply emerged. But consequent methodological naturalism does not accept that theory, either; and, according to atheists, the world is eternal, and the great collapses and explosions of the world happen cyclically.

Currently the most popular version of theistic evolution accepts only the first divine act of causing the "big bang," after which evolution is purported to have developed everything on its own, under some vaguely understood sense of "providence." However, theistic evolutionists do not provide any reason to set a limit to God's direct work in the world at this very point. Moreover, the Church teaches the direct creation of a human soul each time a new human is conceived. Perhaps this makes the limits imposed by theistic evolution even more arbitrary. If we believe in special creation of human souls and a multitude of miraculous events in the history of salvation, then it is difficult to say why we should exclude a multiplicity of supernatural creative acts in nature over billions of years. So far, science has not been able to offer a credible explanation of the origin of the universe, of the first life, or of the different kinds of life. The question of whether science is at all capable of answering these questions remains open. Thus, there are no decisive reasons, stemming either from theology or science, for the Church to agree with Darwin's theory and accept the natural development of all biodiversity. It belongs to natural science to study *how* the world works, but it is beyond its scope to say *where* it came from. The origin of species is right in the middle of that debate. Undoubtedly we still need to wait to see the ultimate result of the controversy over evolution and creation.

Pope Francis's Address to the Pontifical Academy of Sciences

On October 27, 2014, Pope Francis attended a plenary session of the Pontifical Academy of Sciences, which included the unveiling of a bronze statue in honor of Pope Benedict XVI. In his speech to the members of the PAS, Francis mentioned the topic of evolution. First, he observed that scientists were addressing "the highly complex topic of the evolution of the concept of nature."[132] Then the pope warns that when reading the Genesis account of creation one may "imagine that God was a magician, with such a magic wand as to be able to do everything." However, according to the Pope, "[I]t was not like that. God created beings and left them to develop according to the internal laws that He gave each one, so that they would develop, and reach their fullness." God gave His

132. This and all subsequent quotations are from the American translation available on the Zenit website: http://www.zenit.org/en/articles/pope-francis-address-at-inauguration-of-bronze-bust-of-benedict-xvi (March 3, 2015).

creation autonomy; He is not a "demiurge or a magician, but the Creator who gives being to all entities." Francis continues:

> The beginning of the world was not the work of chaos, which owes its origin to another, but it derives directly from a Supreme Principle who creates out of love. The Big-Bang that is placed today at the origin of the world does not contradict the divine intervention, but exacts it. Evolution in nature is not opposed to the notion of Creation, because evolution presupposes the creation of beings that evolve.

At the end of the address the pope mentions the origin of man, which, he observes, brings "a change and a novelty." Furthermore, he ties this notion to Genesis:

> When, on the sixth day of the Genesis account, we come to the creation of man, God gives the human being another autonomy, a different autonomy from that of nature, which is freedom. And He tells man to give a name to all things and to go forward in the course of history. He renders him responsible for creation.

As in the other recent papal statements concerning evolution, here also one may see a lack of clear definition of the word "evolution." In fact Francis speaks here about the evolution of "the concept of nature [Italian: *concetto di natura*]," which makes things even less clear. We do not know whether the message referred to the "meta-problem," that is, evolution of the concept of nature, or to the evolution of nature itself. But even assuming the latter (which the following context demands) we still cannot be sure what kind of evolution within nature the pope meant to signify.

By saying that God is not to be imagined as "magician with a magic wand," Francis dismisses naïve interpretations of Genesis, wherein God would appear as a somewhat chaotic wizard making things here and there without any deeper plan or room for secondary causation. But the dismissal of the naïve interpretations does not help to establish whether the traditional creationist view belongs to those interpretations. It also does not tell us whether God created some elements of the universe directly and immediately or left everything to secondary causation. Therefore, this statement fails to address the crucial questions of the current debate, unless one assumes that all creationist interpretations of Genesis are naïve, and demand imagining God as a magician.

Perhaps some creationists see God as a quite unpredictable magician. On the young earth view, for instance, God must have directly created fossils in the strata, as well as all other signs of the old age of the universe, over the course of the period of creation understood as six natural days. This interpretation brings to mind a god who deceives people, leaving them with multiple signs of a history that never happened. However, the young earth view is not the only interpretation of Genesis that acknowledges God's supernatural activity in the formation of the universe. Progressive creationism, for example, recognizes the signs of the old universe as true, and sees supernatural formation over long periods of time as God's way of perfecting nature to a point where nature—left to its internal laws—would never get by itself. On this view (shared by many saints and Doctors, such as St. Ambrose) God is not a magician, but rather an artist, or a painter who perfects creation with every touch of the brush.

Francis contrasts the vision of God as magician with the vision of God who "created beings and left them to develop according to the internal laws." However, this juxtaposition misses some important distinctions. For instance, many Enlightenment philosophers proposed a deistic vision of God, who is "so great" that He does not work upon the effects, but only the causes of the effects. In this view God becomes just a "great Architect," a "cause of causes," and not a Christian God who knows and devises all particular things in the universe. (See our earlier discussion of Erasmus Darwin's views.) Presumably the pope does not wish to promote the deistic vision of God; but without such an explanation, his words remain ambiguous and vulnerable to misinterpretation. After all, God *is* the One, who can do anything, even work as a magician if He so wishes. The way he actually works in Genesis seems to be far from just "leaving the things to development according to the internal laws."

The concept of God's work as presented in the papal address seems to support the common opinion of theologians, known as theistic evolution—that is, the idea that God created the universe in the first moment and then left everything to develop according to created laws of nature.[133] Two statements seem to support this view: First, the one already quoted, that God "created beings and left them to develop according to the internal laws"; second, his claim that "The evolution in nature is not opposed to the notion of Creation, because evolution presupposes the creation of beings that evolve." Both statements point to the idea that God created the universe out of nothing by his supernatural power and left it to natural evolution. Creation *ex nihilo* is recognized by science as the "Big Bang," a theory positing a temporal beginning of the universe, which originated from a singular point of infinite density and temperature. This theory, in the pope's words, "does not contradict divine intervention but exacts it."

Nevertheless, the pope's support for theistic evolution is not as obvious as one would expect. In both statements Francis speaks about the creation of *beings* (plural) and their further evolution. A straightforward reading brings to mind the Augustinian idea of creation rather than the one maintained within theistic evolution. According to Augustine, God created all things—that is, dif-

133. For more on our understanding of theistic evolution see Chapter Two, under "The Arena of the Current Debate."

ferent beings—at once, and then they developed (evolved) according to their specific natures. Augustine's idea implies separate creation of species, even if in a hidden (enveloped) form. There is no room for transformation of species or universal common descent—the essential points of theistic evolution. Francis's address seems to favor the Augustinian idea over theistic evolution because he talks about creation of beings—many different beings—and their further development. In any case, these papal statements are not clear enough to establish one of at least two possible interpretations. Only more precise understandings of the notion of evolution could help to determine whether Francis supports theistic evolution or the Augustinian idea of the one-time creation of different beings.

The same problem applies to the idea of the non-opposition between the notions of Creation and evolution. One can easily imagine the notion of creation in such a way that it excludes the notion of evolution—and, in fact, many scholars over centuries have so understood it. For example, if creation is taken as an immediate, supernatural act, which brings something out of nothing (without preexisting matter), then it excludes the notion of evolution understood as natural process that assumes the pre-existence of matter, laws, and perhaps other secondary causes. The very ideas of direct and indirect action are logically exclusive. But if evolution means only "change over time" within the natural order, and creation means "God's work in the universe," then the notions are not in opposition. They simply signify the same reality as observed from different standpoints. Therefore, again, the papal statement turns out to be too general to interpret unambiguously.

The last issue pertaining to the topic of creation is the origin of man. Francis speaks about the "autonomy" which created beings received from the creator in order to evolve according to their laws. When it comes to the creation of man, God gives him "another autonomy," which is freedom. God asked man to name all creatures and made him responsible for creation. The pope does not refer to any particular concept of human origins: neither the idea of creation of the human body directly from dust nor the evolutionary origin of the human body from lower animals is mentioned. The whole problem seems to be reduced to "human freedom," which implies that man possesses free will and a spiritual nature. But the problem of human origins as presented in the speech lacks any metaphysical or realistic historical dimension. The Genesis account seems to be almost entirely reduced to moral questions of human responsibility for creation in the course of history. Therefore, this issue also leaves much room for further interpretation. In fact, relying just on this papal address, one cannot say anything about different competing conceptions of human origins.

Altogether, the papal address from October 2014 does not bring any novelty to Church teaching on evolution. It repeats the older claims about non-opposition between the Genesis account and scientific ideas of evolution, but without defining the terms employed or explaining how precisely creation happened. It also lacks some of the crucial distinctions that make the creation/evolution debate possible. Even if a superficial reading of the address seems to support an evolutionary interpretation of Genesis, when one takes a closer look, there is much room left for "creationist" ideas. Specifically, the papal utterance harmonizes with the Augustinian idea of creation, which is not the same as theistic evolution.

10

Looking into the Past: Two Stages in Church Teaching on Evolution

The question we asked at the beginning of this book was: what positions over the last 150 years has the Catholic Church adopted regarding evolution? After analyzing the teachings of popes, Roman congregations, and theologians, we may conclude that the Church has undergone an "evolution" consisting of two distinctive stages.

During the first stage, in response to the theory proposed by Darwin and his supporters, we can see the emergence of a new idea of creation called theistic evolution; i.e., a view according to which God created the world using only secondary causes. Generally those "secondary causes" were biological processes leading first to the creation of "first life," then to the diversity of species, and finally to the formation of the human body. For some propagators of this concept, evolution—understood as an increase in organic complexity—led also to the creation of human consciousness (E. Haeckel). However, the idea that the soul was the result of the evolution of matter was from the very beginning unacceptable in Catholic teaching. In the encyclical *Humani Generis* (1950) Pope Pius XII explicitly rejected this idea. Therefore, the variant theories of theistic evolution endorsed by different authors was subject to different limitations. At the end of the 19th century, Catholic evolutionists usually accepted the direct creation of the first life or the first few species ("polyphyletic evolution") and recognized the direct creation of a rational soul. Despite these significant reservations, the concept of the evolutionary origin of species was rejected by the vast majority of theologians. The most important scholars of that period with regard to the articulation of the "classical" concept of creation included M.J. Scheeben and Cardinals C. Mazzella and E. Ruffini. Theistic evolution applied to the human body was rejected by the Church Magisterium in the teachings of popes, bishops, and supporting congregations. The testimony of this teaching is found in the decree of the Synod of Cologne (1860); Leo XIII's encyclical

Arcanum (1880); the unchangeable stance of the Congregation of the Index against books by R. Caverni (1878), D. Leroy (1895), and J.A. Zahm (1898); the pronouncements of the Pontifical Biblical Commission (first and foremost the 1909 decree on the historical character of the Book of Genesis, chapters 1–3); and the speech given by Pius XII to the Pontifical Academy of Sciences on November 30, 1941. In the third chapter we mentioned that the First Vatican Council also came close to issuing a pronouncement that would rule out evolution of the first humans—man and woman—with respect to both body and soul.

All that evidence, placed in the theological context of the era, shows that the Catholic Church in the late 19th and early 20th centuries presented a defined teaching on creation, which could not be reconciled with Darwin's theory. The main elements of that teaching included three truths: (1) separate formation of species understood as independent natures of living beings (this truth deemed a matter of sound philosophy rather than faith); (2) the creation of the body of the first man from the dust of the earth by direct action of God, without any secondary causes (either material or immaterial); and (3) the creation of Eve from Adam's side—without any contribution of secondary causes (the certainty of the two latter truths being quite high, at the level of ordinary teaching, though some theologians considered them part of the solemn Magisterium). This teaching included also a permanent belief in the direct creation of the soul of the first and all successive humans. At the same time, the Magisterium did not require anyone to believe in the short history of Earth. The 1909 Reply of the Pontifical Biblical Commission stated that the Hebrew word *Yom* used in Genesis 1 may be understood as either a natural day or a different period of time. There has always been good ground for discussion on the matter. It means that the Catholic Church did not condemn, nor did it command, belief in young earth creationism.

A clearly expressed stance on the origin of man was maintained until Pius XII's 1950 encyclical *Humani Generis*. However, as we have shown, certain allowances were made earlier, namely in the 1920s and 1930s, when subsequent publications that sought to combine Catholicism with Darwinian evolution (works by H. Dorlodot and E. Messenger) ceased to be condemned. A substantial change in the Church's approach, the one that opened the second stage of teaching, took place when *Humani Generis* was published. Pope Pius XII shifted the truth about the origin of man from the domain of faith to the domain of scientific research. It was a significant novelty, because up until then it had been believed that science as such could not give a final and definite answer as to where the human body came from; that question was answered by faith, and therefore the main source of knowledge on the matter had been Holy Scripture. Traditional exegesis claimed that the Bible speaks not only about the fact *that* God created things, but also *how* He created them. On the traditional understanding, science could only provide a negative background[1] for the adoption of the truths of faith (i.e., positive knowledge about God). According to Pius XII, however, science possibly can provide explanations regarding the origin of the human body. By allowing such a possibility, the pope opened the way for common acceptance of the idea that God formed the universe using natural processes of an evolutionary character. As a consequence, most theologians *de facto* accepted the "dictatorship of science" and tried to conform interpretation of the Holy Scriptures and, more broadly, any traditional teachings on creation, to scientific theories of evolution.

The issue of evolution returned in the catecheses of John Paul II. In the years 1985–1986, he asserted that evolution, which some researchers accept and others deny, is consistent with Holy Scripture. The basic idea of gradual formation of the human body in a natural process does not in any way contradict faith. To some degree this was an extension of the view already presented by Pius XII in 1950. However, characteristic of the teaching of John Paul II was his emphasis on the finality embedded in the process of evolution. Ten years later, in a speech to the Pontifical Academy of Sciences (1996), John Paul II stated that new scientific knowledge leads to a conclusion that evolution should be seen as more than just a hypothesis. This was only an assessment of the results of scientific research, and thus did not pertain to either faith or morality; it had only a "descriptive" and not a "normative" character. Moreover, the alleged elevation of the status of evolution from a hypothesis to a theory was indirect and related to contemporary advances in the sciences. In the same speech, however, John Paul II emphasized that, since evolution is a theory, it should explain facts. If it ceases to explain facts, it should be rethought. After all, according to the pope, the theory of evolution is not a single specified theory, but rather a set of different theories, which also have their underlying philosophical assumptions.

Until the end of his pontificate (2005) John Paul II never again commented on evolution, even though the debate among scientists and theologians was ongoing, and growing more and more heated. It would seem then that John

1. By "negative background" we mean here the idea that in some cases science can determine the natural causes of phenomena whereas in other cases it cannot. For example, thunderstorms, mountain elevations, and the movements of celestial bodies today find their explanation in scientific theories; there is no need to resort to supernatural causality. However, in other cases, such as miraculous healings, scientists can only say "we do not know how to explain a given phenomenon." In the negation of a natural explanation, science provides a negative background for faith; that is, it shows where natural, scientific reasoning must give way to other forms of knowledge, such as theology. Regarding the origin of species, scientific research can only show that they appear abruptly in history, do not change over time, and that there are no transitory forms between them in the fossil record. These data do not "prove creation," but point to other ways of explaining their origins, that is, to the theological notion of creation.

Paul II's silence on the matter during the last nine years of his pontificate was intentional. One of the reasons might have been an expectation of more arguments on the part of intelligent design proponents. It is probable that the pope was aware of increasing scientific difficulties regarding Darwinian evolution, and in order not to make premature judgment refrained from taking position.

Cardinal Schönborn's op-ed in *The New York Times* in 2005 started a new ecclesiastical debate on evolution. In his article the Viennese hierarch spoke in favor of design in nature and reminded the reader that the Church had never accepted Darwinian evolution. In a series of catecheses given in the academic year 2005–2006, the cardinal returned in many respects to evolutionary views, especially regarding the origin of man. Those statements, though, should not be seen as an acceptance of Darwinism but rather as a great apology for the idea of God's plan in the visible world, even if that plan was to be brought about in the course of a long evolution. A similar approach can be seen in the main pronouncements by Pope Benedict XVI, although in the span of his entire theological activity Joseph Ratzinger proposed a few somewhat different opinions regarding the question of origins. Pope Benedict remained true, however, to the following two ideas: First, the theory of evolution needs to have clearly defined boundaries and cannot become a general theory regarding everything. When it transcends its competences to explain reality, it becomes the enemy of faith and seeks to annihilate it. The pope did not define, however, where that necessary boundary lies. Second, Benedict reiterated on numerous occasions that the world is not the result of chaos or contingent natural events—a belief that constitutes an inherent element of mainstream evolutionary theories. Instead, the world is a work of a higher reason or Logos, even if it emerged as a result of ongoing evolution. In this sense the pope allowed theistic evolution, though without explicit negation of the classical concept of creation.

It is worth noting that the encyclical *Humani Generis* was the only relevant document of the highest rank published during the second period of ecclesiastical teaching on evolution (after 1950). And while up until 1950 the rank of the pronouncements had been relatively high (and those were pronouncements rejecting the theory), after 1950 this trend dramatically lessened. Thus Pius XII's encyclical constitutes a turning point in terms of both content and formal significance. The second period has been a time of slow and moderate acceptance of theistic evolution. It may be described in four points:

1. The Church allows scientific research to answer the question of the origin of man, which implies that the theory of evolution might be true.

2. Even though John Paul II considered evolution as something more than just a hypothesis, the Church has never adjudicated whether the theory is true. On the contrary, John Paul II explicitly emphasizes that the theory might cease to explain facts, at which point it would have to be revised.

3. The Church acknowledges the theoretical possibility of reconciling its teachings on faith and morality with the theory of evolution understood as cosmic, chemical, and biological evolution, as well as the origin of the human body from lower animals. At the same time, it teaches the independent and direct creation of the soul of the first and any subsequent human.

4. The Church rejects any theories of evolution that do not recognize the existence of the fundamental rationality of nature. The Church believes that nature acts in a purposeful manner and that the rationality therein can be detected with reason alone, without the need to employ supernatural truths revealed by faith.

These four points indicate that the Church allows the emergence of the universe as posited within the theory of natural cosmic evolution. They also mean, therefore, that the world might have been formed by secondary causes only, without God's supernatural work. That view, referred to in the literature as "theistic evolution," claims that God created matter in a single act, and then "conducted evolution" to create new beings. The world, thus, is subject to God's general Providence, but God does not intervene in natural processes. Consequently, different species, as well as the body of the first man, resulted from the operation of laws of nature, although the detailed explanation of those laws is, as of now, unknown. This vision of natural history was maintained in the document *Communion and Stewardship*, signed by Joseph Ratzinger, at that time prefect of the Congregation for the Doctrine of the Faith.

Still, we are speaking here of a "moderate," and not a "complete" or "simple," acceptance of theistic evolution. This is because there are three reservations regarding the presented doctrine.

1. The Church has never formally rejected alternative views on the creation of the world, including progressive creationism or even young earth creationism. A Catholic thus may, with clear conscience, question evolution from a scientific point of view. But if he rejects the scientific theory of evolution, there is no reason to accept the theological concept of theistic evolution. Even though theistic evolution was endorsed in *Communion and Stewardship*, that document is not part of the Church's Magisterium (it has only an auxiliary nature). And in the teachings of the popes, the concept is accepted only as a "possibility."

2. As was noted by Bishop Andreas Laun, acknowledging that a scientific theory does not contradict faith does not make the theory true. Therefore, the Church leaves open the possibility of a future revocation of the theory of evolution and of a revision of her own doctrine on creation.

3. It is still unclear how to harmonize scientific macroevolutionary theories in biology with purpose and design embedded in nature as postulated by the doctrine of the Church. Since the 1980s we have observed the emergence of numer-

ous proposals of how to reconcile the randomness of Darwinian explanations with purpose in natural order, but none of them seems sufficient.[2] Therefore, despite the growing number of declarations that there is no discordance between faith and evolution, there definitely remain important questions to settle.

There have been over a dozen ecclesiastical documents that in a direct or indirect manner refer to the issue of evolution. Direct references may be noted in the encyclical *Humani Generis*; the speech by John Paul II to the Pontifical Academy of Sciences (1996); John Paul II's catecheses in the years 1985–1986; the pronouncement of the Synod of Cologne (1860); a speech made by Pius XII to the attendees of the First International Symposium on Medical Genetics (1953); a document of the International Theological Commission, *Communion and Stewardship* (2004); the Vienna catecheses of Cardinal Schönborn; and condemnations of pro-evolutionary books.

Indirect references to evolution can be found in those documents that present positive doctrine regarding the manner of human creation. Apart from older pronouncements, such as Pope Pelagius's confession of the faith (557) and the teachings of the Council of Vienne (1312), the group includes modern documents: Leo XIII's encyclical *Arcanum* (1880), the pronouncement of the Synod of Cologne (1860), and Pope Pius XII's address to the Pontifical Academy of Sciences (1941). All the texts propagating this positive doctrine of the Church spoke of the direct and supernatural creation of the bodies of our first parents, thus ruling out evolution by implication.

Yet another, separate, group consists of documents discuss the interpretation of Genesis. A document of key importance here is the 1909 decree of the Pontifical Biblical Commission on the historicity of the first three chapters of the Book of Genesis. In the same category is a much later document from the Pontifical Biblical Commission, *The Interpretation of the Bible in the Church* (1993). The former talks about the necessity of maintaining the literal interpretation of the Book of Genesis in relation to the creation of man; the latter, in turn, allows the application of a wide variety of different critical and interpretive methods to the

2. Among the most important attempts, one may list the theory of panentheism presented by Arthur Peacocke in *Theology for a Scientific Age* (Cambridge: Basil Blackwell, 1990). The issue is addressed also in J.F. Haught, *Deeper than Darwin: The Prospect for Religion in the Age of Evolution* (Boulder, CO: Wetsview Press, 2003); idem, *The Cosmic Adventure: Science, Religion and the Quest for Purpose* (Ramsey: Paulist Press, 1986); idem, *Science and Religion: From Conflict to Conversation* (Mahwah: Paulist Press, 1995); John Polkinghorne, *Science and Theology* (Minneapolis/London: Fortress Press/SPCK, 1998); idem, *Faith, Science and Understanding* (New Haven: Yale University Press, 2000); Keith Ward, *God, Chance and Necessity* (Oxford: Oneworld, 1996); *In Whom We Live and Move and Have Our Being: Panentheistic Reflections on God's Presence in a Scientific World*, ed. Ph. Clayton, A. Peacocke (Grand Rapids, MI, and Cambridge: Wm. B. Eerdmans Publishing Co., 2004). Other theories were presented by F.R. Ellis (followed by J. Zycinski, *Wszechswiat emergentny*, 21–24); Ian G. Barbour, in *When Science Meets Religion* (San Francisco: Harper, 2000); and S.M. Barr, in *The Design of Evolution*, et al.

text. Pro-evolutionary authors often quote the latter document to justify a figurative interpretation of Genesis 2:7, thereby contradicting the pronouncement of 1909. But the 1909 document was issued before the status of the Pontifical Biblical Commission was changed, and thus it belonged to the teaching office of the Church. Documents issued after 1971, such as *Interpretation of the Bible in the Church*, are not the part of ecclesiastical Magisterium; therefore, they must be interpreted within the limits defined by the *Responsa* from the beginning of the 20th century.

Finally, we shall attempt to juxtapose "pro-evolutionary" ecclesiastical pronouncements with those that are "anti-evolutionary," and compare their levels of theological certainty. Each "pro-evolutionary" pronouncement may support evolution either directly, by claiming as certain that God used evolution when creating the world, or indirectly, by only allowing such a possibility. Similarly, "anti-evolutionary" pronouncements may rule out evolution either directly or only indirectly—namely, by presenting the opposite approach (that of direct creation) in a positive manner. Among "pro-evolutionary" pronouncements, the only document that seems to teach about evolution in a positive manner is *Communion and Stewardship* (2004), issued by the International Theological Commission. Yet the document is only auxiliary to the Church's teaching office. Any other documents that can be deemed "pro-evolutionary" allow evolution only as a possibility. Among "anti-evolutionary" documents, in turn, we may find those that rule out evolution explicitly (e.g., the pronouncement of the Synod in Cologne and all condemnations of books favoring theistic evolution), as well as those that do so implicitly (e.g., Leo XIII's encyclical *Arcanum*, the 1909 decree of the Pontifical Biblical Commission on the historicity of the Book of Genesis 1–3, and Pius XII's 1941 address to the Pontifical Academy of Sciences).

Taking into consideration the levels of theological certainty as defined in the document *Donum Veritatis*,[3] we note that none of the Church pronouncements allowing evolution can be considered as infallible or definitive teaching. In contrast, "anti-evolutionary" documents are rooted in the authentic tradition of the Church, expressed in, among others, Pelagius I's *Solemn Profession of the Faith* (557) or the teaching of the Council of Vienne (1312).

3. *Donum Veritatis* (in *AAS* 80 [1990], 1550–70), an instruction on the Ecclesial Vocation of Theologians published by the Congregation for the Doctrine of the Faith in 1990, contained a new approach to qualifying theological theses. According to *Donum Veritatis* there are four degrees of theological certainty of the pronouncements issued by the Magisterium: 1. Pronouncements made in a definitive way; 2. authentic and infallible teaching of the Magisterium on what concerns morality; 3. neither infallible nor definitive teaching of the successors of the Apostles deepening the understanding of Revelation in matters of faith and morals; 4. magisterial decisions in matters of discipline prudently and conditionally settling disputes. In the previous approach theology had recognized seven degrees of certainty of theological statements (*notae theologicae*) and six censures—that is, degrees of fallacy (*censurae theologicae*).

Conclusion

Contemporary debate in the Church is characterized by pluralism of opinions regarding an understanding of creation. To introduce some order to the discussion, we will define three basic models of the interdependence of science and revelation that can be found in contemporary theology:

Model A	Model B	Model C
Revelation	Revelation	Revelation
progressive creationism	theistic evolution	theistic evolution
theory of intelligent design	Darwinian evolution	theory of intelligent design
science	science	science

The word "science" in the chart above designates knowledge acquired by reason through experimental research concerning the physical universe. Revelation, located at the top of this chart, designates supernatural knowledge; made available to humans by God, first and foremost in Holy Scripture; and relating to the origin of the world and humanity. Science and revelation cannot contradict each other, since, as the faith claims, the book of Nature and the book of Revelation ultimately have the same source. They come from God and they speak of one created reality. Therefore, there must be a perfect concordance between scientific knowledge and supernatural knowledge. The three models show how contemporary theologians are attempting to achieve that unity:

Model A: implies that facts observed in nature are best interpreted by the theory of intelligent design, while the best interpretation of the Genesis account is given by the concept of progressive creationism. Intelligent design and progressive creationism remain in full concordance because the design could have been introduced into nature by direct and supernatural works of God.

Model B: implies that Darwinian evolution is the best interpretation of natural facts, while theistic evolution is the best interpretation of Genesis. This model closely describes the position of, for example, Archbishop J. Zycinski or George Coyne, S.J. Popes John Paul II and Benedict XVI pointed to the difficulty of this model, which is due to the incompatibility between theistic evolution and Darwinian evolution. There is no harmony here, because one natural process cannot be at once both chaotic and teleological, random and purposeful. Nevertheless, recent popes did not explicitly condemn this approach.

Model C: implies that intelligent design is the best interpretation of natural facts, while theistic evolution constitutes a possible interpretation of the Book of Genesis. This model was first introduced at the end of the 19th century by Anglican bishop Frederick Temple (he did not, of course, employ the term "intelligent design" in its contemporary understanding, but in a more general meaning). There is a certain level of concordance between theistic evolution and intelligent design. Such a model is deemed acceptable by some ID theorists. It would seem that the teachings of recent popes (John Paul II, Benedict XVI, and Francis) are closest to this particular model. Its difficulty, however, lies in the evolutionary interpretation of the Genesis account.

All three models contain common elements, as well as elements that make them mutually exclusive. Therefore, by adopting model A, one rules out models B and C, etc. At the same time, they are all currently allowed in Catholic theology. This means that the teaching of the Church is not specified; rather, it accepts completely different, even contradictory, ideas about creation.

Pluralism of opinions has a positive influence on the development of the debate. Unfortunately, a significant number of the most influential theologians treat the issue as if evolution were already an established "dogma." Meanwhile, the evidence of Tradition, as well as contemporary science, again pose the question regarding formation of the world. Did God create matter and energy, with laws pursuant to which, under God's Providence, everything incessantly evolves, heading towards the "Omega Point," towards ultimate self-realization? Or rather, did God create the world, and then during six days decorate it (St. Ambrose), that is, add the bounty of new natures, like a painter multiplying the beauty of creation with each stroke of a brush? And after He completed the act of formation on the seventh day He took His rest, and this is when the history of salvation started, a history in which God also acts, albeit in a different manner. These questions often take a more specific form: Did man evolve from a lower "living matter" (Pius XII) or was he rather formed directly by God from the dust of earth? Was Eve Adam's monovular twin in the womb of the most developed hominid, which had not yet passed the threshold of humanity (J. Zycinski), or did God make Adam fall asleep and take out his rib, from which He Himself formed the first woman, who is the "bone of his bones" (Gen. 2:23)? So far the natural sciences have not provided answers to these questions. What is more, it is very doubtful that the natural sciences are capable of providing such answers at all. We are thus left with theology. If we take into consideration how difficult it has sometimes been in history for the Church to establish certain truths, one may conclude that also in this case the Church, led by the unfailing inspiration of the Holy Spirit, will in future discover the whole truth and will present it in the form of a relevant dogma.

Appendix:

Two Views on the Origin of the Human Body

To understand the theological dispute about human origins we need first to define the two different approaches that have been present in the Church for over a hundred years. The first approach may be defined as "traditional" and the second as "evolutionary."

The Traditional Approach

The traditional approach is the one that prevailed in the Church from virtually her beginning until the mid-twentieth century. It consists of two crucial ideas—special creation of the first human body from the dust of the earth, and derivation of the first woman from Adam's side. Contemporary scholars supporting the evolutionary approach claim that the traditional approach was not well established in the Church, and that the Church Fathers did not understand these two truths literally. If this were the case, the evolutionary approach would not contradict the traditional teaching. Besides, if these truths were not considered truths belonging to the faith, they could be overturned by later scientific discoveries. Therefore, my first task is to show that the Church Fathers (as well as later holy doctors and theologians) indeed understood these two truths literally, i.e., as the real and historical way man emerged. Secondly, we will show that they maintained that these truths belong to the faith and, as such, are immutable.

The first author to whom we shall refer is St. Irenaeus (†202). His testimony is the more important as he was the disciple of Bishop Polycarp, in turn the disciple of St. John the Apostle, the disciple of Christ. The theology of Irenaeus comes from before the synthesis of biblical interpretation with Platonic philosophy. Hence, through Irenaeus, we gain insight into the original understanding of the biblical account, fashioned in the Hebrew rather than the later Greek framework. The main work of Irenaeus, *Adversus Haereses*, provides an overview of dozens of erroneous ideas about God, the world, and the human being, which as early as the second century had already attempted to contaminate Christianity. With regard to the origin of man Bishop Irenaeus writes:

> The protoplast himself Adam, had his substance from untilled and as yet virgin soil *for God had not yet sent rain, and man had not tilled the ground* (Gen 2:5), and was formed by the hand of God, that is, by the Word of God, for *all things were made by Him* (John 1:3), and the Lord took dust from the earth and formed man; so did He who is the Word, recapitulating Adam in Himself, rightly receive a birth, enabling Him to gather up Adam [into Himself], from Mary, who was as yet a virgin. If, then, the first Adam had a man for his father, and was born of human seed, it were reasonable to say that the second Adam was begotten of Joseph. But if the former was taken from the dust, and God was his Maker, it was incumbent that the latter also, making a recapitulation in Himself, should be formed as man by God, to have an analogy with the former as respects His origin. Why, then, did not God again take dust, but wrought so that the formation should be made of Mary? It was that there might not be another formation called into being, nor any other which should [require to] be saved, but that the very same formation should be summed up [in Christ as had existed in Adam], the analogy having been preserved.[1]

It follows not only that God created the first human body from dust, but also that this truth is closely related to the truth of Jesus's formation in the womb of Mary by the power of the Holy Spirit. If Adam had been created differently, according to Irenaeus, the analogy Adam–Jesus presented by St. Paul (Rom 5:19–21) would be invalidated, and this would also challenge the dogma of the virginal birth of Jesus. Thus, Irenaeus connected the divine origin of Jesus with the belief in the direct formation of Adam's body.

This kind of reasoning was known in the earlier theology as an *analogia fidei*: the belief that some truths of faith can be derived by analogy from others. The removal of one truth of faith would cause collapse of others, because they all constitute a kind of net, a *nexus mysteriorum*. From these principles (*analogia fidei, nexus misteriorum*) it follows that if the human body's formation from clay is only a figure of speech, then Jesus's formation in Mary's womb by God is also just a figure. But the Church understands Jesus's formation by supernatural power of the Holy Spirit not as a mere metaphor, but as a true, physical, and historical event. Therefore, in Irenaeus's view, Adam's formation from clay should also be understood literally and historically. Elsewhere Irenaeus presented another analogy (*analogia fidei*):

> That [God] is powerful in all these respects, we ought to perceive from our origin, inasmuch as God, taking dust from the earth, formed man. And

1. Irenaeus, *Adversus haereses*, Book III, ch. 21, n. 10 (PG, t. 7/1, c. 954–955). Quotation after: *The Ante-Nicene Fathers*, vol. 1, *The Apostolic Fathers with Justin Martyr and Irenaeus*, ed. A. Roberts, J. Donaldson (New York, NY: Cosimo 2007), 454; online edition: www.ccel.org/ccel/schaff/anf01.html (March 5, 2015)

> surely it is much more difficult and incredible, from non-existent bones, and nerves, and veins, and the rest of man's organization, to bring it about that all this should be, and to make man an animated and rational creature, than to reintegrate again that which had been created and then afterwards decomposed into earth (for the reasons already mentioned), having thus passed into those [elements] from which man, who had no previous existence, was formed.[2]

This passage again proves that the bishop of Lyons did not understand the creation of man from the dust of the earth as a metaphor but as the actual way in which Adam's body was formed. In addition, this manner of Adam's creation proves the omnipotence of God, because only God could have created all parts of the human body from nothing. The formation of man is depicted here as the opposite of decomposition—man returns to the earth after death in the same way as the first man was formed out of dust. Again, Irenaeus justifies one truth of faith, namely resurrection of the body, with another—immediate creation of the first human body. Since God had once already formed the human body out of dust, how much easier it will be for Him to restore the same body from ashes to life! Using this analogy, Irenaeus argues for the resurrection of bodies, on the basis of a proper understanding of the origin of the first human body.

In another place Irenaeus criticizes the doctrines of the Gnostics Saturninus and Basilides, who claimed:

> [Man] was accordingly formed [by angels], yet was unable to stand erect, through the inability of the angels to convey to him that power, but wriggled on the ground like a worm. Then the power above taking pity upon him, since he was made after his likeness, sent forth a spark of life, which gave man an erect posture, compacted his joints, and made him live.[3]

There is a striking similarity on essential points between the ancient Gnostics and modern theistic evolutionists. According to both, the human body was produced not immediately by God but by "secondary causes," such as angels (as the Gnostics held) or "evolutionary processes" (as contemporary theistic evolutionists hold). In both doctrines, the "living matter"—that is, some kind of bizarre or lame animal, currently called a "hominid"—receives a "spark" from heaven that transforms it into a fully human being.

In the same spirit as St. Irenaeus spoke Cyril of Jerusalem (†387). Arguing against the Jews, who rejected the truth of the virginal birth of Jesus, he argues:

> But let us take what is yet a greater wonder than this. For that bodies should be conceived, even if wonderful, is nevertheless possible: but that the dust of

2. Ibid., Book V, ch. 3, n. 2; PG, vol. 7/2, c. 1129.
3. Ibid., Book I, ch. 24, n. 1; PG, vol. 7/1, c. 674.

> the earth should become a man, this is more wonderful. That clay molded together should assume the coats and splendors of the eyes, this is more wonderful. That out of dust of uniform appearance should be produced both the firmness of bones, and the softness of lungs, and other different kinds of members, this is wonderful. That clay should be animated and travel round the world self-moved, and should build houses, this is wonderful. That clay should teach, and talk, and act as carpenter, and as king, this is wonderful. Whence, then, was Adam made? Did not God take dust from the earth, and fashion this wonderful frame? Did not God taking dust from the earth wonderfully fashioned this figure? Is then clay changed into an eye, and cannot a virgin bear a son. So what? Clay is transformed into an eye, and the virgin will not beget the son? What is more impossible according to human judgment yet happened and what is possible in itself could not have happened?[4]

We see that St. Cyril is not using metaphorical language here. He speaks about clay as the material out of which the members of the human body were formed. About the origin of Eve, Cyril writes:

> Of whom in the beginning was Eve begotten? What mother conceived her without female mother? The Scripture says that she was made out of Adam's side. Is Eve then born out of a man's side without a mother, and is a child not to be born without a father, of a virgin's womb?[5]

Just like Irenaeus, St. Cyril backed up the truth of the virginal conception of Jesus with the truth of the origin of Adam. If Cyril had taken metaphorically the description of the creation of Eve from Adam's side, then the formation of Jesus in Mary's womb should be considered merely a metaphor too. Instead, Cyril's starting point was the obvious notion (for him and for the Jews) of Eve being molded from Adam's side. The argument had an *a fortiori* logic—if something more difficult (i.e., the formation of man from dust or of woman from Adam's side) had been accomplished by God, and we believe in this, why could God not accomplish something less difficult, like the formation of Jesus in Mary's womb, and why should we not believe in it? Cyril and Irenaeus considered the virginal conception of Jesus to be something "less difficult" because God did not need to create any new species, but only an individual of the previously created human species. God could have molded Jesus from clay, as in the case of Adam, but then the human nature of Jesus could be doubted. Thus, to show us that Jesus has a truly human nature and that no new species can arise after creation has been completed, Jesus is born of a human female: Mary.

St. Gregory of Nyssa (†394) also had no doubts regarding the immediate creation of the first human body:

4. Cyril of Jerusalem, *Catechesis XII*, 30, PG, t. 33, c. 763.
5. Ibid. *Catechesis XII*, 29, ibid., c. 761.

> If it had been simply written: He made, you would think that man had been made as were the wild beasts, the sea monsters, the plants, the grass; but so that you may understand that thy nature is superior to that of the other beings, Moses explained God's proper and singular art in thy creation: God took dust from the earth. He said what God had done, and then he added how He had done it: He took dust from the earth and of it He formed man with His own hands.[6]

St Gregory's words contradict the contemporary claim that the creation account says only *that* God created the world, but it does not say anything about *how* He did it. According to the contemporary claim, the Bible tells us only that the human species had a temporal beginning sometime in the ancient past, but it does not say anything about the way the human body emerged. This approach was completely foreign to the Church Fathers. As we see in the quoted fragment, Gregory of Nyssa found an answer to the question of *how* in Genesis and, for him, it was *the way* of human emergence, namely the "proper and singular art of creation," which constitutes the exceptional dignity of humans.

Likewise, St. John Chrysostom († 407) had no doubts that the first man emerged through an immediate and supernatural formation out of the dust of the earth:

> God formed man taking dust from the earth. See also in this the honor given. He did not take anything else from the earth but dust, the least thing on the earth, as it were, and by His command He changed that dust of the earth into the nature of the body. In the same way as He produced the very substance of the earth, when it did not exist, so now, by His will, He changes dust of the earth into a body.[7]

Chrysostom does not speak metaphorically in this passage. He speaks of the dust God had taken in terms of the material that served to make man. He underlines that God "had not taken anything else but dust." Moreover, Chrysostom compares the creation of the human body to the creation of matter in the act of *creatio ex nihilo.* The later scholastic tradition would speak about three supernatural acts of God in human emergence: (1) the creation of matter out of nothing in the beginning of time; (2) the formation of the human body out of dust of the earth; and (3) the infusion of the soul, which is the form of the living body. All three acts are supernatural and no secondary causes are involved in them.

Another Father who confirms this Christian understanding of human origins is St. Cyril of Alexandria († 444):

6. Gregory of Nyssa, *Oratio II*; PG, t. 44, c. 281.
7. John Chrysostom, *Homily XIII*, n. 1–2; PG, vol. 53, c. 105.

> Since God created this world in such wonderful harmony, He also enriched our nature with various benefits: first He made that which was not, and having formed it, He honored it: He changed the dust, at His will, into the nature of man, and to the common clay He gave beauty and, at the same time, the soul.[8]

And similarly, St. John Damascenus (†749):

> [God] creates with His own hands man of a visible nature and an invisible, after His own image and likeness: on the one hand man's body He formed of earth, and on the other his reasoning and thinking soul He bestowed upon him by His own inbreathing [...]. Body and soul were formed at one and the same time, not first the one and then the other.[9]

And

> The earliest formation [of man] is called creation and not generation. For creation is the original formation at God's hands, while generation is the succession from each other made necessary by the sentence of death imposed on us on account of the transgression.[10]

In the first quotation, St John Damascenus speaks in unequivocal terms about earth as the substrate out of which the human body is made. He also claims that body and soul were created at the same time, which clearly contradicts the modern idea of the body being prepared by evolution and an ultimate infusion of the soul. In the second quotation, Damascenus distinguishes between direct creation of the first man and man's later generation by parents. In the first creation human nature comes immediately from God, and his body is formed out of the ground. Every subsequent human being is created directly by God regarding his soul, but regarding his body is created indirectly, through generation. It is obvious that since the first human body did not come about through generation, but through creation, the Damascene's view excludes human descent from any animal ancestor.

Ephrem the Syrian (†373)[11] and Tertullian (†ca. 220)[12] wrote in the same vein. St. Ambrose (†397) in turn also testified that the creation of Eve from

8. *De Incarnatione Domini II*, PG, vol. 75, c. 1420.

9. *De Fide Orthodoxa*, Book II, ch. 12, PG, vol. 94, c. 920.

10. Ibid., ch. 30, PG, vol. 94, c. 975.

11. "Formed as was this man [namely, the body of Adam, having been composed of red slime] it was animated and constituted with ineffable power, and then decorated with a vestige of the Holy Spirit: we could not have been enriched with the divine image in any other manner." St. Ephraem Syri, *In Genesis II* in *Opera Omnia*, vol. 1 (Rome: 1787), 133.

12. "And God formed man the clay of the ground. He now became man, who was hitherto clay. And He breathed upon his face the breath of life, and man (that is, the clay) became a living soul; and God placed the man whom He had formed in the garden. [...] The clay, therefore, was obliterated

Adam's side is not a metaphor, but indicates the true manner of how the first woman came into existence:

> This is not indeed in vain: that woman does not derive from the same earth from which Adam was molded, but from a rib of the same Adam; so that we might know that the nature of the body in man and in woman is single, and the fount of human nature is but one.[13]

St. Jerome (†397) explicitly states that the supernatural beginning of Adam is a truth of faith:

> Now what I say is just this: does anyone believe in God the Creator? He cannot believe unless he first believes that to be true which is written of His Saints: that Adam was fashioned by God, that Eve was made out of a rib and from his side, that Enoch was translated. [...] He who does not believe all these things and the others that have been written about the Saints, will not succeed in believing in the God of the Saints.[14]

It is worth quoting one more testimony, by a lesser-known Church author of ancient times, which confirms our claim that belief in the direct formation of Adam was common in early Christianity. As St. Peter, bishop and patriarch of Alexandria, martyred in 311, asserts:

> Now we have thought it necessary to explain the things which pertain to the first man, who is of earth and earthy, being about, namely, to demonstrate this, that he was created at the same time one and the same, although sometimes he is separately designated as the man external and internal. For if, according to the Word of salvation, He who made what is without, made also that which is within, He certainly, by one operation, and at the same time, made both, on that day, indeed, on which God said: Let us make man in our image, after our likeness (Gen 1:26). Whence it is manifest that man was not formed by a conjunction of the body with a certain pre-existent type. For if the earth, at the bidding of the Creator, brought forth the other animals endowed with life, much rather did the dust which God took from the earth receive a vital energy from the will and operation of God.[15]

According to St. Peter, it is manifest that man was not formed by conjunction of the body with a certain pre-existent type. This means that none of the species that already existed could serve as any form or prototype to make the

---

and absorbed into flesh. When did this happen? At the time that man became a living soul by the inbreathing of God—by the breath indeed which was capable of hardening clay into another substance, as into some earthenware, so now into flesh." *De Ressurectione Carnis*, PL, vol. 2, c. 801–804.

13. Ambrose, *De Paradiso*, cap. X, 48, PL, vol. 14, c. 298.

14. Jerome, *In Epist. ad Phm.*, PL, vol. 26, c. 609.

15. *Of the Soul and Body*, in *The Writings of the Fathers Down to A.D. 325*, vol. 6: *Ante-Nicene Fathers*, ed. by A. Roberts, J. Donaldson (Peabody: Hendrickson Publishers, 1995), 283.

human body. On the contrary, according to the saint, if the earth brought all animals at the bidding of the Creator, it is even more fitting that dust taken by God from the earth became a living body by God's "will and operation." St. Peter underlines two truths: that it was dust of the earth that was used by God, and that this event happened instantaneously at God's command.

An important testimony of Catholic orthodoxy from the end of the Patristic period is the confession of faith pronounced by Pope Pelagius I (†561). The papal creed is not just the opinion of one theologian, but a solemn profession of Church doctrine. The pope first pronounced it in a letter to King Childebert I (February 3, 557), and then repeated it in the letter *Vas electionis*, addressed to the entire Church. Pelagius writes:

> I confess [...] that all men from Adam onward who have been born and have died up to the end of the world will then rise again and stand before the judgment-seat of Christ, together with Adam himself and his wife, who were not born of other parents, but were created: one from the earth and the other from the side of the man.[16]

Thus in his confession of faith the pope excludes the possibility of polygenism and confirms the direct creation of man according to both the body and the soul. It is all the more clear because he excludes the possibility of the first man having descended from a parent (*qui non ex aliis parentibus nati sunt, sed alter de terra, altera autem de costa viri creati sunt*).[17]

In medieval times the same doctrine was clearly taught by the Scholastics. For example, St. Albert the Great (†1280) teaches:

> We must say that as regards the body of the first man—according to both the teachings of the Saints and the Catholic Faith—neither was it proper nor could it have been made except by God Himself.[18]

16. Cf. DS 443. Cf. Denzinger-Schönmetzer, *Enchiridion Symbolorum Definitionum et Declarationum*, ed. 34 (Freiburg: Herder, 1967), 155, no 228a.

17. Pro-evolution scholars could try to reinterpret the papal creed in order to make it compatible with the evolutionary origin of the human body. According to the most common claim, the human body evolved from lower animals, but the soul was separately created (the concept called "special transformism"). Pope Pelagius I says that our first parents were not born of other parents. However, the evolutionary hypothesis does not claim that they were born of parents (which implies human ancestors), but from animals, like the hominids, that were used only as matter (preexistent living matter) for the infusion of the human soul. At first glance the pope did not exclude this option. However, if we read the whole sentence, we see that Pelagius juxtaposes "being born of parents" and "being created from earth and rib." It is obvious that in this context the papal words must be interpreted literally, as referring to the material out of which the first humans were created. It is even more obvious if we consider what the pope could have had on his mind—for obviously he wanted to exclude any other way of human emergence than creation from earth.

18. Albertus Magnus, *Sum. Theol.* p. II tract. 13, q. 75, *In II Sentent*, dist. XVIII, a 2, in *Opera Omnia*, vol. 27 (Parisiis: 1894), 312–313.

The holy doctor makes it clear that there were no secondary causes in the formation of the human body—it was made by God himself. In turn, St. Bonaventure (†1274) explains the miraculous way of woman's beginning:

> One might doubt that woman was created from the rib by the same miracle as the multiplication of five loaves and others. You have to clearly say that the formation of woman was miraculous.... Woman was miraculously created from a rib, not because it happened against the ordinary course of nature or against nature, but because it was done by God's power acting beyond nature.... The chief reason why God formed Eve in that way is really twofold: first, because that way of forming her is above the power of nature; second, in order that man should, in both sexes, have as his direct goal and as the object of his entire love Him by whom he knows himself to be directly made.[19]

Bonaventure sees the origin of woman as a miracle, that is, as an event that happened not according to any laws of nature but through a special divine activity working beyond nature. The holy doctor explicitly states that this way of forming woman, namely from Adam's rib, was beyond the power of nature. Thus both man and woman were made *directly* by God. This truth has also a theological significance: Because both sexes were made directly by God, both sexes refer their entire love to God as their Maker. In another place Bonaventure describes the origin of man:

> True faith teaches us to hold the following about the human body in the original state of creation. The body of the first man, formed out of the dust of the ground, was created subject to the soul and proportioned to it in its own way.[20]

Firstly, the saint says that the formation of man is a matter of faith. But if it is a matter of faith, it cannot be disproved by any scientific investigations. Secondly, he says that the human body was fashioned from the dust of the ground in such a way that it was from the beginning proportioned to receive the human soul. This truth is independently confirmed by metaphysical reasoning, whereby this particular body may be animated only by this particular soul.

The decrees of the Council of Vienne (1311–1312) also shed some light on human origins. The council employs another analogy of faith to explain the origin of the Church based on the origin of Eve:

> [We openly profess] that in this assumed nature the Word of God ... permitted his side to be pierced by a lance, so that from the outflowing water

19. St. Bonaventure, *In Secundum Librum Sentent.* Dist. XVIII, a. 1, q. 2; a. 2, q. 3, in *Doctoris Seraphici S. Bonaventurae Opera Omnia*, vol. 2 (Quaracchi: 1885), 454; cf. 436–437.

20. *Breviloquium*, Pars 2, cap. 10, in *Opera Omnia*, vol. 5, 227–228.

> and blood there might be formed the one, immaculate and holy virginal mother church, the bride of Christ, as from the side of the first man in his sleep Eve was fashioned as his wife.[21]

Conciliar teaching is the highest authority of the Church and cannot be considered fallible.[22] The only way this teaching could be reconciled with the evolutionary story would be through a highly metaphorical interpretation of the phrase "as from the side of the first man in his sleep Eve was fashioned." But this kind of interpretation is hard to accept because the very wording points to a literal interpretation (the event happened during Adam's sleep) and because the conciliar fathers did not understand this account of woman's emergence metaphorically.

Next, there is a quite detailed teaching on human origins from the two greatest Doctors of the Church—St. Augustine and St. Thomas Aquinas. St. Augustine's authority has often been invoked by supporters of the evolutionary approach, and St. Thomas Aquinas is regularly cited because his doctrine is a synthesis of many centuries of tradition in theology and philosophy. In a few of his works, St. Augustine treats of the truth about the origin of man. In *On Genesis against the Manichees* (*De Genesi contra Manichaeos*), he accuses the Manicheans of failing to comprehend how the human body was formed from the dust of the earth, and how on this basis they exclude the original immortality of man:

> These enemies of the books of the Old Testament, looking at everything in a fleshly, literal-minded way, and therefore always getting everything wrong, are in the habit of commenting sarcastically even on this point, that God fashioned man from mud. What they say is: Why did God make man from mud? Did He not have anything better, celestial material for example, from which to make man, so that He was reduced to making him, so fragile and mortal, from the muck of the earth?[23]

Furthermore, St. Augustine asks:

> What in any case was so strange or difficult for God, even if He did make man from the mud of this earth, about contriving a body for him that would not have been subject to decay, had man kept God's commandment and not been willing to sin? After all, if we say that the beauty of the sky itself was

21. Council of Vienne, Decrees, 1, DS 901; http://www.dailycatholic.org/history/15ecume4.htm (March 7, 2015).

22. Rev. B. Harrison convincingly argues that this conciliar statement establishes the creation of Eve from Adam's side as a solemn teaching of the Church. See: B.W. Harrison, "Did Woman Evolved from Beasts? A Defense of Traditional Catholic Doctrine," *International Catholic Symposium on Creation, October* 24–25, 2002, *Rome, Italy* (Kolbe Center: 2002), 161.

23. *De Genesi contra Manichaeos*, II, 7, n. 8, PL, vol. 34, c. 200.

> made from nothing or from unformed material, because we believe its Craftsman to be all-powerful, what is so odd about the possibility of the body, which was made from any sort of mud you like, being made by the all-powerful Craftsman of such a kind that before man's sin it would never cause him any trouble or excruciating pain?[24]

In the same book, St. Augustine comments on Gen 2:7 ("And the Lord God formed man of the slime of the earth: and breathed into his face the breath of life, and man became a living soul"). Here he considers three accounts of man's origin. According to him, the biblical text should be interpreted as stating that there was a clay model of man, and God infused the soul into that body. The soul might have been created previously, but existed in God's mouth, i.e., in Truth or Wisdom, or it might have been created at the moment of infusion into the body. It might also have been that man was created already possessing both soul and body, and then the Divine breath "activated" the soul itself, thus making man "a living soul."[25] In each of these solutions, St. Augustine assumes the formation of a clay substrate of the human body, and the enlivening of the existing model.

In his most extensive commentary on Genesis (*De Genesi ad litteram*), St. Augustine writes, interpreting the same verse (Gen 2:7):

> *God formed the man dust of the earth or mud of the earth*—that is, from dust or from mud of the earth—*and breathed, or puffed, into his face the breath of life, and man was made into a living soul* (Gen 2:7). He was not then predestined, because that was done before all ages in the foreknowledge of the creator; nor then causally either started in his finished completeness or finished completely at the starting stage, because that was done at the start of the ages

24. Ibid. There is a striking similarity between some Manichean claims and contemporary Christian evolutionists' statements. Manicheans found it impossible for God to have formed the body from the dust of the earth and made it immortal. As J. Zycinski writes: "It is hard to resort to fantastic suppositions that any of our ancestors had had any possibility of avoiding biological death." What is most probably meant here is spiritual death, as there is no reason to consider a variant of evolution precluding biological death (*Wszechświat emergentny* [*Emergent Universe*], 120). For Zycinski, the evolutionary origin of man would have excluded the possibility of his biological immortality. In this view, man was never immortal, and the death mentioned in the Bible should only be interpreted as spiritual death. However, the *Catechism of the Catholic Church* states that "As long as he remained in the divine intimacy, man would not have to suffer or die" (376, cf. 402, 418, 1008).

25. "[I]f he was still only a body, we must understand the soul being joined to the body in this place, whether it had already been made but was so to say in God's mouth, that is, in his Truth or Wisdom, or whether it was made at the moment when God blew the spirit of life into that clay model; in this case God's so doing would signify his actual work of making the soul in the man by the spirit of his power. If on the other hand the man who had been made was already body and soul, God's breathing into him added sensation to the soul itself when the man was made into a living soul—not that God's breathing was turned into the living soul, but that it got to work on the living soul" (*De Genesi contra Manicheos*, II, 8 n. 10, op. cit., c. 201).

> in the primordial ideas when all things were created simultaneously; but he was then created in his own time, visibly in the body, invisibly in the soul, consisting as he does of soul and body.[26]

Augustine, then, adheres to a theory of formation adopted from the Stoics and Neoplatonists, who proposed that everything had been made in the beginning in the form of primordial reasons or causal principles (Latin *rationes seminales*, Greek *logoi spermatikoi*). The theory was supposed to address the philosophical problem with which he had struggled while analyzing the creation account from Genesis. Augustine finds it difficult to harmonize two truths—that God created various things successively, in a chronological order, which the Bible calls the six days, and that God is perfect and all He makes is perfect. In Augustine's mind, the temporal succession in creation associates with the emanationist concepts of pagan philosophy and seems to make God's work imperfect. This is why he looks for a metaphysical model for the Christian interpretation of the Book of Genesis, which would help him avoid pagan errors. The idea of primordial reasons (*rationes seminales*) seems to answer the problem of the perfectness of God's creative activity while also leaving room for the gradual appearance of all new things, including man.[27]

Nevertheless, this concept and its underlying assumption that God had created all things simultaneously according to their kinds are not in harmony with Darwinian evolution. In Augustine there is no emergence of one species from another, eventually forming the "tree of life" presented by Darwin. Nor does Augustine mention the natural (based on secondary causes), gradual emergence of any nature. In his view the laws of nature might have revealed some natures, but generated none of them. As regards the direct formation of man from the dust of the earth, Augustine is even more certain than in the case of other creatures:

> On the sixth day man was made to the image of God, made indeed, male and female. . . . They will ask me: In what way later on? I will answer: visibly, with the appearance of the human constitution as we know it—not however born of parents, but he from mud, she from his rib.[28]

And:

> But in what manner did God make him [Adam] from the mud of the earth? Was it straightaway as an adult, that is, as a young man in the prime of life? Or was it as he forms human beings from then until now in their mothers'

26. *De Genesi ad litteram* VI, 12, n. 22, PL, vol. 34, c. 348.

27. Cf. M. Fiedrowicz, Introduction to *Saint Augustine: On Genesis* (New York: New City Press, 2002), 19–20.

28. *De Genesi ad litteram*, VI, 6, n. 10, c. 343.

wombs? There is no one else, after all, who does this but the one who said, Before I formed you in the womb, I knew you (Jer 1:5), so that the only thing proper to Adam was that he was not born of parents but made from earth."[29] Conclusion: "Adam was not made otherwise when he was formed from mud already in adult manhood" (*perfectae virilitatis*).[30]

Augustine, similarly to other Church Fathers, juxtaposes the generation and the creation of man. According to him, the first man was not born, but made by God from earth in a perfect form, that is, as an adult, not an embryo. His vision therefore excludes the theistic evolutionists' concept of the first man being supernaturally formed in the womb of the last hominid. The Bishop of Hippo presents the same doctrine in *The City of God* (*De civitate Dei*). When discussing the manner of man's creation, he writes:

> When God had formed man out of the dust of the earth, [...] He made also a wife for him, to aid him in the work of generating his kind, and her He formed of a bone taken out of the man's side, working in a divine manner. For we are not to conceive of this work in a carnal fashion, as if God wrought as we commonly see artisans, who use their hands, and material furnished to them, that by their artistic skill they may fashion some material object. God's hand is God's power; and He, working invisibly, effects visible results. But this seems fabulous rather than true to men, who measure by customary and everyday works the power and wisdom of God, whereby He understands and produces without seeds even seeds themselves; and because they cannot understand the things which at the beginning were created, they are skeptical regarding them—as if the very things which they do know about human propagation, conceptions and births, would seem less incredible if told to those who had no experience of them; though these very things, too, are attributed by many rather to physical and natural causes than to the work of the divine mind.[31]

In this fragment Augustine confirms that man was made from dust and woman from Adam's side. Interestingly enough, he says that woman was given as an aid to generate his kind, which implies that one kind cannot generate another, but always generates the same kind. Some, however, do not believe that man was made in this way. And to them Augustine replies that the same people would not believe in how a human is conceived and born, if they didn't

29. "Sed quomodo fecit eum Deus de limo terrae; utrum repente in aetate perfecta, hoc est virili atque juvenili, an sicut nunc usque format in uteris matrum? Neque anim alius haec facit, quam ille qui dixit, Priusquam te formarem in utero, novi te (Jr 1:5): ut illud tantum proprium habuerit Adam, quod non ex parentibus natus est, sed factus ex terra" (ibid., VI, 13, n. 23).

30. Ibid., VI, 18, n. 29.

31. *De civitate Dei*, XII, 23, PL, vol. 41, c. 373.

know it from their own experience. Therefore, Augustine understands formation of the first man from earth and the first woman from Adam's rib literally.

We also find in Augustine a quite explicit answer to the idea that natural generation can mutate an individual in such a way that it finally becomes a new species. This idea constitutes the core of Darwin's theory. At one point Darwin wrote: "Natural selection can act only by the preservation and accumulation of infinitesimally small inherited modifications, each profitable to the preserved being; and as modern geology has almost banished such views as the excavation of a great valley by a single diluvial wave, so will natural selection, if it be a true principle, banish the belief of the continued creation of new organic beings, or of any great and sudden modification in their structure."[32] Augustine, in contrast, was certain that the accumulation of minor changes in a given species would never lead to the emergence of an entirely new nature:

> For the same divine and, so to speak, creative energy, . . . gave their roundness to the eye and to the apple; and the other natural objects which we anywhere see, received also their form, not from without, but from the secret and profound might of the Creator. . . . I attribute the creating and originating work which gave being to all natures to God. . . . And although the various mental emotions of a pregnant woman do produce in the fruit of her womb similar qualities—as Jacob with his peeled wands caused piebald sheep to be produced—yet the mother as little creates her offspring as she created herself. Whatever bodily or seminal causes, then, may be used for the production of things, either by the cooperation of angels, men, or the lower animals, or by sexual generation; and whatever power the desires and mental emotions of the mother have to produce in the tender and plastic fœtus corresponding lineaments and colors; yet the natures themselves, which are thus variously affected, are the production of none but the most high God.[33]

32. Ch. Darwin, *The Origin of Species*, 95–96.

33. *De civitate Dei*, XII, 25, c. 374. The idea of the universe having itself possibly participated in creation was also addressed by St. Augustine: "We have nothing to do with those who do not believe that the divine mind made or cares for this world. As for those who believe their own Plato, that all mortal animals—among whom man holds the pre-eminent place, and is near to the gods themselves—were created not by that most high God who made the world, but by other lesser gods created by the Supreme, and exercising a delegated power under His control—if only those persons be delivered from the superstition which prompts them to seek a plausible reason for paying divine honors and sacrificing to these gods as their creators, they will easily be disentangled also from this their error. For it is blasphemy to believe or to say (even before it can be understood) that any other than God is creator of any nature, be it never so small and mortal. And as for the angels, whom those Platonists prefer to call gods, although they do, so far as they are permitted and commissioned, aid in the production of the things around us, yet not on that account are we to call them creators, any more than we call gardeners the creators of fruits and trees." Ibid., XII, ch. 24.

Thus, according to Augustine, none of the changes in generation, whether caused by nature or by angels, can produce entirely new species. Even though Augustine does not mention natural selection, the core of his argument excludes Darwin's idea of random variations as the source of advantageous novelty that if subjected to natural selection would ultimately lead to the emergence of new species.

Thomas Aquinas held a similar view on the origin of man. He discusses the direct creation of the first human body in *Summa Theologiae*, questions 91 and 92. In the first article of question 91, Aquinas asks if the body of the first man was made from the clay of the earth (*de limo terrae*). Answering in the affirmative, he explains why it was not made from fire or water, or heavenly bodies, or other substances regarded in his time as more perfect than earth. In the next article he argues that the human body had been made directly by God, without the aid of any other powers—neither of heavenly bodies (which in the Middle Ages were regarded as higher efficient causes of natural processes), nor of angels:

> The first formation of the human body could not be by the instrumentality of any created power, but was immediately from God.... Now God, though He is absolutely immaterial, can alone by His own power produce matter by creation: wherefore He alone can produce a form in matter, without the aid of any preceding material form. For this reason the angels cannot transform a body except by making use of something in the nature of a seed.... Therefore as no pre-existing body has been formed whereby another body of the same species could be generated, the first human body was of necessity made immediately by God.[34]

In the same article, St. Thomas admits that angels might have provided some assistance in the creation of man—gathering the required dust of the earth in the appropriate place, just as they will gather human ashes in the proper place before the resurrection. Therefore, Aquinas excludes the action of created causes (secondary or instrumental) in the formation of the human body. The exclusion of higher causes (both material and spiritual) is an argument *a fortiori* against the participation of mutation and natural selection, which fall into the category of accidental physical (lower) causes.[35]

Aquinas also refers to St. Augustine. According to the bishop of Hippo, man—as regards his body—was made at the beginning in the form of some primordial reason. Thomas comments on this view: "But what pre-exists in the

34. *S.Th.*, I, 91, a. 2, corp.

35. In question 92, Thomas writes further: "The natural generation of every species is from some determinate matter. Now the matter whence man is naturally begotten is the human semen of man or woman. Wherefore from any other matter an individual of the human species cannot naturally be

corporeal creature by reason of causal virtues can be produced by some corporeal body. Therefore the human body would be produced by some created power, and not immediately by God."[36] Next, Thomas—elaborating upon Augustine's view—states that a primordial reason may exist in creatures in two ways: (1) it may take the form of both active and passive potency—which applies to things that can be made by a previously existing being; or (2) it can possess the passive potency only—and this, according to Augustine, was the form it took in the human body. Therefore, the body could have only been made by God.[37] Apparently, Aquinas suspends the question of the correctness of Augustine's idea as such, because, even if one accepts Augustine's view consistently and entirely, it does not deprecate the idea of God's direct creation of man from clay. This is because, in the concept of *rationes seminales* (whatever this should signify), the body only exists in the potency to come into being—and a passive potency at that—thus requiring direct divine action in order to become actual.

Furthermore, commenting on Genesis 2:7 ("And the Lord God formed man of the slime of the earth: and breathed into his face the breath of life, and man became a living soul"), Thomas excludes two mistaken views on the origin of man. One of them assumes that God first made the human body and only later infused a soul. The claim that God created a body without a soul or a soul without a body would stand in conflict with the perfection of the first creation, as both are part of human nature. Meanwhile, the prevailing modern theological doctrine about the origin of the human body assumes that God added a soul to a body which he had earlier "prepared" in the course of evolution. This view is directly refuted by Aquinas. The other fallacious opinion argues that God created the body and the soul simultaneously, and the words about the "breath of

generated. Now God alone, the Author of nature, can produce an effect into existence outside the ordinary course of nature. Therefore God alone could produce either a man from the slime of the earth, or a woman from the rib of man" (*S.Th.*, I, 92, a. 4, corp.). And: "Matter is that from which something is made. Now created nature has a determinate principle; and since it is determined to one thing, it has also a determinate mode of proceeding. Wherefore from determinate matter it produces something in a determinate species. On the other hand, the Divine Power, being infinite, can produce things of the same species out of any matter, such as a man from the slime of the earth, and a woman from out of man" (ibid., 92, a. 2, ad 2).

36. Cf. *S.Th.*, I, 91, a. 2, 4. In the same article, Thomas also writes that the movement of the skies (which means natural causation) is the cause of natural changes, but not such that occur in spite of nature: "The movement of the heavens causes natural changes; but not changes that surpass the order of nature, and are caused by the Divine Power alone, as for the dead to be raised to life, or the blind to see: like to which also is the making of man from the slime of the earth" (ibid., a. 2, ad 3).

37. "Secondly, in passive potentiality only; that is how pre-existing matter can be produced by God. And in this sense, according to Augustine, the human body pre-existed in the previous work in their causal virtues" (*S.Th.*, I, 91, a. 2, ad 4).

life" refer to the gift of the Holy Spirit. However, according to Thomas (following Augustine), such an approach is excluded by the biblical text. The words about the breath of life do not refer to the spiritual life but to the animal life (*non ad vitam spiritualem, sed ad vitam animalem refert*). How, then, should this verse be interpreted? Thomas states that "by breath of life we must understand the soul, so that the words: He breathed into his face the breath of life are a sort of exposition of what goes before; for the soul is the form of the body."[38] In this way, Thomas solves the problem of the substantial unity of form and matter in the human being: there is no time when the body can exist without a soul, although the body itself was formed from clay by the power of God, and subsequently transformed into a living human body in the strict sense, which emerged at the moment of being connected to the independently created soul.

The doctrine of Thomas Aquinas on creation was confirmed in the 20th century by Pope Pius X in his motu proprio *Doctoris Angelici*:

> The opinion of certain ancients is to be rejected which maintains that it makes no difference to the truth of the Faith what any man thinks about the nature of creation, provided his opinions on the nature of God be sound, because error with regard to the nature of creation begets a false knowledge of God; so the principles of philosophy laid down by St. Thomas Aquinas are to be religiously and inviolably observed, because they are the means of acquiring such a knowledge of creation as is most congruent with the Faith of refuting all the errors of all the ages, and of enabling man to distinguish clearly what things are to be attributed to God and to God alone.[39]

We learn from the papal document that the teaching on the nature of creation is not accidental to faith. On the contrary, it influences our image of God. In the context of the modern discussion about creation and evolution, this principle means that our account of God's creation of nature also influences our understanding of God's nature. For example, if one believes that God worked in nature only through secondary causes (indirectly), the image of God in his thinking would differ from the one we get when believing in God's supernatural and direct causation in the formation of the universe. According to the pope, "error with regard to the nature of creation begets a false knowledge of God." The pope encourages us to observe the philosophical principles of Aquinas, because they are most congruent with faith and help refute all errors. In saying this, the pope also highlights the fact that Aquinas's teaching enables us to clearly define what things should be attributed to God alone. And according to Aquinas, the formation of the human body could only be the work of God.

38. *S.Th.*, I, 91, a. 4, ad 3.
39. *AAS*, 6 (1914), 337.

Therefore, the papal document implicitly supports the idea that the human body was formed supernaturally by God from the dust of the earth.

The concept of the direct formation of the human body developed over the centuries in Catholic theology. Francisco Suarez, representing the period of late Scholasticism, witnessed the reception of medieval thought in the 16th- and 17th-century Church. This *doctor eximius* (doctor exceptional and pious), as Benedict XIV has called him, precisely articulated the thought of his times:

> I am speaking about that body as it was then made and prepared for the reception of the soul. When a man is formed by way of natural generation, the organization of the body and its orderly arrangement are the result of the natural power at work in generation. But, natural propagation apart, such a result cannot come from any created agency whatever, whether elemental, or celestial, or from all of them together. In the first man, obviously, the organizing of the body was not produced by natural generation; its author, therefore, could be none but God alone.[40]

Again, we see that the theologian distinguishes two ways in which the human body has emerged. One is through natural generation, which applies to every newly born man; the other applies uniquely to the first man alone, in whom the organization of the body was not from natural generation but directly from God.

According to the principles of the development of theology, the truth about the direct formation of the human body by God's power was specified in various ways by the theologians of subsequent centuries. By the second half of the 19th century, the traditional concept had reached its mature form. Cardinal Camillo Mazzella (1833–1900) believed that the emergence of man assumed three moments of supernatural divine action: (1) the creation of matter; (2) the formation of the body; and (3) the infusion of the soul.[41] One of the most prominent theologians of the 19th century, Matthias Joseph Scheeben (1835–1888), whose repeatedly reissued works provided the foundation of the education of the German-speaking clergy, argues in his main work, *Handbuch der Katholischen Dogmatik*:

> As to the body of man, the Church, basing her doctrine on its revealed origin, teaches that it is composed of earthy or material elements; that its organization as a human body is not the result of either chance or the combined action of physical forces, but is formed after a clearly defined Divine Idea, either directly by Divine action, as in the case of the first man, or indirectly through the plastic force of generation. Hence we cannot admit the descent

40. Francisci Suarez, *De Opere Sex Dierum*, lib. III, cap. 1, n. 6 in *Opera Omnia*, vol. 3 (Parisiis: Apud Ludovicum Vivés, 1856), 172–73.

41. C. Mazzella, *De Deo creante*, 4th ed. (Roma: Forzani, 1896), 343–74.

> of man from ape-like ancestors by a process of gradual organic modification, even supposing that God directly created the soul when the organism had acquired a sufficient degree of perfection. Even apart from Revelation, sound philosophy will never admit that such a transformation of the types of organic beings is possible as would be required to arrive at the human organism. The astonishing unity in the immense variety of organisms is conclusive evidence of the Divine Wisdom of the Creator, but it is no evidence whatsoever of a successive transformation of the lower into higher organisms.[42]

Scheeben's position was supported by most theologians at the turn of the century, among them: Cardinal Thommaso Zigliara, Pietro Caterini, Enrico Buonpensiere, Gustave Lahousse, Gabriel Huarte, Giovanni Perrone, Gerard van Noort, and Joseph Pohle.[43] The famous German theologian and historian Christian Pesch wrote in 1908 that

> among the old theologians there was never any doubt in this matter, but rather all of them, for dogmatic reasons, held that Adam was taken from the dust of the earth and Eve from his side. When, therefore, that new theory (namely, moderate transformism) was put forward almost all theologians immediately gave as their judgment that it cannot be reconciled with Catholic doctrine.[44]

Similarly, Michael Hetzenauer, the consultant to the Papal Biblical Commission and professor of biblical exegesis at the Lateran University, claims:

42. Based on the English translation of Scheeben's work: J. Wilhelm, T.B. Scannell, *Manual of Catholic Theology based on Scheeben's Dogmatik*, vol. 1, 4th ed. (London: Kegan Paul, Trench, Trübner, 1909), 397.

43. Th. Zigliara, *Propaedeutica ad sacram theologiam in usum scholarum*, 4th ed. (Roma: S.C. de Propaganda Fide, 1897). P. Caterini, "Come entrino la fede e la teologia nella questione trasformistica," *La Civiltá Cattolica* 11, no. 3 (1880), 279–80. On the teaching of E. Buonpensiere cf. Chapter Two, under "The Intervention of the Congregation of the Index." G. Lahousse, *De Deo creante et elevante* (Bruges: Beyaert [et al.], 1904). G. Huarte, *De Deo creante et elevante* (Roma: Universitá Gregoriana, 1935). Lahousse and Huarte believed that the truth of direct creation cannot be called either *de fide definita* or *de fide catholica*, but is *de fide divina* (it is not defined as a truth of faith but belongs to supernatural faith [ibid., 156]). G. Perrone, *Praelectiones theologice*, vol. 3, *De Deo creatore*, 25th ed. (Mediolani: C. Turati; Genuae: Darius J. Rossi, 1857). Two years before the publication of Darwin's *The Origin of Species*, Perrone stated that the doctrine that the bodies of our first parents had been formed directly by God is an object of faith (ibid., 79). As Van Noort writes: "Adam and Eve, both in body and soul, were formed by God, without the use of evolution. On its own, the expression *special creation of man* used in the decree of the Papal Biblical Commission leaves room for a certain amount of freedom, but the expression *formation of the first woman from the first man* clearly excludes all evolution from Eve's body. However, no reasonable person would accept that Adam's body was made through evolution, while the body of Eve was not." Cf. *Tractatus de Deo Creatore* (Amstelodami: C.L. Van Langenhuysen, 1903), 115. J. Pohle, *Lehrbuch der Dogmatik* (Paderborn: Schöningh, 1905), 424ff. (Last issued in 1952).

44. Ch. Pesch, *Praelectiones dogmatice*, vol. 3, *De Deo creante et elevante. De Deo fine ultimo*, 6th ed. (Friburgi Brisgoviae: Herder, 1925), 87.

> [T]he opinion of the transformists—according to which the body of some species of brute beast became so perfect, by continual evolution, as to be apt to receive the rational soul, and thence that Adam's body was not formed immediately from the slime of the earth, but only mediately, in that God infused the rational soul into one of the brute beasts originally formed from the earth—is contrary both to the constant tradition of the Church and to the clear doctrine of Holy Scripture.[45]

Achilles Ratti, later Pope Pius XI, addresses the issue of the origin of man in his doctoral thesis *De hominis origine quoad corpus*, (*The Origin of Man Regarding the Body*). He proves that according to divine revelation our first parents (both in body and soul) were created by God himself, not through some kind of "cooperation," but by virtue of a direct and simple act. With respect to the body, however, the divine action was not strictly creative (meaning *ex nihilo*), as God used the dust of the earth he had previously created from nothing.[46] Moreover, the opinion of the evolutionary origin of the human body was explicitly rejected by Hurter, Bartmann, Egger, Palmieri, Janssens, Dupasquier, Berti, Hugo, and others.[47]

What was probably the last Catholic theology textbook to present the special creation of the human body as Church teaching was published in 1952 in Spain. The authors, Spanish Jesuits, devote twenty-nine pages to the classical doctrine. They criticize the evolutionary approach and argue—based on Church documents—that evolutionism applied to the human body is unmaintainable. The authors also evaluate the meaning of scientists' attempt to disprove that truth:

> Natural sciences (biology, paleontology) offer their own contribution to solving the issue of human origin. If it was solidly confirmed by means of scientific evidence that the human body is the result of evolution, then theologians would undisputedly have to acknowledge this fact. However, the evolution of man is far from being absolutely determined; in reality it remains merely a hypothesis, and a highly inconceivable one, as even scholars themselves maintain. Among them are to be found some who refute it ada-

45. M. Hetzenauer, *Annotationes de formatione terrae hominisque atque de modo diluvii* (Roma: Pontificio Seminario Romano Maggiore, 1925), 13 and 17.

46. A. Ratti, *De hominis origine quoad corpus*. This work was later used by Father F. Sala as the basis for dogmatic lectures; it was published as *Institutiones positivo-scholastice theologiae dogmaticae*, 5th ed. (Mediolani: ex Typografia pontificia S. Josephi, 1899), 197–211. The primary thesis of the future pope reads: "As it follows from Revelation, the first parents, not only regarding their souls, but also their bodies, were created by God alone. Not simply through the concourse [the cooperation and accidental convergence] of created causes, but through direct and immediate action, though not creative. (*Constat ex divinis revelatione, primos parentes non modo quoad animam, verum etiam quoad corpus, conditos fuisse ab ipso Deo, non per simplicem concursum, sed per actionem directam et immediatam, licet non creativam*)."

47. Cf. E. Ruffini, *The Theory of Evolution Judged by Reason and Faith*, 137.

mantly, whereas others are willing to regard it as to some extent likely, or perhaps find it obscure, or at least not more probable than the other conflicting ones. Since this theory cannot be granted any scientific validation, scholars would not only be obliged to surmount all the obstacles connected with transformism, but would also have to prove that the first man could not have been conceived in any other manner.[48]

The authors recognize the role of science in settling the question of human origin. They nevertheless claim that, even if all scientific and philosophical problems in the evolutionary hypothesis were resolved, this would still not be enough to disprove special creation. In other words, simply presenting an alternative scientific explanation to the theological concept of creation does not inevitably invalidate the theological concept of creation. What scientists would need to do, according to the Spanish Jesuits, is to prove that any other way of human emergence, such as special creation, is not possible. This, however, is impossible within the scientific enterprise. We can see, therefore, that the authors implicitly deny the capacity of science to disprove special creation.

Taking into account this great cloud of witnesses, we may conclude that, at least until the early 20th century, direct creation of the first human body was commonly accepted as the ordinary Magisterium of the Church. However, something then began to change in Catholic doctrine. Over the next thirty years, the assessment of Cardinal Mazzelli, who wrote that "the ones currently calling themselves transformists are in vain trying to overturn or deprecate this most certain truth,"[49] would be proved false.

The Evolutionist Approach

In modern times the animal origin of man was first proposed by Thomas H. Huxley (1863), and subsequently by Ernst Haeckel (1868) and Charles Darwin (1871).[50] Among Catholic theologians, this claim provoked questions about Tradition, Church doctrine, and the interpretation of the biblical account of creation. In earlier times, figurative readings of Genesis 1–2 were endorsed by, for example, Tommaso de Vio (also known as Gaetani or Cajetan, 1469–1534), though there is no proof that he would have accepted the evolutionary origin of

48. Cf. I.M. Dalmau, I.F. Sagüés, *Sacrae theologiae summa*, vol. 2 (Madrid: Biblioteca de Autores Cristianos, 195[illegible]), 506–34.

49. "Primi parentes, prout ex divina revelatione constat, non modo quoad animam, sed etiam quoad corpus, immediate a Deo conditi sunt. . . . Quam certissimam veritatem frustra evertere aut infirmare nituntur qui nunc audiant Transformisti." C. Mazzella, *De Deo creante*, 353–54.

50. T.H. Huxley, *Evidence as to Man's Place in Nature* (London: Williams and Norgate, 1863); E. Haeckel, *Natürliche Schöpfungsgeschichte* (Berlin: G. Reimer, 1868); and *Anthropogenie oder Entwickelungs-geschichte des Menschen* (Leipzig: Verlag von Wilhelm Engelmann, 1874); C. Darwin, *The Descent of Man.*

Adam's body.[51] Cajetan's opinion was adopted by a known exegete and initiator of many modern trends in biblical studies—Joseph Marie Lagrange (1855–1938). Other exegetes, such as Franz von Hummelauer and Gottfried Hoberg,[52] believed that it is indeterminable whether Eve was really made from Adam's rib or this was just a figurative way of speaking. According to Hummelauer, Augustine also had doubts on the issue. However, the two views of the origin of the body of the first woman (creation vs. evolution) are so similar that—according to the German exegete—they are both acceptable. Some scholars thought it possible to recognize such an interpretation of the creation of Adam, which would permit the evolutionary origin of his body; but in the case of Eve, the literal description would have to be accepted.[53]

As we have seen (Chapter Four), the first Catholic to formulate a thesis about the possibility of reconciling the evolutionary origin of man and Christianity was the British biologist St. George Mivart.[54] Afterwards, the same thesis was promoted by Dalmace Leroy, O.P. and Father John A. Zahm. Henri Dorlodot spoke about the compatibility of Darwinism and Catholicism in general, and the matter of the origin of man was most extensively developed by Rev. Ernest Messenger. The latter's main work, *Evolution and Theology* (1932), was subtitled *The Problem of Man's Origin,* and indeed two-thirds of the book was an attempt to harmonize the evolution of man with Holy Scripture, the doctrine of the Holy Fathers and Doctors, Scholastic theologians, and Church decrees. Messenger writes:

> If we consider this question simply from the point of view of abstract possibility, then it is difficult to see on what grounds we could deny to God the power to produce elementary organisms able to act as instrumental causes in

51. "Cogor ex ipso textu et contextu intellegere hanc mulieris productionem, non ut sonat littera, sed secundum mysterium, non allegoriae, sed parabole" (In Gen. 2:21). After: M. O'Connor, "Rhetoric and the Literary Sense: The Sacred Author's Performance in Cajetan's Exegesis of Scripture" in *Faithful Performances: Enacting Christian Tradition,* ed. T.A. Hart and S.R. Guthrie (Aldershot: Ashgate, 2007), 114.

52. F. von Hummelauer, *Commentarius in Genesim* (Parisiis: Sumptibus P. Lethielleux, 1908), 150. G. Hoberg, *Die Genesis* (Freiburg im Breisgau: Herder, 1908), 36. Hummelauer refers to the early commentary by Augustine, *De Genesi contra Manicheos* (2,12,17). Commenting on Hummelauer's stance, Cardinal Ruffini states that the Fathers were unanimous in interpreting the text on the creation of Eve in the strict, literal sense. Even if we agree that St. Augustine had some doubts in his early commentary (which Ruffini rejects), he explains them in his later works. Cf. Ruffini, *Evolution Judged by Reason and Faith,* 121–22.

53. E.g., W. Schmidt, who was the editor of *Anthropos.* His opinion is quoted in A. Lemmonyer, *La Révélation primitive et les données actuelles de la science d'apres l'ouvrage allemandé du R.P.G. Schmidt* (Paris: Gabalda, 1914), 137.

54. A relevant fragment of his writings was quoted when discussing Mivart's views (ch. II, 2, a). However, this short assertion was the only statement by Mivart in which he accepted the evolution of the body, and the thread was not developed further in his book.

> the production of man, more or less as this power is possessed by the sexual elements, but with the difference that in the case of the former the seminal power would reach its term only after a series of successive generations and mutations. In such a hypothesis, nothing would happen by chance or accident in the eyes of God, whose Providence governs all things.[55]

One might say that Messenger expresses the essence of the modern theistic evolutionary understanding of the origin of man. According to this view, the main force generating the human body is embedded in the material element—seeds or genes—which, under the influence of various more or less random circumstances, was transformed over the course of many generations into a body similar or identical to that of a human. However, from the theological point of view, the whole evolutionary process was subject to general divine providence. When the material substratum reached an appropriate degree of self-organization, God infused it with a directly created, immaterial soul. Messenger described this process in the following way:

> It is God who truly acts throughout, and when a secondary cause acts, God concurs in the effect and makes it to be produced by the secondary cause, in the measure in which it is possible for a secondary cause to produce. Now, in order that human generation should arrive at its term, that is to say, in order that a new human nature shall be produced, it is necessary that a new soul should be created. In this precise act of the creation of a spiritual and immortal soul, no created being can participate as an efficient cause properly so called.... The condition required for human generation, namely, the creation of the immortal soul, proceeds from the Divine activity alone, without any intrinsic collaboration on the part of the causality of the parents.[56]

Nevertheless, as regards the creation of Eve, Messenger accepts her direct formation from the body of Adam: "It is our considered and definite belief that Eve was really formed from Adam. In other words, the *formatio primae mulieris ex primo homine* is literally true, as affirmed by the Biblical Commission. Indeed, this is so certain and so clearly taught both in Scripture and Tradition that it may well be *de fide*."[57] The standpoint accepting the evolutionary origin of Adam but also the direct formation of Eve from Adam's side seemed most unreasonable and unjustified to Cardinal Ernesto Ruffini, who even called it an absurdity.[58] Therefore, as time passed, the majority of evolutionary theologians rejected Messenger's reservation, deciding that Eve was not physically taken

55. E. Messenger, *Evolution and Theology*, 91.
56. Ibid., 89–90.
57. Ibid., 252.
58. E. Ruffini, *Evolution Judged by Reason and Faith*, 123.

from Adam, but rather in the way "an image is taken from a model."[59] This metaphor, however, explained nothing from the biological or historical point of view.

The evolutionary generation of Adam's body became the most developed thread within the framework of theistic evolution. Most Catholic evolutionists accepted—after Messenger—the fact of an "ontological leap" that had occurred upon the infusion of a rational soul. For instance, Messenger thought that we cannot speak of any gradual evolution of consciousness of the first people. This was quite different from the views of Darwin and Haeckel, who classified the human races, identifying them as more and less developed according to their physical or mental capabilities.[60] For Haeckel, peoples differ in intellectual capacity according to the current evolutionary stage of their race. Haeckel, indeed, even speaks of many human species. Messenger, on the other hand, believes that if

> we introduce the moral or ethical point of view, then it must be admitted that there is a serious difficulty, not precisely against the origin of man by natural evolution considered in the abstract, but against the account of this origin as it is generally set forth by evolutionists. This applies especially to their ideas about the slow development of human mentality. Even from the merely philosophical point of view, it would seem difficult to believe that for many centuries and according to the primary intention of nature there could have existed a series of intelligent beings incapable of choosing their own end.[61]

However, Messenger failed to see that the problem of hominization starts not when the creation of the human soul is questioned, but immediately after the classical doctrine regarding the origin of the human body is abandoned. Thus there appeared in the evolutionary view a certain divergence between atheists

59. Such was the standpoint presented by, e.g., Father Charles Hauret. Cf. idem, *Origines de l'univers et de l'homme d'après la Bible* (Paris: J. Gabalda, 1950), 237.

60. In his second book (*Natürliche Schöpfungsgeschichte*, 1868), published three years before Darwin's *The Descent of Man*, Haeckel identifies 22 intermediate stages in the lineage of man, from Monera to "ape-men" to "man-apes" to humans. Furthermore, within the category of "human species" he identifies twelve races, each representing a different stage of evolution. See E. Haeckel, *The History of Creation* (New York: Appleton and Company, 1887), 2:308n. The considerations of Haeckel, Huxley, and Darwin gave rise to the later concepts of racism, eugenics, and euthanasia in Europe and the USA. The existence of a strict ideological and historical correlation between Darwinism and Nazism was proved, e.g., by R. Weikert, particularly in his *From Darwin to Hitler: Evolutionary Ethics, Eugenics and Racism in Germany* (New York: Palgrave Macmillan, 2004). Darwin himself stated prophetically in 1871: "At some future period, not very distant as measured by centuries, the civilized races of man will almost certainly exterminate, and replace, the savage races throughout the world." Ch. Darwin, *The Descent of Man*, 2: 201.

61. *Evolution and Theology*, 92.

and theists concerning an "ontological leap" in the emergence of human exceptionality. Consequently, atheistic evolutionists did not accept the equality of human beings, whereas theistic evolutionists attempted to defend the thesis that the animal nature was substantially changed when it was "hominized." As Messenger argues:

> If we pass from philosophical considerations to the theological hypothesis generally received today that Adam was constituted in the state of sanctity and justice from the first moment of his existence, then we may safely conclude that God would certainly have caused the virtuality existing in nature to produce a human being with fairly high mental development, without passing through the phases of inferior humanity supposed by Darwin and the evolutionists generally. If Adam was capable of sinning gravely, then he must have had the organism of a real *homo sapiens*.[62]

On this occasion, Messenger does not even hesitate to use the expression "special influence of the First Cause" in the formation of man, provided that this term does not rule out the operation of secondary causes. However, it is easy to notice that Messenger's view contains a certain aporia. On the one hand, it assumes the natural origination of man through evolution, while on the other it accepts divine intervention, the sudden improvement of nature, and, in his own words, "the acceleration of evolutionary development."[63] Eventually he even states that, so far, there had been no convincing proof that man had actually evolved.[64]

Messenger's view led to troublesome questions about the borders between the operation of God and the operation of nature (as well as between God and nature as such), and between the soul and the body. It is thus no surprise that

62. Ibid., 93. The author also asserts that "It is [truth] *de fide* that Adam committed a grave sin, and that he sinned as the head of the human race. He must, therefore, have sinned by a truly human act, that is, by a free act on the part of his will, with the concourse of his higher organic faculties." Ibid., 98.

63. "Divine Providence would have arranged things in such a way that the first human being should possess a brain sufficiently developed, in the adult stage at any rate, to enable its owner to discern between moral good and evil. . . . If this should be thought impossible without the special influence of the First Cause, then it would be best to hold that the First Cause did in fact intervene at the proper time in order to accelerate the development necessary. This supposition would not mean that the virtuality of the human race was no longer found in the organisms from which the first man issued, nor that he did not arise as an effect of this virtuality. For the First Cause has the power of making secondary causes produce their own proper effects in a manner different from the normal." Ibid., 93.

64. Ibid., 275. In sum, Messenger entertains three possible moments of divine intervention in the generation of man: (1) creation of the soul—although he rather regarded it as a manifestation of "ordinary" divine providence; (2) elevation of both the body and the soul to a supernatural status; (3) in the formation of the first human body, although in his opinion science is unable to determine whether this was the case. Ibid., 276.

the lines between supernatural and natural activity indicated by Messenger were perceived by other theistic evolutionists as quite arbitrary. Over time, theistic evolutionists adopted an increasingly "naturalistic" vision of the formation of man, along with a number of phases in the development of pre-human species called hominids.[65]

We may safely conclude that at the end of the 19th century there were two theistic models of the origin of man—one speaking of his direct creation in terms of body and soul, and the other proposing the evolutionary generation of the body and direct creation of the soul. The supporters of the former view argued that it was positively taught by the Church Fathers and Scholastics and endorsed by the documents of the Magisterium. The proponents of the second view argued that there was no conflict between these sources of Catholic doctrine and the evolutionary origin of the first human body. The latter, however, were divided as to the limits of nature's capacity in the formation of Adam's body and the manner of formation of the first woman.

65. This was the standpoint represented by, e.g., Józef Zycinski (J. Zycinski, *Wszechświat emergentny* [*Emergent Universe*], 73–77). It is worth noting that in 1996, John Paul II endorsed the concept of an "ontological leap" that was closer to Messenger's viewpoint. See John Paul II, "Message to Pontifical Academy of Sciences in Connection to the Session 'The origin of life and evolution' of 22 October 1996," in *AAS*, 89 (1997), n. 6.

Bibliography

Abbott, A. "Papal Confession: Darwin Was Right about Evolution." *Nature* (31 October 1996): 393(6603).

Acta et decreta Concilii Provinciae Coloniensis. Coloniae, 1862.

Acta et Decreta Sacrorum Conciliorum Recentiorum: Collectio Lacensis. Volume 7. Freiburg: Herder, 1890.

Allen, J.L. "Benedict's Thinking on Creation and Evolution." *National Catholic Reporter* 6 no. 1 (September 2006). http://www.nationalcatholicreporter.org/word/word090106.htm#one.

———. "Pope Cites Teilhardian Vision of the Cosmos as a 'Living Host.'" *National Catholic Reporter* (28 July 2009); http://ncronline.org/print/14207

———. "Schönborn and Science vs. Theology." *National Catholic Reporter* 41 (22 July 2005); http://www.nationalcatholicreporter.org/word/pfw072205.htm.

Appel, T.A. *The Cuvier–Geoffroy Debate: French Biology in the Decades before Darwin*. Oxford: Oxford University Press, 1987.

A.M. "Das neue Biblische Handbuch." *Benediktinische Monatschrift* 31 (1955): 49–50.

Arber, W., N. Cabibbo, and M.S. Sorondo, eds. *Pontificiae Academiae Scientiarum Acta* 20. Ex Aedibus Academicis in Civitate Vaticana: 2009.

Armachano, I.U. *Annales Veteris Testamenti a prima mundi origine deducti* in *The Whole Works of the Most Rev. James Ussher, D.D.* Vol. 8. Londini: 1650.

Artigas, M., T.F. Glick, and R.A. Martinez. *Negotiating Darwin: The Vatican Confronts Evolution* 1877–1902. Baltimore: John Hopkins University Press, 2006.

Auletta, G., M. Leclerc, and R.A. Martínez, eds. *Biological Evolution: Facts and Theories: A Critical Appraisal* 150 *Years after* The Origin of Species *March* 3–7, 2009. Roma: Gregorian & Biblical Press, 2011.

Axe, D., and A. Gauger. "The Evolutionary Accessibility of New Enzyme Functions: A Case Study from the Biotin Pathway." *Bio-Complexity* 1 (2011): 1–17.

Baldwin, J.T. "God and the World. William's Paley Argument from Perfection Tradition: A Continuing Influence." *The Harvard Theological Review* 85, no. 1 (Jan., 1992): 109–20.

Barbour, I.G. *When Science Meets Religion*. San Francisco: Harper, 2000.

Barnett, S.A. et al., eds. *A Century of Darwin*. London: Mercury Books, 1962.

Barr, S.M. "The Design of Evolution." *First Things* 156 (October 2005): 9–12.

Bartynowski, S. *Apologetyka podręczna: obrona podstaw wiary katolickiej i odpowiedzi na zarzuty*. 1911; reprt. Te Deum, 2001.

Beer, G. de. *Homology: An Unsolved Problem*. Oxford: Oxford University Press,

1971.

Bégouën, H. *Queues souvenirs sure le movement des ideas transformistic dans les milieux catholiques suivi de la mentalité spiritualiste des premiers homes*. Paris: Bloud & Gay, 1945.

Behe, M. *Darwin's Black Box: The Biochemical Challenge to Evolution*. New York: Free Press, 2006.

———. *The Edge of Evolution: The Search for the Limits of Darwinism*. New York: Free Press, 2007.

The Biblical Commission Document "The Interpretation of the Bible in the Church": Text and Commentary. Roma: Editrice Pontificio Instituto Biblico, 1995.

Bishop, B.E. "Mendel's Opposition to Evolution and to Darwin." *Journal of Heredity* 87 (1996): 205–13.

Black, D., P.T. de Chardin, C.C. Young, and W.C. Pei. *Fossil Man in China: The Choukoutien Cave Deposits with a Synopsis of Our Present Knowledge of the Late Cenozoic in China*. Peiping: Geological Survey of China and Section of Geology of the National Academy of Peiping, 1933.

Bonomelli, G. *Seguiamo la ragione*. Milano: 1898.

Bergounioux, F.M., and A. Glory. *Les premiers hommes: précis d'anthropologie préhistorique*. Toulouse: Didier, 1943.

Boyer, C. *Tractatus de Deo creante et elevante*. Roma: Pont. Univ. Gregoriana, 1957.

Brandi, S.M. "Evoluzione e domma." *La Civiltá Cattolica* 17, no. 5 (1898): 34–49.

———. "*Evoluzione e domma*: Erronee informazioni di un Inglese." *La Civiltá Cattolica* 18, no. 6 (1902): 75–77.

Breuil, H., and R. Lantier. *Hommes de la pierre anciene*. Paris: Payot, 1951.

Brooke, J.H. "The Wilberforce–Huxley Debate." *Science and Christian Belief* 13, no. 2 (2001): 127–41.

Brucker, J. "Bulletin Scripturaire." *Études* 28 (Septembre–Decembre 1891): 488–97.

———. "L'origine de l'homme d'après la Bible et le transformism." *Études* 26 (Mai 1889): 28–50.

Caldwell, S. "Pope Sacks Astronomer over Evolution Debate." *Daily Mail* (23 August 2006). http://www.dailymail.co.uk/news/article-401950/Pope-sacks-astronomer-evolution-debate.html

Callender, L.A. "Gregor Mendel: An Opponent of Descent with Modification." *History of Science* 26 (1988): 41–75.

Carroll, W.E. "Creation, Evolution, and Thomas Aquinas." *Revue des Questions Scientifiques* 171, no. 4 (2000): 319–47.

Caruana, L., ed. *Darwin and Catholicism*. London: T&T Clark, 2009.

Catholic Encyclopedia. 15 volumes. New York: The Encyclopedia Press, 1907–1912.

Caterini, P. "Come entrino la fede e la teologia nella questione trasformistica." *La Civiltá Cattolica* 11, No. 3 (1880): 279–80.

———. *Dell'origine dell'uomo secondo il transformismo: Esame scientifico filosofico teologico.* Prato: Giachetti, 1884.

Caverni, R. *De' nuovi studi della filosofia: Discorsi a un giovane studente.* Firenze: Carnesecchi, 1877.

Chaberek, M. "Tomasz z Akwinu a ewolucjonizm: Polemika z tezami P. Lichacza i W.E. Carrolla." *Filozoficzne Aspekty Genezy* (2012); online at http://www.nauka-a-religia.uz.zgora.pl/index.php?action=tekst&id=228

———. *Dell'antichitá dell'uomo secondo la scienza moderna.* Firenze: Cellini, 1881.

Chambers, R. *Vestiges of the Natural History of Creation.* 2nd edition. New York: Wiley and Putnam, 1845.

Chardin, P.T. de. *Christianity and Evolution.* Translated by R. Hague. New York: Harcourt Brace Jovanovich, 1971.

———. *The Heart of the Matter.* Translated by R. Hague. San Diego: Harcourt Brace Jovanovich, 1978.

———. *Man's Place in Nature.* London: Fontana Books, 1971.

———. *The Phenomenon of Man.* Translated by B. Wall. New York: Harper, 1959.

Clayton, Ph., and A. Peacocke. *In Whom We Live and Move and Have Our Being: Panentheistic Reflections on God's Presence in a Scientific World.* Grand Rapids/Cambridge: Wm. B. Eerdmans Publishing Co., 2004.

Cloyd, W. "Vatican Scholars to Include Intelligent-Design Theory in Meeting." *Citizen-Link* (30 August 2006). http://www.discovery.org/a/3724.

Collins, F. *The Language of God.* New York: Free Press, 2006.

Confessore, O. *L'americanismo cattolico in Italia.* Roma: Studium, 1984.

Cowell, S. *The Teilhard Lexicon.* Brighton, Portland: Sussex Academic Press, 2001.

Coyne, G. "God's Chance Creation." *The Tablet* (6 August 2005). http://www.thetablet.co.uk/article/1027

Cuvier, G. *Essay on the Theory of the Earth.* 5th edition. Edinburgh-London, 1827.

Dalmau, I.M., and I.F. Sagüés. *Sacrae theologiae summa*, vol. 2. Madrid: Biblioteca de Autores Cristianos, 1952.

Dalrymple, G.B. *The Age of Earth.* Stanford: Stanford University Press, 1991.

Darwin, C. *The Descent of Man and Selection in Relation to Sex.* London: J. Murray, 1871.

———. *The Life and Letters of Charles Darwin, Including an Autobiographical Chapter.* Volume 2. Edited by F. Darwin. London: John Murray, 1887.

———. *The Origin of Species, by Means of Natural Selection, or the Preservation of Favoured Races in the Struggle for Life.* London: John Murray, 1859.

Darwin, E. *The Temple of Nature or, the Origin of Society: A Poem, with Philosophical Notes.* Baltimore, 1804.

———. *Zoonomia or the Laws of Organic Life.* 2nd edition. Vol. 1. London, 1794.

David, F. [David Fleming]. "Review of Evolution and Dogma." *Dublin Review* 119 (July–October 1896): 245–55.

Dawkins, R. *The Blind Watchmaker.* New York: W.W. Norton, 1986.

———. *Climbing Mount Improbable*. New York: Norton, 1996.

———. *The God Delusion*. New York: Mariner Books, 2008.

Dembski, W. *The Design Revolution*. Nottingham: Inter-Varsity Press, 2004.

———. "The Explanatory Filter: A Three-Part Filter for Understanding How to Separate and Identify Cause from Intelligent Design." http://www.arn.org/docs/dembski/wd_explfilter.htm.

———. ed. *Mere Creation Science Faith and Intelligent Design*. Nottingham: Inter-Varsity Press, 1998.

———. *Remarkable Exchange between Michael Ruse and Daniel Dennett*. http://www.uncommondescent.com.

Denton, M. *Evolution: A Theory in Crisis: New Developments in Science are Challenging Orthodox Darwinism*. London: Burnett Books, 1985.

Denzinger, H., and A. Schönmetzer. *Enchridion Symbolorum, Definitionum, Declarationum*. Freiburg: Herder, 1966.

Descartes, R. *The Principles of Philosophy*. Translated by J. Bennett. http://www.earlymoderntexts.com/pdfs/descartes1644part3.pdf.

Dorlodot, H. *Darwinism and Catholic Thought*. Translated by E. Messenger. London: Burns Oates and Washbourne, 1922.

Dwight, T. *Thoughts of a Catholic Anatomist*. New York, London: Longmans Green & Co., 1911.

Edwards, W. *Des Caractères physiologiques des races humaines considérés dans leurs rapports avec l'histoire, lettre á M. Amédée Thierry*. Paris: Compère Jeune, 1829.

Enchiridion Biblicum. Documenta Ecclesiastica Sacram Scripturam Spectantia: Auctoritate Pontificiae Comissionis de Re Biblica edita. Roma: Apud Librariam Vaticanam, 1927.

Euvé, F. *Darwin et le christianisme: vrais et faux débats*. Paris: Buchet-Chastel, 2009.

Fiedrowicz, M. Introduction to *Saint Augustine: On Genesis*. New York: New City Press, 2002.

Fitzmyer, J.A. *To Advance the Gospel: New Testament Studies*. 2nd edition. Grand Rapids: Wm. B. Eerdmans, 1998.

Flannery, M.A. *Alfred Russel Wallace: A Rediscovered Life*. Seattle: Discovery Institute Press, 2011.

Flew, A., and G.R. Habermas. "My Pilgrimage from Atheism to Theism." *Philosophia Christi* (Winter 2004): 197–212; http://www.epsociety.org/library/articles.asp?pid=33.

Frederick, Lord Bishop of Exeter. *The Relations between Religion and Science: Eight Lectures Preached Before University of Oxford in Year* 1884. New York: Macmillan and Co., 1884.

The Fundamentals: A Testimony to the Truth. 12 volumes. Chicago: Testimony Publishing Company, 1910–1915.

The Fundamentals [abridged]. Grand Rapids: Kregel Publications, 1990.

Gage, L. P. "Can a Thomist Be a Darwinist?" In *God and Evolution*. 187–202. Seattle: Discovery Institute Press, 2010.

———. "Darwin, Design and Thomas Aquinas: The Mythical Conflict between Thomism and Intelligent Design." *Touchstone* 23, no. 6 (Nov/Dec 2010): 23.

Gage, L.P., and R.C. Koons. "St. Thomas Aquinas on Intelligent Design." In *Proceedings of the American Catholic Philosophical Association*, vol. 85 (2011): 79–97.

Gauger, A., D. Axe, and C. Luskin. *Science and Human Origins*. Seattle: Discovery Institute Press 2012.

Giertych, M. *O ewolucji w Parlamencie Europejskim*. Kórnik, 2007.

———. "Papiez o ewolucji." *Opoka w Kraju*, No. 20(41), (December 1996): 1–2.

———. "Wokól ewolucji." *Opoka w Kraju*, No. 22(43), (May 1997): 3–5.

Gilson, E. *From Aristotle to Darwin and Back Again*. Translated by J. Lyon. Notre Dame: Notre Dame University Press, 1984.

Glick, T. F. *What about Darwin?* Baltimore: The John Hopkins University Press, 2010.

González de Arintero, J. T. *La evolución y la filosofía Cristiana: Introducción general y Libro primero, La evolución y la mutabilidad de las especies orgánicas*. Madrid: Librería de Gregorio del Amo, 1898.

Gould, S. J. *Rocks of Ages: Science and Religion in the Fullness of Life*. New York: Ballantine Books, 1999.

———."Smith Woodward's Folly." *New Scientist* (5 April 1979): 42–44.

Granat, W. Dogmatyka. *Bóg Stwórca; Aniołowie—Człowiek* (Lublin: TN KUL 1961).

Greene, J.C. *Darwin and the Modern Worldview*. Baton Rouge: Louisiana State University Press, 1961.

Grison, M. *Problémes d'origines: L'univers Les vivants. L'homme*. Paris: Letouzey et Ané, 1954.

Guibert, J. *Les Origines, questions d'apologétique. Cosmogonie. Origine de la vie, origine des espèces, origine de l'homme. Unité de l'espèce humaine. Antiquité de l'espèce humaine. État de l'homme primitive*. Paris: Letouzey et Ané, 1896.

Haeckel, E. *Anthropogenie oder Entwickelungs-geschichte des Menschen*. Leipzig: Verlag von Wilhelm Engelmann, 1874.

———. *Last Words on Evolution*. Translated by J. McCabe. London: A. Owen, 1906.

———. *Monism as Connecting Religion and Science*. Translated by J. Gilchrist. London: Adam and Charles Black, 1894.

———. *Natürliche Schöpfungsgeschichte*. Berlin: G. Reimer, 1868.

Halaczek, B. "Ewolucja pogla dów teologicznych na ewolucje." *Slaskie Studia Historyczno-Teologiczne* 31 (1998): 17–25.

Harrison, B.W. "Early Vatican Responses to Evolutionist Theology." *Living Tradition* 93 (May 2001). http://www.rtforum.org/lt/lt93.html

Haught, J. F. *The Cosmic Adventure: Science, Religion and the Quest for Purpose*.

Ramsey: Paulist Press, 1986.
———. *Deeper than Darwin: The Prospect for Religion in the Age of Evolution.* Boulder, CO: Westview Press, 2003.
———. *God after Darwin: A Theology of Evolution.* Boulder: Westview Press, 2000.
———. *Science and Religion: From Conflict to Conversation.* Mahwah: Paulist Press, 1995.
Hauret, Ch. *Origines de l'univers et de l'homme d'aprés la Bible.* Paris: J. Gabalda, 1950.
Hedley, J.C. "Dr. Mivart on *Faith and Science.*" *Dublin Review* (July–October 1887): 401–19.
———. "Physical Science and Faith." *Dublin Review* 123 (July–October 1898): 241–61.
Heneghan, T. "Pope to Debate Evolution with Former Students." *Reuters* (30 August 2006).
Henke, R. "Aufrecht aus den Baumen." *Focus* 39 (1996): 178.
Hennenberg, M. "Brain Size/Body Weight Variability in *Homo Sapiens*: Consequences for Interpreting Hominid Evolution." *Homo* 39 (1990): 121–30.
Hess, P.M.J., and P.L. Allen. *Catholicism and Science.* Westport: Greenwood Press, 2008.
Hetzenauer, M. *Annotationes de formatione terrae hominisque atque de modo diluvia.* Roma: Pontificio Seminario Romano Maggiore, 1925.
Hilbert, M. "Darwin's Divisions: The Pope, the Cardinal, the Jesuit and the Evolving Debate about Origins." http://www.touchstonemag.com/archives/article.php?id=19-05-028-f.
Hildebrand, D. von. *The Devastated Vineyard.* Translated by J. Crosby and F. Teichert. Chicago: Franciscan Herald Press, 1973.
———. *Trojan Horse in the City of God.* Manchester, NH: Sophia Institute Press, 1993.
Hoberg, G. *Die Genesis.* Freiburg im Breisgau: Herder, 1908.
Hooper, J. "The Pope Prepares to Embrace Theory of Intelligent Design." *The Guardian* (27 August 2006).
Horn, S.O., and S. Wiedenhofer, eds. *Creation and Evolution: A Conference with Pope Benedict XVI in Castel Gandolfo.* San Francisco: Ignatius Press, 2008.
House, H.W., ed. *Intelligent Design 101: Leading Experts Explain the Key Issues.* Grand Rapids: Kregel Publications, 2008.
Hoyle, F. "Hoyle on Evolution." *Nature* 294 (12 November 1981): 104–5.
Hoyle, F., and Ch. Wickramasinghe. *Evolution from Space: A Theory of Cosmic Creationism.* New York: Simon & Schuster, 1984.
Huarte, G. *De Deo creante et elevante.* Roma: Universitá Gregoriana, 1935.
Hugueny, E. *Critique et Catholique*, vol. 1. Paris: Letouzey et Ané, 1912.
Hulsbosch, A. *God in Creation and Evolution.* Edited by M. Versfeld. New York: Sheed and Ward, 1965.

Hummelauer, F. von. *Commentarius in Genesim*. Parisiis: Sumptibus P. Lethielleux, 1908.
Huxley, T.H. *Evidence as to Man's Place in Nature*. London: Williams and Norgate, 1863.
———. *Evolution and Ethics and Other Essays*. New York: Macmillan, 1894.
———. *Lectures and Essays*. London: Macmillan and Co., 1903.
International Catholic Symposium on Creation, October 24–25, 2002. Rome: Kolbe Center, 2002.
International Theological Commission. *Communion and Stewardship: Human Persons Created in the Image of God*. http://www.vatican.va/roman_curia/congregations/cfaith/cti_documents/rc_con_cfaith_doc_20040723_communion-stewardship_en.html.
The Jerome Biblical Commentary. New Jersey: Prentice-Hall, 1968.
Johnson, J.W.G. *The Crumbling Theory of Evolution*. Brisbane: Queensland Binding Service, 1982.
Jones, S. *England and the Holy See: An Essay towards Reunion*. London: Longmans, 1902.
Kleinhaus, A. "De nova Enchiridii Biblicii edition." *Antonianum* 30 (1955): 63–65.
Kopczynski, S. "Rediscovering the Decrees of the Pontifical Biblical Commission." *Living Tradition* 94 (July 2001); http://www.rtforum.org/lt/lt94.html
Krauss, L.M., F. Ayala, and K. Miller. "Open Letter to Pope Benedict XVI." (12 July 2005). http://academic.regis.edu/mghedott/lettertobenedict.htm.
Kulisz, J. *Teilhardowskie rozumienie grzechu*. Warsaw: ATK, 1986.
Kwiatkowski, F. *Filozofia wieczysta w zarysie*, vol. 2: *Filozofia bytu. Filozofia swiata nieorganicznego. Filozofia duszy*. Kraków: WAM, 1947.
Lahousse, G. *De Deo creante et elevante*. Bruges: Beyaert [u.a.], 1904.
Lamarck, J.B. *Zoological Philosophy*. Translated by I. Johnston. Nanaimo BC: Malaspina University-College, 1999.
Landau, M. *Narratives on Human Evolution*. New Haven, London: Yale University Press, 1991.
Lane, D.H. *The Phenomenon of Teilhard: Prophet for a New Age*. Macon, GA: Mercer University Press, 1996.
Lanpo, J., and H. Weiwen. *The Story of Peking Man: From Archeology to Mystery*. Translated by Y. Zhiqi. Hong Kong and London: Oxford University Press, 1990.
Laun, A. "Evolution and Creationism: Theological Considerations." *Daylight* 34 (April 2004): 5–11.
Leith, B. *The Descent of Darwin: A Handbook of Doubts about Darwinism*. London: Collins, 1982.
Lemmonyer, A. *La Révélation primitive et les données actuelles de la science d'apres l'ouvrage allemand du R.P. G. Schmidt*. Paris: Gabalda, 1914.
Lenartowicz, P. "Czy Papiez uznal wiarygodnosc teorii ewolucji?" *Na początku…*, (1/82) (1997): 7–11.

———. *Elementy filozofii zjawiska biologicznego*. Kraków: WAM, 1986.

———. *Ludy czy malpoludy: problem genealogii czlowieka*. Kraków: Wyzsza Szkola Filozoficzno-Pedagogiczna Ignatianum, 2010.

———. *Phenotype-Genotype Dichotomy: An Essay in Theoretical Biology*. Roma: Pontificia Universitas Gregoriana, 1975.

———. "O 'cudach' probabilistycznych, czyli fakt selekcji i odmowa poznania tego faktu." In *Vivere et Intelligere*. Wybrane prace Piotra Leartowicza SI z okazji 75-lecia jego urodzin. Edited by J. Koszteyn. Kraków: Wyd. WAM, 2009: 569–608.

———. "O starozytnosci czlowieczenstwa." *Kwartalnik Filozoficzny* 33 (2005): 35–59.

———. "O wczesnych stadiach ewolucji czlowieka." In *Czlowiek i swiat: Szkice filozoficzne*. Edited by R. Darowski. Kraków: WAM, 1972.

Leo XIII. *Testem benevolentiae*. http://www.papalencyclicals.net/Leo13/l13teste.htm.

Leroy, D. *L'évolution restreinte aux espèces organiques*. Paris: Delhomme et Briguet, 1891.

Linnaeus, C. *Philosophia botanica*. Stockholm, 1751.

———. *Systems*. Leipzig, 1748.

Louis, C. *Rome and the Study of Scripture: A Collection of Papal Enactments on the Study of Holy Scripture together with the Decisions of the Biblical Commission*. 7th edition. St. Meinrad: Abbey Press Publishing Division, 1964.

Lubac, Henri de. *La pensée religieuse du Pére Teilhard de Chardin*. Paris: Aubier, 1962.

———. *Teilhard de Chardin: The Man and his Meaning*. New York: Hawthorn Books, 1965.

———. *Teilhard et notre temps*. Paris: Aubier, 1971.

Lyell, C. *Principles of Geology: An Attempt to Explain the Former Changes of the Earth's Surface, by Reference to Causes Now in Operation*. 3 volumes. London: 1830–1833.

Major, L.E. "Big Enough to Bury Darwin." *The Guardian* (23 August 2001).

McKeough, M. *The Meaning of rationes seminales in St. Augustine*. Washington, DC: Catholic University of America, 1926. http://www.guardian.co.uk/education/2001/aug/23/highereducation.peopleinscience

Marcora, C. *Corrispondenza Fogazzaro–Bonomelli*. Milano: Vita e Pensiero, 1968.

Maritain, J. "Teilhard de Chardin and Teilhardism." *U.S. Catholic* 33 (1967): 9–10.

Marthaler, B.L. et al., eds. *New Catholic Encyclopedia*. 2nd edition. 15 volumes. Washington, DC: Catholic University of America Press, 2003.

Mayr, E. *Animal Species and Evolution*. Cambridge: Cambridge University Press, 1970.

———. *Systematics and the Origin of Species from the Viewpoint of a Zoologist*. New York: Columbia University Press, 1942.

Mayr, E., and W.B. Provine, eds. *The Evolutionary Synthesis*. Cambridge: Har-

vard University Press, 1998.
Mazzella, C. *De Deo creante.* 4th edition. Roma: Forzani, 1896.
Medawar, P.B. "Critical Notice." *Mind* 70 (January, 1961): 99–106.
Messenger, E.C. *Evolution and Theology: The Problem of Man's Origin.* New York: Macmillan Company, 1932.
Meyer, S.C., S. Minnich, J. Moneymaker, P.A. Nelson, and R. Seelke. *Explore Evolution: The Arguments for and Against Neo-Darwinism.* Melbourne & London: Hill House Publisher, 2007.
Meyer, S.C. *Signature in the Cell: DNA and the Evidence for Intelligent Design.* New York: HarperOne, 2009.
Meyer, S. *Darwin's Doubt.* New York: HarperOne, 2013.
Miller, K.R. "Darwin, Design, and the Catholic Faith." http://www.millerandlevine.com/km/evol/catholic/op-ed-krm.html.
———. *Only a Theory: Evolution and the Battle for America's Soul.* New York: Penguin, 2008.
Mivart, St. G. "Evolution and Faith." *Dublin Review* (July–October 1871): 1–40.
———. "Happiness in Hell." *Nineteenth Century* 32 (1892): 899–919.
———. "The Happiness in Hell: A Rejoinder." *Nineteenth Century* 33 (1893): 320–38.
———. "Last Words on the Happiness in Hell: A Rejoinder." *Nineteenth Century* 33 (1893): 637–51.
———. "Letter from Dr. Mivart on the Bishop of Newport's Article in Our Last Number." *Dublin Review* (January–April 1888): 182.
———. "Notices of Books: *On the Genesis of Species.*" *Dublin Review* (January–April 1871): 482–86.
———. *On the Genesis of Species.* New York: D. Appleton and Company, 1871.
Monod, J. *Chance and Necessity: Essay on the Natural Philosophy of Modern Biology.* Translated by A. Wainhouse. New York: Vintage, 1971.
Moreland, J.P., and J.M. Reynolds. *Three Views on Creation and Evolution.* Grand Rapids: Zondervan Publishing House, 1999.
Muggeridge, M. *The End of Christendom.* Grand Rapids, MI: Eerdmans, 1980.
Murphy, J. "Dr. Mivart on Faith and Science." *Dublin Review* (January–April 1888): 407.
Nadaillac, M. de. "Review: *L'évolution et le Dogme.*" *Revue des Questions Scientifiques* (Juillet 1896): 229–46.
Neuhaus, R.J. *Biblical Interpretation in Crisis.* Grand Rapids: Wm. Eerdmans, 1989.
Newton, I. *Newton's Principia Motte's Translation Revised.* Translated by Andrew Motte, revised by Florian Cajori. Berkeley: University of California Press, 1934.
Noort, G.C. van. *Tractatus de Deo Creatore.* Amstelodami: C.L. Van Langenhuysen, 1903.
O'Brien, J.A. *Evolution and Religion.* 2nd edition. New York: The Century Co.,

1932.

O'Connell, P. *Science of Today and the Problems of Genesis*. Rockford: Tan Books, 1993.

O'Connor, M. "Rhetoric and the Literary Sense: The Sacred Author's Performance in Cajetan's Exegesis of Scripture." In *Faithful Performances: Enacting Christian Tradition*. Edited by T.A. Hart and S.R. Guthrie. Aldershot: Ashgate, 2007.

O'Leary, D., ed. *Roman Catholicism and Modern Science: A History*. New York: Continuum, 2007.

Olson, R.G. *Science and Religion* 1450–1900. Baltimore: The Johns Hopkins University Press, 2004.

Owen, H. "Beyond Creationism: Towards a Restoration of Catholic Creation Theology." *Logos Review* (Summer 2009): 2–7.

Pagnini, S. *Profilo di Raffaello Caverni* 1837–1900. Firenze: Pagnini e Martinelli, 2001.

Paley, W. *Natural Theology*. Boston, 1854.

Papal Addresses to the Pontifical Academy of Sciences 1917–2002. Vatican: The Pontifical Academy of Sciences, 2003.

Paul, H.W. *The Edge of Contingency. French Catholic Reactions to Scientific Change from Darwin to Duhem*. University Press of Florida, 1979.

Peacocke, A. *Theology for a Scientific Age*. Cambridge: Basil Blackwell, 1990.

Perrone, G. *Praelectiones theologice*, vol. 3, *De Deo creatore*, 25th edition. Mediolani: C. Turati; Genuae: Darius J. Rossi, 1857.

Pesch, Ch. *Praelectiones dogmatice*. Vol. 3, *De Deo creante et elevante: De Deo fine ultimo*. 6th edition. Friburgi Brisgoviae: Herder, 1925.

Płonka, T. *Stopniowalność orzeczeń Magisterium Kościoła w nauczaniu Stolicy Apostolskiej podczas pontyfikatu Jana Pawła II*. Warszawa: Instytut Papieża Jana Pawła II, 2011.

Pohle, J. *Lehrbuch der Dogmatik*. Paderborn: Schöningh, 1905.

Polkinghorne, J. *Faith, Science and Understanding*. New Haven: Yale University Press, 2000.

———. *Science and Theology*. Minneapolis/London: Fortress Press/SPCK, 1998.

Popper, K. *Unended Quest*. La Salle: Open Court, 1976.

Rabut, O.A. *God in an Evolving Universe*. Translated by W. Springer. New York: Herder and Herder, 1966.

Ratzinger, J. *Dogma und Verkündigung*. München: Erich Wewel Verlag, 1973.

———. *In the Beginning: A Catholic Understanding of the Story of Creation and the Fall*. Translated by B. Ramsey. Grand Rapids: William B. Eerdmans Publishing Company, 1995.

Richards, R.J. *Darwin and the Emergence of Evolutionary Theories of Mind and Behavior*. Chicago: University of Chicago Press, 1987.

Richards, J. and G. Gonzalez. *The Privileged Planet*. Washington: Eagle Publishing Company, 2010.

Ross, H. *Creation and Time: A Biblical and Scientific Perspective on the Creation-Date Controversy.* Colorado Springs: NavPress, 1994.

Ruffini, E. *The Theory of Evolution Judged by Reason and Faith.* Translated by F. O'Hanlon. New York: Joseph F. Wagner; London: B. Herder, 1959.

Sagan, C., F.H.C. Crick, L.M. Muchin. *Communication with Extraterrestrial Intelligence (CETI).* Edited by C. Sagan. Cambridge: MIT Press, 1973.

Sagan, D. *Debata Benedykta XVI i jego uczniów nad stworzeniem i ewolucją.* [in:] Filozoficzne Aspekty Genezy, 2005/2006; vol. 2/3, 7–17. http://www.nauka-a-religia.uz.zgora.pl/images/FAG/2005-2006.t.2-3/art.08.pdf

Sala, F. *Institutiones positivo-scholastice theologiae dogmaticae.* 5th edition. Mediolani: ex Typografia pontificia S. Josephi, 1899.

Schönborn, C. *Chance or Purpose?: Creation, Evolution and a Rational Faith.* San Francisco: Ignatius, 2007.

———. "The Designs of Science." *First Things* 159 (January 2006): 34–38. http://www.firstthings.com/article/2006/01/the-designs-of-science.

———. "Finding Design in Nature." *The New York Times* (7 July 2005); http://www.nytimes.com/2005/07/07/opinion/07schonborn.html?_r=0.

———. "Schöpfungskatechese und Evolutionstheorie: Vom Burgfrieden zum konstruktiven Konflikt." *Internationale Katholische Zeitschrift* 17, no. 3 (1988): 213–26.

Schulz, H.J. *Wer ist das eigentlich—Gott?* Wien: Buchgemeinschaft "Welt und Heimat," 1969.

Scott, E. "The Creation/Evolution Continuum." http://ncse.com/creationism/general/creationevolution-continuum

Secord, J.A. *Victorian Sensation: The Extraordinary Publication, Reception, and Secret Authorship of Vestiges of the Natural History of Creation.* Chicago: University of Chicago Press, 2000.

Seewis, F.S. "*Evoluzione e Domma* pel Padre J.A. Zahm," *La Civiltá Cattolica* 16th ser., 9 (1897): 201–04.

———. "La generazione spontanea e la filosofia antica." *La Civiltá Cattolica* 16th ser., 11 (1897): 142–52.

———. "Le origini della vita sulla terra secondo il Suarez." *La Civiltá Cattolica* 16th ser., 12 (1897): 168–76.

———. "Review of *De' nuovi studi della Filosofia: Discorsi di Raffaello Caverni a un giovane studente.*" *La Civiltá Cattolica* 10, no. 4 (1877): 570–80; 10, no. 5 (1878): 65–76.

———. Sant'Agostino e la generazione spontanea primitive." *La Civiltá Cattolica* 16th ser., 11 (1897): 421–38.

———. "S. Tommaso e la generazione spontanea primitive." *La Civiltá Cattolica* 16th ser., 11 (1897): 676–91.

Siegman, E.F. "Decrees of the Pontifical Biblical Commission." *The Catholic Biblical Quarterly* 18.1 (1956): 23–29.

Siemieniewski, A. "Postawa Kościoła wobec teorii ewolucji: *Semper Idem.*" *Wro-*

cławski Przegląd Teologiczny 17, no. 1 (2009): 39–58.
Simpson, G.G. *The Meaning of Evolution*. Revised edition. New Haven: Yale University Press, 1967.
Skowron, S. *Narodziny wielkiej teorii: Karol Darwin i jego poprzednicy*. Warszawa: Wiedza Powszechna, 1965.
Slomka, M. "Straszenie Darwinem." *Tygodnik Powszechny* no. 2905 (13 March 2005), http://apologetyka.com/ptkr/groups/ptkrmember/spor/pl/document.2005-03-10.5957624946
Smith, Ch. H. *The Natural History of the Human Species*. Edinburgh, 1848.
Smith, W. *Theistic Evolution: The Teilhardian Heresy*. Tacoma, WA: Angelico Press, 2012.
Spaemann, R., R. Löw, and P. Koslowski, eds. *Evolutionismus und Christentum*. Weinheim: Acta Humaniora, VCH 1986.
Speaight, R. *Teilhard de Chardin: A Biography*. London: Collins, 1967.
Stephen, W. *The Evolution of Evolution: Darwin, Enlightenment and Scotland*. Edinburgh: Luath Press, 2009.
Suarez, F. *Opera Omnia*, Volume 3. Parisiis: Apud Ludovicum Vivés, 1856.
Tax, S., ed. *Evolution after Darwin*. 3 volumes. Chicago: University of Chicago Press, 1960.
Theologus [S. Parravicino]. "Le idee di un Vescovo sull'Evoluzione." *La Rassegna Nazionale* 104 (16 November 1898): 418–20.
Thompson, P.M. *Between Science and Religion: The Engagement of Catholic Intellectuals with Science and Technology in the Twentieth Century*. Lanham: Lexington Books, 2009.
Till, H. J. van. "Basil, Augustine, and the Doctrine of Creation's Functional Integrity." *Science and Christian Belief* 8 no. 1 (April 1996): 21–38.
Verschuuren, G.M. *God and Evolution? Science meets Faith*. Boston: Pauline Books & Media, 2012.
Wallace, A.R., and P. Matthew. *On Naval Timber and Arboriculture, with critical notes on authors who have recently treated the subject of planting*. Edinburgh & London, 1831.
Ward, K. *God, Chance and Necessity*. Oxford: Oneworld, 1996.
Wassmann, E. *The Berlin Discussion of the Problem of Evolution*. London: Kegan Paul, Trench Trubner & Co., 1912.
Weber, R.E. *Notre Dame's John Zahm: American Catholic Apologist and Educator*. Notre Dame: University of Notre Dame Press, 1961.
Weikert, R. *From Darwin to Hitler: Evolutionary Ethics, Eugenics and Racism in Germany*. New York: Palgrave Macmillan, 2004.
Wells, J. *Icons of Evolution*. Washington, DC: Regnery Publishing, 2002.
———. *The Myth of Junk DNA*. Seattle: Discovery Institute Press, 2011.
Wernz, F.X. *Ius decretalium ad usum praelectionum in scholis textus canonici sive iuris decreatlium*, vol. 2, *Ius constitutionis Ecclesiae Catolicae*. Rome: S.C. de Propaganda Fidei, 1899.

Whitcomb, J.C., and H. Morris. *The Genesis Flood: The Biblical Record and its Scientific Implications.* Philadelphia: Presbyterian & Reformed, 1960.

Wilhelm, J., and T.B. Scannell. *Manual of Catholic Theology based on Scheeben's Dogmatik*, vol. 1. 4th edition. London: Kegan Paul, Trench, Trübner, 1909.

Wolf, H. *Index: Der Vatikan und die Verbotenen Bücher.* München: Beck, 2006.

Zahm, J.A. *Evolution and Dogma.* Chicago: D.H. McBride & Co., 1896.

Zigliara, Th. *Propaedeutica ad sacram theologiam in usum scholarum.* 4th edition. Roma: S.C. de Propaganda Fide, 1897.

Zycinski, J. *Bóg i ewolucja.* Lublin: TN KUL, 2002.

———. "Bóg i ewolucja." *Tygodnik Powszechny* 2478, no. 10 (5 January 1997): 1, 10.

———. *Bóg i stworzenie: Zarys teorii ewolucji.* Lublin: Wydawnictwo Archidiecezji Lubelskiej Gaudium, 2011.

———. "Dlaczego ma mi ubliżać ta wspólnota w genealogii z braćmi, którymi są zwierzęta niższe?" *Tygodnik Powszechny* (12) 17 (March 2009), http://tygodnik.onet.pl/cywilizacja/zaplanowani-i-ukochani-wciaz-ewoluujemy/kf5n7.

———. *God and Evolution: Fundamental Questions of Christian Evolutionism.* Washington, DC: The Catholic University of America Press, 2006.

———. *Wszechswiat emergentny. Bóg w ewolucji przyrody.* Lublin: Wydawnictwo KUL, 2009.

Index

About the Author

Fr. Michael Chaberek O.P., S.T.D., is a member of the Polish Dominican Province, with a Doctorate in Fundamental Theology from Cardinal Stefan Wyszynski University in Warsaw. He has a special interest in the creation/evolution debate, and advocates the renewal of a Catholic theology of creation and a new science/faith synthesis based on sound scientific data and a serious approach to the Holy Scriptures in accordance with long-standing Church Tradition.

Made in the USA
Middletown, DE
11 November 2020

23720377R00217